THE POLITICAL WORK OF
NORTHERN WOMEN WRITERS
AND THE CIVIL WAR,
1850–1872

{ CIVIL WAR AMERICA }   Gary W. Gallagher, editor

The Political Work of

Northern Women Writers
and the Civil War, 1850–1872

LYDE CULLEN SIZER

The University of North Carolina Press   Chapel Hill and London

The paper in this book meets the guidelines for
permanence and durability of the Committee on
Production Guidelines for Book Longevity of the
Council on Library Resources.

Library of Congress Cataloging-in-Publication Data
Sizer, Lyde Cullen.
The political work of Northern women writers and
the Civil War, 1850–1872 / Lyde Cullen Sizer.
p. cm.—(Civil War America)
Includes bibliographical references and index.
ISBN 0-8078-2554-9 (cloth: alk. paper)
ISBN 0-8078-4885-9 (pbk.: alk. paper)
1. United States—History—Civil War, 1861–1865
—Literature and the war. 2. Women authors,
American—19th century—Political and social views.
3. Politics and literature—United States—History
—19th century. 4. Authors and readers—United
States—History—19th century. 5. American literature—Women authors—History and criticism.
6. American literature—19th century—History and
criticism. 7. Popular literature—United States—
History and criticism. 8. United States—Politics
and government—1849–1877. I. Title. II. Series.
PS217.C58 S59 2000   810.9'358—dc21   99-087015

04 03 02 01 00   5 4 3 2 1

Contents

Illustrations

Acknowledgments

THE ROOTS OF THIS project, begun a decade ago, date from a confluence of two events: a lecture by Mari Jo Buhle on Mary Livermore and the American Civil War, and a reading of George Fredrickson's *The Inner Civil War* with John L. Thomas. Bringing it to fruition, however, has—like child-rearing—required a village. Or in this case, many villages.

I cannot thank my teachers enough. Beginning with Jean Amster, John Richards, and Tom Regan, among others at Andover, through John Morton Blum, Jonathan Spence, and Cynthia Russett at Yale, I have been questioned, pushed, and encouraged to learn and appreciate history and literature. At Brown I have even greater numbers to thank, particularly Naomi Lamoreaux, for her wonderful combination of thoughtfulness, professionalism, and warmth; Mary Gluck for her remarkable ability to inspire students with a love for intellectual history; Jim Patterson for his tough standards and rough humor; Howard Chudacoff for his unremitting collegiality to a graduate student teaching for him; Patricia Herlihy for her valued friendship in my last years; and the late William L. McLoughlin, who will always serve me as a model of an intellectual who was also a passionate activist and a truly moral man.

The three teachers who directed me deserve particular mention. Codirector Jack Thomas had the uncanny ability of detecting when I most needed support and encouragement, and when I needed to be reminded, humorously, that "this is not deathless prose." He is a master teacher and a great friend. Codirector Mari Jo Buhle was truly the best editor a student could wish for: clear, always direct, and if necessary, bracingly honest. This book has been immeasurably improved as a result. Jacqueline Jones always managed to pick out the argument from a muddled statement and, with her customary dispatch, would put me on the right track. I take great pride in having been her first graduate student.

My other teachers at Brown were my colleagues. Thanks go to the members of my many writing groups and friends with whom I have shared work, in particular: Lucy Barber, Gail Bederman, Bruce Dorsey, Ruth Feldstein, Elizabeth Francis, Kevin Gaines, Jane Gerhard, Linda Grasso, Matt Jacobson, Dorothee Kocks, Suzanne Kolm, Kate Monteiro, Louise

Newman, John Richards, Lou Roberts, Michael Topp, and David Witwer. Thanks also go to colleagues in my field who shared work and insights with me, among them David Blight, Catherine Clinton, Alice Fahs, Joan Hedrick, Martha Hodes, Polly Kaufman, Louis Masur, Nell Irvin Painter, Rachel Seidman, and Ben Weaver.

Writing groups at Harvard and at Sarah Lawrence helped the project through its many drafts. Tom Augst, Steve Biel, Hildegard Hoeller, Meredith McGill, John McGreevy, Jeff Melnick, Dan Morris, and Vince Tompkins made Harvard a warm and challenging intellectual haven for a year. Steve, a fellow Jack Thomas student, was a particularly good friend. Nancy Sommers, director of Expository Writing, modeled excellent teaching and helped me think about writing in new and productive ways. At Sarah Lawrence College the writing group—Bella Brodzki, Bob Desjarlais, Elizabeth Freeman, Elizabeth Johnston, Paul Josephson, Musifiky Mwanasali, Chiwenye Ogunyemi, Mary Porter, Sandra Robinson, and Komozi Woodard—has sustained me through five years of revision. Other scholars and friends at Sarah Lawrence enriched my intellectual life as well, among them in particular, Persis Charles, Michael Davis, Deborah Hertz, Katie Kent, Judy Kicinski, Priscilla Murolo, Pauline Watts, and especially Carol Zoref. Without Priscilla, in particular, this book may never have been published; I'm grateful to her for pushing me to protect precious writing time.

Judy Kicinski, good friend and Sarah Lawrence librarian, has helped me a million times, finding information, reading text, and offering crucial advice. John Hay and Rockefeller librarians, particularly in interlibrary loan, gave me much needed assistance along the way. Gordon Sterling, Eric Alacan and his staff, Elizabeth Johnston, and Tim Gardner have supported me technically in moments of crisis, and all the time. Dean Barbara Kaplan, from the first, never wavered in her support for this project, both emotional and financial; I am deeply grateful. Thanks also to Sarah Lawrence College for the Marilyn Simpson Grant, which gave me needed release time to work on the final version of the manuscript.

My students have also made this work possible. I thank all my research assistants over the years, including Michele Erfer, Amanda Hartzler, Christina Saraceno, Kate Shaughnessy, L. B. Thompson, and most especially, Emily Park and Corinna Buchholz, who aided me in the frantic last weeks. Other students have unofficially pushed me to think in new ways, among them Shana Agid, Tracy Blanchard, Melissa Crowe, Dahlia Ellison, Jeff Gnecco, Desiree Greene, Amanda Guma, Chrystie Hill, Kristen Hill, Ilsa Lund, Paula Mauro, Reenie Mulvaney, Randy Myer, Mary Reynolds,

Mariana Romano, Erica Ryan, Kyes Stevens, Jennifer Tammi, Andy Teranova, Deborah White, and Jamison York.

On the day my twin sons were born, Lewis Bateman called to tell me that the manuscript had been accepted for publication. He pushed me to finish, despite the chaos, and without his persistence and belief there would be no book. To my anonymous readers goes much credit; because of their intelligent and close readings this is a better book. Much thanks also goes to project editor Mary Caviness; this is a clearer and more accurate book because of you.

A series of friends and family gave generously of time, support, and encouragement that was not strictly (or only) intellectual. Thanks must especially go to Barbara Atwell, Steve Biel, Elizabeth Francis, Elizabeth Freeman, Susan Guma, Matt Jacobson, Katie Kent, Eileen Kurtis-Kleinman, Nick Kliment, Stephanie McKenna, Pam and Roger Mailloux, Louise Newman, Felicity Nitz, Chiwenye Ogunyemi, Alice Olson, John and Nancy Richards, Heidi Steinitz, Gordon Sterling, Michael Topp, Ben Weaver, Marje Weishaar, and Anne and Larry Whitten. During revisions, I needed even more help, given my growing family. That help came from many, among them Grace and Cathy Cullen, Georgia and Greg de Vaney, Beverly Fox, Elizabeth Johnston, Mary La Chapelle, Ilsa Lund, Leah Olson, Mary Porter, Marilyn Power, Prema Samuel, Pauline Watts, Janet Wigfield, Janice and Brian Williams, and Ellen and Patrick Young. Chelsea Chaffee, Kristen Hill, Andrea Ohlson, Christina Saraceno, along with mainstays Padmini Amarasiri, Lara Haggar, Shanti Liyanage, and Heather Winn, especially, have made being an intellectual and a mother compatible identities. To Jim Cullen senior I owe a particular debt: I will never stop being grateful for the years of Wednesdays he gave to his eldest grandson, allowing me to work.

My family has been ever present and greatly supportive. I began the research for this project at "The Warner Hilton" in Washington, D.C. and have visited regularly since. Unfortunately Uncle Sturgis will never see the book he helped make happen, but as the family's genealogist and historian, he would be proud. To Aunt Hilda and Aunt Alice, I salute you: your wisdom and example helped me at crucial junctures. My parents, intellectuals and activists, are my models for scholarly work (and parenting), my brothers and sisters-in-law have been forgiving of stress and constant in support, and to my sister and best friend, Judy, particularly, fellow traveler in colleges, thank you.

My greatest thanks go to Jim Cullen, my partner and kindred spirit, and to the sons he helped me to make, James Faust Cullen, and now

Grayson Sterling Sizer Cullen and Ryland Bailey Sizer Cullen. Jim's imagination and humor are so well woven into this work that it would be impossible to unravel. Without him, my intellectual and emotional life would be greatly diminished. And Jay, Grayson, and Ryland, whom we also tend together, have brought me much happiness and further insight into the joy of learning.

The history of the war—which has never yet been truly written—is full of heroism in which woman is the central figure.

The social and political condition of women was largely changed by our civil war. Through the withdrawal of so many men from their accustomed work, new channels of industry were opened to them, the value and control of money learned, thought upon political questions compelled, and a desire for their own personal, individual liberty intensified. It created a revolution in woman herself, as important in its results as the changed condition of the former slaves, and this silent influence is still busy. Its work will not have been accomplished until the chains of ignorance and selfishness are everywhere broken, and woman shall stand by man's side his recognized equal in rights as she is now in duties.

—Elizabeth Cady Stanton, Susan B. Anthony, and Matilda Joslyn Gage, eds.,

A History of Woman Suffrage (1882)

And I shall not confine myself to my sphere. I hate my sphere. I like everything that is

outside of it,—or, better still, my sphere rounds out into undefined space. I was born

into the whole world. I am monarch of all I survey.

—Gail Hamilton (Mary Abigail Dodge), *Skirmishes and Sketches* (1865)

{ I N T R O D U C T I O N }

My Sphere Rounds Out

Northern Women and the Written War

THE START OF THE Civil War found Chicagoan Mary Livermore in Boston tending her sick father. "It was a time of extreme and unconcealed anxiety," she wrote in 1889, when "the daily papers teemed with the dreary records of secession." Nevertheless, she and her father were amazed and heartened at Boston's swift response, and this minister's wife and mother of two joined the swelling tide of activism. "If it be a question of the supremacy of freedom or slavery underlying this war," she remembered thinking, "then I pray God it may be settled now, by us, and not be left to our children. And oh that I may be a hand, a foot, an eye, a voice, an influence, on the side of freedom and my country!"[1] Livermore's memoirs, which chronicled her work in the U.S. Sanitary Commission, testified to the breadth and depth of her contribution to the Union cause.[2] The war, for her, was a life-changing event, impacting on her views, her work, and her subsequent life. Given the dramatic quality of this change, Livermore was not so much representative as suggestive of the war's transformative possibility for writers and actors alike.

Writing of Livermore and others in 1882, the authors of the *History of Woman Suffrage* confidently asserted that the Civil War had "created a revolution in woman herself, as important in its results as the changed condition of the former slaves, and this silent influence is still busy." This revolution occurred after men left for the battlefield, when "new channels of industry were opened to [women], the value and control of money learned, thought upon political questions compelled, and a desire for their own personal, individual liberty intensified." The history of the war, they further argued, "which has never yet been truly written—is full of heroism in which woman is the central figure."[3]

Such celebrations of women's achievements in wartime began with the first shots at Fort Sumter and had become the sentimental norm by the 1880s and 1890s. Among the writers of this alternative history of the war there was agreement: "woman" had offered "a hand, a foot, an eye, a voice, an influence, on the side of freedom and [her] country," and this offering had created "a revolution in woman herself." The majority of the writers on the subject, with some important exceptions, were middle-class white women primarily from the Northeast.[4] The texts, illustrations, and narratives, and through them the explanations of the war's meaning they offered to the public and to posterity, filled popular magazines, pamphlets, autobiographies, and novels throughout the war period to the 1870s, when they almost entirely disappeared until a new flowering returned in the 1880s.

For all the celebration of women's participation and its corresponding emancipatory effect, however, a few women writers described the actual consequences of the war in grim terms. Elizabeth Stuart Phelps, who came of age as a writer during the war, perhaps more accurately captured its meaning when she remembered in her 1897 autobiography a country "dark with sorrowing women."[5] In the North alone 320,000 men were killed, and thousands more were maimed or died later from wounds or illness brought home from the front. It was unlikely that any woman was without a relative, friend, or acquaintance lost to the war.

These were not only emotional costs. The war created widows but few jobs to help them survive. As historian J. Matthew Gallman puts it, this was no "earlier generation of 'Rosie the Riveters' moving into new branches of heavy industry"; those jobs open to women tended to be

Mary A. Livermore (1820–1905). Along with Jane Hoge, Livermore was appointed by Dorothea Dix to recruit female nurses soon after the war began. Soon thereafter she and Hoge ran the Northwestern Sanitary Commission in Chicago, overseeing the gathering and distribution of material to Union soldiers across the West. Livermore wrote about these experiences in a postwar memoir, *My Story of the War* (1890). (Photo from Brockett and Vaughan, *Woman's Work in the Civil War.*)

female defined, low paying and too few, sought by desperate women who were compelled by their circumstances to take lower and lower wages or compensation. Without savings, and even with them, many women had to depend on kin and neighbors to support themselves and their children. The number of children in New York City almshouses alone, Gallman reports, "jumped by 300 percent during the war."[6] Northern wartime newspapers regularly included stories, both actual and fictional, of women who had been found starving and ill, their soldier husbands killed in the war or simply unable to support them.

Many women faced a profoundly difficult postwar life. African American women, if freed from bondage by the war's end, soon were enmeshed in economic peonage in the South and squeezed by the lack of economic opportunity in the North, often limiting them solely to demeaning and low-paying domestic work.[7] Women's suffrage organizers, hopeful that the war would prove a revolution in man as well as woman, hoped in vain. The Fifteenth Amendment, passed by the states in 1870, explicitly included only African American men as new voters despite women's patriotic efforts throughout the war.[8]

The public social conventions of womanhood were not discernibly loosened in the decades that followed; in fact, the reverse may be true. White middle-class women were more likely to teach in high schools, clerk for the government, and nurse in hospitals after the war, but these gains were in many cases won before the war, or represented only a small advance overall for women seeking employment. Greater numbers of women flocked to the factories of the postwar North, but it is likely this would have happened despite any wartime advances. In any case, conditions in many places worsened as Yankee workers were replaced with immigrants.[9]

It is true that some women who had participated in the war went on to create careers for themselves afterward—Mary Livermore, for example, became a lecturer and her family's main source of income, while Clara Barton founded the Red Cross—yet these were the exceptions. The rule remained: women in the mid-nineteenth century had few options for employment or for public or political power. If the war had produced a revolution in "woman's sense of herself," it had produced no immediate corresponding revolution in society or in material conditions. Why, then, the widespread incantations of the war's transformative meaning?

One can begin to understand the gap between public rhetoric and social reality by considering that the Civil War was a time when middle-class women came to believe that they had an acknowledged stake in a national ordeal of overwhelming importance, a personal stake in national politics. By the end of the war, many believed they had a right to a place in the history books, and they continued to believe this even after they became aware that their stories might never be written by the male scholars of the war. Despite economic and social reversals, despite the constricting fabric of conventional society, a personal and cultural vision of possibility evolved and was remembered. Although it was necessarily a limited and constructed vision, it was no less real for that.

The contours of this vision of woman's role in society during wartime emerged early in the newspapers, magazines, and novels of the war period. This written and public women's war became the site for cultural struggle over the meaning of the many divisions in Northern society. Within the dominant ideology of separate spheres, which prescribed appropriate behavior for both women and men, Northern women writers debated, contested, and confirmed their understanding of their role in wartime, as well as in national society, in more general terms. In the literary mass market they actively engaged in what Jane Tompkins calls "cultural" and Mary Poovey calls "ideological" work, finding an appropriate place of power and autonomy despite societal limitations.[10] Here they acted in their own arena of cultural politics, remaking and interpreting societal norms to achieve their own ends.

The work of women writers during the Civil War era was intended to move their readers: to shore up traditional ideas, to rearrange them, or to change them altogether. This idea, that minds can be worked upon by words, stories, and images, was related to the prewar insistence upon the power of moral suasion. It represented the ongoing power of the concept for middle-class women readers in the North, which, given an expanded literate public, was quite an audience. This work was emphatically political—meaning that it participated in the power relations in society—if it was rarely directly partisan: it entered a terrain of national concern, offering an interpretation of the nation's needs and fears.[11]

This effort toward creating a consensus—what I call a rhetoric of unity—was a common aspiration of Northern women writers during the 1850s. It was a claiming of a common purpose as the sections firmly defined themselves against each other: to wage a war successfully they had to see themselves in some sense as fundamentally different. In the early war years, this work was crucial to the Union effort to motivate a fractured populace to concerted effort. This rhetoric of unity, most successful in 1861 and early 1862, was no longer as effective by midwar, given the strains of the conflict. Afterward, women (and men) again adopted it for varying political purposes and in varying ways, using it largely to center the nation around ascendant middle-class capitalist values.

Political Work

Rhetoric, or the art of persuasion through language, only works when it draws upon a powerful common longing; without such longing, it is utterly ineffectual. The war formally began after a decade in which Northern women expressed a growing desire to be respected, understood, and valued by their society for their public as well as their private opinions.[12] This effort toward meaningfulness and a new form of self-respect was also in many cases a drive toward greater class and racial control. It represented an effort to define a universal womanhood that could provide both credibility and power to women, yet it defined women in ways that would most—or only—benefit the middle-class whites for whom such a definition was possible.

The wartime and the postwar period drew special attention to men specifically and to gender arrangements generally. Such a phenomenon was not unique to the Civil War. War, of course, tends to dramatize societal understandings of gender difference.[13] As political scientist Jean Bethke Elshtain argues, "[T]o men's wars, women are backdrop. . . . Women's involvement in war seems to us . . . inferential, located somewhere offstage if war is playing."[14] For women struggling to express a political voice, the war posed immediate and real challenges, even as it created opportunities.

In Civil War stories written by women, it was almost always a woman who played what the authors of *History of Woman Suffrage* later called the "central figure." Instead of accepting their offstage relation to war, they described the war's crucial events as happening where they were located, be it at home well away from the fighting, in a hospital in Washington, D.C., or on the battlefield itself.[15] And as Elshtain argues, "[T]o tell the tale gives power to the teller; he or she is implicated in the narrative and honored as a risk taker, for such one must be to tell this story." Women gained new social power in telling such stories.

Moreover, these stories have particular meaning for the culture, both now and then. In moments of national definition, trauma, and change, the power of the teller increases exponentially. "[S]ocieties are, in some sense, the sum total of their 'war stories': one can't think, for example, of the American story *without* the Civil War, for that war structured identities that are continually reinscribed."[16] If the Civil War was, as Shelby Foote suggested in Ken Burns's documentary film series *The Civil War*, the "crossroads of our being," how did women imagine that crossroads?

The tools of contemporary cultural theory can help the historian reconstruct the diverse meanings that once resided at this imaginative crossroads. The first step in this process is to recognize the complexity, even the ambiguity, of what may now seem to be simple texts. The elegies scattered throughout mainstream newspapers, as sentimental and lachrymose as they tended to be, had political implications, however muddled. As theorist Stuart Hall writes, "Popular culture is one of the sites where . . . [a] struggle for and against a culture of the powerful is engaged; it is also the stake to be won or lost *in* that struggle. It is the arena of consent and resistance."[17] This culture of the powerful was not only capitalism but also the accepted gender conventions of society, and the two were at times in conflict. Women's writings revealed a constant tension between "consent and resistance" to that society.[18]

Within the stories, poems, and narratives of the war, as well as within this rhetoric of unity itself, there was no real political consistency. That this would be true, however, is consistent with much popular or mass culture at that time and since. Writing of another "contested terrain," that of the nineteenth-century dime novels, historian Michael Denning argues that "these stories, which are products of the culture industry—'popular,' 'mass,' or 'commercial' culture—can be understood neither as forms of deception, manipulation, and social control nor as expressions of a genuine people's culture, opposing and resisting the dominant culture. Rather they are best seen as a contested terrain, a field of cultural conflict where signs with wide appeal and resonance take on contradictory disguises and are spoken in contrary accents."[19] In the stories of wartime women, conventional and transgressive messages spar even within the same text, where a yearning for self-expression is coupled with a rhetoric of unity that flattens difference. Rather than opposing the dominant culture and its ideologies of womanhood, writers manipulated those ideologies, first one way and then another, along a spectrum of cultural politics contained within accepted bounds.

These political negotiations took place in a variety of cultural forms, including poems, stories, novels, narratives, essays, and letters to the editor. None of these forms ipso facto established a singular meaning. As historian George Lipsitz persuasively argues, genre implies no inherent message. "Popular culture has no fixed forms," he writes, "individual artifacts of popular culture have no fixed meanings: it is impossible to say whether any one combination of sounds or set of images or grouping of words innately expresses one unified political position."[20] Poems and short stories, domestic and realist novels, narratives and essays all demonstrated ideas in conflict rather than particular visions in themselves.

Lipsitz's work also helps explain the complicated relationship between cultural forms and politics. In some sense, of course, all writing is inherently political: it expresses a set of assumptions, a viewpoint or viewpoints, each of which can be analyzed in terms of political ideology and meaning.[21] "Culture," Lipsitz argues, "can seem like a substitute for politics, a way of posing only imaginary solutions to real problems, but under other circumstances culture can become a rehearsal for politics, trying out values and beliefs permissible in art but forbidden in social life."[22] This concept of cultural expression as political rehearsal is central to understanding what women undertook in writing about the Civil War. In some instances, this approach was practiced explicitly; in other instances, it was practiced covertly.[23] In all these cases, women revealed through their cultural work their political understanding of society. They "tr[ied] out beliefs and values" that would be impermissible in stark unadulterated form—in Congress, for example—with a woman speaker.[24]

What I identify as the political work of women, then, was neither direct, nor purely radical or conservative, nor consistent in its messages, nor specific to a genre. Rarely in the North did any true consensus hold, even in the edited arena of public writing. For all that, however, certain patterns emerged, if only in the breach. Women writers used the opportunity to speak in the pages of literary magazines, political and religious newspapers, novels and stories, to change the way the nation saw the task it was undertaking. They wrote out of a collective longing for a meaningful place in the polity, even if it meant denying a similar place to another woman. This was their political work.

Separate Spheres Ideology

In order for women to write publicly, they had to begin with some obeisance to separate spheres ideology, whether or not that ideology had any material relevance to their lives. Whatever concerns beyond the limits or possibilities of this ideology they might hold—about the conditions of the working class, about the indolence of the rich, about the baleful influence of the Slave Power, about racial stereotypes, or about religious adherence among soldiers far from home—were refracted through an apologia for speaking or writing for the public.

Two ubiquitous themes emerged during the prewar years in the public writing of women, although they were never agreed upon. The first of these was slavery, and, after 1863, race. Throughout the war, an important minority of women writers insisted that the moral meaning of the war could only be the end to slavery, and that women were appropriately called upon to enter politics and to make that happen as the natural arbiters of morality. A few African American women, Charlotte Forten and Frances Ellen Watkins Harper among them, wrote both with and against the grain of gender convention to affirm and interpret their roles as women and as African Americans in white society. Yet the majority of writers on issues of slavery and race at this time were white, and their varying political perspectives shaped their understanding of the meaning and urgency of emancipation.

Secondly, a new recognition of class difference and the limits of gender solidarity emerged during the late 1850s. This strengthened throughout the war, particularly after 1863. Not surprisingly, class issues took on new relevance for middle-class women concerned about national unity as well as eager to establish a vision of universal womanhood. Most ended the war with a stronger sense of the middle-class values they deemed most crucial to the nation's recovery, thereby criticizing both ruling-class and working-class women. For a few major young writers these distinctions were ones to overcome. Class injustices became the defining problem in their writing during and especially after the war, heralding a new movement into the social protest novel of the 1870s and 1880s.[25]

With few exceptions, all of these themes were explored by Northern middle-class women within an overarching framework of separate spheres ideology. Women described the world in terms of complementary arenas of power, some of which were seen as possibly permeable (class and, to varying extents, gender) and others of which were not (race). This ideological construct, which grew in influence with the shifts in economic life in New England and the Northwest in the early years of the century, had solidified as the central social matrix of the emerging Protestant middle class by the 1830s. Within this construct men and women were understood to occupy distinct social spaces.[26] Men were to dominate and control a public "sphere," while women were to supervise and inhabit a private "sphere." Although the ideology implied parity, there was an assumed hierarchy of importance and power: public life was where change happened and was the arena of history. Private life, by contrast, was a timeless arena of domesticity and piety, where women took on a familial rather than individual identity. Men made history; women made families.[27]

By the early 1850s, however, the social arrangements that limited women were under challenge. In 1848 a group of women gathered in Seneca Falls, New York, to protest the legal, political, and societal liabilities of womanhood. Despite public ridicule, they continued to meet, give lectures, and organize petitions throughout the 1850s. Other reformers, some of whom were connected to this movement, published magazines, including the *Una* and *Sibyl*, directed toward reform of conventional social norms.

A few individual writers questioned separate sphere ideology explicitly. "Men and Women," an essay published in the *National Era* in 1859, was an ironic but nonetheless critical piece of this literature. In it, Mary Abigail Dodge, or Gail Hamilton, laughingly scorned the tired "platitudes" concerning "woman's opportunities for self-sacrifice, moral heroism, silent influence, might of love, and all that cut-and-dried woman's-sphere-ism." Give women rubber boots to walk in the rain, take away their constricting clothes (and, by implication, codes), she wrote, and free them from themselves, and you will give them more power than any platitudes. Her mother, it seemed, was shocked by her writing and the criticism it generated. In a private letter, Dodge was anything but conciliatory and remained frank about her purposes as a writer. "I wish you to understand that if I write much I shall probably meet with a great deal of opposition," she wrote, "for I shall express views which run counter to popular conviction, so if you faint now, you will have a catalepsy by and by when worst comes to worst."[28]

As Dodge implied, popular conviction supported separate sphere ideology. In a typical letter to the editor of the *New York Ledger* in 1860, for example, "Gula Meredith" wrote of "Woman's True Position" in no uncertain terms. "Woman can best understand woman's nature," she wrote, "and it is against our nature as against our reason to be seen in the Pulpit, at the Bar or the Polls. Woman's sphere is to elevate, to purify, to teach, and her empire is home."[29] Sarah Josepha Hale, editor of the popular *Godey's Ladies Book*, would surely have agreed.

The ideology of separate spheres was understood and applied in widely divergent ways, however. Dodge said as much in "A Spasm of Sense," an essay published in the *Atlantic Monthly* during the war. "But without any suspicious lunges into that dubious region which lies outside of woman's universally acknowledged 'sphere' (a blight rest upon that word!)," she wrote ironically, "there is within the pale, within the boundary-line which the most conservative never dreamed of questioning, room for a great divergence of ideas."[30] Dodge was right: what any study of the North from the 1850s to the 1870s reveals is a divergence of ideas, yet ideas still limited by boundary lines.

Tangled within separate sphere ideology were assumed ideologies of class and race. As with gender, there was an implied hierarchy of value, even at the same time that middle-class white women proclaimed a universal womanhood. For example, when Gula Meredith argued that women could only work in professions that kept them largely in the home, she excluded many women even while professing to speak for all.

The ideology of separate spheres was intimately connected with its material and economic context. Meant to explain and justify the new lives of women in an industrializing region, separate spheres played a crucial part in middle-class formation.[31] The ideology itself allowed for a standardization of domestic values controlled by the middle class, which Catharine Beecher in her 1841 *Treatise on Domestic Economy* so clearly understood.[32] As historian Christine Stansell argues, "Within the propertied classes, women constituted themselves the moral guardians of their families and their nation, offsetting some of the inherited liabilities of their sex. Laboring women were less fortunate."[33] That middle-class women owed their position to fortune rather than to virtue went unacknowledged by most of the women writers of the period. To acknowledge that notion, of course, would be to undercut their claims to universal moral authority.

By writing on issues of great national concern and by professing to speak for all women, middle-class white women writers were continuing the work of class formation, the political work central to their understanding of the war. Their stories, essays, and narratives constructed an appropriate standard of behavior meant to create and sustain national unity. At the same time, these women were protecting their own claim to legitimacy and respectability despite their stepping, if only with their words, into a public and, by implication, a political arena.

The ideology of separate spheres also assumed whiteness. In their writing, white women rarely if ever extended their assumptions to encompass black women, who were by implication thought literally beyond the pale of respectable womanhood.[34] At the same time, antislavery writers insisted that a natural sense of universal womanhood meant a shared sisterhood, albeit a sisterhood of unequals. As with gender and class, here was an implied and unquestioned hierarchy. White middle-class women were to succor their bereaved and wronged sisters, both African American and white working class, and thereby give themselves power and legitimacy. This rhetoric of unity was not democratic, despite its claim to a kind of democracy.

African American women were well aware of the racial limitations of the ideology of separate spheres. As historian James Horton has shown, the Northern antebellum African American community in Philadelphia found it impossible to accommodate to this ideology on a daily basis. With remunerative labor for African American men severely limited, and that for women generally domestic and thus outside the home, the result was an added yoke of oppression.[35] Literary historian Hazel Carby has argued that African American women explicitly challenged the ideology of separate spheres by reconstructing a new vision of womanhood that affirmed their racial community.[36] African American women exposed the fortune and privilege that allowed white middle-class women their claims of moral authority, and claimed their own moral authority through their experience of injustice.

The political work of Northern women writers, white or African American, rich or poor, was in writing an alternative history and narrative of the war. This story was written through a matrix of gender, class, and racial assumptions. If the white mainstream ideology of separate spheres was not broken by the war, at the end of the war it was severely bent and adjusted; its reimposition in the postwar years, enabled by a celebratory story of patriotic women now eager to return to domesticity, was never complete. The public war dialogue on women, African American slavery, and class demonstrated both the ideology's inherent elasticity and its clear limitations. Yet for many the war served as a transformative moment, a revolution in the *understanding* of woman herself.

In some sense, women—other than those few hundred that historians estimate cross-dressed and fought as men—could never truly understand what Walt Whitman called the "real war."[37] (Nor could he, never having faced combat.) In letters home, North and South, soldiers reiterated again and again how impossible the job of translating the horror and chaos was, even as they kept trying to do just that.[38] The reasons Union soldiers gave to their kin and friends for fighting, despite that horror, were in general not those women offered in letters or—what is under scrutiny here—more public documents. This was not, in general, because of an acknowledged "timorous nature," as historian James M. McPherson finds one postwar novel suggesting; women publicly described their work during wartime as requiring enormous courage, if only the courage to let their loved ones live up to their expressed ideals.[39]

Women, these sources suggest, had a complicated relationship to the ideals of republicanism that both motivated men to fight and sustained men even through the dark endless days of the midwar and the grueling bloodbaths of 1864. In many ways women clearly participated in the value systems expressed by the war-torn North, and they wondered publicly whether the North could sustain the character necessary for republicanism. Their work celebrated sacrifice, and often claimed that such sacrifice was necessary to reestablish virtue in a wavering nation.[40] In a sense, white middle-class women's effort to create a rhetoric of unity was part of a larger national effort toward consensus. As historian Earl J. Hess argues, "Northerners . . . stressed the viability of free government, seeing proof that ideological consensus could unite individualistic people in a common cause, focus their energy on a central purpose, and give them the motivation and strength to endure."[41] Particularly for women like Lydia Maria Child, Jane Swisshelm, Mary Abigail Dodge, and others trained (or self-taught) in the tradition of republicanism and liberalism, these were powerfully motivating ideas.

Other women did not demonstrate the same confidence in the power of republicanism, liberty, or the belief in progress to sustain them. Women's relationship to republicanism was uneasy, given their subordinate status within it: as dependents, at least ideologically, their voices were not meant to be heard in a national public context, just as their political ideas, represented by the vote, were not accepted. Similarly, the ideology of individualism, held in tension with republicanism, was problematic as well. Embraced by some, it was emphatically rejected by others as a kind of dismissal of the connections and responsibilities of family and community. As a result, women had diverging positions on the reigning ideologies supporting the Union war effort, even as they claimed a public space in the discussion of the war's necessity and purpose.

This is not to say that Northern women were not patriotic—many, given their work, sacrifice, and words, decidedly were—but their relationship to war, fought at a distance, claiming family members to whom they were deeply committed, and based on an ideological system within which they fit at times poorly, was distinct from men's. For women there seemed to be no ruling consensus on the meaning of Union, or on the cause of the strife. For many of them—with crucial exceptions—the question was not always how to justify the sacrifice but how to endure it.

That uneasy relationship to the national struggle can help explain women's constant reference to their "place": even to speak in support of the ideological meaning of the war effort was to disturb its internal logic, and yet not to intervene in the crisis consuming the nation seemed to lack virtue as well. Their rhetoric of unity, then, was a kind of offering: women would be a virtuous backbone for the battlefront, stalwart in the face of loss, not quite dependent, if never independent, yet claiming space in the national crisis. The problem was, however, that this ideological offering could not sustain the material and political differences among Northern women: its rhetoric only briefly had resonance for the wider public.

THIS BOOK EXPLORES two separate and related histories of the war in order to illuminate the revolution Northern women writers claimed for their sex. First, this is a history gleaned through literary works designed for public consumption, focusing on political issues in the writing of Northern women from 1850 to 1872. This history suggests a gradual and contested shift from sentimental to realistic writing, demonstrated within as well as between texts. Women writers continued to see their work as moral activism throughout the period, periodically changing the objects of their struggles but not their commitment to moral suasion itself. During this period in literary history as well, women writers moved from what literary critic Susan K. Harris calls the exploratory to the later didactic novel, a move that meant a changed understanding of womanhood and social possibility, as well as a discernible lifting of some of the boundaries of woman's sphere, if only fictionally.

Secondly, and equally as important, this work offers an intellectual portrait of nine popular women writers by following them and their work

"Eminent Women," from a collection of photographs of famous women writers of the nineteenth century. These women never actually sat for the picture together (although many of them met and read each other's work). Among those pictured here are women who wrote regularly on the issues of war, including Phelps, Moulton, Alcott, Howe (author of the famous "Battle Hymn of the Republic"), Stowe, and Livermore. (Photo used by permission of the Schlesinger Library, Radcliffe College.)

through the war years and afterward. These include Lydia Maria Child, Harriet Beecher Stowe, Fanny Fern, Mrs. E. D. E. N. Southworth, Frances Ellen Watkins Harper, Gail Hamilton (Mary Abigail Dodge), Louisa May Alcott, Rebecca Harding Davis, and Elizabeth Stuart Phelps. Among the dozens of women writers who broached the war topic—some popular and others virtually unknown—these nine seemed both exceptional and representative, covering varied audiences and overlapping generations. An analysis of the lives and writing of these women demonstrates the transformation in thinking and writing that the Civil War meant for working writers. The war moved writers of an older generation to a more active politics while helping to establish the new confident voices of a younger generation coming of age during the late 1850s and early 1860s.

These nine were exceptional, for Northern women, primarily because they were writers, earning their living and often supporting their families on income from published work. They were also exceptional in their politics: it is very unlikely that Northern women as a whole were as committed to the end of slavery as these writers were. Yet they were also, in a sense, representative, or at least resonant for their readers: these were women whose work was sought out and eagerly awaited, reprinted in numerous magazines and newspapers, and referred to in lesser-known novels in an offhand way, as if the readers would immediately see and understand the references. If these were not the politics of the readers, they were at least positions readers wanted to know about and ponder. Their work appeared, also, in the more progressive venues: to publish a woman writer on any issue approaching politics was a kind of political statement by editors and publishers. Given these venues—papers like the *New York Ledger*, magazines like *Atlantic Monthly*—the politics of these nine women were representative.

The Civil War and the sectional issues that preceded it offered women writers the opportunity to enter into debates of national significance. Even if using the back door of cultural documents, women joined a political dialogue. Their heroines, whether autobiographical or fictional, were meant to inspire and influence their readers; even the most sensationalist works had didactic—and political—purposes. These writings demonstrated an ongoing and consistent effort to redefine in an outward motion the limits of women's sphere. As essayist Mary Abigail Dodge wryly wrote in 1865, "I shall not confine myself to my sphere. I hate my sphere. I like everything that is outside of it,—or, better still, my sphere rounds out into undefined space. I was born into the whole world. I am monarch of all I survey."[42] This book explores how the writings of women reached out into public life during this tumultuous time, "round[ing] out into undefined space," and touching their hearts, as Oliver Wendell Holmes put it, "with fire."[43]

. . . and now I am at it again, for nothing but deadly determination enables me ever to write; it is rowing against wind and tide.

—Harriet Beecher Stowe, from Charles Edward Stowe, ed.,

Life of Harriet Beecher Stowe (1889)

{ CHAPTER ONE }

Rowing against Wind and Tide

How Women Wrote

"YOU SAY I MUST NOT worry about you. I cannot help it," Sarah Fales wrote in July of 1861 to her son, Edmund, from their farm in Middletown, Rhode Island. Later she asked that he not forget to write "and let us know how you fare and have you got stockings enough and what have you got for shirts." Apparently he didn't forget, and when she heard that his purple shirt had faded, she promised him a plaid. Fales was a farmer's wife, and, given her letters, clearly one with some education. Edmund was her only child. Her letter to him on the eve of battle may have been like many, although relatively few letters from home were saved. In it Fales reveals her fear, her sense of patriotic necessity, and her desire to maintain the domestic bonds that connect her to her only child, leading her to worry, for example, about purple shirts fading.

Mixed in with, and inseparable from, the domestic was the political. "This war, disguise it as we may, is a terrible reality," Fales wrote to her child, just days before he would fight in the first battle of Bull Run. "It is sad to think how many lives have been and still will be sacrificed before it is over." She was well aware of the town's fears and, with her husband, lamented its response. "You ask how the Middletown boys feel about the draft," she wrote. "I do not know much about the boys, but some of the men have been terribly frightened." They proposed, in a town meeting, to hire Irishmen from the railroad contractor to make up the requisite numbers. "Father says," she added, "there will be no drafting as long as there is a dollar left in the town. What do you think of that for patriotism and love of country? In such times of danger as these we have reason to be thankful it is not so everywhere." The implication that Irishmen could be hired to fight from the railroad contractor offers its own message: if their boss could thus determine their life's choices, this made wage work much like Southern slavery.

When the government threatened to draft her husband, however, Fales was adamant. At forty-six, he was a year over the age limit, but his name had gotten put on a list for drafting. When an official from the draft board came to her door, she "told the man he could take [his name] off again." And when Edmund was considering whether to reenlist in early 1863, his mother deferred the matter to his own judgment, saying only that this didn't reflect her "personal feelings," for "a mother's love would plead for her boy."[1]

Sarah Fales's letters both reveal and obscure her political position on the war. As the more literate one in the family—"Father says a part of my writing is for him," she says—Fales was responsible for representing the family and community's news. Her representation of that world revealed her intimate knowledge of the farm's workings, the townspeople's angst, and even of battlefield strategy (she was critical of the Peninsula campaign, saying she was glad when "the army has got back this side of the river again. I hope they won't try to take Richmond that way again this winter").

Yet it is never entirely clear what inspires Fales's national loyalty. While she respects her son's commitment deeply—as a boy he is acting more honorably than the men, she implies—she uses no explicitly republican language of virtue, nor does she seem moved by the concept of Union.[2] Love of country, and one senses that means a literal love of the earth she tends, and love of her son, and his courage, seem to mean more to her than any more abstract ideals. After Edmund has been gone for two years, she feels he has earned the right to pride and respect, and her personal feelings "plead for her boy."

These letters tellingly reveal the enormous amount of work Sarah Fales routinely did, and the ways in which she, too, aided the war effort. It is clear she took over some of what were once Edmund's tasks, particularly the husbanding of his favorite sheep, "Morry," who appears in a few letters as mischievous and always hungry. She tells Edmund about the hoeing of the garden, the milking, the harvesting of corn and hay, about when his vines were producing grapes and when his bees were swarming. Despite her anxiety that the boxes of food she sent him would get mislaid, she made sure to send only those things that would not spoil "for some time unless some one spoiled them by helping themselves to them." And she knew of his entire wardrobe, from the faded purple shirt to the number and condition of his stockings.

Fales was a relatively well-off rural farmer's wife in the most urban of states: Rhode Island. In some sense, however, she is clearly representative of many Northern women and their relationship to the Civil War. Her contribution was a son, the clothes on his back, boxes of food and other supplies, and letters that cheered and teased and informed. In a life that included hard labor, from the hoeing of the garden, to the tending of chickens, sheep, ducks, cows, and bees, to the making and mending of shirts, these sacrifices are significant indeed.

TO UNDERSTAND THE contributions of writing women to the cultural and political life of the nation during the 1850s and 1860s, the lives of Sarah Fales and women like her must form the backdrop. Women writers did not stand outside of the duties that shaped the lives of their contemporaries. Their sense of the nation's problems—gleaned from conversations, sermons, lectures, letters, newspapers, and magazines—came from time stolen from their daily concerns. Writing about those problems represented additional time stolen, even for women who supported themselves and their families by writing. In weighing the meaning of that writing, one must also consider what helped and hindered its production.

Not surprisingly, what distinguishes the nine main writers considered here from Sarah Fales and others like her was the degree of their domestic involvement: unlike Fales, none of them was a farmer's wife, although a few knew and participated in the rituals of growing vegetables and tending livestock. These nine women thought of themselves, and were thought of, as writers; they were often if not always the primary breadwinners for their families; and they tended to live in or near urban areas in the Northeast. This chapter will serve as an introduction to them, and to the lives that informed the work they and others like them did during the Civil War era.

Like Sarah Fales, Harriet Beecher Stowe was besieged by competing demands on her time. In the early 1850s she was surrounded by children. Of her seven offspring, six were living, one an infant that still woke in the middle of the night. Stowe and her husband had just moved to Brunswick, Maine, from Cincinnati, Ohio, where much of her family still lived. In a letter to a friend Stowe humorously sketched the contours of her life: "Since I began this note I have been called off at least a dozen times; once for the fish man, to buy a codfish; once to see a man who had brought me some barrels of apples; once to see a book-man; then to Mrs. Upham, to see about a drawing I promised to make for her; then to nurse the baby; then into the kitchen to make a chowder for dinner; and now I am at it again, for nothing but deadly determination enables me ever to write; it is rowing against wind and tide."[3] Stowe was "called off" by multiple priorities: to feed her family, both immediately—chowder for dinner—and in the long term—barrels of apples; to see a "book-man," which could mean to buy books for herself, her husband, or her children, since she was undoubtedly responsible at least in part for their education; to give "Mrs. Upham," presumably a neighbor, what she'd promised, indicating both her inclination and perhaps her perceived responsibility to the community; then to nurse her baby, a regular and insistent demand.

Despite this context of chaos, responsibility, and familial isolation, Stowe was deeply interested in national politics. So when her sister-in-law Isabella Beecher wrote, "if I could use a pen as you can, I would write something that would make this whole nation feel what an accursed thing slavery is," Stowe's response was both troubled and inspired. She sent a message back thanking her sister-in-law for her note, promising that as soon as the baby slept through the night, and providing that she lived, she would do it.[4]

That note of self-pity and anxiety—if she lived—represented real fears. Another of the nineteenth century's most popular writers, Elizabeth Stuart Phelps, lost her mother when she was around Stowe's age. In her autobiography, Phelps attributes her mother's death to the confluence of domestic and literary duties, duties that literally killed her:

Now she sits correcting proof-sheets, and now she is painting apostles for the baby's first Bible lesson. Now she is writing her new book, and now she is dyeing things canary-yellow in the white-oak dye—for the professor's salary is small, and a crushing economy was in those days one of the conditions of faculty life on Andover Hill. Now—for her practical ingenuity was unlimited—she is whittling little wooden feet to stretch the children's stockings on, to save them from shrinking; and now she is reading to us from the old, old red copy of Hazlitt's "British Poets," by the register, upon a winter's night. Now she is a popular writer, incredulous of her first success, with her future flashing before her; and now she is a tired, tender mother, crooning to a sick child, while the MS. lies unprinted on the table, and the publishers are wishing their professor's wife were a free woman, childless and solitary, able to send copy as fast as it is wanted. The struggle killed her, but she fought till she fell.[5]

If Harriet Beecher Stowe and Elizabeth Stuart Phelps went on to experience lives more like that of a "free woman" in the 1850s and 1860s, they and Sarah Fales shared a world where women's work—even for the privileged middle class—was never done.[6]

To appreciate the "deadly determination" of Northern women who wrote for a public audience during the 1850s and 1860s, then, it is important to appreciate the dailiness of their lives, that tide they rowed against. Not only does this daily ritual suggest what they had to overcome and explain the small amount produced by any one woman writer—with important exceptions—but it suggests the priorities of their lives, what they were routinely fighting for and against. To do political work was to take time away from the domestic and the familial, the values most significant in their immediate context. In addition, it suggests the connectedness of any woman's political and domestic life, the connection between a faded purple shirt and the nation's destiny on the battlefield, between ideas about Morry and his yen for crackers and about the meaning of patriotism and love of country. Despite the ideology that ruled Northern middle-class women's sense of the public world, the political and domestic were not separate spheres, they were literally on the same page.

Northern women's intellectual and cultural work differed considerably from that of middle-class Northern men. For those men, writing constituted the bulk of their daily work, and they did not have to excuse their appearance on a public stage. If public and private, domestic and political were never as bifurcated as convenient historical categories have posited, women still frequently began or ended the literary work with an apologia tendered on the basis of their sex, or lack of experience, or both. And the domestic work alone separated what was possible, if it did not somehow shut off women's political and intellectual work.

The North was in the process of transformation as these women bought codfish, sewed plaid shirts, and whittled little wooden feet to stretch out socks. These shifts were more dramatic than those in the South in the 1850s, and they had deep-seated effects. Lines between classes were hardening; urban areas were developing; and immigrants were arriving in ever greater numbers, even as the political conflict between North and South intensified. The developers of the Lowell mills who had predicted that the industrial world would never come to this promised land had long since been proven wrong. Those transformations—in work, in play, and in civic life— had significant consequences for the reading and writing lives of women.

Wind and Tide: The Obstacles and Inspiration of Political Work

In March of 1850 Lydia Maria Child wrote to a wealthy friend of hers with a proposition. For a number of years she had lived apart from her husband and boarded with friends in New York, first as she edited the *National Anti-Slavery Standard* and then while she wrote *The Progress of Religious Ideas*. Now she wished to reunite with David, who had come back from out west after fruitlessly trying to make money. Aware that if she intended to live with her husband again she would have to support them both (he never seemed able to make money), Child asked her friend Ellis Loring for assistance. If he would buy a small property of three or four acres of land, she and David would work the land and pay rent. Ultimately, she hoped, they would buy the farm from him.

A year later she wrote again, to apologize for being unable to pay the rent: David had gone into debt; wood had cost more than she had bargained for; and the land was rocky and filled with tree stumps. They'd had to replace a drain to their sink, which had been made of wood (and hence rotted), to repaper the inside of the house, and to fix the window fastenings. She wished, she wrote to Loring, that she could transfer all her savings and earnings (in royalties) to him, by some legal form, in order to protect them from David's mismanagement, but she feared how discouraged David would be if he discovered her plan. She closed by begging Loring to destroy the letter.[7]

Child's letter suggests the concerns that many women faced, from the practical problems of water (the drain) to the more complicated ones of financial management. When functioning as a housekeeper, which all nine writers did for much of the next twenty-five years, they had to negotiate the many difficulties of running a household in the mid-nineteenth century while carving out time and a space for intellectual work. They had to either cook or supervise three meals a day; make or buy, and then wash weekly, the clothes for spouse, self, and children; heat and light the house, as well as clean it; and all the while bear, raise, and educate, and sometimes nurse and mourn their children.

Food was women's constant preoccupation. As the 1850s began, what people ate shifted given their geographical region. In the Northeast, this meant white rather than sweet potatoes, pork as the meat of choice rather than beef, and lots of corn. Lettuce and other leafy vegetables spoiled easily and thus were not generally eaten in any great quantities. Bread, either flat, like pancakes, or yeast bread, which was considerably harder to make, was served with almost every meal. Before the decade was over finely ground "white" flour was more widely available and easier to use. Ironically, this was no advance for harried cooks: it often meant higher expectations for baking previously special rolls, pastries, and cakes on a regular basis. Those more elaborate confections, along with white bread, generally signaled class aspirations and distinctions.[8]

Fruits and most vegetables had to be canned fairly swiftly after the harvest—the Mason jar was introduced in 1858—and this involved several days of added work.[9] (Not until the 1860s were store-bought canned goods regarded with anything but suspicion.) Meals were cooked over the fire or the newer ranges and cookstoves, which went through many changes during this period. By 1850, fires were most often coal-burning, although Child mentioned her husband cutting wood, which was, at the time, too green for burning. Both forms of fuel required constant tending, including gathering it and watching that it burned evenly below brick ovens for baking or meat. Cleaning out the ash and blacking the stove were also frequent tasks.

These newer closed stoves, which gave kitchens—and homes in general—much more heat in winter and summer, were often deadly. In *House and Home Papers*, which Harriet Beecher Stowe published as the war was ending, she wrote ironically about the threat of carbon monoxide poisoning from these fuel- and labor-saving new stoves. "[I]n thousands and thousands of cases it has saved people from all other human wants, and put an end forever to any needs short of six feet of narrow earth which are man's only inalienable property."[10] Stoves created work, too. Ash and soot covered all surfaces during the winter months, and can help explain the ubiquitous spring cleaning, where all windows, walls, closets, bedding, and furniture covering were washed, repaired, and replaced.

Yet stoves, and with them, furnaces, *did* improve some mid-nineteenth century lives considerably, if only by making them more comfortable in the winter. They also encouraged a communal life in those months, as, for example, Phelps and her brother snuggled up to a register and listened to their mother read a story in the example above. By midcentury they were available to upper-class and a growing number of middle-class homes; the working class, as with most of the new improvements of the nineteenth century, went without.

In a given week, women not only had to cook three times a day, but they also had to wash their family's clothes, generally on Monday (Sunday was customarily the day to change clothes for the week). Laundry was one of the most dreaded tasks of a mid-nineteenth century's woman's life, and often a neighbor's daughter was hired to help. It required multiple steps: stained clothing needed soaking in advance, and then to be scrubbed, rinsed, and boiled. The garment was then rinsed again and if needed, dipped in starch, wrung out either by hand or with a hand-turned wringer, and then hung to dry. The next day, clothes and linen would be ironed. The most time consuming and taxing part of the laundry was not even the scrubbing but the moving of water from the source (rarely nearby) to the kitchen and out again. Making or purchasing soap and starch took even more time or forethought, as would the dyeing of cloth.

Happily for the middle-class woman, by 1850 the weaving of cloth in the home had largely become a thing of the past, given the development of factories in Pawtucket, Lowell, and Lawrence. But until well after the Civil War, women still made clothing at home, generally with the help of seamstresses, who would cut out and fashion the garment, leaving the needlework for women to do almost every evening. Louisa May Alcott, marveling at her first bedroom alone (a short-lived luxury), mentioned her workbasket beside her desk as a matter of course. Men's clothing became ready-made well before women's, but sizes were not standardized until after the wartime press for uniforms. Sarah Fales, for example, still made all of Edmund's clothes at home.

If cloth was available, it was still very costly. Women not only sewed new clothes but repaired and refashioned old: socks with large holes were made small for children, and if they shrank, as in Phelps's mother's experience, they were stretched for further use. Sleeves that had faded were turned and used again. When Jo March of *Little Women* burns her dress by crowding too close to the fire, she simply has to stand with her back to the wall at a party until she can repair it; wardrobes were understandably small even in the middle class.[11] In Fanny Fern's semi-autobiographical novel,

Ruth Hall, her protagonist's in-laws demand that her husband's clothes be given to them after his death—including the suit he was married in.

A central element in this matrix of work were the children. As more and more production moved outside of the home during the nineteenth century, higher standards for child-rearing and a virtual cult of motherhood became common for the middle class. Fathers had less influence on and less time with their children, and it was assumed that all emotional and spiritual guidance would come from women. Most of their intellectual life initially came from mothers, too, if middle-class children also went to school, either in the developing common school system or at private academies. Elizabeth Stuart Phelps's mother, who read literary classics to her children, was relatively unusual: mothers most often used the Bible, along with a growing children's literature and old favorites like John Bunyan's *Pilgrim's Progress*. Yet middle-class mothers took this educating very seriously. Harriet Beecher Stowe ran a little school in her home in Maine as the 1850s began and read all of Sir Walter Scott's novels in order to teach English history to her children.[12]

Once they reached ages five and six, children could often be as much a help as a hindrance. They generally began to help with domestic work, even in middle-class homes, sometimes by watching the younger children, sewing, chopping vegetables, and setting tables. When older they carried wood, coal, and water in addition to carrying messages. At the same time, mothers worked hard at inculcating middle-class values in their children with the tending of these chores, teaching them the social rules of manhood and womanhood and the virtues of self-discipline and hard work.

Death rates for children in the antebellum North were understandably high, given a dearth of medical knowledge, hazardous living conditions, and the unavoidably divided attention of most mothers. Cholera, typhoid, and flu took many parents and children, among them Fanny Fern's husband, Louisa May Alcott's sister, and Harriet Beecher Stowe's two-year-old child. (Another of Stowe's sons died later in the 1850s by drowning.) Complications in childbirth led to both maternal and infant deaths (Phelps's mother died this way). Well before the war, women were too often acquainted with death in their immediate family; what the war did was to make otherwise quite personal and sometimes protracted deathbed scenes distant and quick, and as a result, unfathomable.

The roots of women's war work went deep into the domestic lives that preceded it. Nursing family members was a regular occupation, and writing women, like their contemporaries, often remembered times in their lives based on the illnesses they presided over. Mrs. E. D. E. N. Southworth, a single mother living in Washington, D.C., in 1846, remembered the constancy of "keeping school and keeping house." While writing her breakthrough novel *Retribution*, published in 1849, her son was gravely ill, and she managed it only "before and after school hours, at night and in the intervals when the sick was sleeping, or at least free from pain."[13]

Lydia Maria Child underscored the strenuous dailiness of the work in a list she compiled of her achievements of 1864. In addition to sewing and writing she:

> Cooked 360 dinners.
> Cooked 362 breakfasts.
> Swept and dusted sitting-room and kitchen 350 times.
> Filled lamps 362 times.
> Swept and dusted chamber & stairs 40 times.

That she saved this record for herself and posterity indicates Child's sense of the bitter, unending reality of domestic work, mixed with pride in her productivity.

Domestic work was crucial to both the familial economy and to the development of industrial capitalism. Historian Jeanne Boydston adds up the benefits that accrued to a household run by a frugal and able house-keeper, who could be expected in any given year to sew and mend, cook and clean, make and repair household materials from featherbeds to quilts to window fasteners, to judiciously shop and tend to children, to nurse, and in some cases to take in boarders or relatives. "The exact value varied from woman to woman," she argues, "but it would seem judicious to conclude that the labor of a middle-class wife might easily be worth upwards of $700 a year to her household."[14] Middle- and working-class men were encouraged to marry; in marrying they made an important and lasting investment, and saved significantly on boarding costs.

Housework was crucial to the larger economy, and inseparable from the family. Because women routinely worked in the home earning that $700 a year, sometimes even after a day of factory work, employers could depress wages for both women and men. And, as Boydston points out, women's cash value was "embedded in the collectivity of the family." There was little if any way women could earn the same amount outside the home, despite their production of its value. Because those services were so often "free," they were rarely marketable. Women's dependence upon the family, like industry's on her, was, as Boydston put it, "acute."[15]

Bereft of men, women could swiftly find themselves in terrible circumstances. Before she became famous as Fanny Fern, Sara Willis (later Parton) was widowed when typhoid carried off her husband. Prior to that time she, her husband, and her two remaining children (her first child died) were living in a boardinghouse in comfortable circumstances. Willis, for example, had no cooking to do, and it was likely that the boardinghouse also laundered her family's clothes along with the linen. Yet with her husband's death Willis assumed his debts, and all their assets went to paying them. Neither her family nor his would adequately support them, and almost overnight she found herself destitute, living on bread and milk and trying to support herself by sewing.[16]

In Louisa May Alcott's autobiographical novel, *Work*, published after the war, her orphaned protagonist leaves her aunt and uncle's home and sets out to make a living for herself. The novel demonstrates a few of the possible occupations available to middle-class women in the nineteenth century, among them teaching, sewing, acting as a "companion" to upper-class young women, and nursing. None paid well, and few even well enough to permit any degree of comfort for a middle-class woman living independently of a family.

Like Sara Willis, many writers began with other occupations, most typically teaching. In 1850 Frances Ellen Watkins (later Harper), who would subsequently become a well-known African American poet, left her home in Baltimore in order to teach sewing at the Union Seminary in Columbus, Ohio. Two years later she went on to Little York, Pennsylvania, for another teaching job. In 1853 a law passed in Maryland made it impossible for her to go home: free blacks in that state were made vulnerable to sale as slaves.[17] Mary Abigail Dodge, an essayist who wrote as Gail Hamilton, also began as a teacher at the Ipswich Female Seminary in Massachusetts, which she had attended as a student. Even though she was thought to be a particularly good teacher, she found the job constricting and underpaid, and she left it to teach and supervise Gamiliel Bailey's children in Washington, D.C. Her connection to Bailey, the editor of the *National Era*, served her well; his national magazine had originally published *Uncle Tom's Cabin*.[18]

GIVEN THE HEAVY constraints on women, the question remains: how *were* they able to write? The answer is common to all: only with a great deal of support from other women, both emotional but more to the point, physical.[19] Harriet Beecher Stowe's sister-in-law may have encouraged her to speak out about the strengthened Fugitive Slave Act, but Stowe was also blessed with the help of various young women. Although her servants helped her instead of entirely relieving her from work, such aid enabled her to find time for her writing. Lydia Maria Child, with no children, was more mobile (though she stayed in one place throughout most of the war period) and lived during much of her earlier career in boardinghouses, where crucial house and laundry tending was often cared for by another woman.

As writing came to be a priority for these women, they could sometimes shift their familial priorities. When Lydia Maria Child wrote to Ellis Gray, asking him to rent a house for her and her husband, she told him she would not be able to move there at first. She would send her husband on ahead while she finished the book she was working on. New York offered greater proximity to the libraries she needed, and she did not want to move her papers, as she had had to previously.[20] Elizabeth Stuart Phelps, after writing her first book shivering in an unheated room covered with her mother's shawl, wrote many of her subsequent ones in a little one-room house built for her in the backyard by her father.

Even given assistance from servants, boardinghouse keepers, and family, women writers still had to buck convention to write. This was almost equally true for those writing novels with only covert political messages. In *Knowledge Is Power*, historian Richard Brown analyzes the ways in which women received and interpreted public knowledge. While female literacy equaled male literacy by the 1830s, women's education was limited by strictures on *what* they could read, strictures they often internalized. Lucy Breckenridge, for example, a young Southern woman, wrote in her diary of the 1860 novel *La Femme*, by Jules Michelot, "I do not like that kind of reading . . . it scares me of myself, and makes me rebel against my lot."[21] In this regard, Breckenridge, a wealthy white Southerner, was like many of her contemporaries. As Brown notes, "Nearly all the information to which she enjoyed access, whether through conversation, observation, or letter, through public speech or printed matter, focused on private life—especially social manners and personal emotional states—thereby reinforcing the central doctrine of separate spheres."[22] This might help to explain the very personal and moral ways that many women understood patriotism and the war effort.

Ironically, however, that doctrine was undercut by the very exclusion it created and sustained. The "information environments" Brown describes were woman-centered, allowing for discussion and resistance to emerge when clothed in domestic settings and with sentimental language. If "history, politics, natural philosophy, and a host of other subjects interested particular women . . . it was the world of sentiment that religion and the novel both expressed, which held priority."[23] Novels from the late eighteenth century were intended to inform and instruct as well as offer an escape from drudgery, and women both read them and wrote them with those goals in mind.

First, of course, these women had to get their work published. A market revolution in publishing made the careers of writing women possible, much as their domestic lives constrained it.[24] As the technologies of printing presses, typesetting, and paper improved, so did the commercial viability of supporting American literary efforts. Publishers managed to shed some of their dependence on English reprints with the development of viable publishing houses in America. By the 1840s and 1850s, literary monthlies like *Harper's* (1850), *Putnam's* (1853), and the *Atlantic* (1857) joined story papers like the *New York Ledger* (1855).[25] Many of these periodicals depended on women writers to increase and sustain their business.

Literate adults underwrote this literary outpouring. "The democratic goal of universal literacy in the new republic was translated into broadened opportunities for education," historian Mary Kelley argues, "with the result that approximately 90 percent of the adult white population, men and women, entered the literate category during the first part of the nineteenth century."[26] As historian Susan Geary explains, "[T]he new literary patron was the common man, man in the mass." This transformation of readership was "finally and fully accomplished" in the 1850s, she argues, "for it was then that the publishing industry finally found itself able to manufacture and distribute books in large quantities quickly, cheaply, and efficiently."[27]

Novels—the most widely accepted form of popular culture in the early nineteenth century, and scorned by intellectuals and ministers for that reason—came to dominate the literary marketplace by midcentury. With the introduction of patents, or copyrights, and competition for the stories of popular authors came greater remuneration. "For the first time," Kelley finds, "the American writer could consider the possibility of linking creative effort with vocation."[28]

Women played a central role in this emerging literary culture. As readers and consumers they exercised increasing control over the marketplace, dictating its direction through their purchasing habits. By the 1850s, some writers were able to support themselves and their families with their pens. Susan Warner's *The Wide, Wide World* became the best-selling novel in American history in 1850, eclipsed only by Harriet Beecher Stowe's *Uncle Tom's Cabin* in 1852. By the end of the decade Fanny Fern had written the militant *Ruth Hall* and Mrs. E. D. E. N. Southworth had serialized one of her most popular novels, *The Hidden Hand*.[29]

The novelists were not alone. Louisa May Alcott, Rose Terry (Cooke), and Louise Chandler (Moulton) began writing short stories in the 1850s, as Frances E. Watkins (Harper), Lucy Larcom, and Julia Ward (Howe) were publishing their poetry for the first time. Mary Abigail Dodge wrote her first essays for publication in this decade. Jane Swisshelm, Ann S. Stephens, and Dr. Lydia Hasbrouck, among others, joined Sarah Hale in the editing of newspapers and magazines in the 1850s. This subversion of male prerogative caused at least Swisshelm some amusement. Her first paper, the *Pittsburgh Saturday Visiter* [sic] "was quite an insignificant looking sheet," she remembered, but it still shocked men. "[N]o sooner did the American eagle catch sight of it," Swisshelm wrote, "than he swooned and fell off his perch."[30]

The American eagle seemed to swoon at transgressions of subject matter as well as form during the 1850s. As an editor from the *North American Review* wrote in 1851, "[A]part from the consideration, that a female author puts much of her personal individuality into her work, being more prone to express emotions than ideas, it may be said that in taking *any* public stand for praise or for blame, a woman risks more than a man." Over a decade later an anonymous essayist in *The Knickerbocker* made a similar observation, writing that some men found women's trespass on issues of metaphysics or philosophy an "unpardonable sin." "These little men are pallid with terror," the essayist wrote, "and they run up and down the sidewalk and the forum, crying: Woman is 'unsexing' herself; she is stepping out of her 'sphere!'" The issue of sphere, the writer concluded, is a simple one: "for the inevitable test of sphere is success. What man or woman can do, and do well, God doubtless intended they should do."[31]

The political and intellectual work of women, then, came before, during, and between the tasks of domesticity, tasks even the more privileged among middle-class women writers had to undertake. This domestic and familial world provided the lens through which women saw and understood politics; they did not have the leisure of their male writing contemporaries. Yet the circumstances of each woman writer, both those at the center of this work, and those that only occasionally inform it, were also specific to them, and it is to those more specific circumstances that we now turn.

Nine Rowers

At the beginning of the 1850s, the nine Northern women who form the core of this study of the Civil War spanned forty-two years in age. The oldest, Lydia Maria Child, was forty-eight in 1850 and frankly confessed in a letter that she had expected to die that year, having foreseen it in a dream.[32] The youngest, Elizabeth Stuart Phelps, was six and would lose her mother and adopt her mother's name two years later. The others—Harriet Beecher Stowe, Fanny Fern, E. D. E. N. Southworth, Frances Ellen Watkins Harper, Rebecca Harding Davis, Louisa May Alcott, and Gail Hamilton—ranged in age from thirty-nine to seventeen.

These women were chosen not because they are, somehow, representative of all Northern middle-class women, or even Northern women writers. Rather it is their distinctiveness that identifies them: they wrote consistently during the Civil War period (or began writing then); they produced multiple novels, essays, poems, letters to the editor, or stories about the war; and they persevered despite the "wind and tide" of their individual lives. Most were white. Most supported themselves and their kin solely through writing. None of these women was particularly wealthy in 1850, although Harriet Beecher Stowe became so as her fame increased, and some of them—Lydia Maria Child and Fanny Fern—were at times quite poor. Other women, some of whom left only their byline on a few poems or stories, crowd around these nine when reporting the history of the war and the decades that preceded and followed it.

These women were unusual not only in their writing. As noted before, only Lydia Maria Child, the oldest among them, ever helped run a farm the way Sarah Fales did. Unlike the majority of their contemporaries, many of them lived in urban or semi-urban areas. Not surprisingly, most of these women had some experience of formal schooling, and all, save Elizabeth Stuart Phelps, were teachers or tutors themselves before becoming writers. Of the nine, seven married and five had children, which is slightly less than representative.

What was also unrepresentative (although this is harder to measure) was the position these writers took on issues of slavery and race. All nine acknowledged and deplored in some way the severe bifurcation in the nation along racial lines, although only Child, Stowe, Harper, and Davis made it a central theme in their writing during the war years. The eight white women depicted here were as deeply affected by racial consciousness as Frances Ellen Watkins Harper; their whiteness had for them an implicit wage, allowing them entry into the publishing world in a way generally not possible for African American women.[33] Stowe, for example, used slave narratives to write *Uncle Tom's Cabin*, and Lydia Maria Child acted as an editor for Harriet Jacobs's *Incidents in the Life of a Slave Girl*. Davis, Southworth, and Harper grew up in slave states, where the reminders of their free status would be evident on a daily basis. Fanny Fern's fictionalized autobiography, *Ruth Hall*, was likened to a slave narrative in a review, but her triumph as a very well paid writer of editorials for the *New York Ledger* would never have been possible for an African American woman. In short, all these authors used, and were directly affected by, race.

Regionally, New England had the greatest influence on these women: of the nine, six grew up and were educated there. The three who were not— E. D. E. N. Southworth (Maryland and Virginia), Frances Ellen Watkins Harper (Maryland), and Rebecca Harding Davis (Virginia)—consistently and deliberately wrote about the South, seemingly as a kind of corrective to New England arrogance even as they supported the Union.

Perhaps the best way to organize a swift recovery of these writer's lives is to group them both generationally and regionally, given the significance of these influences. In one cohort, then, would be Lydia Maria Child, Harriet Beecher Stowe, and Fanny Fern. Although Child was nine years older than Stowe and Fern (who were born the same year), and although her religious training and beliefs could not have been more different from Stowe's, these women grew up in a New England undergoing fierce change, both industrially and socially. Their shared nexus was the Commonwealth of Massachusetts, a state both radical and conservative, eager for change and deeply resistant to it. The Massachusetts of Gail Hamilton, Louisa May Alcott, and Elizabeth Stuart Phelps, by contrast, was one where industrialism's presence was well established and class lines had hardened. These women grew up with more conveniences, more access to education, and a greater sense of middle-class respectability, if much stayed the same.

New England Mothers: Introducing Child, Stowe, and Fern

By 1850 Lydia Maria Child had distanced herself from the antislavery community and felt old and tired. Born in 1802, she was nearing fifty when the Compromise of 1850 was passed, and she must have believed all her years of antislavery work were making no headway against popular prejudice. Her strongly argued and influential essay on slavery, *An Appeal in Favor of That Class of Americans Called Africans*, squelched her promising literary career in 1833. Although two collections of editorials on city life, *Letters from New York*, revived some of her earlier fame, she was now immersed in a constant round of what she found to be deadening domestic work. Child had struggled financially at almost every turn, her idealistic but improvident husband, David Lee Child, hindering rather than helping their survival.

Lydia Francis (she adopted the name "Maria" when she was christened) was born in Medford, Massachusetts, the youngest child of David and

Susannah Francis. Her father was a baker, known for his well-loved "Medford Crackers." Child had little formal schooling: a local "dame school" was followed by "Miss Swan's Seminary" for a year. Her brother, Convers, by contrast, attended Harvard and later became a professor at the Divinity School there. After Susannah Francis's early death in 1814, Lydia was sent to live with an older married sister in Maine. Despite her lack of schooling, she was reading Homer, John Milton, and Sir Walter Scott by the time she was fifteen.[34] Three years later, Lydia moved to live with Convers and his wife in Watertown, Massachusetts.

From the first, Lydia Maria Francis was a writer, although the interest in antislavery reform that would ultimately come to dominate and define her life came later. Unlike Stowe, for example, Child's career did not so much take off as revive in the 1850s. Her cultural and political work had begun when she was twenty-two, after she heeded a call for a truly American literature. Her impulse then, as later, was toward historical inquiry: the 1824 novel *Hobomok*, which lambasted Calvinism and offered a daring interracial marriage between an Indian youth and a Puritan maid, was set in Salem, Massachusetts, in the early 1600s. If in the end the Indian relinquishes both his love and his child to the immigrant Europeans, the work was still shocking in the context in which it was published. The clarity and edge of its voice and the interest of its story gained the fledgling writer entry into a literary Boston, albeit one that would rudely shut seven years later. Child followed *Hobomok* with another historical novel, *The Rebels, or Boston before the Revolution*, in 1825. The following year she began to edit the country's first magazine for children, *Juvenile Miscellany*, and in 1829 her well-loved *The Frugal Housewife* was published.

In 1831 the course of Lydia Maria Child's life changed dramatically. The radical abolitionist William Lloyd Garrison, Child later wrote in a letter, "got hold of the strings of my conscience and pulled me into reforms. . . . Old dreams vanished, old associates departed, and all things became new."[35] In 1833 Child made a definitive break with the genteel community that had enjoyed her magazine, novels, and advice book when she wrote *An Appeal*, a pamphlet tracing the history of antislavery activism and denouncing efforts at colonization. Important members of the antislavery community, including Wendell Phillips, Thomas Wentworth Higginson, and Charles Sumner, credited it with drawing them into the antislavery fold. Public reaction was swift and negative. The prospering *Juvenile Miscellany* failed in the following year, and Child's subsequent books attracted significantly smaller audiences than her earlier works.

Ironically, Child would soon be subject to criticism that she was too moderate. In 1841 she went to New York to edit the *National Anti-Slavery Standard*, the organ of the American Anti-Slavery Society, but left two years later amid charges that the paper was compromising too much by attempting to attract more mainstream antislavery activists to the cause. Indeed, for all her admiration for Garrisonian principle, Child herself was a consensus builder who sought to encourage any kind of political action that would aid in the destruction of slavery. In a letter to a friend, dated March 6, 1843, she wrote despairingly of the divisions in the antislavery community: "[I]t comes more and more forcibly and clearly to my mind, that we are fighting in the spirit of *sect*; a spirit which I abhor, in all its manifestations."[36] Her vision embraced a more widely defined understanding of civic virtue, one that included radicals and moderates alike.

It was not until later in the 1850s that Lydia Maria Child's flagging spirits revived, drawing her again into political activism. The notorious beating of Senator Charles Sumner by Representative Preston Brooks, one inspired by Sumner's passionate speech about the violence in Kansas and the culpability of Southerners (including Brooks's uncle), was one catalyst. She did not sleep for two nights after hearing of the attack. "If my eye-lids started to droop, I started up, shuddering with some vision of murdered men in Kansas, or of Charles Sumner, bleeding and dying," she told a friend in a letter. "If I had only been supplied with any safety-valve of *action*, to let off the accumulating steam!"[37] Child's safety valve would be in writing, in exercising a political voice. She used her knowledge of the past antislavery struggle in the United States and elsewhere, her detailed recall of the chronology of political events, and a cool and straightforward tone to persuade less through feelings than through rational argument.[38]

If, for Child, the 1850s were a time of renewed activism, for Harriet Beecher Stowe they were a beginning. Stowe's intensity and conviction grew out of her sense that slavery was un-Christian and that she had a moral duty to stop it. It was hardly surprising that Stowe felt the answer to the problem was in religion, or that she felt some custodial responsibility for the nation. She herself was the daughter, sister, and wife of many prominent ministers. Her New England background, her ease with having a public eye on her family, and her pride in her Yankee heritage gave Stowe both self-confidence and arrogance about her vision for America. Although her demeanor before and even after *Uncle Tom's Cabin* was modest, as befit a Victorian lady, this sense of the rightness of a Beecher diagnosing the national ills helped her write a panoramic story and then defend it with evidence gathered from newspapers, congressional speeches, and slave narratives in *A Key to Uncle Tom's Cabin*.

By the 1850s, however, Stowe's confidence in the ministers of America had weakened (with the notable exception of those in her own family). In a letter to a friend she described her anger over their craven response to Daniel Webster's call for calm and the Compromise of 1850, which included the newly strengthened Fugitive Slave Law. "To me it is incredible, amazing, mournful!" she wrote.[39] It was this perception of a failure of manhood and religious will, and the overpowering sense of moral crisis, that served as Stowe's defense for her political life throughout the 1850s. In a March 1851 letter to Gamaliel Bailey, Stowe claimed that before then she had felt "no particular call to meddle" with the subject of slavery, but now "the time is come" when all must speak, "even a woman or child." The "peril and shame" of the country demanded it, she wrote, "and I hope every woman who can write will not be silent."[40]

Despite her political knowledge and literary sophistication, Stowe was at heart a religious visionary. *Uncle Tom's Cabin* portrays a Christ-like figure, Uncle Tom, who spreads love as his ministry and is forgiving even after being mortally wounded. In fact, Uncle Tom is in some sense more God-like than even Christ, for he does not cry out in despair before accepting his fate. His faith converts his fictional oppressors, just as Stowe meant to convert her actual readers. In a letter to Frederick Douglass, written as she was at work on *Uncle Tom's Cabin*, Stowe was clear in her assessment of the national crisis and her hopes for its resolution. "I have looked all the field over with despairing eyes," she wrote. "I see no hope but in Him. This movement must and will become a purely religious one."[41]

Sara Willis Parton was more secular than Stowe, and less earnest than Child; her work was characterized by sharp political and social satire mixed with an occasional sentimental platitude. Fanny Fern, as Parton came to be known both professionally and personally, was something of a maverick; she had no religious status from a ministerial family, nor was she enmeshed in a variety of antislavery communities.[42] Despite the success of her later novels *Ruth Hall* and *Fanny Ford*, Fanny Fern was primarily an editorialist. Her short sketches considered a wide range of topics, among them women's rights, the condition of workingwomen, and national politics. Her racial politics are little known but can be inferred from her relationship with Harriet Jacobs, an escaped slave and author of the first full-length Southern slave narrative written by a woman.[43] Jacobs's daughter Louisa Matilda briefly came to live with Fern and was treated as one of the family.[44]

Fanny Fern had a difficult birth. As part of a writing family she might have had a great deal of help breaking into the profession. Like Stowe, she

Sara Payson Willis Parton, a.k.a. "Fanny Fern" (1811–72). The best-selling novelist and newspaper columnist earned one of the highest salaries at the time for her biting editorials in the *New York Ledger*. (Photo used by permission of the National Portrait Gallery, Smithsonian Institution.)

was born in 1811 but otherwise provides a remarkable contrast to the sober Harriet. Willis was considered a "handful" as a girl and was sent to Catharine Beecher's Hartford Female Seminary at least in part to get her out of the house (she met Catharine's sister Harriet there). When she returned at nearly twenty, her education became domestic, but it failed to tame her. Six years later, in May 1837, Willis married a kindred spirit, Charles Harrington Eldredge, called "Handsome Charlie" by his friends.[45] Until 1844, Sara Eldredge's life was happy, if marred by her husband's unsuccessful business career. Over the next two years, however, she was to lose five relatives: sister, mother, daughter, sister-in-law, and husband. After Eldredge's death, Sara struggled to support her two remaining daughters with minimal help from her father and father-in-law. When they encouraged her to marry Samuel P. Farrington in 1849, a man she did not love, she eventually gave in.

This proved to be a terrible mistake. Her new husband was jealous and abusive, and in 1851 she left him, subjecting herself to ridicule and contempt from her family and the family of her first husband. Without help, and burdened with adulterous slander spewed by Farrington, Sara turned to her pen for financial security and eventually for solace. On June 28, 1851, her first short piece was published in the Boston story paper *Olive Branch*. "The Model Husband" was an ironic exposé of the foibles of men.[46] By September of that year Fanny Fern was born—an ironic gesture toward sentimental writers with alliterative names—and came to be Sara Willis Eldredge Farrington's literary and eventually de facto name for the rest of her life.

The frank voice of "The Model Husband" was indicative of Fanny Fern's later style and politics. It was humorous and caustic, with a scathing realism about double standards between the sexes that was intended to startle and amuse her readers. Fern's subject was domestic relations, and she seemed to respect few boundaries. And it worked. Fern's impact, although not financially remunerative for some years, was immediate. The day following its initial publication her piece was picked up by exchange with a prominent Boston newspaper.[47] By the end of the year Fern was also writing for the *True Flag*, another Boston paper. In the two years that Fern wrote for the *Olive Branch* its circulation soared.[48] By 1855 she was being courted to write a weekly column for the *New York Ledger* by the savvy Robert Bonner, who paid her one hundred dollars a column, or more than any previous columnist, man or woman. She was joined there by Mrs. E. D. E. N. Southworth in 1856.

Although Lydia Maria Child, Harriet Beecher Stowe, and Fanny Fern were produced by New England within nine years of each other, each represents a distinct political and intellectual position. Child was very much an activist, despite her hiatus for seven years from organizational antislavery; she was also childless and had been the primary breadwinner since marriage. Stowe was deeply religious, and had she been a man, would clearly have been a minister: her political work was always in some sense a sermon, intended to move a Christian nation to moral political acts. Fern was a rebel, from both organizational activism and religious orthodoxy; her work was intended to question verities rather than impose them.

Northern Borders: Introducing Southworth, Harper, and Davis

Southworth, Harper, and Davis grew up under the tutelage of New England but outside its direct orbit: Southworth and Harper in Maryland, and Davis in Wheeling, Virginia, which would defect to the Union when it became West Virginia during the Civil War. As a result, while clearly Unionist, their work had a more nuanced reading of the South, and a more critical reading of the New England North.

Mrs. Emma Dorothy Eliza Nevitte Southworth (1819–99). E. D. E. N. Southworth was a best-selling novelist of sensationalist fiction before, during, and after the Civil War. *Fair Play* (1867) and *How He Won Her* (1868), a two-volume novel, portrays four women, two Northern and two Southern, caught in the tumult of the war. One cross-dresses and fights for the Union; another nurses for the Union, renouncing a Southern fiancé; another is forced out of her native South and works in hospitals in Washington; and a fourth dies tragically while riding (as a woman) beside her Confederate husband. (Photo used by permission of the Emma Dorothy Southworth Collection (#8315), Clifton Waller Barrett Library, Special Collections Department, University of Virginia Library.)

Rather than the religious imagery of Stowe, or the essays of Child and Fern, Mrs. E. D. E. N. Southworth used fast-paced and dramatic tales to illustrate her national and social concerns. Her work was set in Maryland or Virginia (with the occasional jaunt to New York City or Washington, D.C.) and depicted a world where slavery was constant, class divisions between whites were visceral and unavoidable, and adventure could be had by young women of standing. What made her novels Unionist in spirit was the celebration of free labor ideology at their heart; the implicit critique of slavery (clouded by her use of pervasive racial stereotypes); and her celebration of a kind of ordered republicanism associated with Northern culture (and attributed to many Northern characters).

By 1849, when her first book-length story, *Retribution*, was published in the *National Era*, Southworth had begun to draw an audience. It was a difficult beginning. Emma Dorothy Eliza Nevitte was born December 29, 1819, eight years after Harriet Beecher Stowe. Although she spent much of her early life in Washington, her mother was from Maryland and her father from Virginia. Nevitte lost her father in 1823 and grew up under the tutelage of a stepfather, Joshua L. Henshaw, who ran an academy in Washington. At age sixteen she left school, returning as a teacher. In 1840 she married Frederick Hamilton Southworth, an inventor, and moved to Prairie du Chien, Wisconsin. By 1844 she was back in Washington, D.C., apparently abandoned by her husband, supporting herself and their two children by teaching in the public schools and later becoming a school principal. While writing *Retribution*, which she began in 1846, she was "keeping school and keeping house."[49]

Perhaps not surprisingly, given her background and struggle for subsistence, Southworth consistently wrote on the issue of social class in her novels throughout the 1850s and 1860s. Her vision was both conservative and progressive. She suggested that the American Dream, of status and wealth, was possible even for those who come from low or mixed birth, provided they had the intelligence and the drive to rise through education and hard work. Her proto–Horatio Alger stories revealed more persistence than luck and expressed great confidence in society's ability to judge and reward integrity and virtue. At the same time, without irony, Southworth illustrated great class differences that comfortably remain in place. Her critique of society only came when honorable individuals failed to get accepted, and this rejection never blighted her heroines (more often heroes), but only checked them on their inevitable rise. Here was a fantasy and vision that appealed to a wide audience and continued to appeal for over forty years.

Frances Ellen Watkins Harper's poetry, by contrast, reached a small but far more radical audience, where it, too, had a great appeal. Unlike Child, Stowe, Southworth, and Fern, Frances Ellen Watkins was not married by 1850, and did not have her first child until the early 1860s. Rather than children, her life was filled with the necessity for other kinds of labor. Born into a free black family in Maryland in 1825, Watkins was orphaned at age three. No records exist of the name of her mother, or of whom her father might have been. Watkins was raised by an aunt and an uncle, the Reverend William Watkins, who founded and ran the William Watkins Academy for Negro Young, a school known for its emphasis on biblical studies and stern discipline. Watkins attended until she was thirteen. From then on she seemingly had sole responsibility for her upkeep, working as a domestic worker, sewing and caring for children, and eventually teaching in other Northern states. At the same time she wrote poetry and prose, and in 1845 she published her first book, *Forest Leaves*.[50]

The Compromise of 1850, much as it enraged white Northern antislavery activists, had an even more direct effect on Watkins and her family.[51]

The strengthened Fugitive Slave Law offered remuneration to those who would capture and turn over fugitive slaves to their Southern owners. Even free blacks were in danger, for all that slave owners needed in order to claim their "property" was a signed affidavit, for the purported slaves could not defend themselves in court. Given this context of personal danger to family and students, Watkins's uncle was forced to shut down his school, and he and much of his family moved to safety in Canada.[52]

Frances Ellen Watkins's background had a direct impact on her writing. Her sadness at the loss of her mother was replayed in her poems on the anguish of the slave mother. The religious training provided by her uncle gave her work a serious and evangelical cast.[53] And her anger at the nation for its injustice to her people sustained her political work throughout her lifetime. Upon the grave of a free man sent into slavery for entering Maryland, Watkins wrote, "I pledged myself to the Anti-Slavery cause."[54] She went on to write for abolitionist papers and, after moving to Boston from Philadelphia, was hired as an antislavery lecturer.

A few of Watkins's most reprinted early poems were responses to Harriet Beecher Stowe's *Uncle Tom's Cabin*, a novel that to some degree mirrored Watkins's religious and political position at the time. In a poem "To Mrs. Harriet Beecher Stowe," Watkins thanks her explicitly for making the nation *feel*: "I thank thee for the kindly words / That grac'd thy pen of fire, / And thrilled upon the living chords / Of many a heart's deep lyre." In another poem in response to the novel, however, Watkins moves beyond Stowe's politics of individual conversion and notes the hypocrisy of a nation of slaveholders: "Oh! how shall I speak of my proud country's shame? / Of the stains on her glory, how give them their name? / How say that her banner in mockery waves— / Her 'star spangled banner'—o'er millions of slaves?" Without Stowe's familial arrogance, Watkins still claims America—"my" proud country—but her critique is sharper. Watkins cannot speak of pride, glory, or patriotism without irony, whereas Stowe's novel on a basic level assumes that the institutions are sound, needing only right-feeling hearts in the individuals to guide them.[55]

Like Stowe, Watkins set out to make the nation feel, and she did so largely with vignettes that highlight the internal pain of slavery and the shared humanity of slaves. "The Slave Mother" begins by startling the reader with this pain: "Heard you that shriek? It rose / So wildly on the air, / It seemed as if a burden'd heart / Was breaking in despair." The reader is drawn through the mother's and her son's agony as he, her "only wreath of household love," is torn from her. The effect is profoundly unsettling, the narrator returning to the opening stanza to explain: "No marvel then, these bitter shrieks / Disturb the listening air: / She is a mother, and her heart / Is breaking in despair." The grieving woman is "mother" as well as slave; her pain is real and understandable.[56]

Watkins's voice was both sentimental and political. Her poems, the product of a religious and an oral tradition, were written in a style meant to be read aloud, with dramatic flourish and consistent rhythm. They are the evidence of a deeply Christian worldview and allowed Watkins to become a lay minister of sorts. Like most other popular poets writing at the same time, including Whittier and Longfellow, Watkins intended her poems to inspire and to teach. Her underlying message was the power of woman's love. In one poem this power even sways the judgment of God. In "The Syrophenician Woman," an anguished mother pleads with the "Saviour" to spare the life of her dying child. Her faith and passion astonishes and persuades him.

Watkins's style had great resonance with an antislavery audience. *Poems on Miscellaneous Subjects*, first released in 1854, was published in both Boston and Philadelphia and was so successful it was reprinted in Boston that year and again in both cities the following year. By 1857 it was advertised as having sold 10,000 copies. In addition, many of Watkins's poems were printed and reprinted in abolitionist newspapers (including the *Aliened American*, *Frederick Douglass' Paper* and the *Liberator*) before being published in book form.[57]

Rebecca Harding Davis's work, like Southworth's and Harper's, was profoundly shaped by the ills of her immediate context. While an abolitionist, Davis explored the condition of the white working class, and their antebellum "war," beginning with her early realist (or what one critic calls "metarealist") novella, *Life in the Iron Mills*. Davis was very aware of her audience—in this case the readers of the *Atlantic Monthly*—and her wartime work was produced to enlighten its powerful and reformist readers. It rebuked those who imagined that transcendence was possible or that self-realization meant anything to a degraded worker. "I am going to be honest," the narrator of Davis's *Life in the Iron Mills* tells the reader earnestly, "This is what I want you to do. I want you to hide your disgust, take no heed to your clean clothes, and come right down with me,—here, into the thickest of the fog and mud and foul effluvia. I want you to hear this story. . . . There is a secret down here, in this nightmare fog, that has lain dumb for centuries: I want to make it a real thing to you."[58]

Life in the iron mills of western Virginia was as close to a real thing for Rebecca Harding as it could be for a middle-class woman. Although she was born in Pennsylvania in 1831, Harding (later Davis) grew up in Wheeling, Virginia, after the age of five. From there she watched the workers as they filed down to work in the mills and the Conestoga wagons as they moved to the West filled with pioneers. In 1845 she returned to Pennsylvania to attend the Washington Female Seminary, graduating three years later as valedictorian. She then returned to Wheeling to help her mother with her four younger siblings. In "the intervals of that all important cooking," Harding wrote for the Wheeling *Intelligencer*, acting briefly as its editor in 1859. Still, Harding confessed to James Fields at the *Atlantic Monthly*, "Whatever I wrote before the Iron Mill story I would not care to see again—chiefly verses and reviews written under circumstances that made them unhealthful. I would rather they were forgotten."[59]

Before Harding's next work was published the nation plunged into war. Unlike most of the other women writers in this study, Harding had no geographical distance from the war with which to elevate it into a millennial struggle. Western Virginia was a battlefield for much of the struggle, and stories of innocent women, children, and old men killed, hurt, or driven out of their homes by both Union and Confederate soldiers were common. When in March 1862 Harding visited the North and heard Bronson Alcott hold forth to the Concord literati and their Virginian guest on the war's meaning, she was disgusted. "I had just come up from the border where I had seen the actual war; the filthy spewings of it; the political jobbery in Union and Confederate camps; the malignant personal hatreds wearing patriotic masks, and glutted by burning homes and outraged women; the chances in it, well improved on both sides, for brutish men to grow more brutish, and for honorable men to degenerate into thieves and sots," she recalled in her autobiography. "War may be an armed angel with a mission, but she has the personal habits of the slums."[60]

Harding's trip north had many important consequences for her life and work. The most obvious was that she met a young editor at *Peterson's Ladies Magazine* with whom she had been corresponding since he had written her an admiring review of *Life in the Iron Mills*. Not only did their exchange allow Harding to begin a profitable relationship with *Peterson's*, but she married her admirer, Lemuel Clarke Davis, on March 5, 1863. The Davises settled in Philadelphia, starting out in the home of Clarke Davis's sister. Other consequences were not so obvious. The Concord literati whom Harding met convinced her even more strongly of the significance of her regional perspective; she was western, loved bigness, celebrated democracy, and stood at the gateway to the dangerous beyond. She also rejected the Transcendentalism of Emerson and others as self-realization at the expense of the oppressed. "Their theories," she wrote in her autobiography, "were like beautiful bubbles blown from a child's pipe, floating overhead, with queer reflections on them of sky and earth and human beings, all in a glow of fairy color and all a little distorted." It lacked "some backbone of fact," a backbone needed to make positive change in society.[61]

Her trip north also made Harding feel a part of a literary community of women, and her letters attest to her interest in the work of her contemporaries. Although she was dismayed by Bronson Alcott, she warmed to his daughter Louisa May. Louisa May Alcott told Harding that she had gone to Concord and back to get her only decent gown in order to attend a Boston fete the Fields were hosting for their Virginian guest. In her autobiography years later, Davis recalled seeing in Alcott "that watchful, defiant air with which the woman whose youth is slipping away is apt to face the world which has offered no place to her." In a letter to Annie Fields (wife of James Fields, Davis's editor) in 1864 Davis praised Alcott's *Hospital Sketches* for the experience that is so clearly revealed in them; not surprisingly it is her realism—"she knows hospitals"—that earns Davis's respect. While Davis did not record ever meeting Mary Abigail Dodge, she did compliment her writing to Annie Fields as well, calling it "western": "Rough, democratic, hardy, common sense is the strength of western people and if she had belonged out there we'd have crowned her the genius of it—."[62]

All three writers viewed their political terrain through the lens of their context: for Southworth, there was more to admire about the South, even as she uncritically heralded free labor ideology. For Harper, the South represented slavery and the North a kind of exile; until the war ended she could not return to her birthplace. For Davis, transplanted Southerner, seeing the war firsthand made her particularly wary of any truisms or platitudes about glory: war, she might have said, is hell.

New England Daughters: Introducing Hamilton, Alcott, and Phelps

The youngest of these writers had an easier time becoming established: their predecessors, Stowe, Southworth, and Fern, particularly, had made lucrative careers for themselves despite sometimes unconventional or unpopular views. Hamilton, Alcott, and Phelps all grew up knowing of these examples and thus did not have to imagine and create a space for themselves as self-supporting writers.

Gail Hamilton (born Mary Abigail Dodge) wrote with a clear sense of purpose: she wanted to change people's minds. From the first her writings were laced with admonition. In a letter to her mother, in March 1860, Dodge addressed her mother's fears concerning a forthright essay she had submitted to the *Congregationalist*. "I wish you to understand that if I write much I shall probably meet with a great deal of opposition, for I shall express views which run counter to popular conviction, so if you faint now, you will have a catalepsy by and by when worst comes to worst," she not very consolingly wrote. "There is an undercurrent of feeling that will sustain me. I *want* to upheave and overturn. Land needs to be sub-soiled, as well as top-dressed."[63]

Dodge was equally candid about her transgression of cultural boundaries. "Didn't my politics look splendidly in print?" she asked her mother in a letter in 1858, of her essay "Men and Women." "I flatter myself that it was particularly well done. Do you want me to write as if I were a man, or should I let the cloven foot appear in case it should be inconvenient to conceal it? (I don't mean am I to write like the —— but like a woman? I am afraid you will say it is all one in my case)."[64] Her definition of politics, in this case, widens the definition well past partisan stances, and she assumes her mother will understand; more than other women writers of the time, Hamilton *self-consciously* engaged in political work.

Dodge, born in 1838, was the seventh and youngest child in her family. She was raised on her father's farm in Hamilton, Massachusetts, and was well educated by nineteenth-century standards, leaving the village school for a boarding school in Cambridge at twelve, and then on to the Ipswich Female Seminary.[65] From 1850 to 1858, Dodge taught at a succession of schools, including Catharine Beecher's Hartford Female Seminary. In 1858 she moved to Washington, D.C., at the urging of Gamaliel Bailey, who had begun publishing Dodge's work in the *National Era* two years earlier. Dodge acted as the governess of Bailey's children and lived with him and his wife while contributing to the *Congregationalist*, the New York *Independent*, and the *Atlantic Monthly*. In 1860, after Bailey's death, Dodge returned to Hamilton to live with her mother for the next eight years, thus viewing the Civil War with some geographic detachment.

From the first Mary Abigail Dodge was intrigued with both politics and literature. Her letters to family members attest to lively debates and discussions over the implications of national policy, as well as to a certain New England arrogance. Still, Dodge wished to hear the opposition, if only to reject it. In 1854 she wrote home: "I wish you would once in a while send me a Kentucky paper—Pro-slavery if possible—I think it is well to look at both sides of the question. My very soul has been stirred within me the last few months by that most unmanly, demoniac Nebraska Bill. I cannot believe that men who have trodden our free Puritan soil, and breathed our pure mountain air, can suffer themselves to become minions of slavery."[66] In 1852, Dodge wrote of her intellectual preferences, recommending them to her mother's attention and suggesting again the small world in which these writers orbited. "Have you ever read 'The Wide, Wide World,' or 'Queechy,' or 'Uncle Tom's Cabin'?" she asked, "If you have not, I advise you to do it, especially the latter. They are well worth your attention, though they are stories." She also praised the New York *Tribune*, a "most excellent" paper, "a little ultra perhaps in some things, but right on the two great questions of the day, slavery and temperance."[67]

Dodge became well known by her literary contemporaries, including Harriet Beecher Stowe, whom she had praised to her mother. Not all of them found her to their immediate liking. Louisa May Alcott met her in 1863 and described her as overconfident and unfashionable. "Too sharp & full of herself," Alcott mused. "Insisted on talking about religion with Emerson who glided away from the subject so sweetly and resolutely that the energetic lady gave it up at last. She wore a brown hat all evening and was very queer."[68] Alcott's preference went to another writer she had met with the same Concord literati, "Miss Harding."[69] Still, in a letter to a friend about an essay of Gail Hamilton's, Alcott was far more complimentary.[70]

Hamilton appealed to as diverse a crowd as the forthright Fanny Fern, the evangelical Harriet Beecher Stowe, and the realist Rebecca Harding Davis, all of whom appreciated her style and message.[71] In a short biographical sketch of Dodge for her husband's collection *Eminent Women of the Age*, Fern humorously catalogued Dodge as "a lady, at whose mention stalwart men have been known to tremble, and hide in corners; who 'keeps a private graveyard' for the burial of those who she has mercilessly slain; who respects neither the spectacles of the judge, nor the surplice of the priest; who holds the mirror up to men's failings till they hate their wives merely because they belong to her sex." Stowe was taken by Dodge's character as much as her words, calling her "large-hearted & simple minded & good as she can be."[72]

Louisa May Alcott was considerably less righteous than her contemporary; her memory of New England seems far more nuanced and critical. When the war began she was twenty-nine, and although she was already established as a writer by then, her war work brought her into the public eye and made possible her later fame. Born in 1832, in Germantown, Pennsylvania, to Abigail and Bronson Alcott, Louisa May was the second of four daughters, like the Jo March figure in her semi-autobiographical work, *Little Women*. All four children, although particularly the first two, studied with their father, an educational reformer and Transcendentalist. Alcott lived much of her life between Concord and Boston, writing to support both herself and her family. She was, as her father called her, the "son" of the family and never married.

Throughout her career as a writer, Louisa May Alcott led a curious double life. On the one hand she sought the approval of the literary circles in which she lived—her family was financially supported by Ralph Waldo Emerson, she had a youthful crush on neighbor Henry David Thoreau, and Nathaniel Hawthorne lived next door. On the other hand, in order to make the money that she needed, and to exorcise her own demons, she wrote blood-and-thunder tales, too, under various pseudonyms.[73] She began publishing in the 1850s, when she was in her twenties, and although she was known in Boston reformist circles—she also wrote about John Brown for the *Liberator*—it was not until she published her semi-autobiographical narrative of nursing in Washington, *Hospital Sketches*, that she gained wider attention.[74]

As the war opened Louisa May Alcott grew impatient with the life of water-carrier, stove-watcher, and sewer that was the norm for the midcentury Northern middle-class woman. In November 1862 she decided to move beyond lint-gathering and sewing for the soldiers. "Thirty years old," she observed pointedly. "Decided to go to Washington as a nurse if I could find a place. Help needed, and I love nursing, and *must* let out my pent-up energy in some new way." In December she left with the Hawthornes as escort, "feeling as if I was the son of the house going to war."[75] When she returned to Concord she adapted the letters she had written home into a short fictionalized novella and published it in the Boston *Commonwealth*.

Like Lydia Maria Child and Harriet Beecher Stowe, Alcott adopted a frank and confident style, and wrote through and with gender conventions to discuss the political and social issues of the day. Her fictional sketches, however, used a light ironic touch that Child's passionately serious letters did not. Alcott's easy and humorous depiction of the transgression of numerous social boundaries and her likable and competent narrator "Tribulation Periwinkle" gracefully suggested all kinds of opinions women were supposed to keep to themselves.

Elizabeth Stuart Phelps was perhaps the youngest major writer to have been personally affected by the Civil War; she was only seventeen at the firing on Fort Sumter, twelve years younger than Alcott. She dates the beginning of her adult literary self with the beginning of the war: the first chapter of her autobiography, "Wartime: First Stories," opens with the effect of the war on Andover, the men's boarding school where her father taught, and ends with her choice of a literary life. Phelps frankly admits that she needed external confirmation in order to have the confidence to write; if her first story had been rejected, she said, she would never have written another. Yet that story, of "a poor and plain little dressmaker, who lost her lover in the army," was accepted, as what Phelps called "the beginning of anything like genuine work for me."[76] It was an important beginning, despite its short length and sentimental tone. "A Sacrifice Consumed" contained the seeds of Phelps's later career: it suggested the economic hardship of women workers, the legitimacy of their struggle, and the solace a loving rather than a stern God could offer.

Phelps was well trained to interpret the religious meaning of the war. Born in Boston, Massachusetts, in 1844 to the Reverend Austin Phelps and Elizabeth Stuart Phelps, Mary Gray Phelps (who took her mother's name after her death in 1852) grew up surrounded by the renowned Andover seminary where her father moved to teach sacred rhetoric and homiletics. She was educated at Abbott Academy, a private girls' school, and then Mrs. Edwards' School, where she was trained in a curriculum similar to many men's colleges of the day. Her religious training was rigorous and orthodox, including tutoring in theology by an Andover professor.[77]

From birth Phelps had been surrounded by literary influences as well. But when Ralph Waldo Emerson visited Andover and her Chaucer Club, she drew his scorn by confessing she found Chaucer did not take hold of her as current events did. Emerson then asked what she would read—the 'Morning Advertiser?' " The pupil felt rebuked but unrepentant, and although she recognized that the Concord sage saw her and her environment as "enslaved in superstition" and "barbaric," she implied that she had herself little use for Transcendentalism.

Phelps, instead, believed strongly in the political work of women. Harriet Beecher Stowe, who during the war lived at Andover, where her husband then taught, was a model of "the greatest of American women." The rest of Andover, not having accepted even the concept of an "eminent woman," looked askance at Stowe, but Phelps held to her own opinion. Phelps was also affected by younger writers. In her 1867 story "At Bay," she paid tribute to the writer who introduced her to the grit and struggle of a West Virginia mill town, not knowing that this was Rebecca Harding Davis.[78]

UNLIKE THE WRITERS discussed above, Sarah Fales left for historians only her letters to her son as evidence of her politics. Yet the travail of her life, often described only in social histories, frames and makes meaningful the lives of her contemporaries, writers such as Stowe, for example, who, like Fales, sent a son to war. In order to write, women had to find time and space in lives crowded with domestic duties and social expectations. They had to believe in their own ability to make sense of the public world—most often through private lives—and in their own right to do so.

In order to speak on political issues, even within the eagerly bought pages of a story paper, a lady's magazine, or a reform journal, a woman writer had to establish a respectable and respected place. Women writers manipulated, challenged, defended, and ultimately reworked the "women's sphere" of domesticity and family, taking up, in the process, the sectional issues of the 1850s. Those were implicitly and explicitly issues of class, or a critique of the North, and issues of slavery, or a critique of the South, in a larger argument about the meaning of America, with a hovering African American (or in some cases Irish American) presence. It is to the content of their work that I will now turn.

We rejoice that the barriers to woman's equality are being thrown down, or overleaped; we are glad that she now has the press at her command, and may, if she will, stir up the mighty mass of people to give heed to her behest's. We only wish there were more of them willing to devote their talents to the good of the sex, and the moral elevation of their race; and we can only hope that the spirit which has enkindled in the breast of the few, may pervade the many, and that they may fully consider the part which it is their duty to take in arresting the terrible evils which have spread to such a fearful extent over our beloved country.—"Raising a Voice against Indignities," *The Lily* (April 1850)

CHAPTER TWO

Raising a Voice

The Civil War Begins in the 1850s

WELL AFTER THE Civil War's end, Harriet Beecher Stowe's son recorded her reminiscences, including in them an account of her visit to the White House in December of 1862. In what is perhaps an apocryphal story, President Abraham Lincoln was said to have greeted her with an exclamation, framed as a question: "So this is the little lady who made this big war?"[1] That greeting, never corroborated by outside sources, has been retold many times—though not, significantly, by Stowe's most recent biographer, Joan Hedrick, who may have doubted its veracity.[2] In this story is encapsulated much of the intersecting political struggles of the 1850s.

That the story may be entirely apocryphal, and that a careful historian and biographer therefore might leave it out, does not discount its importance as memory. Stowe remembered Lincoln saying these words, and she remembered it as her due, a pleasantry with some heft. Recorders thereafter did homage to her and to Lincoln in echoing the phrase, as if saying: "Here's the Great Emancipator sharing the glory of his courageous act, on the eve of its enactment."

Whether accurately remembered or not, the phrase is in some sense true. Stowe *was* literally "little," relative to Lincoln's stature, and she was, as a woman, *little* politically, to the President's *big*. Her views, as a nonvoter, were not those Lincoln had to track most carefully. As a woman she was not intended to make policy, to make war; that she did is conferred as a kind of gift, a paternal nod. Crucially, Stowe was also, as Lincoln recognized, a "lady," and by then largely free from the grueling domestic labor that had previously dominated her days; and the fact of her class status had everything to do with how she saw her world (which is not, of course, all that surprising).

That Stowe "made this big war" is far more arguable: no one person, not even Lincoln or Jefferson Davis, could be said to have made the Civil War. But Stowe's rendering of public opinion, her "making" politics into a moral act (and thus bequeathing it to women), did help to make war come, a war that was all about the unstated but still very present issue of slavery.[3] The politics she offered in *Uncle Tom's Cabin* suggested a world shaped by Christian, Northern, and middle-class values, and represented the most successful effort at cultural and political unity of the 1850s, even as its publication spurred dozens of "anti-Tom" novels North and South.

In order to tell the story of Northern women's politics of the Civil War—their "political work" of writing—one must start in the 1850s, for it was then (if not earlier) that the war was in a sense "made." Despite the rigors of their respective lives, this "making" was a matter of deep concern. In a section of the country diverse in its attachments and its public opinion, to make any sort of consensus—even one simply of book sales—was a matter of some real moment. Hence, any political discussion by women, even discussion deeply embedded in cultural documents, was attended to with sustained analytic rigor and questioning. Here was a popular culture with consequences: what a Harriet Beecher Stowe or a Harriet Jacobs, a Fanny Fern or a Rebecca Harding Davis said was carefully written and carefully read.

The dialogues, debates, and juxtapositions that follow indicate the struggle within the North (and its divergence from the South), even as women writers there worked to find some common ground. Four concep-

Harriet Elizabeth Beecher Stowe (1811–96). The author of *Uncle Tom's Cabin* (1852), Stowe continued writing on issues of morality, slavery, and politics through the 1850s and the Civil War. (Photo used by permission of the National Portrait Gallery, Smithsonian Institution.)

tual and authorial pairings track both ongoing struggles between writers— about women's proper place, about slavery and race, and about the nature of political work—and the growing sense of urgency in the 1850s itself. Each pairing is a kind of debate that would continue throughout the war years and afterward, and represents not so much a constituency of people, or even the overall literature of the period (which, on the whole, may have been less contested), as a collection of ideas about politics and political work. The first, set in the early years of the decade, suggests two responses to the slavery question: patience versus action. Stowe wishes to act; Southworth, though troubled by slavery, offers no such urgent message. The second, in the middle of the decade, suggests two renderings of women's politics: one based on independent action, the other on influence. The third, subsequent to John Brown's raid and between a Northern and two Southern writers, maps out the escalating anger of the decade. The fourth suggests the ways in which the concerns of reformers—on racial and wage slavery—were linked in the minds of an insightful few, and this linking would reappear in the postwar period.

These four juxtapositions are intended to reveal the complexity and contentiousness of public opinion, even among literate Northern women; the force of public events on their political understandings and consequent writing; and the way in which they joined in the "making" of a "big war," ever aware of their status as "little ladies." The 1850s, from the appearance of *Uncle Tom's Cabin* to *Incidents in the Life of a Slave Girl*, published just afterward in April 1861, represented a real movement in the depth and rigor of women's political writing, as women authors worked to unify the North behind a moral purpose.

Stowe and Southworth: Slavery and the Proper Work of White Women

In order to make the nation's public work the logical work of women, writers had to construct that world carefully: first they had to portray it as immoral—not a difficult thing to do—and then they had to describe how the domestic world (the world of women) was not only connected to it but also a necessary agent of its transformation. This was trickier, because the ideals of separate sphere ideology suggested an almost tangible boundary between men's and women's worlds. E. D. E. N. Southworth and Harriet Beecher Stowe both undertook the challenge of making the vision of a domestic world that which should shape the national and public world. They were not the first women writers to do so, but they were among the most popular.

Southworth, as noted in Chapter 1, came to writing out of dire need and with a thorough education, both in personal tragedy—she lost a father early in childhood and a husband early in marriage—and in man's inability to protect women. She wrote at the bedside of an ill son, and her effort to change the way the public world felt must have seemed to her intimately connected to a personal one. Like *Uncle Tom's Cabin*, *Retribution* was published in the *National Era*. In contrast to Stowe's bombshell of two years later, *Retribution* only marginally concerned slaves. Its title was meant to inspire fear of the eventual response of God (and, one imagines, the slaves themselves) to the domestic evil that the institution of slavery encouraged. As in Stowe's work, slavery in Southworth's writing spoke more to white women's concerns than to black women's.

Retribution suggests many of the patterns of Southworth's developing literary and political style. Most significantly, perhaps, the book has two main female characters, representing a strict dichotomy and moral lesson. In a pattern that would persist in her later work, virtue and ethnicity were married: the native white character was instinctively good, the nonnative, instinctively evil. Hester Grey is plain, simple, and quiet, has great powers of love and self-sacrifice, and little perception. Juliette Summers (an Italian orphan adopted by an Anglo family) is bright, beautiful, and alluring, with great intellectual powers cleverly hidden. After meeting in a boarding school, the wealthy and lonely Hester befriends the destitute but crafty Juliette. Years later, Juliette comes to visit Hester and her guardian-turned-husband. Unbeknownst to Hester, her husband falls passionately in love with Juliette and waits half-impatiently for Hester's consumption to kill her. When it does, he marries Juliette, but although they both love each other, their distrust of one another kills that love. Juliette eventually elopes with a European duke and is later beheaded. Hester's daughter, through love and constancy, redeems her father and emancipates all her slaves despite financial ruin.

The reader is supposed to identify with the simple, loving, and wronged Hester, the image of conventional womanhood, and to abhor the powerful Juliette. Yet even here, at the beginning of Southworth's writing career, the message is less clear than it seems. In a passage in which Hester sits thinking (while her husband is waiting for her to die), she considers the current debate over women's rights. "They must not only change the laws of the land, but the laws of woman's nature, before they can improve upon Divine Providence by changing her relations," she muses, never identifying "they." "Talk of women's rights—women's rights live in the instincts of her protector—man. Woman's subordination of love is not only a law of nature, a law of revelation, but a doctrine of all inspired books since the Bible."[4] The irony here is plain. The instincts of Hester's "protector" will not save her but hurry her to the grave. Women, then, must *not* simply subordinate themselves to love but must act to protect themselves and to further the good of the nation. Hester's daughter, the hope of the future, will do just that, but not so much in the service of social justice—slavery here is not depicted as a deep moral wrong—but in the service of her own redeemed and politicized white womanhood.

The sins of the South will bring misery to the nation, Southworth argues implicitly. "I have tried to show you how from the sin, domestic infidelity and treachery, sprung inevitably the punishment, domestic distrust and wretchedness," she concludes, describing both home and nation. If "Human and Legal" retribution can be averted through concealment, and "Divine" by repentance, "Moral" retribution must be suffered, "and that, not by the arbitrary sentence of a despot, but by the natural action of an equitable law, old as Eternity, immutable as God."[5]

Even given Southworth's title and the freeing of the slaves at the end of the novel—a radical act in 1849 in the embattled South—her political work in this novel is not primarily about or for African Americans. She suggests with her positioning of the issue a reluctance to directly confront the implications of her work. *Retribution* suggests that a moral universe tilted off balance will right itself at the expense of all, yet this might argue a political complacency, for if God will right the imbalance, what imperative does she suggest to the reader? Ultimately there is a sense of powerlessness here rather than a drive for perfectionism: Southworth will expose the wrong that slavery brings, but she does not have Stowe's confidence in the nation's ability to right it.

Southworth's arguments are directed at white concerns and needs and only tangentially consider the wrongs done to slaves. Her African American characters are in most cases caricatures, like many of her other stereotyped characters, though in less diverse or provocative ways. Only on a few occasions does Southworth offer slave characters who are drawn respectfully—although she drew few characters without some poke at their foibles, the exception being middle-aged white women.[6]

With *Retribution* Southworth imagined a world in which white women's goodwill ultimately outweighs white men's evil, and where women's good is buttressed by God's will. Yet this is a vision that is profoundly influenced by individualism: no group consciousness of women awakens here, nor a consciousness of a shared oppression with African Americans, however skewed. Ultimately the world *will* right itself, and good people will get their due, but it may take the moral guiding hand of a virtuous (white, native-born) woman.

STOWE WOULD NOT entirely disagree. Her long serialized novel, *Uncle Tom's Cabin*, was an explicit political act in a way Southworth's was not. There was a righteousness in Stowe's work, a focus on injustice, that gave it an altogether more radical cast. In addition, the South for Stowe was an alternative moral landscape, not simply another part of a flawed society. Despite her professed interest in reaching a Southern audience with her charmingly mistaken characters like Augustine St. Clare, or her brutal Northerner-turned-Southerner, Legree, the lines of a moral world are drawn geographically in Stowe's novel in unmistakable ways. In addition, here God is still in the whirlwind, but readers were urged to start now, to take responsibility, to act. There is an urgency and an implacability that Southworth's romance lacks, if the underlying vision of white women's moral work is shared.

In *Uncle Tom's Cabin* Stowe responded to the strengthening of the Fugitive Slave Act, a provision of the Compromise of 1850 meant to appease angry Southerners. The compromise was intended to resolve the tension raised by the spoils of the Mexican War, a war sought largely by Southerners, who were eager to expand slavery, and rejected by many Northerners, who were wary of such expansion. While the compromise offered concessions to the North—California as a free state, the banning of the slave trade in the District of Columbia—it was rightly interpreted by many Northerners as anything but a "compromise" in its addition of a strength-ened Fugitive Slave Act. The passage of this part of the compromise brought many who had been sitting on the fence over the issue of slavery into an antislavery position, and helped push Stowe on to the writing of *Uncle Tom's Cabin* at the urging of her sister-in-law.

Stowe may have gone to church one Sunday with this urging in mind, and she remembered emerging with a story that she felt would move the nation. In February of 1851, at communion in the Bowdoin College chapel in Brunswick, Maine, Harriet Beecher Stowe had a vision, as she later explained. "[L]ike the unrolling of a picture," her son wrote in her biogra-phy, she saw a stalwart African American man beaten to death by his white master and his master's brutal henchmen. After his master left him bleed-ing, the slave transcended both his pain and the great wrong done him to forgive his oppressors before he died. When Stowe returned home, she wrote the incident down and read it to her family, who wept with her. The American public, which she considered her larger family, was also deeply affected by Stowe's translation of her vision in *Uncle Tom's Cabin*. With this evangelistic, political, racial, and moral polemic, Stowe fired a shot that was, in a sense, comparable to the ones that began the physical Civil War in Kansas and at Fort Sumter.

Harriet Beecher Stowe's vision that cold February in Maine sprang from a belief that the best way to influence politics was through the heart, not the head: she intended to "stir up [a] mighty mass of people," to "consider the part which . . . is their duty," for "the moral elevation of their race." Stowe perceived the nation as facing "terrible evils," evils imposed and experienced by whites as well as blacks. Her yearning to be of service to the nation, to join ranks in fighting these evils, grew from a desire to place women and love at the center of social change that celebrated ascen-dant middle-class values and that assumed a moral white America.

The two journeys of the novel, one toward freedom and the other toward death, represented Stowe's conviction that the social organization of the North was more morally sound than that of the South. In the first and most significant of the journeys, Uncle Tom is taken farther and farther south and away from his moral compass and domestic peace (on Legree's plantation he has to struggle to maintain his religious balance), and Eliza and George escape to the North, toward a moral compass and domestic peace (though they would tellingly only find it back in Africa). That one journey is passive and the other active is also telling: the South is a place from which Christian people, especially blacks, need to escape. With a vision couched in these terms, especially one with such popular appeal, compromise seems unlikely. Can one compromise with the devil? Can one do so in a world so evil that it taints even the well-intentioned Augustine St. Clare?

In *Uncle Tom's Cabin* and other novels, poems, and stories of the early 1850s written by white women, imaginative use of the institution of slavery made reference first to the claims and dilemmas of white women. On some level this is understandable if still problematic: they were intended to move whites to action, and spoke to whites' self-interest. Written by women who mainly had no experience of slavery and only minimal contact with African Americans, free or enslaved, this work dealing with the issue of slavery created a vision of white womanhood, a position on class hierarchy and individuality—one about which Northern women and Southern women argued. So, for example, the slave Topsy was meant primarily to demonstrate the hidden nobility of St. Clare and fundamentally to force the Northern Miss Ophelia to recognize her shortcomings. Topsy's abuse, her separation from her mother, is clearly part of the story but is not its plot.[7]

In the beginning of the 1850s, the intentions of Stowe's political work were clear: thoughtful white people needed to act to end this domestic and familial outrage, to cleanse their souls and their country (Stowe was at this time a colonizationist) of this immense wrong. This was her answer to what many in the North called the Slave Power: Northern white women's love is stronger than legislation. If the character of Senator Bird could make the laws, a reproachful look from his moral wife—which worked to impel him to save Eliza and her child—could help him break them. And women needed to make those reproachful looks.

Despite their shared antislavery aims, Southworth and Stowe reveal differing assumptions in their work. Stowe makes her case by emphasizing the similarity between blacks and whites: Eliza, for example, loves her child like "you" do, and like Senator Bird does. Southworth draws blacks and whites separately; her intention is to show the moral goodness of whites who free their slaves, not the social injustice that demands such action. And Stowe also sees the connections within communities; her novel is about family, and its centrality to moral life. Southworth focuses on individuals; her families tend to be rent with conflict, not bound by loyalty. That Stowe is a Northerner, and Southworth a border state Southerner perhaps is no surprise given these assumptions and this historical moment.

If the "little lady" was to speak politically (as well as to give meaningful looks), questions remained concerning where and how she should do this. The clash between members of a women's rights community over women's proper interpretation of her place coalesced around the work of two writers in 1854 and 1855: Fanny Fern (Sara Willis Parton) and Elizabeth Oakes Smith. Fern, who became one of the century's most popular writers, was juxtaposed with the far less well known activist Elizabeth Oakes Smith.

Women writers fought hard over the issue of their "sphere." While suffragists were few in number, the scope of the issue associated with them—the so-called woman question—was not. In his survey of magazine literature from 1850 to 1865, historian Frank Mott calls the question "ubiquitous," appearing not only in "the magazines designed mainly for the women themselves, but [in] quarterlies, monthlies and weeklies of all descriptions."[8]

The contested nature of the issue of women's sphere, even for those women writers who were the most liberal in their thinking, was made particularly clear in a series of reviews of Fanny Fern's semi-autobiographical novel, *Ruth Hall*. Played out in the pages of the women's rights paper the *Una*, this debate over the proper voice of a woman writer demonstrates that even ultra-reformist women adopted no single political strategy. Elizabeth Cady Stanton, one of the century's most outspoken reformers, championed *Ruth Hall*, describing it as a woman's slave narrative. Caroline Healey Dall, an editor of the *Una* and an outspoken historian and intellectual on her own, espoused many of the views of the Transcendentalist Margaret Fuller. Her reaction to *Ruth Hall* was one of dismay, and she substituted Elizabeth Oakes Smith's *Bertha and Lily* as a more appropriate reformist novel.

In the concern that Stanton and Dall showed these novels is an acknowledgement of the important political work that they did and the clashing interpretations of the ends of that work. The audience for these novels (and authors) differed widely. *Ruth Hall* was one of the decade's (and the century's) best-sellers; by 1854, Fanny Fern had established herself as a major new voice in Boston, one that had reached other cities through regular newspaper exchanges. *Bertha and Lily* was the first novel of the reformer Elizabeth Oakes Smith, the mother of five sons and wife of humorist Seba Smith. Elizabeth had been writing since the 1840s, but before 1854 she had been known primarily for her stories, essays, historical sketches, and a popular long poem, "The Sinless Child." Far more than Fern, Oakes Smith was an avowed reformer, both in dress and in voting rights for women. *Bertha and Lily* was well received by the reform community but failed to reach the larger mainstream audience Fern commanded.[9]

Neither *Ruth Hall* nor *Bertha and Lily* could have been written before the mid-1850s; they are radical statements, allowable only in a context of women's rights conventions and arguments over women's appropriate place. They assume an antislavery position, along with a certain understanding and position about women's right to independence and women's powerful effects on society. Juxtaposed with the more conservative and religious writing of best-selling novelist Susan Warner, whose *Wide, Wide World* more overtly promotes a kind of submission to duty and God's will, these novels reveal a wide disparity even within the women's rights reform position at the radical end of the spectrum of opinion on separate spheres.

And yet these two novels are remarkably different. *Ruth Hall* is a version of Sara Parton Willis's life story, minus only her ruinous second marriage (which would appear in *Rose Clark*). Unlike most other women's novels of the period, there are few long descriptive sections and little romantic or expressive language in this novel. Fern does what she says she will do in the opening pages: she enters people's homes, records what is happening frankly and briskly, and moves on to the next vignette. This relatively short and fast-paced novel breaks conventions in other ways as well: it begins with a marriage, proceeds to widowhood, and ends with financial independence. It describes the selfishness of professing Christians and the crass manipulativeness of supposedly loving relatives. It glories in the eventual success of a woman and celebrates her popularity with her public. And it offers no change of heart based on the influence of a moral woman on an erring man; men are either good or bad but are ultimately not redeemable. Its message is that women can and must earn their own way and should expect little from relatives, and that the only way to make change happen is through exposing wrongdoing.

Bertha and Lily, by contrast, is both more and less startling. From the beginning, Oakes seems to have a greater ambition for the meaning of her work; in her preface she presents her novel in the hopes that it will "contain some significant words on questions of vital import to the growth of humanity." In the course of her novel she touches on the issues of fallen women, women's right to education, the stifling quality to woman's assumed conventional behavior, the evils of slavery, the weakness of religious instruction and ministerial failure, and the moral bankruptcy of almshouses and prisons. Her heroine, Bertha, is a fallen woman of enormous virtue, godliness, and self-confidence. Bertha's task in the novel is to redeem the overly erudite minister, Ernest Helfstein, and to teach him through the power and influence of a strong and intellectual woman. She does this both by personally encouraging him to adopt two children from the almshouse (one of whom will turn out to be Bertha's lost and illegitimate daughter) and with pointed speeches.[10]

Undoubtedly there were those who would agree with both implied positions: that women should safeguard themselves through financial independence, and that they should make positive change through their strong and unabashed influence on men. But the implications of each conflict are significant, as well: Fern offers a world in which each woman stands alone, on her own power; Oakes a world where the community moves toward a collective vision, where no one stands alone. One is distrustful and capable; the other trusting and strong-minded.

Reviewers were very aware of these implications. "In the name of womanhood, I thank Fanny Fern for this deeply interesting life experience," Elizabeth Cady Stanton wrote after reading *Ruth Hall*. The virtue of the novel was its unflinching exposure of erring men: "Heaven has witnessed these petty tyrannies in the isolated household long enough. When woman does at length divest herself of all false notions of justice and delicacy, and gives to the world a full revelation of her sufferings and miseries—the histories of all other kinds of injustice and oppression will sink into utter insignificance, before the living pictures she shall hold up to the unwilling vision of domestic tyrants." What *Ruth Hall* can do, she added, is give a useful "restraining fear" to tyrannical relatives, lest they be exposed to a "discerning public." Further, Stanton criticized the *National Anti-Slavery Standard* for its severe review, asserting that Fern's was as much a slave narrative as Frederick Douglass's, and no tyranny should go "unknown and unrebuked."[11]

It was not so much Fanny Fern's exposé that bothered women reviewers but the manner in which it was offered. This was personal and deliberate, and it was the loss of self-control and womanly generosity that Caroline Healey Dall rebuked. This was not the kind of reform or reformer Dall wished to see promoted, for Fern returned tyranny with exposure, and not with the love and kindness even an erring father deserves. For Dall, then, the notions of justice and delicacy that Stanton called false, she called true, and she held even oppressed women to them.[12] Smith's novel, which retained an argument for woman's loving, religious, and compassionate nature even as it critiqued the stranglehold that this "nature" argument might suggest, earned her approval. If Smith wished to turn the world over, to substitute women for men as ministers of love, to allow women to express opinions, to hold money and have ambition, she did so without abandoning a sense of the world's perfectibility, without, like Fern's protagonist, becoming cynical—or knowing.

The political implications of these novels, despite their similar positions on women's right to financial and personal independence, revolved around the novels' adherence to the *spirit* of separate spheres ideology. If women wrote with love and charity, they could be trenchant in their recommendations. If they wrote to expose, in a spirit of revenge or righteousness—if they revealed a sense of their right to speak that was too assured—they might hurt the cause, and turn away women not yet ready for such forthright claiming.

By the mid-1850s the decade represented in a sense a shifting from one of these positions to the other. In women's writing there was a palpable shift in the acceptable, from a novel of love like *Uncle Tom's Cabin*, in which the title character prays for the souls of his murderers, to a novel like *Dred*, Stowe's also, in which the title character promises vengeance if justice is not served. This shift came as a result not only of public discussion but largely out of growing anxiety and anger within the North at large. Given the growing numbers of immigrants in the North, and the more aggressive and defensive Slave Power in the South, concerned white women believed that they had to act to establish the moral centers for social and political life. At midcentury many still struggled to use love and not violence, but to do so they expressed a need for increased vigilance on women's part, a greater sense of their complicity and hence their duty.

When the Kansas-Nebraska Act came up in Congress, Harriet Beecher Stowe urged women to work against what she saw as the threatened spread of slavery northward. The act, which ended a geographic settlement of the issue of slavery established by the Missouri Compromise in 1820, allowed territories to choose their status, slave or free, by popular vote. This opened up the vision of slavery expanding farther north, and giving the South additional power in the Senate. This heightened an existing sense of outrage. Very public fights over fugitive slaves were taking place in the streets of the North, most notably that over Anthony Burns, who in 1854 was escorted back to slavery by Federal troops after an angry Boston mob attempted to free him. Many, even previously conservative Northerners, were sickened and radicalized by the event.[13]

In "An Appeal to the Women of the Free States of America, on the Present Crisis in Our Country," Stowe beseeched women to throw the weight of their influence for "the cause of free principle." "Women of the free states!" she exhorted, "the question is not, shall we remonstrate with slavery on its own soil? but are we willing to receive slavery into the free States and territories of the Union?" In a prophetic sentence for 1854 she observed, "We are on the eve of a conflict which will try men's souls, and strain, to their utmost tension, the bonds of brotherly union which bind this nation together."[14] Stowe was not alone in her fears, but her call explicitly to women to see and make sense of the costs of national legislation was pointed. The edge to her words, her sense of dread, grew more common as the decade closed.

Stowe told her readers that to avoid the apocalyptic destiny that will surely follow, women must act. Her first duty was "*for herself* thoroughly to understand the subject, and to feel that as mother, wife, sister, or member of society, she is bound to give her influence on the right side." As Christian women, however, their job was to soothe tensions while creating moral solutions: women's politics would be one without the contentious political wrangling. "While, then, we seek to sustain the cause of free principle unwaveringly, let us hold it also to be our true office, as women," she wrote, "to moderate the acrimony of political contest, remembering that the slaveholder and the slave are alike our brethren, whom the law of God commands us to love as ourselves." For the sake of slaves and slaveholders, children, country, and liberty, Stowe concluded, "let every woman of America now do her duty."[15] Her duty, by 1854, was to intervene in political life.

Two years later Stowe included in her column in the New York newspaper *the Independent* the letters of a Kansas emigrant to his mother in Massachusetts. In "Mothers of the Men in Kansas," published the month after the raid on the town of Lawrence by Missourians, Stowe returned to her appeal to Northern women with even more urgency. "Women and mothers of the Free States," she asked, "what counsels can you give to your sons and brothers in times like these?" Like the brave men of Kansas, women, too, had a role to play. "Shall these brave men be striken [*sic*] down and defeated, while your voice can persuade one to go to their help—while you can solicit material aid to send to their assistance?"[16] The answer, of course, was no.

Child versus Wise and Mason: Speaking for the North

A longtime activist of the more direct and forthright sort, Lydia Maria Child was disgusted and tired after two decades of struggle against slavery. An avid reader of newspapers, and very politically aware, Child tracked the partisan changes that encouraged a regional politics. By 1856 some Northern women were looking to the Republican Party, and particularly to candidate John C. Fremont, to right the balance of power in the government. In August, Lydia Maria Child wrote to her friend Sarah Shaw of her newfound excitement over partisan politics: "Our hopes, like yours, rest on Fremont. I would almost lay down my life to have him elected. There has never been such a crisis since we were a nation. If Slave-Power is checked *now*, it will *never* regain its strength. If it is *not* checked, civil war is inevitable; and, with all my horror of bloodshed, I could be better resigned to that great calamity, than to endure the tyranny that has so long trampled on us." "And 'our Jessie,' bless her noble soul!" Child continued, referring to Jessie Benton Fremont, the presidential candidate's wife. "Isn't it pleasant to have a *woman* spontaneously recognized as a moral influence in public affairs? There's *meaning* in that fact."

Jessie's importance to the campaign stirred Child's desire for the vote. "What a shame that *women* can't vote!" she wrote exuberantly. "We'd carry 'our Jessie' into the White House on our shoulders, *would* n't we? Never mind! Wait a while! Women-stock's rising in the market. I shall not live to see women vote; but I'll come and *rap* on the ballot-box. Won't *you*? I never was bitten by politics before; but such mighty issues are depending on *this* election, that I cannot be indifferent."[17] Child, like Stowe, was now even more convinced that women could act in politics with a singleness of moral vision that many men lacked. And her claim that she was "never bitten by politics before" only refers to partisan politics: Child may not ever have been indifferent. What had changed was her sense that others had joined her in her passion, that "women-stock's rising."

Clearly Child was not alone in her excitement over Jessie Fremont, or her sense that Jessie was her husband's greatest asset. That a candidate's wife would be so noted was profoundly unusual. The campaign slogan "Give 'em Jessie!" and a popular advertising note, "Fremont has got a better half, / And what must be the whole?" almost denigrated Fremont on his wife's behalf. A rendition of "Oh! Susannah," adapted for the campaign, had as its chorus: "Rise, bold freemen, / Rise from hill and dale; / Your watchword, 'Jessie and the Right,' There's no such thing as fail!" The Democratic candidate, bachelor James Buchanan, was faulted for his lack of a moral or charming wife. "A rusty old codger, who ne'er—as 'tis said," Republicans sang, "had children to speak of, and never was wed."[18] Fremont lost the campaign, but the Republicans established themselves both as a sectional party and as a national force to be reckoned with. They also were connected to a rising sense of women's political stake in national politics, or those politics that could be read as having a moral significance.

The tone of women's writing on slavery was changing. Far more than ever before, it reflected the accelerating pace of national events and the apocalyptic overtones of public discourse. To some extent, women were themselves becoming radicalized, with increasing polarity between the North and the South. As with men, there were also moderates, and they still retained some influence, particularly following the secession crisis of 1860–61. But they would ultimately be overwhelmed by a rising tide of war that engulfed the nation.

Although by 1859 Child had had a long and productive writing career, it was, ironically, her correspondence that led her to her greatest victory. Like many in the North, although she was initially repulsed by John Brown's resort to violence in his brief capture of the arsenal at Harpers Ferry, she came to see his act as that of a properly revered martyr.[19] On October 26, 1859, she wrote a letter to John Brown's jailer, Governor Henry Alexander Wise of Virginia, asking him to deliver a letter to Brown and, if possible, to be allowed to come and care for Brown during his final days. She claimed that she and "all my circle of abolition acquaintances were taken by surprise" by the events at Harpers Ferry, and although a believer in peace principles, she "and thousands of others feel a natural impulse of sympathy for the brave and suffering man."[20] Despite Child's deferential beginning—"I have heard you were a man of chivalrous sentiments"—her letter was understood and read as a direct attack on the South and its institutions.

Wise fired back his own, suggesting that of course she could visit—"Virginia and Massachusetts are involved in no civil war"—although it might not be prudent. He vowed to protect her, for, he wrote, "I could not permit an insult even to woman in her walk of charity among us, though it be to one who whetted knives of butchery for our mothers, sisters, daughters and babes."[21] But, he said, her sympathy and that of her ilk had inspired Brown to his crime, and he was doubtful that Brown's action would have come as a surprise.

Child took up his challenge in her reply. If she had the constitutional right to visit Virginia, as Wise had said, this was a rare instance of the efficacy of the Constitution. "Your constitutional obligation, for which you profess so much respect," she wrote, "has never proved any protection to citizens of the Free States, who happen to have a black, brown or yellow complexion; nor to any white citizen whom you even suspected of entertaining opinions opposite to your own, on a question of vast importance to the temporal welfare and moral example of our common country."[22] She then listed several outrages perpetrated against various individuals in the

South who had expressed antislavery opinions. Further, she accused Wise of his own treason, quoting his 1842 speech in Congress in which he "threatened to trample on the Constitution and break the Union, if a majority of the legal voters in these Confederated States dared elect a President unfavorable to the extension of Slavery."[23]

Finally, after giving Wise a history of the abolitionist movement, Child accused *him* of provoking the raid at Harpers Ferry: "You may believe it or not, Gov. Wise, but it is certainly the truth that, because slaveholders so recklessly sowed the wind in Kansas, they reaped a whirlwind at Harper's Ferry." The South had weakened the Union "beyond all power of restoration." Among the "free, enlightened yeomanry of New England . . . a majority . . . would rejoice to have the Slave States fulfill their oft-repeated threat of withdrawal from the Union." The South's immoral character was revealed through its connection to slavery; and the question of morality was at the center of Child's response. "The moral sense of these States," Child wrote, "is so outraged by being accomplices in sustaining an institution vicious in all its aspects; and it is now generally understood that we purchase our disgrace at great pecuniary expense." If the wish to separate is in earnest, she concluded, "the hearty response of millions" would be, "Go, gentlemen, and 'Stand not on the order of your going, / But go at once!' "[24]

Governor Wise published the letters in a Virginia paper; the New York *Tribune* then picked them up and published them on November 12, 1859. Child, writing to the *Tribune*, added the letter she had written to Brown and his response. The final letters of the later-collected *Correspondence* were added in mid-December. Mrs. Margaretta Mason of Virginia, the wife of the Virginia senator who had fathered the strengthened Fugitive Slave Act in the Compromise of 1850, wrote a reply to Child's letters to Mason and to Brown; Child responded in kind. The *Liberator* published the correspondence in full on December 31, 1859; they were made into an Anti-Slavery Society pamphlet in early 1860. It sold 300,000 copies, representing the pinnacle of Child's popularity.[25]

The interchange between Mason and Child focused on the duty of women to their communities and the nation at large. Mason's letter to Child implicitly accused her of "unsexing" herself, of not deserving the name of woman. Pointedly, Mason began without a salutation, asking instead: "Do you read your Bible, Mrs. Child?" From one middle-class Christian woman to another, this question cast aspersions on Child's central perceived duty as the moral arbiter of her home. Mason questioned Child's priorities with her morals: "*You* would soothe with sisterly and motherly care the hoary-headed murderer of Harper's Ferry! A man whose aim and intention was to incite the horrors of servile war—to condemn women of your own race, ere death closed their eyes on their sufferings from violence and outrage, to see their husbands and fathers murdered, their children butchered, the ground strewed with the brains of their babes."[26] Mason went on to attack Child's activism, asking why she did not aid the many poor around her. Implying that Child was not a true woman because she neglected her own community to meddle in others, Mason concluded that "no Southerner ought, after your letter to Governor Wise and to Brown, to read a line of your composition, or to touch a magazine which bears your name in its lists of contributors; and in this hope for the 'sympathy,' at least of those at the North who deserve the name of woman."[27]

Child again used a moral argument in defending her right to speak of politics in her response to Mason's letter. "[S]urely we, as a portion of the Union, involved in the expense, the degeneracy, the danger, and the disgrace, of this iniquitous and fatal system, have a *right* to speak about it," she wrote, "and a right to be *heard* also." The South does not even allow the other side to speak, she argued, perhaps referring to the gag rule of the 1830s in Congress, which tabled all petitions regarding slavery. "In this enlightened age," Child argued—aiming her own barb at Mason's morals— "all despotisms *ought* to come to an end by the agency of moral and rational means. But if they resist such agencies, it is in the order of Providence that they *must* come to an end by violence."[28]

Finally, Child addressed Mason's attack on her middle-class womanhood. For herself, and "all of the women of New England," she claimed, "it would be extremely difficult to find any women of our villages who do *not* sew for the poor, and watch the sick, when occasion arises." Instead of Christmas gifts of gowns given in lieu of just payment for services, she added, "we pay our domestics generous wages." With a parting shot, Child remarked that she had "never known an instance where the 'pangs of maternity' did not meet with requisite assistance; and here in the North, after we have helped the mothers, *we do not sell the babies*."[29] There, for Child as for Stowe, was the rub: what made Stowe's Eliza leap the ice flows of the Ohio River was central to the moral position of Northern antislavery women. When politics came between mother and child, women had a right to act.

CHILD'S WORK AS AN antislavery writer was particularly significant in the years after John Brown's raid. Emboldened by his example, but hoping to avoid the bloodshed she had seen looming on the horizon for years, Child reenlisted in the antislavery effort. Her *Correspondence* was perhaps the most significant of her writings since her 1833 pamphlet *An Appeal on Behalf of that Class of Americans Called Africans*; in the later pamphlet she captured the mood of her community both in bewailing the violence of Brown's action and in giving to Brown a martyr's status. By predicting civil war, and bidding the South to go, she made dramatically obvious what had been said more covertly in many other forms before.[30]

Child's writings were significant in their refusal to extend apologies for her actions. By the late 1850s, rationales for writing or speaking were no longer as central as they had been for women antislavery writers, although they did remain constant throughout the war. As Jane Swisshelm told audiences in 1858, "[W]omen *ought* to meddle in politics," and "such 'meddling' d[oes] not . . . unsex . . . and unfit [them] for domestic duties." "The 'strongest women' of all ages," she continued, "made the best wives, the best mothers, and combined most of the true womanly instinct."[31]

Unfortunately, however, the best women were not coming forward, and it was this failure, not John Brown's, that concerned Child most. In a letter to William Lloyd Garrison defending Brown's right to choose violence, she argued that Brown's act was necessary because those who chose to use moral suasion had not worked hard enough: "Instead of blaming him for carrying out his own convictions by means we cannot sanction, it would be more profitable for us to inquire of ourselves whether we, who believe in a 'more excellent way,' have carried our own convictions into practice, as faithfully as he did *his*. We believe in *moral influence* as a cure for the diseases of society. Have we exerted it as constantly and as strenuously as we ought against the giant wrong, that is making wreck of all the free institutions our father handed down to us as a sacred legacy?" Child's work, inspired by Brown, was nevertheless undertaken to avoid the methods he espoused.[32]

Jacobs and Davis: The Web of Racial and Wage Slavery

A final pairing, two works published literally on the eve of war, demonstrates the consciousness of this interconnected political world by two of the decade's most trenchant women critics: Harriet Jacobs, as "Linda Brent" in *Incidents in the Life of a Slave Girl*, and Rebecca Harding Davis in her novella *Life in the Iron Mills*, both published in April 1861. These texts reveal what is often assumed in the texts of Northern women: if political critiques of slavery at the beginning of the decade eschewed note of the ills of free labor, by the decade's end careful critics noted their marriage. These were less popular works, written by women on the edge of their respective societies, yet they uncover the unstated assumptions of what had become the mainstream and reveal them as false. Here both North *and* South are condemned for their oppression of the working classes, black and white alike, and implicitly, at least, they give the North no undisputed moral high ground. Perhaps most importantly, these texts indicate the direction of postwar women writers, some of whom claimed a direct link between the problems of slavery and wage labor. Since slavery had ended, they argued, the next challenge was in supporting workingwomen.

Lydia Maria Child's other major project on the eve of the Civil War was editing Harriet Jacobs's *Incidents in the Life of a Slave Girl*. Jacobs, an articulate, self-educated African American woman, both appropriated and revised the male slave narrative tradition.[33] She was clearly aware that her authority as a fugitive slave was itself a political tool. In her construction of self, then, Jacobs crafted a depiction that would both appeal to and provoke an abolitionist audience.

Child's letters reveal that she suggested few changes for *Incidents* and that she shared Jacobs's political views. "I have very little occasion to alter the language," she wrote, "which is wonderfully good, for one whose opportunities for education have been so limited. The events are interesting, and well told; the remarks are also good, and to the purpose." Child copied a great deal of it over, however, switching the order of the narration in a few places to make it more clear. She was quick to tell Jacobs that she need feel no undue gratitude: "I should not take such pains, if I did not consider the book unusually interesting, and likely to do much service to the Anti-Slavery cause. So you need not feel under great personal obligations. You know I would go through fire and water to help give a blow to Slavery. I suppose you will want to see the M.S. after I have exercised my bump of mental order on it; and I will send it to you direct, a fortnight hence."[34] She asked Jacobs to write more about Nat Turner's insurrection, perhaps because of her own experiences regarding John Brown. The only major revision Child suggested was to omit the last chapter on Brown. "It does not come naturally to your story, and the M.S. is already too long," she explained. Jacobs took her advice.[35]

Child praised the narrative and Jacobs herself to her wider community, and tried to drum up support for it. She predicted its usefulness as a political text; *Incidents* documented the evils of slavery rather than simply argued about them. To John Greenleaf Whittier she wrote: "I am glad you liked 'Linda.' I have taken a good deal of pains to publish it, and circulate it, because it seemed to me well calculated to take hold of many minds, that will not attend to *arguments* about slavery. The author is a quick-witted, intelligent woman, with great refinement and propriety of manner."[36] The narrative, however, released in late 1860, was not given much attention by either the *Liberator* or the *National Anti-Slavery Standard*, perhaps because of the press of events in the approaching war.[37]

The relationship between Jacobs and Child was highly unusual for the mid-nineteenth century. In her letters to Jacobs, Child does not seem to take on the conventionally maternal role that many white women adopted in their writing about African American subjects, both actual and imagined. Her matter-of-fact tone seems little short of professional, exchanged from one reformer to another. Nor did Child earn anything as a result of the relationship; all the proceeds from *Incidents* went to Jacobs. Though initially unsure about approaching Child, Jacobs found her "a whole souled Woman." "We soon found the way to each other[']s heart," she wrote to Amy Post. "I will send you some of her letters which . . . will better describe her than my poor pen."[38]

Jacobs was fully able to appreciate Child's generosity and respect because she had experienced far less satisfying interactions with other white women. She began the process of publication of her narrative by having both her friends Cordelia Grinnell Willis and Amy Post approach Harriet Beecher Stowe about taking her daughter Louisa with her to England when she went on a tour after publishing *Uncle Tom's Cabin*; Louisa might then have interested Stowe in Jacobs's narrative. Stowe replied to Willis by including Post's letter, saying that Louisa would be spoiled by all the attention in England, hinting perhaps that she would not pay for her expenses, and questioning if Jacobs's story was true. If it was true, she wanted to use it in her *Key to Uncle Tom's Cabin*. In sending Post's letter to Willis, Stowe revealed more to Willis than Jacobs had, embarrassing Jacobs and giving her no great impression of Stowe's manners or delicacy. That Stowe submitted her story to a white woman for verification indicated her distrust, and Jacobs was well aware that as a black woman and a domestic she did not receive the respect and consideration a white middle-class woman would. Both Willis's and Jacobs's subsequent letters to Stowe were never answered.[39]

Incidents in the Life of a Slave Girl was intended to use a life—Jacobs's own— as an example of political work, to inspire the Northern populace to action. In it, Jacobs challenges several systems of meaning: the slave system, separate sphere ideology, middle-class norms, and racism.[40] Yet she also demonstrates, in a few passages, the ways in which North and South are connected by the oppression of the ruling class. In her autobiography Jacobs described the Nat Turner revolt and its effects on her neighborhood when she was a child. Jacobs knew that the houses of free blacks would be searched for arms, and she knew that the appearance of middle-class respectability enraged whites, especially those who could not afford the material goods that established that respectability. Her weapon was class—and she clearly betrayed her own animosity—yet if "the low whites . . . exulted in such a chance to exercise a little brief authority," it was only because they did not reflect "that the power which trampled on the colored people also kept themselves in poverty, ignorance, and moral degradation."[41] These oppressions were linked, she told her Northern white audience (who, on the verge of war, would be very ready to believe it and hope for a wedge between rich and poor whites). If in her trip to England much later Jacobs contrasted wage slavery with racial slavery (like Child, she emphasized that families were not sold away), she did this in no spirit of denial. The enemy of the slave and the workingwoman was the same: the ruling class.

Davis's *Life in the Iron Mills* makes the same point, yet its function is more evident in the text. Early in her exposé of the working conditions of millworkers in West Virginia, the narrator muses on her childhood fancy of the "weary, dumb appeal on the face of the negro-like river slavishly bearing its burden day after day," a similar sight to the one she now sees, on the streets of the mill town as the "slow stream of human life creep[s] past, night and morning, to the great mills."[42] Yet the narrator recognizes her mistake later: "My fancy about the river was an idle one: it is no type of such a life." The river is able to move on (like wealthy whites); if it is "stagnant and slimy" here, "odorous sunlight" awaits around the next bend. It is the trapped—slaves and workers alike—who are to be pitied, the narrator implies.[43]

Life in the Iron Mills, which captured the imagination of *Atlantic* readers in 1861, revealed the tragedy of wasted lives and hope unrealized. It was a significant work both in establishing Davis as a brilliant literary voice and in introducing a new note in fiction on issues of class. A worker in the mills, Wolfe is an artist of great passion and untutored skill. A young deformed woman, Deborah, also a worker, loves Wolfe and steals money from a visitor to the mills to allow him to realize his ambition. Wolfe is found with the money and jailed, and, unwilling to implicate Deborah, he kills himself. Davis takes the reader through Wolfe's struggle over whether to keep the money as he sits watching middle-class churchgoers. "His brain, greedy, dwarfed, full of thwarted energy and unused powers, questioned these men and women going by, coldly, bitterly, that night. Was it not his right to live as they,—a pure life, a good, true-hearted life, full of beauty and kind words? He only wanted to know how to use the strength within him. His heart warmed, as he thought of it."[44] Just as writers like Stowe asked the same of Eliza, fleeing with her son to keep him safe, Davis asks for Wolfe: Was it not his right?

Davis sought to show Wolfe as everyman, simply pursuing what was taken for granted by the more fortunate—a chance at life and access to clean air and green hills. She also demonstrated an understanding of the huge gulf between the classes. The visitor to the mills whom Deborah robs is Davis's vehicle for exploring this gulf. Mitchell, a thoroughbred gentleman, recognizes Wolfe's talent through his sculpture of a woman reaching out, hungry for life. When Mitchell turns to his brother-in-law Kirby, the owner of the mill, and asks what he will do with Wolfe's talent, Kirby answers for all capitalists. "The Lord will take care of his own; or else they can work out their own salvation. I have heard you call our American system a ladder which any man can scale. Do you doubt it? Or perhaps you want to banish all social ladders, and put us all on a flat table-land?"[45] The speaker assumes that hierarchy is proper: if the world is a ladder, then vast wealth and exploitation can be justified through presumed merit. Yet the speech is ambiguous, too: Kirby taunts the listener with his own theory of free labor. Does he really want an equal system if it could jeopardize his own position?

Davis's story profiled an American system that blocked opportunity and middle-class people who were largely indifferent or thoughtless in their charity. This was a direct critique of the free labor ideology espoused by Abraham Lincoln, and suggested by the constant references to his "log cabin" past. When Kirby asserts that there are limits to his responsibility to Wolfe, Mitchell (and Davis) clearly disagree. A compassionate but crudely naive doctor, standing there, feels that a coin and a kind word would help Wolfe, but Mitchell knows better. The people will rise, he argues, for "reform is born of need, not pity. No vital movement of the people's has worked down, for good or evil; fermented, instead, carried up the heaving, cloggy mass."[46] In the end a kindly Quaker woman helps Deborah when she is released from prison; only in this way is there any positive change. The Quaker woman offers opportunity and equality, not paternalism or advice.

Davis makes other efforts to recall to the reader the connection between these oppressions. Kirby, the mill owner's son, is the brother-in-law to Mitchell, a dilettante who has come south to study the "institutions" of a slave state. The two and a few other ruling-class men congregate near the working station of Wolfe, a workman-cum-sculptor, whose case they discuss idly. Kirby tells his friends that he feels no responsibility for the wasted lives of his workingpeople: his responsibility ends with their paycheck, and he chooses not to think beyond that. "I wash my hands of all social problems,—slavery, white or black," he tells them.[47] For Kirby, the two systems are linked, and both are irrelevant in a capitalist world: he chooses not to think of his own complicity. "Money has spoken!" his brother-in-law says later.

At the end of the story, as Wolfe watches the street from the jail he sees a "mulatto girl" following her mistress. She is laughing, but her "bright eyes" look out "half-shadowed," and he yearns to sculpt her, like he did the hungry workingwoman.[48] It is when he realizes that he will never again sculpt, that his artistic life is dead, that he completely despairs and kills himself.

In the context of the prewar North, Davis's marrying the ills of capitalism and slavery made sense politically for a number of reasons. By 1861 Northerners were more comfortable with such an indictment, if only because it justified going to war against the Southern aristocracy. Yet Davis and Jacobs, by linking the two, were also suggesting a class analysis of the relationship between North and South (connected by the marriage in *Life in the Iron Mills*, which links Kirby and Mitchell), which went further than public opinion would. In the making of moral war, a making begun by a "little lady" (among others) in 1851 and 1852, there was little room for such a complex critique.

THE EVENTS OF THE 1850S triggered a growing sense of war's inevitability, and even its necessity. Stowe's own political line was hardening. The frankly partisan and sometimes belligerent tone of her published letters to the New York *Independent* were nowhere near as generous as *Uncle Tom's Cabin*: Senator Bird, by 1861, would not just be a good-hearted but mistaken man, corrected by the lure of domestic harmony. With a circulation of seventy thousand by early 1860, the political-religious *Independent* had become one of the most widely read and thus most influential papers in the country.[49] Rather than speaking in the voice of domestic fiction—political and powerful in its way, as *Uncle Tom's Cabin* can attest—Stowe took on a stern and specifically political language. Her articles attest to the growing sense of crisis.

Like Child, Stowe was intrigued by the machinations of politics—but only when they revolved around a moral principle. She supported Lincoln and the Republican Party as the party most likely to achieve a moral victory. Her allegiance was tempered, however, by her knowledge of the Republicans' shortcomings. In "What God Hath Wrought," published on November 15, 1860, Stowe admitted that she was "aware that the Republican Party are [*sic*] far from being up to the full measure of what *ought* to be thought and felt on the slavery question." But on this "great moral principle," which has made this election "like no other one," they, at least, "are for *stopping the evil*—and in this case to arrest is to cure."[50] Ultimately, she argued, it was not national politics at all that made change happen. "Our faith," Stowe wrote, "is not in politicians or fleets or armies or elections or Presidents any further than they are indications of His mighty will who hath sworn to break every yoke, and let the oppressed go free." Since God has opened the hearts of the nation to antislavery, however, it is the duty of the antislavery community, Stowe reminded her readers, to "take every advantage of the open eye and ear of the community to keep pure truth in circulation."[51]

"[T]he capture of Burns, the outrages in Kansas, and the attack on Charles Sumner," Lydia Maria Child wrote a friend in September 1857, "roused from the depths of my nature feelings, of whose existence I was not aware." Although she was an avowed pacifist, recent events had inspired in Child an unforeseen anger. "For the first time in my life," she continued, "I felt that I *might* be driven to deeds of blood, when all hopes of justice from the laws, and aid from public sympathy was denied to the fugitive slave."[52]

She was not alone. Far from quelling controversy, the capture and return of slaves like Anthony Burns (and Dred Scott three years later) only divided the nation further. Meanwhile, out in the territory of Kansas, underhanded tactics in drafting a state constitution, random violence, and systematic terror turned the future state into the first battleground of the Civil War. Not even the supposedly gentlemanly halls of government itself were immune; many Northerners were shocked not only at Sumner's beating but at the numbers of gleeful Southerners sending Brooks new canes, and the triumphant reelection of Brooks after he resigned from the House in the aftermath of the incident. Millions of Americans were becoming convinced that war was inevitable—and that it would come at a cost. "Mary Langdon" (Mary Green Pike)'s heroine Ida, in her 1854 novel *Ida May; A Story of Things Actual and Possible*, reflected the sense of impending doom. "[H]umanly speaking," Ida says, "it seems impossible that slavery should cease, except by a convulsion disastrous and fearful as the earthquake, which alone can overthrow vast boulders."[53]

Some saw in this series of events the quickly approaching end to slavery.

Harriet Beecher Stowe confessed to Child in 1861 that she was "convinced that slavery would be overthrown."[54] In April 1859 Frances E. Watkins also predicted that the hand of God would soon right the wrong of slavery. She wrote in a letter to Oliver Johnson, editor of the *National Anti-Slavery Standard*: "Is it a great mystery to you why these things are permitted? Wait, my brother, awhile: the end is not yet. The Psalmist was rather puzzled when he saw the wicked in power and spreading like a Bay tree; but how soon their end! Rest assured, that, as nations and as individuals, God will do right by us, and we should not ask of either God or man to do less than that."[55]

With the battle joined at Fort Sumter, the need for union in all its senses took center stage. Debate over the meaning of women's political work, among those who already believed in it, had no space in a North that suddenly had real need of women's support. The first year of war was characterized by anxiety over the potential mischief that war would inevitably bring. Even so, the war brought an uneasy consensus, a rhetoric of unity out of the conflict of the 1850s, which seemed to express the anxiety that compelled it far more than any real agreement.

What Can Woman Do?—title of a piece in the *Sibyl* (1862)

The first thing which I wrote, marking in any sense the beginning of what authors are accustomed to call their "literary career,"—I dislike the phrase and wish we had a better,—was a war story.—Elizabeth Stuart Phelps, *Chapters from a Life* (1897)

{ CHAPTER THREE }

What Can Woman Do?

The Rhetoric of Unity, 1861–1863

"OF COURSE THE TOWN is in a high state of topsey turveyness, for every one is boiling over with excitement & when quiet Concord does get stirred up it is a sight to behold," Louisa May Alcott wrote to a friend in May of 1861. "All the young men & boys drill with all their might, the women & girls sew and prepare for nurses, the old folks settle the fate of the Nation in groves of newspapers, & the children make the streets hideous with distracted drums and fifes."

Despite the cheeriness of her letter, in the privacy of her journal, Alcott revealed a restlessness with the assumed tasks of women and men, age and youth. "I've often longed to see a war, and now have my wish," she confessed, adding, "I long to be a man, but as I can't fight, I will content myself with working for those who can."[1] And so Alcott took up the most effective weapons at her disposal: first, her needle and then her pen.

The war sharply separated the spaces of men and women, the old and the young. Women and girls continued their work—sewing—and scraped lint for nurses to use on men's wounds.[2] The war brought to them familiar tasks and unfamiliar fears. In the excitement and fervor of the first months of war, women sought to understand where their anticipation and anxiety would fit. They brought to the war traditional and ceremonial images of women: those who bravely sent men into battle, those who waited stoically, those who sewed and bestowed flags and uniforms, those who carried on. These were the images that supported the war effort most conventionally, in ways that emphasized unity.

Yet mixed with those were newer and more daring images: of Florence Nightingale, who in the 1850s made a name for herself and for women-nurses in the Crimea; of vivandières, women on the battlefront who assisted men and sometimes carried the colors (though rarely carried weapons); even of Molly Pitcher, who fought in a battle during the Revolutionary War. The rhetoric of unity, so necessary in wartime, *allowed* a larger room for play, even as it emphasized conformity: if women could successfully argue that their political and cultural work was intended to benefit the Union, paltry considerations of etiquette would ring false.

Alcott expressed a widely shared feeling among Northern women: that their tasks in wartime would—and for many, *should*—differ from men's. She also suggested in her journal both the preponderance of standard responses to war and national crisis that would emerge in the early war years, and her own impatience with them. In this regard, too, her response was typical of many wartime writers. From the most respectable magazine writers to the most sensational dime novelists, women writers in the early days of war explored the conventions of gender, searching within them for levers of power.

At the same time, writers provoked by the national crisis of the 1850s grew ever more pointed in their critique of the moral direction of society. They answered the perennial question of the early war years—what can women do?—with a public remonstrance to political leaders. Here, they said, in published articles, stories, poems, and editorials, is what women *are* doing. These two groups of writers moved closer during the war years, as the vanguard radicalized by the 1850s and a larger mainstream of women writers focused ever more closely on women and their relationship to social and political life.

What women largely did not do, however, with the exception of anti-

Louisa May Alcott (1832–88). Alcott found her voice with *Hospital Sketches*, a fictionalized account of her experience as a nurse in Union Hotel Hospital in Georgetown. She went on to use that voice in her successful series of books aimed at girls, beginning with *Little Women* (1868), which was set in the Civil War era. (Photo used by permission of the National Portrait Gallery, Smithsonian Institution.)

slavery activists, was to ruminate publicly on the cause or the meanings of the war. They offered few celebratory words on behalf of "Union," nor did they generally invoke the legacy of the Revolution, as men North and South did.[3] Once the war began, middle-class writing women settled down to the task of making a place for themselves that gave dignity and power to their part of the national struggle.

Indeed, the early war years were an oasis of consensus in the North, as limited as it was. Women writers were united in their support for the war (given editors wary of being thought disloyal, this is perhaps not surprising), and their calls for women's action and a celebration of national honor were uncomplicated. North and South, honor for men meant risking death; North and South, honor for women meant sacrificing family.[4] Yet in many stories published in the war, honor also meant risking societal displeasure.

What Women Did

Women's varied activities on behalf of the war effort formed the backdrop for their writing. The domestic duties that filled their lives, from water-carrying to sewing, were enhanced by the absence of men and the addition of now further claims on their time. As historian Mary Elizabeth Massey notes, if the conflict began with women asking what they could do, it ended with many answers.[5] Their choices, from conservative to radical, were regularly debated in newspapers and magazines throughout the war years. In such actions (and in the commentary on them), women challenged the limits to acceptable social behavior. They organized vast efforts at relief beginning at the local level; they placed themselves in jeopardy to nurse wounded soldiers despite resistance; and some intrepid or foolhardy few acted directly in the bloody drama as soldiers, scouts, and spies.[6]

Most women working for the war effort in the North never had to leave home to do so. Soldier's aid societies, originally designed to provide local regiments with food, clothing, and medical supplies, flourished in villages, towns, and cities across the North from Boston to Chicago.[7] Women gathered in numbers to sew together, or simply produced finished goods on their own and packed them to send south. Massey has estimated that within two weeks after the firing on Sumter there were 20,000 such societies functioning North and South. Northern civilians and government officials acted early to coordinate the efforts of local societies. By late April of 1861, 2,000 to 3,000 war workers gathered in New York to create the Woman's Central Association of Relief, an organization with a twenty-five-member board, twelve of whom were women.[8] In St. Louis, one woman noted that "every loyal household became a soldier's aid society."[9]

Although the greatest numbers of women assembled boxes of clothing, foodstuffs, and reading matter for the army, others began to work on behalf of the destitute families of soldiers and the fleeing slaves. A Michigan woman wrote in her diary that "we have a Ladies' Loyal League here in town for the benefit of soldiers families, that is needy ones, that don't have enough to be comfortable." A supper with a "fancy table and grab bag" raised money, only some of which was intended for sick and wounded soldiers.[10] The freedmen's aid movement began in February 1862 with the creation of the Boston Education Commission, which also involved many women, including Lydia Maria Child. Child wrote to her friend Sarah Shaw that she was "greatly interested" in the new organization and that she planned to "do all I can for it." "It is refreshing," she continued, "to find *some* green spots in our blood-red landscape."[11] Child went on to give, in some cases more than she could comfortably afford.[12]

Other women took on tasks new to them as the war commenced, in some cases more out of necessity than choice. U.S. Sanitary Commission worker Mary Livermore recalled riding through the farming districts of

Wisconsin and Eastern Iowa on calls of business relating to her war work and noting their transformation in one crucial respect. "Women were in the field everywhere," she wrote, "driving the reapers, binding and shocking, and loading grain, until then an unusual sight. At first it displeased me, and I turned away in aversion," she confessed, but after watching their ability she grew proud. One young woman explained to Livermore her rationale: "I tell mother that as long as the country can't get along without grain, nor the army fight without food, we're serving the country just as much here in the harvest-field as our boys are on the battlefield—and sort o' takes the edge off from this business of doing men's work, you know."[13]

When women left home to work on behalf of the war—particularly if they were unmarried or unescorted—they risked public censure for doing "men's work." This was particularly true of the career that American women captured during the Civil War: nursing. Even though the renowned English nurse Florence Nightingale was heralded by the press, this praise did not always translate into increased opportunities for women. Samuel Gridley Howe seemingly had no qualms about this inconsistency. After encouraging Nightingale personally, he continued to frown on his wife Julia's efforts both in writing and speaking. He told her that "if he had been engaged to Florence Nightingale, and had loved her ever so dearly, he would have given her up as soon as she commenced her career as a public woman."[14] Despite Howe's objections—which one imagines were repeated in many households—hundreds of women worked in both established and makeshift hospitals, on transport ships and in their own homes when the war and its wounded came to them. Not surprisingly, this struggle over propriety in homes and hospitals was also fought in the war literature throughout the North.

A few women created jobs for themselves near the battlefield when official channels gave them little scope. Among them were such well-known figures as Clara Barton, who brought enormous loads of supplies to the front during the war as well as personally supervising efforts to locate missing soldiers after the war.[15] Mary Ann (or "Mother") Bickerdyke eventually affiliated herself with the U.S. Sanitary Commission, but began as an independent agent and never truly gave up that status. Her self-defined duties included nursing on the battlefield, establishing diet kitchens for wounded soldiers, and overseeing the work of surgeons. When approached by an army surgeon that Bickerdyke had accused of misconduct, General Ulysses S. Grant was reported as saying, "My God, man, Mother Bickerdyke outranks everybody, even Lincoln. If you have run amuck of her I advise you to get out quickly before she has you under arrest."[16] Other women, such as Belle Z. Spencer, the wife of a Northern officer fighting in the West, followed their husbands to camp and worked there in any capacity that was necessary. Spencer worked in the hospitals in Cairo, Illinois, but her most unusual work was on behalf of starving Southern refugee families, primarily composed of women and children, who flooded the Federal camps.[17]

Fewer in number but perhaps looming larger in the public imagination were women who acted as men in the wartime drama either as spies or as soldiers. Here was an outright rejection of separate spheres ideology—and even of gender difference. The Northern press was full of the exploits of Southern women spies early in the war, particularly after the arrest and imprisonment of first the well-known Washington socialite Rose Greenhow and then the younger Southern lady Belle Boyd. The North had fewer public spies, and probably fewer undetected ones as well, but the ranks on each side were estimated to have hidden up to 300 women in uniform during the war.[18]

When known, such activities received severe censure. As Massey notes, "Women spies made excellent newspaper copy and even those from prominent families received no mercy from the press. If not referred to outright as prostitutes, they were accused of having clandestine relations with specific officials, of being a 'Cleopatra,' 'seductress,' 'courtesan,' or 'insane.'" Northern newspapers "were even more outspoken than those in the Confederacy," she asserts.[19] Not that they were entirely without defenders. When the Seventeenth Illinois made Mrs. Belle Reynolds a "major" after she got caught in the crossfire at Shiloh and performed meritorious nursing work, a sympathetic *New York Ledger* editorialist made clear that Reynolds was not attempting to "unsex or unsphere" herself. She is "not an amazon," the editor asserted, "but a true and tender wife and woman, and a ministering angel to the sick and wounded." In addition, the editorialist warned off any incipient bloomerites: "Lest the strong-minded sisterhood who affect male attire should imagine that the fair major wears regimentals and a sword, it is proper to state that she dresses like a *lady*, and while exhibiting the most glorious qualities of her *own* sex, does not claim the attributes of the other."[20]

The character of the struggle antislavery activist women fought changed dramatically from 1861 to 1865. From the beginning of the war the institution of slavery began to crumble; by 1865 it was in shambles. In the South, slave women worked to end slavery in any way they could. Their first priority was their children and their families, and this commitment dictated their choices and their efforts on behalf of the Union. When one woman overheard her mistress bewailing a Yankee victory, she remembered, "from that minute I started prayin' for freedom. All de res' of de women done the same."[21] Slave women also undercut the authority of mistresses left alone by slowing their work speed, by using sass to further discomfit and disempower them, and by taking the first opportunity to join Union camps nearby. One slave remembered leaving soon after she heard about the Emancipation Proclamation. "We done heared dat Lincum gonna turn de niggers free," she remembered, "Ole missus say dey warn't nothin' to it. Den a Yankee soldier tole someone in Williamsburg dat Marse Lincum done signed de mancipation. Was winter time an' moughty cold dat night, but ev'ybody commence gittin' ready to leave. Didn't care nothin' 'bout Missus—was goin' to Union lines."[22]

A few African American women are known to have worked directly on behalf of the war effort; one can assume there were many more. Once African American men were allowed to enlist in 1862, Sojourner Truth helped in recruitment drives despite her advanced age. Susie King Taylor, who traveled with her husband's regiment, worked as a laundress and occasional nurse when needed.[23] Harriet Tubman worked as a spy and scout during the war, guiding at one point the enormously successful Combahee River Expedition, which liberated over 700 slaves. She also worked as a nurse and aided destitute fugitives that were perpetually swelling Union army camps.[24]

Northern antislavery women's aid for these efforts took the form of participation in freedmen's aid societies and individual efforts to offer food, clothing, and medical supplies for fugitives. Among the first to send material to the contrabands was Lydia Maria Child, who in November 1861 sent a big box of clothes, books, and sewing supplies to Fort Monroe in Virginia.[25] She also worked in the Emancipation League, an organization established in September 1861 by Massachusetts abolitionists to affect public opinion. One of her efforts on this score was to persuade John Greenleaf Whittier to write a war song to inspire and educate the soldiers to their true moral aim in fighting.[26]

In late 1863 Elizabeth Cady Stanton and Susan B. Anthony joined forces to establish the Women's National Loyal League. As historian Wendy Hamand notes, "The league was an organization dedicated to a radical principle—the abolition of slavery—and was based on the idea of female participation in the political sphere."[27] In her manifesto "To the Women of the Republic," Elizabeth Cady Stanton made an appeal to women to join the league, invoking their patriotism and adherence to the ideology of separate spheres. Like many of her contemporaries, she recalled the heroism of the republican mothers of the Revolution.

That this was the most radical effort by Northern women on behalf of the slave was clearly understood by the press, most of which was silent or critical of the league's activities, which included gathering a huge petition protesting slavery to present to Congress.[28] Even without the issue of woman suffrage, these women were identified and maligned for their political viewpoints. Despite this resistance, however, the league collected over one hundred thousand signatures by early 1864. By a year after its formation the league had more than doubled that number.

Many women antislavery writers were doubtless aware of the league's activities. Most approached the issue of emancipation from a more conservative political position than did Anthony and Stanton; few were self-described women's rights activists. Still, they undertook similar efforts of moral suasion. Like petitions and speeches, the writing of antislavery women was politically motivated and constituted its own form of cultural activism. Antislavery women hoped through their words to direct the attention of the nation to the forces of moral righteousness that necessitated the violence, and by so doing to inspire further efforts to end both slavery and the war.

The writers who form the focus of this chapter were aware of the choices their sisters (and, in many cases, each other) were making. They wrote prominently in mainstream women's publications like *Peterson's Ladies Magazine* and *Arthur's Home Magazine*, as well as reform magazines with a national audience such as the *Atlantic Monthly*, the *Continental Monthly*, and the *Sibyl*.[29] They were frequent contributors to mainstream magazines with a wider constituency, including *Harper's New Monthly Magazine* and the *New York Ledger*. Their essays and short narrative pieces also appeared, although less frequently, in the pages of largely political newspapers such as the New York *Independent* and the Boston *Commonwealth*.

The nine writers at the center of this study were only a few among many and must be understood as working within a much larger literary community. Important women writers worked for many of the mainstream family and story papers, offering an ongoing commentary on women and the Civil War, among whom were Virginia Townsend, Ann S. Stephens, Louise Chandler Moulton, Ella Rodman, and Harriet E. Prescott. Still others offered glimpses of wartime work with narratives of their experiences. These included nurses, like Georgeanna Woolsey, and antislavery activists, like Charlotte Forten and Augusta French. Others, poet Julia Ward Howe and novelists Delphine Baker and Metta Victoria Victor among them, presented reworkings of ideas current in the contemporary press.

These writers spoke to the issue of what woman could do—both properly and improperly—to aid the war effort. They saw their efforts as important cultural and political work. Mary Dodge expressed to Henry James of her satisfaction in being called to this kind of work because of its public character. "I thank God that instead of giving me a wash-tub, or a needle, or a broom to work my work with," she wrote in 1864, "he has given me a pen, and a whole country for my family."[30] Her writings included "Courage!," a tract explicitly written to revive flagging Northern morale. Women's writing, from didactic and bracing, to sentimental and emotion-filled, was crucial war work, too.

From the first days of war, women writers predicted that the conflict would transform women's place in society and sought to convince their audiences as well. In a letter to Dr. Lydia Sayer Hasbrouck, editor of the *Sibyl*, published in that magazine in June 1861, a writer with the initials S. J. F. penned the hope that "the war will cause an upturning of things in general," ending with women being "recognized in the Constitution."[31] Fanny Fern was sure a change was coming. In January 1862 she wrote in a column that "there's one thing certain. This war won't leave women where it found them, whatever may be said of men."[32] Nine months later, Hasbrouck added, "We have one hope from this state of affairs for women— that circumstances will force her to develop her true native resources. Only thus can she profit from surrounding ills."[33]

Yet for all their hopes, Northern women writers were also aware of the difficulty and pain that war would impose, even as they wrote their most patriotic and hopeful missives. The war required great courage, women hastened to write, even from those left behind. Men—the focus of war energy—were not the only ones to sacrifice or suffer. In "Who Are the Brave?" published in October of 1861, Gertrude Karl wrote, "Oh yes! It is brave to go and die / And tis brave to stay and say good-bye."[34] In 1862 an essayist in the *Continental Monthly* recorded how homes were devastated. "In far-off humble households," the author wrote, "sleepless nights and anxious days are passed, of which the world never knows; and every wounded and crippled soldier who returns to family and friends, brings a lasting pang with him."[35]

By the end of the war this perception of the shattering effects of war on families had sharpened into an implicit critique.[36] As Caroline Cheseboro' candidly wrote in 1864, "When War takes hold of women, the touch is not tender."[37] If this touch was truer of the Unionist Southern heroines in many war stories, it was also described as reaching homes farther north.[38] In retelling the story of Jenny Wade, a heroine of Gettysburg who refused to leave her home on the battlefield (she was baking bread for the soldiers), Mary Eastman mocked the notion that women could be somehow separated or protected from war. "But not for woman, scenes of war!" Jenny Wade sarcastically replies to a Rebel soldier who is urging her to leave. "Then why bring scenes of war to her? / For show me, of our land, a part / Without a desolated heart."[39]

The war was thus a cultural as well as a military battleground. Women fought over the limits to their sphere, a sphere already within the war's reach. They pondered the meaning of their experiences. When women refused to wait passively and chose to adopt the new tasks of war—organizing aid societies, nursing, or even fighting—they faced opposition from those who feared, as Virginia Sherwood put it, any "mode of development" that might "unsex or unsphere" them. Against this tendency, women writers explored new models for women. On some level this was propaganda, but unlike the war stories of later wars, this literature was not funded by the government and represented no entirely consistent position. As the heroine of Metta Victor's 1862 dime novel, *The Unionist's Daughter*, told a Southern soldier, "Our standards of womanly excellence differ."[40]

Leave-Taking and Waiting: Early Stories of Patriotism

Let not the same supineness that so long cried peace, when there was no peace, now induce us to undervalue the present crisis. We are in for a long pull, and a strong pull, and need to take breath and begin with a will. . . . Our sons and brothers whom we are sending take their lives in their hands, and may never return; but this is a cause to die for.—Harriet Beecher Stowe, *Independent* (April 1861)

On April 25, 1861, the New York *Independent* published a piece by Harriet Beecher Stowe seemingly intended specifically for women. In it she emphasized the work that they needed to do by acknowledging the extent of the sacrifice to come. Her terms were purposefully collective: "We are in . . ."; "Our sons and brothers." A "long war" was ahead, in which many would lose lives and family, whatever cause they espoused. Stowe, like many of her peers, did not write to move men to go to war but to urge women to take on the work of war: to send their kin, and to begin to accept their loss. "We thank God," she wrote, for mothers that cheer on their sons, for young wives that have said "go" to their husbands, for widows who have given their *only* sons.[41] By creating (or reestablishing) the image of the stoic woman at home, Stowe and other writers took up their own work: inspiring women, and thus men, to fight.

This patriotic image—often referred to as the Spartan or the Roman mother—was a powerful icon in the wartime literature. This woman was stalwart and confident; she offered her men up to war with few if any tears, believing that national good was more important than personal preference. She greeted their deaths with the same stoicism, calling it glorious to die for one's country. The power of this particular patriotic appeal would wane appreciably over the next four years. Early wartime stories focused on the moments of greatest trial for the patriotic woman and offered examples of heroic behavior.

The decision to enlist and the moment of leaving was central in the stories written in the first two years of war. Although details differed, the outlines of the struggle were clear: men rarely left without acceptance and support, but it was their duty to leave, and woman's to stay home and wait. As one soldier-hero says to his reluctant fiancée in the *New York Ledger*: "Men must act, now, and women must suffer. It *must* be so, darling. Tell me if you are willing to show yourself a true little patriot, and bid me God speed?"[42] The fiancée in question is not patriotic but learns to become so after her lover has left and is wounded during the battle at Fort Donelson. The reader is allowed to feel superior to the selfish girl by recognizing what her true course of action should be before she does.

The key element of this scenario—the waiting—generated its own set of literary descriptions of frustration with the conventions of womanhood. Women counteracted the passivity of the notion of waiting in several ways. Some writers invested it with tremendous meaning: as literary critic Kathleen Diffley argues, waiting constituted a holding together of the family homestead and thus a maintenance of a crucial social order.[43] Other writers described the active tasks they took on at home that signified their connectedness with the battlefront. In "The Army of Knitters," an anonymous author stresses the threads that bound home and soldier together:

We rouse to the rescue! We've mustered in thousands!
    We may not march on in the face of the foe:
Yet, while ye shall tramp to the sound of the battle,
    Foot to foot we'll keep pace wheresoever you go!

Ay, soul on soul, are we knitted together!
    By link on link, in one purpose we're bound!
God mete us the meed of our common endeavor.
    And our differing deeds with one blessing be crowned![44]

Only later would others use the waiting to explain why they had to undertake new and more challenging tasks, and leave home. One 1863 heroine tells her father frankly, "I am tired of this life; of this slow, inactive, wearing life, with its leaden hours, and its great loss and grief eating into my soul. I want to do some work, to render some service for my country."[45] She goes to Washington and becomes a nurse.

If these early war stories of leave-taking and waiting are the most conservative of the war years—women rarely challenge the limits of the home, only seeking to enhance the work done within them—they are imbued with a sense of power. In a number of stories published in the *New York Ledger* in the early war years women reject one suitor for another whose politics are more patriotic—despite their wealth or class status.[46] They also challenge the sense that the war has more ramifications for men than for women: their stories are meant to illustrate and sympathize with their intended women readers. Fanny Fern's 1862 article "Soldiers' Wives" is clear on this point (but assumes all later historians will be men): "When the history of this war shall be written (and *that* cannot be *now*), let the historian, what else soever he may forget, forget not to chronicle this sublime valor of the hearthstone all over our struggling land."[47]

Some of these early stories of war, particularly those written before 1863, center on the image of woman as the more stronger patriot, the one who had to use all her power to urge men to do their duty. Ella Rodman's "A Daguerreotype in Battle" tells the familiar story of a woman with two lovers. One companion, wealthy, accomplished, and urbane, talks of "art" and little else. The other, a distant cousin, is honest and quiet and determines to go to war as a private. When asked for her hand by the first, the woman refuses, saying: "If I ever love, it will be to one who has shown himself willing to sacrifice everything for his country."[48] She ultimately marries the private, who is promoted for valor. In an anonymous poem, "A Loyal Woman's No," a similar scenario emerges of a man rejected because of his politics (among other things). The narrator of the poem tells her suitor she is not his "because you are not man enough / To grasp your country's measure of a man! / If such as you, when Freedom's ways are rough, / Cannot walk in them, learn that women can!"[49] In each case the model soldier is the private, the one who chooses a democratic meritocracy as a challenge, and who refuses to use class privilege to evade patriotic duty.

If Stowe, Rodman, and the anonymous poet were committed to the cause from the first, other authors described the sending of men to war as a more painful and less immediate decision. By admitting the pain of the patriotic woman, however, they make it no less heroic. In 1864 one writer wrote impatiently, "Talk of Spartan mothers and Roman matrons, it reads well, I admire them, but truth compels me to say that of all the mothers I have known who have given sons to this war, the utmost stretch of heroism has been to say, 'If it *must* be I will try to bear it.' "[50] Choosing a different strategy than the straightforward essay Stowe used in the New York *Independent*, fiction writers still described their heroines as steadfast only after their difficult decisions have been reached. Ultimately, it seems, these authors forgave women for their ambivalence if they recognized their duty and carried it out.

Despite the sentimental tone of most of these stories, they are remarkably realistic in depicting scenes that could very well have occurred in the middle-class households of their readers.[51] What these authors offer is the image of the "true woman," who, in being generous, loving, but most of all brave in the face of sorrow, can inspire men to be manly. This is nowhere more clear than in popular *Atlantic* writer Rose Terry Cooke's 1862 story "A Woman." When Cooke's heroine hears of the shooting at Baltimore as troops moved south, she anticipates her fiancé's wish to go to war, and comes to tell him that she will support him in his decision and marry him before he goes, if he wishes. Cooke's heroine loses the husband and goes to work in the Washington hospitals and is acknowledged by the doctor in her ward as a "true heroine" and by the narrator as a "true woman." Cooke's title, "A Woman," reinforces the notion that *all* women have within them the seeds of their own heroism; her story is intended to bring those seeds to flower.[52]

Louise Chandler Moulton, a well-known Boston short story writer, wrote several stories on this theme. Her sentimental tales are also clearly didactic in intent. In "Buying Winter Things," she describes a valiant young woman who admits to her admiring cousin that her bravery is "a hard struggle."[53] In another story, "Captain Charley," Moulton allows the reader to see a widow agonizing over whether to let her only son enlist. The widow's first thought is for herself, that she would have no one left if he were to die. Yet, she questions, "Had she any right to deprive the good cause of the blows that stout right arm could strike?" Although she ultimately decides to let him enlist and is initially soothed by her faith in everlasting life and her belief in the cause, the days of waiting take their toll, and then "all her faith in Heaven, all her belief that she had done right, could not ease her longing and her heartache."[54] (Her son, injured in battle and wanting to die, wills himself to live for his mother's sake.)

In an anonymous *Harper's* story, the difficulty of such decisions is even more vividly depicted. Annie, an older woman who after years of waiting for a cad is finally engaged to a cousin who truly loves her, is asked to give up her new fiancé to the war. Even as Annie takes courage from her fiancé's words—"This is no time for a man to be at home, no time for a woman to be a coward"—she feels how wrenching and lonely the war really is. Annie may even find this experience more significant for women than the cause that separates the North and the South: "Hard hard it was! Myriads of us all over this struggling, bleeding country know how hard; and know that even at this deadly crisis we could hold open arms to rebel women, and weep with them in the divine reconciliation of mutual sorrow."[55]

Wartime stories and poems suggested that waiting was even harder than enlisting, but it was an inevitable role for women and one they accepted even as they despised it. In "Buying Winter Things," a character named Nan learns to let go of her fiancé and throws herself into war work as her cousin Gertrude has. "My offering, like yours," Nan writes to Gertrude, "is on the altar. Come to me and teach me how to *wait*." The narrator intrudes at this point with a stark question: "How long will these women, and many more besides them, have in which to learn that long slow lesson? With what grand results, to them, to all, will the waiting be crowned at length? God knows."[56]

The juxtaposition of a woman's waiting and a man's action—"he was taken and I was left"—implied a clear sense of frustration and despair by the middle of the war. This was the aspect of patriotism that women writers most often challenged. Some female characters in these stories suggest that they, too, would go, if they only could. In Moulton's story "Kitten," the heroine tells her sweetheart, "It is hard, Ralph, to say I am willing to risk what is so much more to me than life; but if I were a man I should go, so I can not complain that you should go in my stead."[57] Another heroine, from the short story "My Thanksgiving," hears that her fiancé is missing and desperately wants to go look for him—although she concedes finally that it would not be proper. "Oh, how I wished then to be a man!" she cries.[58] In Harriet E. Prescott's *Atlantic* story, "Ray," the title character, a crippled but brave young man, asks his family friend Vivia if she wishes she were going to war. "Yes," she answers, "There is something in it, isn't there?" Ray responds, "You'll sit at home and your blood will boil! What keeps you women alive? Darning stockings, I suppose."[59]

The question of what the patriotic woman could actively do rather than passively suffer loomed large in the stories of war by 1863. Moulton's heroines, among others, express their yearning as a response to the pain of giving their sweethearts and kin up to war. "When I had given him up I longed to do something myself," Gertrude tells her cousin in "Buying Winter Things."[60] She turns to benevolent work and buys clothes and food for the poor and families of soldiers instead of new clothes for herself. Other Moulton heroines turn to nursing when their sweethearts or husbands die or are reported missing. In "Captain Charley," a widow learns of her son's wounds and travels alone to Washington to take care of him. Moulton adds an ironic twist when she suggests that "it is strange how much strength is in the weakest and most loving type of woman in the hours which try men's souls."[61]

Other authors suggested similar or related tasks for women during the war. In "Tableaux Vivants," Katherine Williams's narrator describes her soldier's aid sewing group and suggests that if men worked as hard and as cohesively as women did the war would already be over: "We look back on our record with the proud consciousness that if Secretaries in the Cabinet and Generals in the field had wrought toward their object with the same harmony and enthusiasm that we gave to ours, the 'ninety days' would be very nearly over."[62] Williams was not alone in suggesting that the men did not work as well as some women. Belle Z. Spencer, who worked intermittently in the hospitals of the western theater, wrote in 1864 a "true story" of a young woman who lost father, brother, and husband to the war but kept on working in area hospitals until her own health broke down. On a boat en route to Washington, D.C., Spencer confronts an officer who in referring to this woman had rudely commented on "the habit women had of following the army." "I would to heaven, Sir," Spencer responds, "that every man under the Government may have worked half as earnestly and effectively as she has! I trust you will do so."[63] By defending the young woman, of course, Spencer is also defending herself—from the officer and perhaps from a skeptical reader.

Many women wrote to inspire their audience to specific tasks. In "One Day," Alice B. Haven wrote of her character Nell Reed's struggle to encourage a friend to work on behalf of the wounded at a hospital nearby. Reed is not exactly a nurse but ministers to the soldiers' other wants, cooking delicacies for them, writing letters to kin, and bringing them fresh flowers. In the story Reed is criticized for neglecting her family—which she hotly denies—and for drawing undue attention to herself, and yet she perseveres with the support of her husband, who is too sickly to go to war himself. Her friend, Mrs. Chandler, learns the "lesson of the day" and is moved by what she sees: "She knew it was but a tithe of the crimson harvest of war . . . Not only in the portion to which we are learning to limit our devotion, but in that where the wind of this whirlwind was sown, strong men were bearing the anguish of pain and death, and women the *heavier burden* of suspense and breaking hearts; and she went out of the sunshine of her own undimmed life into the shadow of theirs, and so fulfilled the law of Divine sympathy and love."[64] The reader, of course, is another Mrs. Chandler, and Haven adroitly answers her imagined objections within her text.[65]

These and other early war stories established the boundaries of women's appropriate patriotic behavior while stressing the power of their influence. Women—unified by this common experience—had to let their husbands, sons, and lovers go, but these moments of crisis demonstrated their underlying strength and their connection to the nation.[66] Their position, confined to the home and to waiting, often had an edge of bitterness. What these stories shared was a clear sense of women's role at the center of both the war's meaning and the war's sacrifice. As the war progressed, however, that center would shift.

A Woman-Centered Understanding of War: Delphine P. Baker and Metta V. Victor

In 1862 two novels were published using the war as their central concern and women as their primary actors; they were the first two such novels in a coming flood.[67] They were significant in the ways they differed from the rather more conservative stories of waiting that largely defined the first years of war. With Louisa May Alcott's 1863 *Hospital Sketches*, discussed below, they illustrate a move away from giving power only through conventional understandings of women's role, while using the patriotic push of early war to create a wider scope for their political work.

The audiences for these novels differed widely, demonstrating the breadth of concern for the woman question during wartime. Delphine Paris Baker's allegorical novel (or novella) *Solon, of the Rebellion of '61* was published by a small Chicago press; she signed it only "Delphine" and wrote in a sentimental style for what one imagines was a limited middle-class (and abolitionist) audience.[68] By contrast, Metta Victoria Victor's novel, *The Unionist's Daughter: A Tale of the Rebellion in Tennessee*, published in Erastus Beadle's enormously successful dime novel series, was sensationalist in style and meant explicitly for as wide an audience as possible.

Also dissimilar were the backgrounds of Baker and Victor. Delphine Paris Baker, about whom little is known, was a lecturer on the sphere of woman and women's education in the western states before the war. Although Baker grew up in New England, her home was in Chicago as the war began. With the first casualties Baker turned her attention to the plight of disabled soldiers, starting a monthly paper, the "National Banner," to support her efforts. By 1866, after false starts and delays, she was able to engineer the passage of a bill to support the establishment of an asylum for the disabled at Point Lookout, Maryland. Not surprisingly, despite her persistence and work, she was not invited to become a trustee nor given any official post at the asylum she helped found.[69]

Metta Victoria Fuller (Victor) grew up in Ohio and moved east as an adult. Unlike Baker, at no time did she draw specific attention to her views on the status of women in society outside of her novels, yet her life was lived in the public eye. In 1844, at age thirteen, Fuller published her first story, thus commencing a life of enormous literary productivity. By the 1850s she was writing reformist novels, beginning with the popular *The Senator's Son; or, The Maine Law: A Last Refuge*. In 1856 she married Orvile James Victor, an editor, and between 1857 and 1872 she bore nine children. At the same time she assisted her husband in editing the *Cosmopolitan Art Journal*, in 1860 taking over both that and the *Home*, a monthly magazine. Although the *Home* folded after only a year and a half, Victor's career was assured by her connection with its publishers, Beadle and Adams. One of Victor's most famous dime novels was the mock slave narrative of Christmas week on a Southern plantation, *Maum Guinea, and Her Plantation "Children,"* published in 1861. Victor went on to write after the war, but the tone of her writing changed as the national appetite did, shifting from reformist in the 1850s to satirical in the late 1860s and 1870s.[70]

What connects Baker's and Victor's work is their insistence on women's central relevance to the greater war story: Baker, in giving women agency in defining the war's meaning, Victor, in describing women experiencing war's deprivations and acting on its challenges. Both also offer relatively unfettered and decisive heroines, even though both also end with woman and her sphere of home reestablished. These novels represent the change in the central female character in the war fiction that developed in the following years from the strong but waiting woman to the active and challenging woman. This was an important portent both for women's war literature and for women's literature in general.

Baker's preface to *Solon* opens with a statement of intent, a common practice in didactic novels of the mid-nineteenth century.[71] Her rather trenchant political statements can thus be hidden behind a veil of acceptable language of piety and modesty. "Should sentiments breathed in the following pages," she wrote, change the hearts of the readers, "grateful to God will be the writer, for the satisfaction that a little good may arise from a humble effort."[72] The story, of a marriage between Solon, the South, and Nora, the North, begins with their threatened divorce. Solon arrogantly expects to hear concessions from Nora, but he will not. The author intervenes in the dialogue to place Solon with other men, who expect angels after they have created demons with their poor treatment of women. "When wilt thou learn, O man!" Baker asks, that "when thou dost seek to tyrannize over her [woman], she will eventually appear in the spirit of a demon, taunting thee with the corroding bitterness of those deep and incurable wounds which thou hast so thoughtlessly inflicted on her heart."[73] It is men, then, who are primarily at fault for the dissolution of the union.

Yet Baker does not excuse woman. Her fault lies with her timidity in attacking the root of the evil in her household. Divorce, or civil war, is "a domestic and political tragedy," brought on by woman's reluctance to involve herself in politics as well as man's destruction of domestic peace. Nora very frankly tells Solon that their marriage has been overshadowed from the first by the "phantom of selfish fear," or slavery. His faults, she continues, "have ever been heinous to my sight, yet the love I bear toward our children [the states] caused my tongue to cleave to the roof of my mouth whenever I sought to reprove thee for thy daring and traitorous acts, and in this respect am I greatly in error." Her father [Lincoln] did not threaten to "meddle with your idols" unless violence was offered to him. In this eventuality, however, he would not back down—nor would she—and "if war must come, let it come!"[74]

To have protected themselves against disunion, women and the nation should have been "strong-minded" long before, Baker argues. Solon represents the recalcitrant husband who demands silence and submission as his due. "There is very little indeed of the gentleness of woman in thy nature," Solon tells Nora reprovingly. "The true woman's heart will submit to any discipline, or 'despotism,' as you term it, rather than lose the confidence and affections of her liege lord," Nora gently interrupts, and equates slavery with alcoholism, both having a destructive effect on the home. Her job is not to stand aside and allow drunkenness but to boldly protect through a "purifying home influence." "Yet when the tempter came," Nora tells Solon, "she who should have grown strong in courage, and thrust the tempter from the household, stood trembling, fearing to resist the entrance of the evil one, lest her husband should deem her 'meddlesome,' or too 'strong-minded.' Seest thou reality in the picture which I have presented?"[75] Solon does not, finally raging, "Silence, mad woman!" and leaving to prepare for war.

What follows is a metaphorical description of the first year of battle, with an emphasis on an upbeat reading of even ghastly defeats. The reader can detect the then current political debates and fears. When Nora is discouraged her father (Lincoln) urges her on, claiming that moral rectitude will win despite difficulty. The dissolution of slavery—which Lincoln has yet to accept as a war aim—is confidently offered by Baker nonetheless. Even the disloyal are mentioned as an inevitability as long as slavery is tolerated. Women are lauded as well, not as strong-minded meddlers, but as gentle helpmates. "Woman, too, the 'weaker vessel,' is taking her part in the struggle," Baker adds in a long passage. "Ever faithful in her good works; self-sacrificing noble woman is denying herself of comforts to add to those of the soldier." "In this great struggle between freedom and despotism," she concludes, "the influence of woman must be as deeply felt as in any former period of the world. She may touch the springs of the nation's power, and call in the most decisive events."[76] Here is the little lady, again, who made a big war.

It is woman and woman's vision, ultimately, that wins. Baker predicts the end of the war will come with the end of slavery, and predicts also a chastened Solon, come once again to beg Nora's hand in marriage. "This generation will never appreciate thy purity and magnanimity of soul, my dear Nora," he says supplicatingly, "but ages to come will bless thy name and laud the efforts which have given back the Union unbroken." Nora blames the "fire eaters" for Solon's defection and accepts him again. Baker intervenes with the story concluded—wife and husband peacefully reunited in a happy home—"hoping that no domestic storm may ever again darken their horizon, or o'ercloud their happiness."[77] It is a comforting fantasy.

The modern reader may be shocked by Baker's sanguine predictions about the war's impending end, knowing with hindsight the years of carnage still ahead. The disjunction between the politically assertive Nora and references to gentle and influential "women" also seems startling. Yet the middle story revealed here is one of the connection between the domestic and political spheres, and the message is clearly one directed at women. To be strong-minded and meddlesome over issues as morally acute as slavery and disunion is not only desirable but necessary in avoiding war and maintaining domestic peace. Women must speak their politics or they will lose their homes.

Metta Victoria Victor's preface also claims a moral rationale for the story that will follow. This story, "literally . . . 'founded upon fact,'" is buttressed by an appendix with newspaper clippings as evidence.[78] Victor offers the story of Tennessee Unionists hounded from their homes, "and if," she says, "in the reading of our story the reader obtains an insight into the shocking social, as well as political disasters which followed in the train of treason in Tennessee we shall have accomplished the leading *purpose* of our labors."[79] Here again the domestic—or "social"—and the political merge, for Victor implies that women are at the heart of the war's experiences and its destruction.

Victor's story centers on Eleanor Beaufort, a beautiful young girl who has previously led a sheltered and easy life. Politics reaches into her home and disorders it forever, causing the loss of Beaufort's innocence, love, and comfort. She is introduced in virginal white and described as having an "ethereal loveliness"; when the chapter ends with "the carelessness of her almost childish girlhood away forever," the point can hardly be more clearly put. Beaufort is challenged on political issues that go to the heart of her future plans. Engaged to the dashing and wealthy Sinclair Le Vert, she must chose him or her Unionist politics. When her choice is clear, Le Vert, like Solon, is flabbergasted at her lack of submissiveness. "Surely, Ella," he exclaims, "you would not hesitate between your lover and a political quibble?"[80]

Ella Beaufort's journey to adulthood leads her through many transformations. The story is set in the South and contains sympathetic but crudely stereotyped slave characters, along with a political rather than a moral call for slavery's end. The issue for Beaufort—and, it seems, for Victor—is always one of civil liberties rather than antislavery. At one point, aghast at the screaming mob outside her house, Beaufort asks her then fiancé, "Why do they call my father an abolitionist? They know, and you know, Sinclair, that there is no truth in the assertion."[81] Even in the end, when her faithful slave Pompey has followed Beaufort north to Cincinnati (as his master, Beaufort's dead father, had allowed), she makes no explicit reference to giving him his freedom, even as it is assumed. His family, of course, does not figure in his plans so much as his loyalty to his mistress.[82]

Far more central to Beaufort's development are both her dawning sense of her own confidence and abilities and her newly found "republicanism" as she rejects the company of the wealthy Le Vert for Beverly Bell, the poor son of a minister who eventually becomes her husband. Beaufort's father is taken away and imprisoned by the Confederates. As he is taken, he tells Eleanor that although he is sorry to leave her alone, "I know you are equal to the emergency." She proves to be so, handling the plantation as if she has been trained for it, and rejecting her to-be sister-in-law's languid response to life. She begins to realize "that the hardest of all work [is] to do noth-ing, mentally and physically."[83]

The true test of Eleanor Beaufort comes with the storming of her house by angry townspeople. Here she learns of her own courage and comes to learn of Tennesseans with whom she has previously never inter-acted: the middle and lower classes. Beaufort prepares for the coming of the mob and is "as cool and as prompt as if she [were] a business man, giving orders for the day." Her slaves, including the stalwart Pompey, who spirits her away when the house is overrun, support her. She is taken to the hideaway of "Turkey Dan," a poor white farmer who has acted as a Con-federate spy to free her father from jail. At this mountain hideout Beaufort meets not only Beverly Bell but others like him, some of the Unionist "party of middle classes, mountaineers and small farmers, with many of the more intelligent planters" who have been forced to flee.[84]

Victor's novel is significant for its effort to be inclusive of all the classes of Tennesseans—even those she herself designates as poor white trash (Turkey Dan). If Beaufort is at the outset from a protected and carefree class, she quickly learns that it is politics rather than class that distin-guishes good from evil. It is the wise Turkey Dan who recognizes Beau-fort's lack of class arrogance as he comforts Bell, who is initially rejected by Beaufort. "Now, Bell," he chides, "you know that little lady is an out-and-out republican, every inch of her. If she don't take up with you, they'll be some other reason."[85] The reason for Beaufort's reluctance, at this point, is her own desire to act in the war: love must come after patriotism.

Stuck in the mountains with a band of fugitive Unionists, Beaufort continues her journey of self-discovery. Here is the central story of Vic-tor's novel. While Beaufort is not as adept as Turkey Dan's wife—who can, he proudly lists, "shoot a b'ar, skin a deer, clean a rifle, kill a pig, or jerk off a snake's head, nigh about as handy as I can myself"—she does escape from guerrillas through the woods, ride as a courier for Beverly Bell, face down and then successfully flee from the band of Confederates she encounters after shooting one of them, and then face prison after she is caught on her way home with no flinching until surreptitiously freed by Sinclair Le Vert. This all while inspiring Bell's religious faith with her own.

What Beaufort has in this middle story is an acknowledged role in the fight, even if, by the end, she returns to love and family. When Beverly first asks her to marry him she says as much, asking him instead for a job. "Oh, Captain Bell," she queries, turning aside his proposal, "if you want to break this stupor, to thaw this ice, give me work to do. What are your secret commissions? Can not you trust some of them to a woman's wit?" After her work as a courier Eleanor decides to become a hospital nurse, and thus begins her slide back to respectability. "The doctors, however much disposed to discredit women-nurses," do not reject the competent Beaufort but come "to rely on her for the careful fulfillment of their most important instructions."[86] When Bell comes to the hospital with a shattered arm, which must be amputated, *she* proposes to *him*. They move ultimately to a cabin in Cincinnati, where she works as a music teacher.

Victor's message to her reader is clear. Women are affected deeply by the war's social and political impact, and their response is to act: as plantation bosses, as intrepid couriers, as careful nurses. In the interest of national unity women also can be "out-and-out republicans" and despite privation will choose correct politics over ease and luxury. Yet Victor's final message, if it does not discount the more adventuresome one before, muffles its impact for the general reader. The more soothing vision comes last, suggesting that women will retreat to domesticity when the turmoil is over, and, like Eleanor Beaufort, they will "put far from [them] the thought of [a lost] home, of the beloved dead, of the uncertain future, setting [their] wom[e]n's heart[s] to the work [they] had chosen, of blessing the life of another."[87] Moral purpose and domestic ease thus sandwich the adventure, risk, and active courage of women.

The Voice of Tribulation Periwinkle: Introducing Women-Nurses

This domestic vision, following an active middle story of courage and ability, contrasts with the story of nurse Tribulation Periwinkle, Louisa May Alcott's humorous "women's rights woman" of thirty, who seeks no husband or romance. That both could capture the fancy of the reading public is significant. In the contested terrain that was the woman question there were varied standards of womanly excellence, even among the more daring heroines. All of these were offered as unifying visions, even as they contradicted each other's purposes. Louisa May Alcott, one of the nineteenth century's most beloved authors, offered up one of the most creative and unusual heroines of the war, and found her voice in her own letters home to her family, written when she herself was a nurse at one of the ghastliest hospitals in Washington, D.C. Her tone, deliberately playful, sought to ease anxiety on the home front about the effect of hospital work on young women, even while offering it as an acceptable alternative to home and family.

Alcott's *Hospital Sketches* was one of the first nursing narratives of the Civil

War. As one that successfully used and at the same time mocked sentimental ways of describing nursing, it garnered considerable attention. Alcott herself was startled. "Much to my surprise," she wrote in her journal,
"[the sketches] made a great hit, & people bought the papers faster than
they could be supplied." *Hospital Sketches* soon came out in book form—two
publishers wanted it—and promptly went through several editions.[88]

In important and consistent ways Louisa May Alcott, through Tribulation Periwinkle, claims and supports conventional notions of "home"
and woman's place within it, echoing other early war writing.[89] The family
life reflected at the novel's beginning is a warm and comforting one, supportive of Tribulation's desire but loving and mournful at her departure.
When Periwinkle first alights at "Hurly-Burly Hotel," she feels a sudden
rush of unease, thinking that she is "very far from home." When the first
wounded come she "indulge[s] in a most unpatriotic wish that I was safe
at home again," but she constructs her transgression as duty: after having
"enlisted" in the war as a nurse she must stand her ground.[90]

Tribulation Periwinkle sets out to make the Hurly-Burly Hotel a comforting home for the wounded, and in her depiction is a justification for
women's place in wartime hospitals. Although fearful at first, Periwinkle
soon adapts a maternal demeanor. Known as the "nurse with the bottle,"
she spreads lavender water freely and sets about washing the wounded of
Fredericksburg as they are brought in, "like any tidy parent on a Saturday
night." Moving from bed to bed with dinner, she indulges the soldiers'
need to retell the battle and their place in it between bites as she feeds
them. Dinner over, she sits beside them as they dictate letters to kin. Their
welcome for her, after only "a little while," gives Periwinkle great satisfaction, "a womanly pride in their regard, a motherly affection for them all."[91]

And yet Alcott, through Periwinkle, managed also to demonstrate the
transgressive nature of her work as a nurse, and her own criticisms of the
social boundaries of womanhood. Her novel begins with a bald statement—"I want something to do"—and there are only a few options open
to her as a woman: author, teacher, wife, actress, nurse. Only the last offers
a combination of adventure and involvement in social issues, and when
Periwinkle looks into "the sisterhood which [she] wished to join," there is
a "Miss General" to whom she speaks in order to become a nurse. In this
sisterhood, the women do not need to be married, she implies in her aside:
"We hear no end of Mrs. Generals, why not a Miss?" When Periwinkle is
accepted as a nurse she announces to her family: "I've enlisted!" and she
describes her mother bidding her goodbye much in the way she might a
soldier son.[92]

Periwinkle's (and Alcott's) work at Hurly-Burly Hotel clearly breaks down any literal definition of separate spheres. There she washes and tends men in various states of undress, acting with strangers as their next of kin as they die. Periwinkle describes herself as shocked when first asked to clean the soldiers coming from Fredericksburg: "If she had requested me to shave them all, or dance a hornpipe on the stove funnel, I should not have been less staggered, but to scrub some dozen lords of creation at a moment's notice, was really—really—." Screwing up her courage, Periwinkle "drown[s] [her] scruples in [her] washbowl" and "clutche[s] [her] soap manfully." Her first patient, a bashful older Irishman, helps her through her initial shyness.[93]

Alcott frankly discusses the liabilities of the life of a nurse, however humorously Periwinkle handles them. Thankfully, Periwinkle adds in her postscript, no disrespect is accorded her in the Hurly-Burly Hotel, although her experience is an exception. "I had been prepared by the accounts of others," she writes, in response to the voiced criticism of her "sisterhood," "to expect much humiliation of spirit from the surgeons, and to be treated by them like a doormat, a worm, or any other meek and lowly article." Instead she meets courtesy and as a result quickly discards the "carefully prepared meekness" she had expected to have to muster.[94]

Louisa May Alcott's stint at the Armory Hospital ended abruptly when she contracted typhoid fever and almost died. Consistent with the practice at the time, Alcott was given calomel, or mercury, which eventually killed her after years of dizziness and nausea.[95] As she wrote in her sketches, the experience changed her life. "I shall never regret the going," she wrote, "though a sharp tussle with typhoid, ten dollars, and a wig, are all the visible results of the experiment; for one may live and learn much in a month. . . . Let no one who sincerely desires to help the work on in this way, delay going through any fear; for the worth of life lies in the experiences that fill it, and this is one which cannot be forgotten."[96] By emphasizing helping "the work" along, Alcott could ease the nation's conscience and muffle her transgressiveness through the use of a powerful rhetoric of patriotism.

Hospital Sketches was very well received. As she wrote to her publisher, the abolitionist James Redpath, she particularly loved seeing "my townsfolk buying, reading, laughing and crying over it wherever I go." Even the august Henry James Sr. approved of the stalwart Periwinkle, writing to Alcott, "It would be tedious to you to hear how much pleasure an old man like me has taken in your charming pictures and how refreshing he found the personal revelation there incidentally made of so much that is dearest and most worshipful in a woman."[97] Other readers more clearly saw the transgressions in her work and her style, one going so far as to suggest that there was undue levity in *Hospital Sketches*.[98] If the *Sketches* never made Alcott much money, she later observed, "it showed me my style."[99]

Political Work through Moral Suasion: Abolitionists Speak Out

How long must this people [enslaved African Americans] wait . . . with this great arrear of crime and injustice unrighted? The time has come when the nation has A RIGHT to demand, and the President of the United States a right to decree, their freedom; and there should go up petitions from all the land that he do it.
—Harriet Beecher Stowe, "Simon the Cyrenian," *Independent* (July 1862)

In the increasingly bitter debate over slavery from the 1830s, antislavery women writers like Lydia Maria Child and Harriet Beecher Stowe consistently constructed their work as a moral undertaking; their style during the early war years was in passionate, didactic prose, mixing rationalist arguments with religious warnings.[100] These writers used the patriotic first years of war as a lever for reform; rather than celebrate glory and honor, they drew attention to the costs as a way of emphasizing the wrong direction the nation had taken in claiming union and not the end of slavery as its goal.

Regardless of the electoral politics of slavery, they argued, attacking it was essential in setting the national house to rights, in defending the purity of women, and in upholding the sanctity of the family. According to this view, women were uniquely capable of such work because of the moral authority they derived naturally as women generally and as mothers specifically. As Baker had insisted in *Solon*, antislavery was not merely an issue in which women had an understandable interest, but one they had an outright duty to support. To fail to act was to be complicit in allowing it to continue.

Antislavery women used this moral justification and the context of wartime to extend their intellectual and political arena. As in the 1850s, where greater numbers of women joined ranks with reformers, the war expanded the discussion of slavery. The war, women reformers argued, could only be justified if fought for a moral purpose. Until that moral purpose was proclaimed there could be no victory. In a letter to the New York *Independent* shortly after Bull Run, Harriet Beecher Stowe claimed that without righteousness of purpose, Northern men would not win—nor would God sanction—Union victory. "Has there been," she asked her readers, "no secret cleaving to the accursed thing which is the cause and sum and soul of the whole war?"[101] Divisions in the North were due, then, to its inattention to the real goals of God's war.

Stowe was not alone in ascribing the war's purpose to God's vengeance for the failure to end slavery. "I recognize the hand of God in the tempest. All we can do is fulfill whatever seems to be our duty, and try to trust in *Him*," Lydia Maria Child wrote to a friend in August of 1861. "Sometimes my patience fails, at other times, faith and hope are re-assured."[102] The *National Anti-Slavery Standard* published a speech by Mary Grew on the same topic that same month. "It is not, and never was," she said, "in this nation's heart to do this thing [fight over slavery]. They may not mean it; but God does, and he, not General Scott, is leading our armies."[103] In "Lights among the Shadows of Our Civil War," from her book of essays *Country Living and Country Thinking*, Gail Hamilton offered a similar message. "We did not enter upon this war for the purpose of abolishing slavery, but every day strengthens the probability that that will be the issue," she remarked presciently. "It is not the end which the government has in view, but it may be the end which God has in view."[104] As the death toll rose, and the end seemed nowhere near, this argument may have seemed more persuasive than ever.

A moral rhetoric of unity thus became a vehicle for antislavery women writers to discuss politics—specifically legislative reform, military strategy, and social norms—throughout the war. Their political writing was closely tied to the historical moment, and it shifted as the direction of war policy did. In these first years of war the object of Stowe and Child in particular was to redirect the nation toward moral and thus justifiable goals. In the explicitness of the language and the pointed political commentary, these antislavery writings represent a departure from the more implicitly political patriotic stories discussed earlier.

By the firing at Sumter, the group of writers introduced earlier had scattered with changing patterns of life. Mrs. E. D. E. N. Southworth, fresh from her enormous success with *The Hidden Hand*, in 1859 took both her children to England until 1862. Although her sentiments on the war were complicated by her Southern birth and did not appear in her novels until 1865, they became clear to her sometimes outraged neighbors on her return. Southworth nailed a flag to the front door of her cottage on the Potomac, insisting that all who would visit her step below it to enter; she also nursed soldiers in her home and reportedly housed President Lincoln on occasion as he traveled to the battlefront.[105] Fanny Fern continued to write for the *New York Ledger*, expressing unalloyed patriotism and vigor in her columns. (This work will be discussed in Chapter 4.) Frances Ellen Watkins married Fenton Harper in 1860 and retreated from public life. She and her husband worked on a farm together near Columbus, Ohio. In 1864, with his death, Harper and her daughter moved east. For the rest of the war Harper worked on behalf of fugitives and freedpeople now streaming north.[106]

Harriet Beecher Stowe and Lydia Maria Child were personally as well as intellectually involved with the war from the first. Stowe's son Fred enlisted with the first wave of volunteers, along with many of Calvin Stowe's pupils at Phillips Andover, where the family now resided. In articles for the *Independent* Stowe described the tremendous effect that the war had on the campus and the patriotic flag-raising ceremonies she attended.[107] Her home was thus surrounded and invaded by war fervor, and she entered the fray heartily in the first years of war in an effort to translate her vision of the war's transformative meaning to the national public. Lydia Maria Child was childless, but the children of neighbors and friends were dressing and leaving for war, a sight that moved her to tears. She went to a meeting after hugging one such soldier goodbye with "moistened eyes," she told a friend in a letter, thinking, "If I could only be *sure* that if he dies, he will die for *freedom!*"[108] One of Child's closest friends, Sarah Shaw, wrote to her about her son, Robert Gould Shaw, throughout the war, mixing personal grief about his eventual death with political commentary on the war's purposes.

That Harriet Beecher Stowe and Lydia Maria Child agreed generally on the meaning of the national context in the early years of war is clear from Child's letters. She and Stowe met at a party in July of 1861. Both were rare party-goers, and they used this occasion to retreat to a corner, where, "with few interruptions," they "succeeded in ignoring the party." They "dived at once into public affairs," Child recalled, "and I found faith and hope stronger than anxiety in her mind." Although Child described herself as hopeful as well, her anxiety seemed equally strong at this time; what distinguished Stowe and Child, it seemed, was the way in which they described the war. Stowe understood the conflict in biblical terms: the South, or the Pharaohs, she predicted, would be "swamped and Israel was to go free." Although Child clearly wished to share Stowe's faith, and did to some extent, she felt herself to be less willing to offer Christian forbearance. "I am surprised to find how indifferent I am to the drowning of Pharaoh's hosts, provided the Israelites get on dry, firm ground," she confessed.[109]

Not surprisingly, perhaps, Lydia Maria Child in the *National Anti-Slavery*

Standard and Harriet Beecher Stowe in the New York *Independent* were two of the most prolific and consistent antislavery writers in the early years of war. Both used letters to the editor as their primary method of persuasion, and both, though counseling idealistic action, were well informed and incisive governmental critics. The harder edge to their writings demonstrated the strength of their conviction that a war for any purpose other than social justice would not be worth fighting. In this form and conviction they were not alone. Editors Lydia Sayer Hasbrouck and Jane Grey Swisshelm and fiction writers like Louisa May Alcott, among others, also sought to sway public opinion through directed and clearly political published letters and editorials.[110]

Lydia Maria Child had steeled herself for war by February 1861. In a letter to a friend she described war as the only alternative to compromise, which would constitute a moral failing. "If the Republicans do *not* yield up all they have gained, I suppose the alternative is civil war," she wrote. If it is a "horrid" alternative, she continued,

> here lies the alarming fact; we must *always* keep on compromising our principles, or else civil war will be threatened; and if we go on in the shameful path we have so long traveled, our free institutions must be everywhere and entirely crushed. Freedom must come up manfully to the struggle, or die by a slow but certain poison. Therefore, much as I deprecate civil war, I deliberately say even *that* is better than compromises of principle, at this momentous crisis. Such epochs come in the history of individuals and of nations, when we are solemnly called upon to decide whether we will serve God or the Devil; and if we choose the latter, ruin is inevitable.[111]

Yet when the war began Child was disappointed; townspeople in Wayland, Massachusetts, where she was living at the time, were all adamant in believing that the war was not being fought over slavery. She noted this in replying to a friend who had claimed that there "was not a booby to be found so stupid as not to know that this war is on account of slavery."[112]

There were no "boobys" to be found in Lydia Sayer Hasbrouck's reform newspaper, the *Sibyl*. Governmental leaders were leading the nation poorly, she argued, and women, if only allowed, could right the moral wrong through politics. "But slavery!" Hasbrouck wrote in May 1861, "thou hast done this fearful thing, and until freed from thy accursed presence this strife will not be truly ended."[113] The following January, Hasbrouck added in another editorial that if given the vote, women would abolish slavery forthwith: "Then, in the present war struggle, we, with thousands of women, would vote the Abolition ticket, while our husbands cruised in the slough of Republicanism. While our husbands hugged to their breasts the 'peculiar institution,' we women would spurn it from the land."[114] In August 1862, Hasbrouck predicted disaster if the president did not end slavery soon. "Slavery or the nation must die," she wrote; "we think it full time that the fact was drummed into the brains of our President. If he does not act on it soon, God only knows what greater humiliations are in store for us as individuals and as a nation."[115]

Other women writers made their political aims equally explicit. Writing in the *Independent*, Harriet Beecher Stowe took aim at England, wondering how a nation that led the international antislavery movement could fail to support the North against the slaveholding South. In a published "Letter to Lord Shaftesbury," an English agitator for antislavery during the 1850s, Stowe defined "what we, the Christian men and women of America, understand by this war." The conflict, she claimed, was the result of English and American agitation against slavery. "We consider that this war is a great Anti-Slavery War, not in form, but in fact; not in proclamation, but in the intense conviction and purpose of each of the contending parties, and still more in the inevitable overruling indications of divine Providence."[116] Child celebrated Stowe's piece in a letter to a friend. "Didn't you like Mrs. Stowe's letter to Lord Shaftesbury?" she asked. "I did, *amazingly*. I thank God for Mrs. Stowe."[117]

Stowe and Child were particularly concerned with government policy toward the fugitive slaves who were flocking to Union camps. Their writing explicitly upheld actions by the political and military leaders they approved, and cast aspersions on those who had disappointed them. In "The Man and the Hour," published in September 1861, Stowe celebrated General John C. Fremont's emancipation of Confederate slaves in occupied Missouri. "Rather than call the slave 'contraband,' which was 'advantageous and ingenious in its day,'" Fremont "makes the just distinction: the *property* of traitors he declares confiscated; their *slaves*, if they have any— free," Stowe wrote.[118] She waxed poetic in commenting on this turn of events. "Earth shall not look on a sublimer sight than that of the Army of the South and West," she predicted, "with freedom to the slave on its banner, as it shall roll majestically down the Mississippi, with the prayers of the oppressed rising like many waters for its success, and the songs of the redeemed ones waving like birds as it passes."[119] Fearing the political ramifications of Fremont's actions in border states, Lincoln remanded the order, however, and other generals persisted in returning slaves to their masters, earning Child's severe displeasure. In January 1862 she angrily wrote to a congressman: "Never had men such a glorious opportunity to redeem a country and immortalize themselves! Never did men show themselves so miserably deficient in all the qualities, which the crisis demanded! When I see the great swelling tide of popular enthusiasm ooze away through the slimy mud of shallow diplomacy, it seems as if my heart would break."[120] In exercising one of the only political privileges she could claim—writing to congressmen—Child sought to influence public opinion by congratulating those who acted in ways she approved.

Lydia Maria Child was not shy about publicly criticizing Lincoln's leadership, and she refused to apologize for acting in a political arena as a woman. In a letter to the president in September 1862, published in the *National Anti-Slavery Standard*, she confronted his failure to draw on the nation's "moral enthusiasm," which was "the mightiest of all forces."[121] This was a matter for women to bring to his attention, she argued. If "it may seem a violation of propriety" for her to write to the "Chief Magistrate," Child wrote, "an American woman of the nineteenth century need not apologize for pleading with the rulers of her country in behalf of the poor, the wronged, the cruelly oppressed."[122] In political issues of moral import women need not be diffident in expressing their outrage, Child insisted, even as she used the language of deference by referring to her trenchant critique as "pleading."

In related political works, short depictions or narrative sketches of slaves were used by early war writers to sway public opinion by playing to people's stereotypical assumptions about slaves' loyalty and childlike trust. Two of these slave depictions stand out for their use of moral goodness to hint at the necessity of political action. In each it is a woman who understands this necessity: in Lydia Maria Child's "How a Kentucky Girl Emancipated Her Slaves," a woman accepts poverty instead of slave ownership; in S. C. Blackwell's "Fugitives at the West," a woman assists fugitives.

These themes are perhaps clearest in Lydia Maria Child's description of Mattie Griffiths's emancipation of her slaves, undoubtedly because Child was describing the interaction of slave and former mistress as an outsider. The essay was a published letter from Griffiths, prefaced by an introductory statement by Child. Griffiths was unusual among Northern white women for her familiarity with African Americans; nevertheless, Child, within the context of the story she relates, constantly reminds the reader of her difference. The *Autobiography of a Female Slave* (written by Griffiths and accepted for many years as an authentic slave narrative) was one of Lydia Maria Child's favorite works, as Child's private letters attest.

As an orphaned Southerner who gave up all her inherited wealth—i.e., her slaves—and moved north for reasons of principle, Griffiths represented the fruition of all Child's hopes for the South. Child recognized and commented on the difficulties of such a choice in "Kentucky Girl." "It required the strongest convictions of duty and the loftiest moral courage to pass through such a social martyrdom," she wrote. "Her womanly nature quailed before it, but conscience was victorious."[123] Morality is necessary for emancipation, Child argued, and maidenly timidity will not stop the most valiant among Southern women. In "Kentucky Girl," Child equated Griffiths with the Grimké sisters, recalling Angelina Grimké's stirring speech to the Massachusetts legislature in 1837. She quoted Grimké's defense of women's right to meddle in politics: "As daughters, wives and mothers, may we not incur fearful liabilities in our country's peril?" Child added, despite the "solemn earnestness twenty-four years ago, the dead body of a soldier is carried past my window to the desolated home of his poor widow."[124] The relevance of such a juxtaposition can hardly be ignored: had progress been made earlier, perhaps such husbands would not have had to die.

Griffiths's actions are thus framed as the glorious result of true morality, a morality unique to women. The Griffiths excerpt at the center of Child's published letter describes the moment when she announces to her slaves that they are free, and gives them their papers of manumission. "It was delightful to watch their countenances," Griffiths recalled, "as they slowly received the idea of personal freedom. It seemed as if they underwent some heavenly transfiguration." She was delighted also to feel so clearly her own power. "Poor creatures!" she lamented, "they embraced my knees, they kissed my hands, they would have covered my very feet with caresses if I would have permitted it." Her slaves, she was quick to add, were extremely loyal and unselfish. Though their first thought was overwhelming joy for themselves, their second was of her: "But when these first ebullitions of feeling were over, they began to think more of me than of themselves." "Now wasn't this very touching?" she asks Child, "Poor, faithful, loving creatures! I can never be forgetful of my duty to their race." While the new freedmen are still "creatures," Griffiths is very careful not to tell them what occupation to take up, or where to settle. "I did not wish to act," she confides, "as if I were their mistress after I had given them their freedom." She did, however, provide them with food and clothing. This is an attitude toward Reconstruction that Child approves and offers as a model to her readers.[125]

S. C. Blackwell's "Fugitives at the West," published in the *Continental Monthly* in May 1862, was comprised of descriptions not of her own freed slaves but of fugitive slaves near her home in Cincinnati—the same place, ironically, where the majority of Griffiths's former slaves settled. For her, as for Child and Griffiths, the moral imperative of ending slavery was a constant underlying theme. Here she offered a narrative that could serve as a model for other women and antislavery sympathizers. Blackwell began her reminiscence by identifying the struggles of African Americans as the site of "every element of romance." "These elements of romance," she added, "with the moral principles lying at their root, were laid ahold of by Mrs. Stowe."[126] In "taking ahold of" her own romantic story, Blackwell described scenes she saw and heard about in Cincinnati, including the oft-told story of a mother who killed her children rather than have them return to slavery.[127] Meeting a minister's daughter who worked on the Underground Railroad, Blackwell agreed to help clothe and feed fugitives on their way north.

In her narrative Blackwell emphasized the bond she felt between herself and Sallie, an African American woman who lived nearby. Their common womanhood offers them a way to connect. In Blackwell's account, Sallie becomes imbued with natural moral sentiments, but they are laced with childlike innocence; she poses no threat to the racial order. If ultimately respectful, Blackwell still began her description by recalling how when she gave Sallie sewing to do, she would return with it and would "sink to the ground, as if utterly exhausted by the walk and the heat, and sitting at my feet, would play with the hem of my dress, as she talked."[128] Like Griffiths, this attitude of grateful subservience was what Blackwell remembered first. Sallie's voice and ideas caught Blackwell's fancy: "There was such magnetic power in her intense earnestness, her strong emotions, and her certain and exultant trust in God and his providence, that it held me spell-bound." On the outside Sallie is "a jolly, ignorant, negro-woman," yet she had a soul that "lay like a glowing volcano beneath that easy, careless Southern manner." And Sallie also had a clear understanding of God's underlying purposes and prophesied the end of slavery brought about by Him. Blackwell often remembered her words, especially now, "when the Lord is shaking the nations."[129] Again, like Child, Blackwell assessed the meaning of Sallie's example in terms of the war. Their messages dovetailed: slaves would act morally, responsibly, and gratefully when freed, and their essential goodness made them worthy of such freedom.

In the first years of the war, antislavery writers directly addressed politicians and governmental leaders whose policies concerned them, while they indirectly offered models of both benevolent behavior for white women and the ultimate subservient and respectful behavior of freed blacks. Both approaches were political in intent, and both relied on a sense of the war's underlying moral purposes and women's inherent knowledge of those purposes. These strategies were developed in keen awareness of an intended audience: editorials prodded the more often male readers of political newspapers, while narratives aimed at women readers of reform magazines.

These more pointed political works emanated from the pens of women who had already cut their teeth on the national problems of the 1850s. For younger or more conservative writers it took the stern gender divisions of a war-torn society to draw them into the melee of cultural struggle. The sense of being left out, left behind, and unheard spurred women of both generations to act and to write. In the first years of war they struggled to find a place of importance that would not challenge entrenched convention. Later, however, many abandoned the sentimental vision of a woman's passive waiting and filled the pages of magazines and novels with more dashing heroines. Still others, reeling from the losses of the battlefield, began to sound a note of discontent and to retreat from patriotism. If an effort at consensus was abandoned by many, at midwar, the rhetoric of unity only became eclipsed somewhat, to be revived after the war's end.

The year 1863 was a pivotal one in the lives of Northern women and women writers and in the literature on war written by women. Mired in a conflict that seemed to have no end, some writers turned to their pens to exhort more patience and virtue from the women at home. Those women, it seemed, were less willing to adhere to any Spartan image of sacrifice. Growing anger from the Northern working class also surfaced in 1863, most violently with the New York draft riot. Although before the war some women had been deeply concerned by the problem of industrial capitalism and the hierarchies of class it created in this supposedly classless society, the clear discrepancies of the national conflict threw this problem into greater relief.[130] Emerging in the early and middle years of war was the arresting voice of Rebecca Harding Davis, who insisted that there was more than one war going on. For abolitionists, the middle year of the war was also a crucial turning point. With the Emancipation Proclamation, early Reconstruction on the South Sea Islands, and the addition of African American men to the Union ranks came a flood of new issues and concerns. Threaded through all of the work of women writers at midwar was this sense of crisis and a corresponding impulse to intervene and redirect America.

Let the war go on, then. If we are not engaged in a righteous cause, may the Lord send us defeat after defeat, disappointment after disappointment, till we weary of fighting against him, and return repentant to his ways.

—Gail Hamilton, "Lights among the Shadows of Our Civil War" (1863)

"You are coming to political economy by a woman's road, Grey."

—Rebecca Harding Davis, "Paul Blecker" (1863)

{ CHAPTER FOUR }

A Woman's Road

Crisis at Midwar

"I AM SICK AT HEART when I hear the word *compromise*," essayist Gail Hamilton wrote in 1862. "The rumors which have sometimes darkened the air seem to have had no foundation; yet, because habit becomes a second nature, I cannot hear them without a thrill of dread."[1] What Hamilton called a "thrill of dread" pervaded the North at midwar. Battles were being lost: by the end of 1862, Bull Run, the Peninsula, and Fredericksburg had all become synonyms for failure. Even ostensible victories, like Antietam, were secured with horrific causalities or lost opportunities. The costs of war, literal and otherwise, were becoming all too evident to Northern writers and other intellectuals, and rumors, such as that of a military coup led by George McClellan, "darkened the air." The appeal of compromise was evident even to those, like Gail Hamilton, who were most dead set against it.

Under the weight of such despair, the unquestioned patriotism of the first year of war ebbed. It became harder to sustain a rhetoric of unity: the North seemed frayed and uncertain of its purposes. Defending a republican ideology, an ideology with profound and enduring meaning for men, seemed less viable for women, especially as the war escalated its human costs. In the end, the moral purposes of such a defense seemed less than clear. In a story by Rebecca Harding Davis, a captured Rebel slaveowner illuminates what Davis believed to be the nature of the schisms within the Union. There was no singular, well-articulated goal, Davis implies, and just as the North seemed on the verge of committing to one—the end of slavery—there seemed to be less consensus than ever. "You have too many slogans," the captive Southerner in Davis's story tells his friend and jailer, a Union captain. "Strong government, tariff, Sumter, a bit of bunting, eleven dollars a month. It ought to be a vital truth that would give soul and *vim* to a body with the differing members of your army. . . . Try human freedom. That's high and sharp and broad."[2] This is Davis's message as well, ironically told through the voice of a Southerner who will be murdered by his own slave. Human freedom has costs, she suggests, costs that still need to be paid.

Women writers on the home front expressed through their public writing an impatience with the seemingly fragmented understanding of the war's purposes. By contrast, Northern men, historians have surmised from hundreds of letters home, seemingly had less trouble agreeing on the war's purposes, even after having experienced combat. If one Pennsylvanian officer admitted being sick of the war and wanting to be home with his wife and child, he also added that "every day I have a more religious feeling, that this war is a crusade for the good of mankind," one he had to fight not only for himself but for his children.[3] Northern men fought for the ideals and opportunities of republicanism and a free labor ideology, but they also fought for each other, and for a sense of manhood. Despite battles, marches, and privation, historian James M. McPherson has found, "if anything, the motivating power of soldiers' ideals of manhood and honor seemed to increase rather than decrease during the last terrible year of the war."[4]

In September 1862, President Abraham Lincoln announced that he would, in a circumscribed way, "try human freedom" on January 1, 1863. This announcement was not, for close observers in the North, unexpected. Few women, besides the politically sensitive Lydia Maria Child,

Mary Abigail Dodge (1833–96), or "Gail Hamilton." Dodge was a popular essayist during the mid-nineteenth century, writing numerous pieces urging courage and stoicism from women on the home front. After the war she became an antisuffragist, believing in limiting the electorate to the educated elite. (Photo from Dodge, ed., *Gail Hamilton's Life in Letters*, vol. 1.)

heralded each step on the road to emancipation (perhaps because the steps were political rather than moral in character). From accepting General Benjamin Butler's clever use of the still demeaning label "contraband," to supporting confiscation acts, to banning slavery in Washington, D.C., and to approaching border states with plans for compensated emancipation, Lincoln edged closer to the moral stance demanded by abolitionists.[5] The preliminary Emancipation Proclamation, announced in the wake of Antietam's carnage, galvanized the antislavery community. If the proclamation, in its current form, was greeted with varying degrees of enthusiasm, even such a limited document put the war on a new footing and gave it entirely new meanings.

Ironically, given women writers' insistence on a moral meaning to the national struggle, this act brought no greater consensus to their understanding of the war's imperatives. While African American reformer Charlotte Forten rejoiced on the South Sea Islands, calling the occasion "the most glorious day this nation has yet seen," her position—surrounded as she was by the very few slaves freed as a result of the proclamation—was unusual.[6] Lydia Maria Child was less pleased. "As for the President's Proclamation," she wrote to a friend when she first heard of it, "I was thankful for it, but it excited no enthusiasm in my mind. With my gratitude to God was mixed an under-tone of sadness that the moral sense of the people is so low that the thing cannot be done nobly."[7] The political purposes mingled with the ethical ones made the president's act repugnant to Child: if it was the right thing to do to end slavery, she felt, it should have been done in 1861 (or much earlier), not in 1863, and then piecemeal.

One of the more common responses, perhaps, was the anxiety Susan B. Anthony noted in her reaction to a meeting of "Loyal Women" in New York City that year. After the implementation of the Emancipation Proclamation, Northerners had to make sense of the document, and they wrangled over it both in the streets of New York and in the pages of conservative and liberal papers. The relationship of class division and slavery was well established: to some, to end slavery meant to abandon the working classes, particularly the Irish. Yet the absence of slavery in the North ironically also was the moral high ground from which Northerners spoke to the English, fearful that they would follow their commercial interests and side with the South.

On the eve of "try[ing] human freedom," however tentatively, Northern women writers' long-sought unity fell apart. It fractured because the uneasy relations between women, so contested in the 1850s, could not overcome the press of changed circumstances and divergent politics of the mid- and late war. Class divisions, always significant, if dismissed by the middle-class writers of the early war, now became a larger part of the national discussion. The central ideologies of the mainstream North—separate spheres and a rejuvenated wartime republicanism—seemed to fit uneasily with women's conceptions of the war's meaning, and women's proper response to it. As the North attempted publicly to come to terms with the consequences of the Emancipation Proclamation, the issues of race, freedom, and potential social equality drew the greatest degree of attention. One of the effects was to divide women writers along political lines. Although many continued to take as their work the creation of the ideal woman-in-wartime, that ideal was now complicated by more obviously diverging beliefs about the war's purposes.

Against this backdrop of military defeat and ideological reorientation, several young writers—among them Hamilton and Davis—began to more confidently find their voices. By midwar their perspectives were well known in their literary communities. Davis, in particular, presaged many of the concerns of the postwar period, using a style and language that would grow in stature. She sought to tell realistic, "commonplace" stories of "to-day" and with this accurate history reflect the perplexity inherent in human life.[8] Gail Hamilton's style, by contrast, represented as much a synthesis of the moralistic past as a working toward the realistic future. Although her voice was self-confident, frank, and abrupt—unusual qualities in a woman writer at midcentury—her recommendations were an unlikely mixture of transcendental self-realization and Calvinist self-restraint.

Midwar crises brought to the fore concerns about the conditions of workingwomen. Such questions would have significant postwar ramifications for the lives and writings of a few important young writers. While the issues were not new—reformers had been addressing them for decades—the middle of the war brought them into sharp relief.[9] Like the heroine in Davis's Civil War story "Paul Blecker," who realizes that she has no option but to marry a man whom she does not love, women writers came to focus on the particular trials of their sex when women were barred by prejudice or habit from independent labor, freedom, or national action. Rising numbers of casualties gave new urgency to fears about economic survival for women. Middle-class women writers, most of whom were self-supporting, drew greater national attention to issues of economic inequity as the war wore on.

However varied their assessments and priorities, all these writers lived and worked in a climate of uncertainty between the summer of 1862 and the end of 1863. Some responded to this climate by directing their messages toward women whose influence they felt could reinvigorate the nation. Others, especially antislavery writers, reacted to the Emancipation Proclamation by shifting the focus of their political messages from the injustice of slavery to the promise of emancipation (the subject of Chapter 5). Finally, and significantly, during the midwar years young writers took up old issues in complex new ways, suggesting that the verities of the past were no longer acceptable or secure.

The political understandings that the work of the midwar period represents were very much shaped by the writers' own material circumstances, by the effects of the war on women and families. The sentimental vision of the stalwart waiter-by-the-gate, the robust enlistment recruiter, and the cheerful letter-writer gave way to visions of women weeping, widows and orphans starving, and nurses, stanching blood, surrounded by the wounded and the dead. As one character put it to another in an *Atlantic Monthly* story by Davis, "You are coming to political economy by a woman's road, Grey."

This "woman's road" was fraught with difficulty. The idea of a meritocratic and republican world, which sustained men facing the greatest of challenges, was shot through with ironies for women. If they were economically dependent on men before the war (and many, especially the writers, were not), women often could not rely on men's incomes during the war. In a world in which they were forced into or chose independence, for some an ideology that demanded deference to political hierarchy did not and could not appeal. Most tried to establish an uneasy path through this ideological tangle, reserving more space for women in a political world through some combination of separate spheres and classic republicanism. Others, perhaps more aware and certainly more concerned about workingwomen's struggle against economic adversity, were more ready to abandon ways of thinking that had little relevance in their lives. This "woman's road," then, lead in several directions, many of which were away from that which men on the battlefront, given differing material circumstances, ultimately chose.

Economic Struggle and Wartime Disillusionment

[The people] have borne, silently and grimly, imbecility, treachery, failure, privation, loss of friends and means, almost every suffering which can afflict a brave people. But they cannot be expected to suffer that such massacres as this at Fredericksburg shall be repeated.—*Harper's Weekly* (December 27, 1862)

Historian James M. McPherson argues that there were three separate turning points in the middle years of the Civil War: Antietam in 1862, Gettysburg and Vicksburg in 1863, and the elections of 1864. Those who were there agreed. "The character of the war has very much changed within the last year," Union general Henry Halleck wrote in March 1863. "There is now no possible hope of reconciliation with the rebels."[10]

The turning point that seemed to most affect the women writers studied here, however, occurred around the time of Antietam and the ensuing preliminary Emancipation Proclamation. Both events had tremendous consequences. The last day of Antietam, while considered by many a nominal victory for the North, was the bloodiest day of the war, leaving 4,100 dead and 18,000 wounded Confederate and Union casualties.[11] The enormity of the loss was manifest to the thousands of visitors to the exhibit of ghastly images of the battle mounted by photographer Matthew Brady in New York.[12] The preliminary Emancipation Proclamation had varying effects. Abolitionists were cautiously optimistic; many Democrats were bitter and angry.[13]

Antietam did not result in any momentum for the Union army. In December of 1862, the Federals were badly trounced by a smaller force of Confederates at Fredericksburg, leaving 12,600 Union casualties. Even a "brave people," a *Harper's Weekly* editor averred, cannot suffer such a "massacre" twice. For the four months that followed, Union soldiers waited for the mud to dry. This interregnum was painful; in the North, the despair and schisms became palpable. Northerners were split in their understanding of the war's aims, angered by the incompetence of their generals, and appalled by the losses that mounted without any visible progress. In a letter to General Ambrose Burnside, who had reluctantly led the fiasco at Fredericksburg in the absence of any apparent replacement for General George McClellan, Quartermaster General Montgomery Meigs wrote frankly, "Confidence and hope are dying."[14]

A divide also opened between those benefiting from the war and those devastated by it. As historian Phillip Paludan has noted, "[W]hen the war began, inequality of wealth distribution may have been at an all-time high."[15] Concessions to wealthy businessmen for their support and contributions and service exemptions for those who could afford to pay the $300 bounty precipitated explosions like the New York draft riots of 1863, where class tensions and racial animosity fused in a violent conflagration that left over a hundred rioters, including African Americans, dead.[16]

Such expressions of rage were of little benefit to workingwomen. Although the war is often cited as a reason for increasing numbers of women in the industrial workplace, their presence as competitors for workingmen actually preceded the war in many cases. Cotton, wool, and paper mills—as well as shoe and rubber companies—already employed women. By 1860, according to the director of the census, women constituted one-quarter of the workers in manufacturing.[17] Women, particularly Irish immigrants and African Americans, were predominantly domestic servants in Northern households. Limited jobs were available to women who desired work at home or who had to work there to care for children (many of whom also worked). Much of this employment was piecework, an exploitative system of pay keyed to production rather than labor. The severity of such conditions led middle-class women to make seamstresses a fixture of stories about poor but still respectable women.[18] Somewhat more genteel women worked in increasing numbers as teachers, numbers of whom would sharply increase as male teachers volunteered for war.[19]

Nevertheless, an estimated 300,000 women entered the workforce during the Civil War.[20] Despite the number of workers who enlisted and the increased production due to wartime demand, however, there were still more workers than there was work. In addition, particularly for sewing women, conditions worsened as sewing machines came into greater use and the price of thread—which subcontractors insisted that workers buy—skyrocketed. In addition, these workers were particularly vulnerable, historian Alice Kessler-Harris has noted, because of their inexperience, their lack of financial support by kin at the battlefront, and the corrosive expectation that true women stayed in the home.[21]

Still, military production did create some new possibilities for women

This Winslow Homer montage foregrounds the despair of Northern women as a female figure sits weeping at the news of the war. A Southern belle, with a slave woman carrying her abundant food, strolls haughtily by emaciated Union soldiers in the upper

workers, albeit limited ones. As the war progressed factory doors opened wider to allow greater numbers of women—more than 100,000 by one estimate.[22] This increase was due not only to the replacement of war volunteers and draftees but also to the expansion of arsenals and war-related manufacturing. Francis Spinner, after his appointment as treasurer of the

right-hand image, reinforcing the sense of the Southern woman's fierce—and in this image, inhuman—loyalty to the Confederacy. (From "News from the War," *Harper's Weekly*, June 14, 1862, in the author's collection.)

United States in 1861, initiated the hiring of women as "government girls," a development that drew the wrath of male critics. Their numbers grew throughout the war to 447 by 1865; by the time that Spinner retired in 1875, women's tenure as government clerks was largely secured.[23] The number of women in other government offices and departments grew slowly as well.

By the end of the war there were women in the Post Office, the Office of the Quartermaster General, the Freedmen's Bureau Offices, the Interior Department, and the Pension Office.[24]

Another growth industry during the war was prostitution. Union camps and the city of Washington swarmed with women bartering sex for money. Paludan, in his study on the Northern home front, comments on the rise of women in jails and prisons, noting that observers were surprised by the numbers of them who had relatives in the war. Economic need, he surmises, was the reason.[25]

Conditions on the home front worsened the already vile state of urban life for the workingwoman and her children. Between 1861 and 1863, the price of a dozen eggs had jumped from $.15 to $.25, cheese had gone from $.08 to $.18 per pound, and potatoes from $1.50 to $2.25 per bushel. Bread doubled in price. As food, housing, and fuel prices rose, wages for workingwomen made no advance. Wages fell for seamstresses during the war as competition between needy women became fierce. Paludan estimates that seamstresses "saw wages go from 17.5 cents per shirt in 1861 to 8 cents per shirt in 1864."[26]

Wives and families living on farms fared marginally better than industrial workers, largely because they rarely had to deal with food shortages. If women were not unaccustomed to working in the fields during harvest, the dearth of men made many women managers and laborers during the entire planting cycle. Other women farmers went about their business with some aplomb, including one Iowa woman who refused to be helped down from her wagon when she came to sell corn, potatoes, and vegetables in town. "I declined their kindness," she wrote, "and said I would get down the same as a man did if I could do a man's work."[27] For many, however, men's work was untenably added to their normal twelve- to fourteen-hour days. One wife was frank about her difficulties in a letter to her husband: "i cant eat nor sleep," she wrote, "my nack hurts me so that i cant stand it to chop hardly at all. i shall have to brake up housekeeping before long. if i was only out of the way folks would take care of my children but to scatter them while im alive is more trouble that i can bare to think about."[28]

Despite bounties and wages, soldiers' families still suffered economically throughout the war. Even if the pay scale was higher for soldiers than what they were accustomed to at home, wages came irregularly, causing severe problems. One woman wrote to her husband, whose pay was long in coming, "i cant write any more for i have no more stamps or paper but write oftener or i shall give up all hopes."[29] In February 1863 the *New York Ledger* ran a piece in its editorial section about a family decimated by war conditions: the wife died of starvation when her husband's pay failed to arrive; he died of wounds.[30]

By July 1863, many working people were fed up with their worsening conditions. Women were among those who participated in the New York riots.[31] Perhaps more significantly, some women began to act in concert in their workplaces to forge more livable conditions for themselves. In August 1863, sewing women in Philadelphia protested to Secretary of War Edward Stanton when those without kin in the army were fired. Several strikes in New York later in the fall were led by women. A few, such as those by umbrella makers and employees of a shoe company, were successful. Most were not, with some employers going so far as to discharge all workers who had participated in the strike.

On November 18, 1863, a group of women seamstresses went even further. Fifty-three of their number met to form the Workingwomen's Protective Union. After its second meeting, the New York *Herald* observed that "the workingwomen of the city are fairly on the move."[32] Conditions continued to worsen, however, and by March 1865 the sewing women of Cincinnati had written to President Lincoln: "We are unable to sustain life for the prices offered by contractors, who fatten on their contracts by grinding immense profits out of the labor of their operatives."[33] Angry at the widening gap in income and the flagrant disparity in the government's treatment of working people and owners, these women still put their hope in reason and in a president who hailed from a log cabin. He did not, however, intervene on their behalf.

There was a crucial difference between the work that middle-class women took up and the desperate straits that working-class women faced. The question that dominated discussions of the war and womanhood in the first years of war—what can woman do?—was based upon an assumption of some leisure and choice. For many women who worked on behalf of the war effort in factories, at home as seamstresses, or as nurses, this expression of self-realization was of secondary concern to simple self-support. And an increasing number of women were forced to consider how they would carry on now that their breadwinner was disabled or dead.

Before 1863, as workingwomen had begun to act out against the war and their conditions, some middle-class writers sought to emphasize the connections of gender over those of class, insisting that womanhood and shared pain united all women. As Mary C. Vaughan explained in a Civil War story of June 1861: "A common grief had for a time annihilated all distinctions of rank or class. The delicate, high-bred wife of the colonel of the regiment, and the daughter of the common soldier, in workingwoman's dress, and with workingwoman's hard hands wiping away the tears that dimmed eyes that strove to look their last on one manly form, drew nearer each other, and exchanged glances of sympathy."[34] Still, stereotypical markers of class and status remained in place: "high-bred" versus "common," "delicate" versus "hard." The effort to create common cause did not lead writers to erase differences but instead merely to describe them as unimportant. With the backdrop of women's labor activism, and the privations that inspired it, such rhetoric could only sound hollow.

By 1863 the confidence in these "glances of sympathy" had waned still further. Women writers responded with multiple remedies. Some, Gail Hamilton among them, used republican rhetoric to call for a strengthened sense of purpose that largely avoided issues of economic or racial strife. Others, fewer in number, sought to break through the assumed dichotomies of good and evil, saint and sinner, and to reveal even further the divisions in society that needed repair, divisions between men and women, wealthy and poor, North and South. Despite differing responses, however, all perceived that there was a crisis in leadership and direction. Their writing was political work: it was meant to give readers a "realizing sense" of what they confronted and what they had to do.[35]

The "Loyal Women of the Nation" were publicly called together by Elizabeth Cady Stanton and Susan B. Anthony in May 1863 to confer about what women might "properly" do to support the government. "In this crisis of our country's destiny," the call read, "it is the duty of every citizen to consider the peculiar blessings of a republican form of government, and decide what sacrifices of wealth and life are demanded for its defense and preservation." Echoing "Paul Blecker," it continued, crying for a moral purpose to the war: "No mere part or sectional cry, no technicalities of Constitution or military law, no mottoes of craft or policy are big enough to touch the great heart of a nation in the midst of revolution. A grand idea, such as freedom or justice, is needful to kindle and sustain the fires of a high enthusiasm."[36] The call set up the parameters of the meeting in advance: it was for those "citizens" who could choose how much wealth to sacrifice, who could get to New York City by May, and who read newspapers. And it was for those who felt that moral purpose was the only defensible reason for revolution—a revolution, perhaps, whose fires needed "[re]kindl[ing]" and "sustain[ing]."

The conversation that followed demonstrated a split among women who wanted women's rights prominent and equal to African American rights and those who wanted them kept separate, lest the animosity raised by women's rights hinder the progress of full emancipation. What all seemed to concede, however, was that there was great anxiety in 1863 over the result of the Emancipation Proclamation and its meaning in determining the war's purpose. As Susan B. Anthony put it: "There is great fear expressed on all sides lest this war shall be made a war for the negro."[37] Her following sentence, "I am willing that it shall be," went unchallenged, although subsequent speakers were not so forthright.

The debate over the war's meaning, and women's proper place within it, raged in 1863, at a time of real fragility and angst in the North. Among middle-class white women writers, this debate again narrowly focused on the interests of those with wealth to sacrifice, and those who determined themselves to be—or desired to be—the keepers of the nation's moral stature, and the guardians of the interests of Southern slaves. Yet even within those parameters there were differences, as there were in the prior decade. What separated the two factions was this acute sense of crisis, and the brief oasis of (partial) consensus. What connected them was a deep belief in the power of moral argument in creating a stable and productive national consciousness.

To Upheave and Overturn: Gail Hamilton Goes to War

Miss Mary A. Dodge (Gail Hamilton) might be styled an essayist, but that would be but a vague term to denote a writer who takes up all classes of subjects, is tart, tender, shrewish, pathetic, monitory, objuratory, tolerant, prejudiced, didactic, and dramatic by turns, but always writing with so much point, vigor, and freshness that we can only classify her among "readable" authors.
—E. P. Whipple, quoted in Coultrap-McQuin, *Doing Literary Business*

For many women, moral argument and the place of a Protestant God in the "whirlwind" of war were deeply connected. Gail Hamilton was one such writer who, throughout the war, presented a "tart, tender, [and] shrewish" voice in the *Atlantic Monthly*.[38] Dodge had joined the Congregational Church at a very early age, and her religious sensibility infused her work. In her first essay on the war, "Lights in the Shadows of Our Civil War," she made clear her position on the relationship between politics and morality. "We do ill when we merge the moral aspects of this war in its political aspects," she wrote. "We must act politically, but we should think morally. And only when our politics are moral can they be truly politic. Good morals may not always be good politics, but bad morals can never be."[39] This essay, and another, "Courage! A Tract for Our Times," illustrated her unswerving stand on the virtue of and necessity for Civil War.[40] The war, she argued, was both punishment and goad from a stern God.

Hamilton's writing was shot through with both an ennobling sense of the power of republican virtue to save the country and the unnerving sense that perhaps the country was not virtuous enough to be saved. Threaded throughout her jeremiadlike prose was the fear that too many Northerners would choose compromise rather than sacrifice. Until Americans repented their great sin in slavery, until they gave up their comfort, money, love, and self to the cause, she asserted, the battles and bloodletting could not—*should not*—end.

By 1863, Hamilton saw herself as a kind of lay prophet who would lead her readership to see the struggle in its true light. But if she was considered by some of her contemporaries to be the logical choice to speak to the women at home, other women writers challenged her vision of the war and womanhood, sparking an impassioned discussion at midwar on the role and responsibility of women and the true challenge facing the nation. That discussion did not break down easily into two sides, nor did each position represent conservative, liberal, or radical perspectives: rather, in each these views mingled, representing instead a deep sense of urgency and division.

Hamilton initiated the debate with "A Call to My Countrywomen," in the March 1863 issue of the *Atlantic Monthly*. "In the newspapers and magazines you shall see many poems and papers written by women who meekly term themselves weak, and modestly profess to represent only the weak among their sex—discussing the duties which the weak owe their country in days like these," she wrote with an air of sarcasm. These poems and papers stressed what women *cannot* do: they cannot fight, because they are not men; they cannot nurse, because of their duty to their children; they cannot write effectively because "they do not know how," and finally they cannot "do any great or heroic thing, because they have not the ability." Having said all this, Hamilton continued, they end their stories with what they can do: pray.[41] Here the lack of space in republican rhetoric for strong and capable women is made manifest, and Hamilton goes on to challenge that understanding of the nation and of the responsibilities of her sex.

Although Hamilton did not discount the importance of prayer, she challenged the implied complacency of the reader who assumed that that was all she could do. Virtuous workingwomen, she suggested, were particularly important as the real moral glue of the nation. "True," she wrote, "women cannot fight, and there is no call for any great number of female nurses; notwithstanding this, the issue of this war depends quite as much upon American women as upon American men,—and depends, too, not upon the few who write, but upon the many who do not." Mrs. Adams, Mrs. Reed, and Mrs. Schuyler were not the only women of the Revolutionary War era who were of importance, she argued; so too were "the wives of the farmers and shoemakers and blacksmiths everywhere." Important women in Hamilton's day, like Mrs. Stowe, Mrs. Howe, or Miss Dix, could not alone save the country, but needed the support of "the thousands upon thousands who are at this moment darning stockings, tending babies, sweeping floors." "It is to them I speak," Hamilton claimed. "It is they I wish to get ahold of; for in their hands lies slumbering the future of this nation."[42]

In this passage, Hamilton encapsulated many of the common concerns of white Unionist women exhorters in the middle years of the war. They shared a sense that gender was at the heart of war's effects, drawing lines through society even as battle lines were drawn on the field.[43] They also saw themselves as participating in a literary dialogue. Most women agreed that their contributions on behalf of the war effort were as important as men's, although *how* women were to be important was the issue at stake. Finally, and significantly, these writers revealed unanalyzed class assumptions. In this instance Hamilton constructed herself as one of the writers of the war, like a Stowe or a Howe, and she envisioned her audience as the virtuous white working classes who needed direction. She assumed, as did her cohorts, that with moral suasion she could trigger a shared set of republican values that would heal the nation's divisions. Rather than indicating any knowledge of the concerns of this class, she presumed to know the ideas and values that would unify it, and thus the nation. In this way she continued the work of the early war years in attempting to motivate or build a national unity around proper womanhood. Yet her vision of this womanhood was muscular rather than demure, bold rather than usefully patient.

"A Call to My Countrywomen," which was later published in pamphlet form, provoked a number of responses. One anonymous pamphlet, published by the Loyal Publication Society, responded to Hamilton directly.[44] "A Few Words in Behalf of the Loyal Women of the United States by One of Themselves" reflects the language and political stance of Harriet Beecher Stowe, although considering Stowe's goodwill toward Hamilton, it seems unlikely that she authored it.[45] Another essay on the subject, "The Ladies Loyal League," by Mrs. O. S. Baker, was published in the *Continental Monthly* in July of 1863. (Hamilton's collected essays, which included "A Call," were reviewed in the same magazine four months later.)

In these essays the authors revealed a similar set of class assumptions, even as they staked out different positions on the degree to which Northern women were living up to the dictates of a virtuous republicanism. Hamilton saw her audience—the hardworking and frugal middle-class woman—as embodying (dormant) virtue and in need of guidance. At the same time, her essay revealed unease about the loyalty of that audience and was an attempt to establish virtuous action. The author of "A Few Words," by contrast, was annoyed by Hamilton's implied critique of Northern women. For this writer, Northern women *were* united in an already established virtuous middle: it was Southern ladies who transgressed appropriate boundaries. Mrs. O. S. Baker, for her part, also attacked the ruling class instead of exhorting the working class or middle class, but her targets resided in the North.

All three assumed that the virtue and moral rectitude necessary to the saving of the country would come from a shared set of middle-class values, values wrapped up in a gendered republican rhetoric. Despite the differing strategies—blame, praise, indicting a common enemy—in effect they were working to shore up the virtue and constancy of the North, using the rhetoric of unity. All three implied with their writing that such a set of values was either disintegrating or under attack, a perspective new to the midwar. What the three essays reveal is not just the passionate response that the war elicited among Northern women, but a sense that the war could only be understood in terms of gender and republicanism, not race or class. Yet the fact that the three writers needed to argue this point revealed growing unease over these divisions.

At the heart of the issue, these women asserted, lay the war's most stark question: if men marched, did women just wait? Where did the virtuous republican woman take *her* stand? Women, naturally and properly distinct from men, had correspondingly different duties, but rather than waiting passively they should wait with an ennobling sense of their moral mission. In accepting, and to some degree celebrating, diverging social roles and the notion of influence, these writers professed a separate sphere ideology that ignored class disparities by offering gender connection.[46]

Even given the common ground, however, the variations between the writers are revealing. In each case the author perceived and addressed a particular problem—workingwomen's enthusiasm in support of the war, Southern versus Northern womanhood, and the evil of antidemocratic actions—while at the same time redefining the meaning of separate sphere ideology. In claiming the values of republicanism, the uneasy fit of new material circumstances and older ideological logic became clear: how, in a culture that celebrated individualism yet still largely denied it to women, were women to value the ennobling virtue of a republicanism that assumed shared property-holding and implicitly relegated women to beneficent and natural dependency?

Gail Hamilton was aware of the complexity of this debate, referring to it regularly throughout her writing career. Essentially Hamilton hearkened back to republicanism by distorting an understanding of separate sphere ideology and claiming a propertied man's place. A writer of considerable force and humor, Hamilton used separate sphere ideology against itself, arguing that the integrity of the domestic sphere required women to work outside it. She also recognized that the umbrella of separate sphere ideology hid potentially conflicting opinions. "There is within the pale, within the boundary-line which the most conservative never dreamed of questioning, room for a great divergence of ideas," she noted in another 1863 essay, "A Spasm of Sense." Two years later, she forcefully asserted, "I shall not confine myself to my sphere. I hate my sphere. I like everything that is outside of it,—or, better still, my sphere rounds out into undefined space. I was born into the whole world. I am monarch of all I survey."[47] That she believed herself a "monarch" represents not only her forceful expansion of women's role, but her deep identification with men and the ruling class.

Yet as Hamilton sought to shed the limits that sexually segregated "spheres" implied, she recognized their power, and in writing directly for women reinscribed them even as she subverted them. The women she sought to inspire to action were at home within the traditional confines of the culture. Hamilton did not urge them to leave but argued instead for a bolder and more assertive definition of the separate sphere. She urged women to speak up for their convictions, to hide their weakness, to be independent instead of submissive. (In so doing, she gave women a power to resist dependency that she never allowed for propertyless males.) Her "Call" went out to those wedged so tightly between the responsibilities of family and community that they felt they could give no more. Yet she insisted that they must. Their first response, sewing, was also necessary but incomplete, for, she wrote, "if you could have finished the war with your needles, it would have been finished long ago; but stitching does not crush rebellion, does not annihilate treason, or hew traitors in pieces before the Lord."[48] Instead, Hamilton asserted, these women must bare their souls, must "come down . . . to a recklessness of all incidentals, down to the rugged fastnesses of life, down to the very gates of death itself." Hamilton called for the "fiery soul" within the gentle mother as a necessary step toward the winning of the war.[49] In speaking to the shared material obstacles faced by middle-class and rural women (those with few or no servants), she sought to create common ground: all physically knew the experience of sewing, of carrying water, of sweeping, and maybe that shared knowledge could build to a sense of a shared purpose.

Hamilton insisted that women adopt a patriotic stoicism and, through their womanliness, inspire manliness in men. "O my countrywomen," she wrote, "I long to see you stand under the time and bear it up in your strong hearts, and not need to be borne up through it. I wish you to stimulate, and not crave stimulants from others." In short, women were needed because of their power over men. Urge men on to war with courage, Hamilton advised, send them letters with home details written cheerfully and regularly, and, above all, "help him bear his burdens by showing him how elastic you are under yours."[50] Hamilton mocked the ideal woman's vaunted fragility, telling the story of a loyal sacrifice: "A gentle, fragile, soft-eyed woman, what could such a delicate flower do against the 'thunder-storm of battle'? What *did* she do? Poured her own great heart and her own high spirit into the patriot's heart and soul, and so did all."[51] Women, though described as fragile, were not fragile at all, and it was time to leave the issue behind.

A sense of urgency suffused Hamilton's essay. The time to rise up with strength was when the future looks dim, when years of war had already taken their toll. "O women," she wrote, "here you may stand powerful, invincible, I had almost said omnipotent." Only virtue—not guns, money, or generals, all of which have already failed—would win the war. If the North lost, it would be "not because of mathematics or mechanics, but because our manhood and womanhood weighed in the balance are found wanting."[52] Like Stowe in *Uncle Tom's Cabin*, Hamilton wanted the nation to *feel* right; only in this feeling would come victory. That feeling was the essence of republican virtue.

For Hamilton, the Civil War was the Armageddon, requiring all the nation's resources. "It is the question of the world we are set to answer. In the great conflict of ages, the long strife between right and wrong, between progress and sluggardy, through the province of God we are placed in the vanguard." Therefore, she urged, "let us have done at once and forever with paltry considerations, with talk of despondency and darkness. Let compromise, submission, and every form of dishonorable peace be not so much as named among us. . . . From every household let words of cheer and resolve and high-heartiness ring out, till the whole land is shining and resonant in the bloom of its awakening spring."[53] "Dishonorable peace" was the biggest danger facing the Union. Hamilton preached her message of sacrifice with all the hardiness of her Calvinist faith. In the end, this fierce struggle would demonstrate the nation's "touchstone of character." Women, no less than men, embodied that character.

But this vision, impressive in its rigor, had limits beyond Hamilton's parochial conception of class. In assuming that all the nation needed was will, Hamilton left no room for those beaten down by the war's effects; she believed that the essential structures of society were just and that the problem came from within—not from ruling-class greed, erring generals, misspent money, too few guns. Workingwomen, struggling for fairness from the government, would hardly have agreed. While Hamilton's political ideology left a great deal for women to do, and assumed that they had great power, it lacked an acknowledgment of the difficulties facing many people, and presumed a shared set of religious and national values.

Such unforgiving didacticism is precisely what irritated the author of "A Few Words," who argued that Hamilton, like others, unfairly juxtaposed Northern with Southern women, assigning to the latter a greater loyalty. Northern women, she implied, *did* share values of frugality, hard work, and Christian modesty; there was no failure of will, no naming of "dishonorable peace" among Northern women. It was *Southern* women who were unrestrained and impetuous, she asserted.

This writer argued that Hamilton's work lacked compassion, self-restraint, and propriety. Prefacing her piece with a long quote from "A Call," the author depicted Hamilton as "one whose sharp dicta are winged with such vehemence that they must doubtless sink deep in every mind within their reach." She suggested that the "soul of fire" that Hamilton invoked resembled the biblical figure "Jael, the wife of Heber the Kenite," who drove a nail through the temple of her "sleeping enemy-guest." That would be "a heroine quite after the Southern pattern," she argued, not that of the more self-controlled North.[54]

The author of "A Few Words" seemed to feel that the carrot of praise, not Hamilton's stick of criticism, would be more effective in mobilizing women. But her passionate defense of Northern women did not simply rely on her reading of Hamilton's piece. Like the other authors, she was addressing an audience of newspaper editors, reformers, and pamphleteers, who she felt had made similar erroneous arguments and assumptions. Her depiction of Northern women (perhaps inflated in their defense) described their tenderness and gentleness, and the influence that these traits might have over more self-confident and independent (republican) men. Such qualities would win the war more surely than Hamilton suggests, and were considerably more fitting to proper womanhood.[55] Finally, what set this writer apart from the other essayists considered here was the explicit statement that the war was being fought over slavery.[56] Only over slavery, an issue of moral rather than political importance, would white women's assertiveness be both justified and imperative.

"Why," the author of "A Few Words" asked both Hamilton and the reader, "should we simulate a 'white heat' if we did not feel it, or see any occasion for it?" The absence of "white heat" was no deficiency but a strength—that of self-control. If Southern women had this heat, it led them only into unwomanly defiance. Northern women should not court newspaper descriptions of their fury. "Public notice they consider not a reward, but a misfortune," the author wrote, "and [they] are ready, when it happens to them, to ask, 'What wrong or foolish thing have I done?'" Tenderness and deference, it was suggested, were what really brought about positive action. "The feelings of Northern women are rather deep than violent," she wrote, "their sense of duty is a quiet and constant rather than a headlong or impetuous impulse."[57] Boldness and assertiveness—characteristic of Hamilton's writing—struck this writer as vulgar.

The author conceded that such restraint had its drawbacks—"it may occasionally circumscribe [women's] influence by lessening the sphere of their example"—but it was nevertheless the essence of proper behavior. "After all, Christian women must be no boasters. When they have 'done all,' they are bound to feel themselves 'unprofitable servants,' and to seek no reward from the applause of men." The many sacrifices of hospital nurses—"no hirelings"—had not been broadcast but were still part of the war's record. Woman's true goodness sprang not from economic contributions but moral impulses—and was limited, then, to a class that could afford such impulses. The appropriate and womanly woman, the writer pressed, would make sacrifices in the true spirit of the martyr; she made no claims for glory and did not seek to profit from it by accruing power. Furthermore, the writer argued, Northern women did not "mistake ferocity or vulgarity for patriotism." This would unsex them. Indeed, "[a]ccording to our Northern creed, when a woman ceases to be a woman, she becomes nothing, or worse than nothing."[58]

According to the author of "A Few Words," women were not to be involved in politics; they were properly dependent in an ideal republican world. If men were aware that the war was brewing, women "walked as in a dream, hoping against hope." When the shots were first fired at Fort Sumter, their dream was dispelled, and "new life came to many an enervated mind and body." Perceiving the need for activity, women entered new pursuits, properly answering that need with quiet but unassuming action rather than passion. They donned unfashionable brown aprons and went to work packing boxes of necessities; they went to the hospitals and became "physicians of all souls," ministering to the needs, physical and spiritual, of Southern and Northern soldiers alike. They renounced extravagance and luxury, and looked to make no profit. These were the tasks and values appropriate to women, not the direct violent actions recorded of Southern women. They were also, clearly, limited to middle-class women: working-class women could not afford to leave home or factory for unpaid jobs in hospitals, and they had no extravagance and luxury to renounce. "Loyal women," like "Countrywomen," were middle class.

Class status and virtuous behavior earned the middle class the right to speak on moral issues of national moment. If in all other political issues women were expected to follow their husbands, the author somewhat inconsistently maintained, women had a responsibility to speak and act against the morally indefensible institution of slavery. Before the war many Southern women of the middling classes, not aristocratic ladies or "poor whites," were against slavery. Yet these women did not speak up; their sacrifices for war were not rivaled by sacrifices for the cause of truth:

> If all the women in the rebellious States who disapprove of slavery, and believe it to be an evil and a sin, had, as with one voice remonstrated against this war for its extension and perpetuity, instead of weakly allowing passion to influence them, without regard to principle or conscience, there would have been no war. If every Southern wife had done her whole duty by her husband, using the "still, small voice" to which God has given such power, in persuading him to listen to reason and duty, rather than to the trumpet-blare of a wicked and heartless ambition, what misery might have been saved![59]

Middle-class women, then, if only in "small" voices, had the power, ability, and responsibility to define moral action, and the ills of war could be blamed solely on white Southern women.

In the conclusion of "A Few Words," the author advised Northern middle-class women more directly. Recommending the creation of "new duties," "new channels for help," and "new modes of evincing our love of country," she still added the caveat "without public demonstration."[60] Staying within the traditional bounds of the separate sphere was the proper thing to do, a guideline to be suspended only when public issues were of overriding moral importance. As in the struggle between Fanny Fern's and Elizabeth Oakes Smith's versions of womanhood, Hamilton's and this author's visions collide at the point of public propriety and political tone.

Even more than Hamilton, then, the author of "A Few Words" assumed that she was addressing a particular audience: the middle classes. In her essay she not only engaged a perceived crisis in confidence but also defined appropriate class behavior. Only if women were not paid, not "hirelings," could their work be truly considered virtuous and laudable, and only the class between the poor and the aristocratic whites of the South could see the moral truth about slavery. Rather than attempting to unify classes with a definition of virtue that derived from the middle class, as Hamilton did, the author of "A Few Words," sought only to unify the middle class as a hedge against inappropriate ideas and actions from outside. Her essay is thus both a product of and a response to the crisis at midwar and the sense of class dislocation.

Unlike Hamilton or the author of "A Few Words," Mrs. O. S. Baker addressed not the middling ranks but the upper classes, who betrayed the war's solidarity by their arrogance. Little is known about Baker, except that she wrote essays on various subjects for both the *Continental Monthly* and the Philadelphia-based *Arthur's Home Magazine*. As a representative of the Ladies Loyal League, which was organized as an attack on upper-class extravagance, Baker sought to establish proper conduct for women during the war; to do so she first had to determine their appropriate role in society.[61] Baker shared with Hamilton and the author of "A Few Words" a desire for change. Like Hamilton's critic, she accepted a conventional understanding of separate spheres. Yet for Baker this implied no particular deference: the spheres were, to her mind, equal in power. The separation between spheres should be complete; women should not seek to unduly influence or inspire men through their words and actions but should maintain direct control over the area reserved for them. Men, she argued, must rule the governmental and political arena, and women the social and humanitarian. Woman's voice, then, was not "small" but resonant in a parallel and equally important way. Here women were not dependent on men for an appropriate understanding of the war's meaning, consistent with an older definition of republicanism. Their economic dependency implied no corresponding moral or intellectual dependence.

Baker's essay was directed at the transgressors of these important limits among women *and* men. Neither should repine at the boundaries set upon them by "the natural laws of means to ends" but should accept important avenues of action "distinctly divided between them." She did not explain how this division was to be maintained, but her implication was that if women did not vote, men should not interfere in reform organizations. While the "existing government is an organized expression of the manhood of the age that founded it," Baker wrote, "the existing society is a like expression of the womanhood of the time." These were separate, she asserted, and if society and government "influence, modify and constantly change each other," they should not overlap.[62] The Ladies Loyal League, Baker implied, did not purport to change politics but focused instead on comparable social and domestic circles.

Women were to use personal influence and support to make change happen. "Cheering, honoring, and aiding in every fit way" both privates and officers; encouraging new enlistments; paying "special honor" to women with kin in the army, especially to those who have lost kin; and frowning on traitors and sympathizers were among her suggestions. (These imply the source of her own sense of urgency: the draft riots, the widows and orphans of war, and the naming of a "dishonorable peace.") Yet finally, and most importantly, for Baker was the cultivation of a "true understanding and appreciation of the principles of our democratic institutions—with a view to their practical social bearing, and consequent obligations upon our sex."[63]

The "anti-democratic social system" of women was at fault for the lack of resolution in the war, Baker believed. One imagines, although it is never mentioned, that the New York draft riots the month before provoked at least some part of this criticism. Women's "pride in ostentation" rather than "simplicity" and their neglect of wounded and sick privates in favor of caring for more wealthy officers impeded the progress of the war and reflected badly on society in general. Class differentiation gave rise to a split in the ranks and in local and national purpose. Something must be done, Baker insisted. "However difficult," she wrote, "it must be accomplished—and by American women, too, for men have no power to lead in such a matter as this: it must be accomplished, or the hope of freedom and progress of humanity will be crushed, and democracy on earth die, even out of institutions of government."[64] "It" was an erasure of class prejudice: in honoring officers and not privates, women were imperiling the war effort and the draft. Even women with no time or money could work in this way, Baker argued, and if their work was in influencing others, they had a power that men lacked to change the course of public opinion. "This work of reforming the spirit and remodeling the customs of society on a simple democratic basis," she concluded, "is one in which every woman— no matter what her condition, nor how circumstanced—is capable of doing."[65] If workingwomen could give up their men to war, and upper-class women could honor them, Baker was suggesting, then draft riots would be a thing of the past.

Like Hamilton, Baker saw women as agents of change, and this agency came through acceptance of and use of separate spheres ideology and a simultaneous reworking of the understanding of republicanism. "Let a controlling majority of our sex throughout the United States thus act," Baker concluded, "and were our threatened Government doomed now to be indeed overturned, the startled world has no cause to despair! For then the women of our land would prove its saviors—for, having recreated society according to the principle of democracy, they would, through the laws of reaction, restore that principle again to American institutions."[66] The flip side to Baker's argument, of course, was an abiding sense of woman's culpability for the "startled world" of 1863.

Three sensibilities at work, one might maintain, will always reveal differences even when they argue a similar action. These women—Gail Hamilton, the anonymous writer, and Mrs. O. S. Baker—did argue for similar actions: for right thinking, for aid and support of the loyal, and for disdain of the disloyal. They understood their world as naturally and, to some degree (Hamilton's caveats aside), properly separated by gender rather than class into different spheres of action, and they claimed dignity and respect for women as the nation's moral centers. At midwar they perceived the country in crisis, divided by class, and wavering in purpose.

Where they differed—and they differed enough, in the pamphleteer's case, to directly challenge each other—was in the meaning and limitations of appropriate womanhood. Gail Hamilton, in perhaps the most widely read essay of the three, supported what some at the time might have called a "strong-minded" approach. She expected all women, despite their condition, to be tough and self-reliant; to accept pain and distress with stoicism; and to speak with self-confidence and passion in support of right action. The author of "A Few Words" described appropriate action for women far more conventionally and expected only the middle class to be morally able to live up to it. Women, according to her, were to act with circumspection, not undue passion. If they needed to speak against their husbands, they should do so with a "still, small voice" on issues of moral relevance. Their sphere was not politics, and they should not stray into it. Mrs. Baker would agree with both writers to some degree, but her understanding of separate sphere ideology and her acknowledgment of the democratic makeup of society made her message more nuanced. For Baker it was a question not of extending a sphere, as was the case with Hamilton, or of deferentially recognizing and acceding to the proper limits of womanhood, as with the author of "A Few Words," but of using limits to insure shared power.

Hamilton and her contemporaries worked on issues of class from a profoundly centered sense of their own class status and agenda. That the war was a necessary evil, that the government was making moral choices, and that women were meant to support and sustain the war and the government were givens. By contrast, a few writers at midwar tried to go beyond their own experiences and see the conflict through the eyes of working-class and rural women. Although this effort at cultural and economic empathy did not, in most cases, shake their belief in the war's legitimacy, these writers did offer a stronger critique of the social and political choices being made by men. Instead of exhorting women to greater effort, they outlined the mistakes made by both men and women.

Class Is Another War: Fern, Townsend, and Davis

Rather than bewailing the lack of unity in the country or seeking to paper over differences of class with similarities of gender, Fanny Fern, Virginia Townsend, and Rebecca Harding Davis set about the business of uncovering inequity in national life, revealing what for Davis was the "mighty hunger" of the oppressed white worker. In their opinion, these people needed no words of wisdom to stir their patriotism; they needed a frank reassessment of their condition and a fair redress of it.

Each of the three writers represented an important position on the issue of the other war the nation was fighting. Fanny Fern had become concerned with workingwomen's issues during the 1850s; she had personally struggled with just that economic insecurity she wrote about. More than perhaps any other woman writer, she had "come to her understanding of political economy by a woman's road."[67] Yet Fern was unhesitatingly patriotic and did not question the war's ultimate purposes or effects. Neither did Townsend. The editor of a conventional Philadelphia literary magazine, Townsend did push the limits she worked within to show the inequity of a workingwoman's lot at midwar. Yet as significant as her position was within its context, it revealed a continued hope for unity that seemed at odds with the class divisions she chronicled. Rebecca Harding Davis had the most original voice among the women writers at midcentury, and her work in the early 1860s deserves particular attention. For Davis, the "mighty hunger" of the oppressed called out from both north and south of the border and from both black and white, and no pat answers could assuage it.

Fanny Fern's descriptions of New York life represented both her desire for a coherent and republican middle-class America and her acknowledgment that it no longer existed. In a column titled "Things I Like to See," she criticized both the genteel class and the working class. On the one hand she liked "a lady who can carry a parcel," on the other "a shop-girl neatly dressed, and without sham ornamentation." But she crossed the lines that genteel women drew to distinguish themselves from other classes. She liked to see "a lady who is superior to the small vanity of perching a lace-cap on the head of her nurse-maid in the street, to make her pass for French or Swede, or to signify by this badge of livery, her servitude."[68] Significantly, she mentioned no women of color among those she "liked to see."

Although Fern never wrote directly of the New York draft riots, her sympathies were clear: she lauded the private from the ranks of the working class and scorned the man of any class who chose not to fight. Her reticence with regard to the riots themselves may have stemmed from several causes: first, she was out of town when the riots took place, and Fern tended to write of the here and now; second, her sympathies would have been severely challenged, as she consistently conflated elitism with disloyalty to the Union cause; and finally, and perhaps most crucially, her editor, Robert Bonner, may have prohibited discussion of the event since readers were likely to have come from both sides of the political fence. Nonetheless, Fern continued her course of patriotic Union support and empathy for the conditions of working people. In September 1864 she sharply criticized those who sought peace with the Rebels without victory. Her Union loyalties were fierce, and she rejected the pricks of her conscience to moder-ate her tone on subjects of war. "Don't you think it wrong for a *woman* to hold up her hands for war?" she imagined being asked. She answered frankly, "Bless you, not I; I enjoy the fight; I am only sorry that, being a woman, I am necessarily counted out. You wouldn't catch me hiring a 'substitute'; in fact, you couldn't get a substitute for *me*."[69] That she imag-ined being challenged as a woman eagerly embracing war spoke to the on-going concern of women writers—that their interest was taboo—and helps explain their constant justifications for entering the wartime dialogue.

Not only should women speak about war, Fern argued, but the conse-quences of war on them begged for acknowledgment. Women bore the brunt of war, particularly poor women, she asserted regularly throughout the midwar years. In "Soldiers' Wives," written in November 1862, she argued that soldiers with their comrades around them, "shoulder to shoul-der," were better off than even wealthy wives left at home. "He has excite-ment," she wrote, "he has praise if he do well; he has honorable mention and pitying tears, if he fall nobly striving." Yet the poor wife of a soldier, left alone with her children, had the most difficult task of all. She did not know where the next meal would come from, got no praise, and worried constantly about the day when her strength would give out. In "Whose Fault Is It?" a far grimmer and more hard-hitting column of June 1864, Fern described *"a little piece of hell"* she found in New York City, where garbage rotted in the streets and pools of blood from the nearby slaughterhouses lay festering. Fern did not blame the "tired mothers" for letting their children near the filth but rather the wealthy businessmen who helped create it. "Alas!" she concluded, "if some of the money spent on corporation-dinners, on Fourth of July fireworks, and on public balls, where rivers of champagne are worse than wasted, were laid aside for the cleanliness and purification of these terrible localities which slay more victims than the war is doing, and whom nobody thinks of numbering."[70] There was another war, Fern implied, with more victims than the military battles being fought, and its perpetrators were selfish capitalists.

Virginia Townsend's writings were in general more sentimental and less hard-hitting than Fern's, but her concern for poor women and their special needs during wartime was clear and sustained. Although she was a fairly well established writer, publishing in different women's magazines and serving as an editor of sorts for *Arthur's Home Magazine*, very little is known about her background. During the war Townsend wrote two extended stories with a working girl as her subject; after the war she wrote a serialized novel—*The Soldier's Orphans*—about a middle-class family laid low by the war. Throughout the war she contrasted the mothers of soldiers from working-class and farm families with those of genteel origins, suggesting in her juxtaposition that the republican core of the nation was instinctively more patriotic.[71] In one of the early historical novels Townsend used the Revolutionary War setting to further cement the vision of a classless, hardworking society in her reader's minds. In *The Battlefield of Our Fathers* she baldly suggested its usefulness to the present in her preface, urging a similar selflessness and valor on her readers.

Townsend insisted, as did Fern and Davis, that the middle class was at fault for not recognizing the conditions under which working-class women worked and that their difficulties were no "paltry considerations." Like Fern, she called for a republican middle, a shared sense of humanity and responsibility. *The Story of Janet Strong*, Virginia Townsend's 1863 serialized novel, explicitly reveals this directive. Janet Strong is an orphaned factory girl who accepts a position as a domestic in the home of a woman named Mrs. Kenneth, only to be seduced and almost ruined by her nephew. Although a reformer, Mrs. Kenneth fails to see her real relation to Janet, for "Janet was to Mrs. Kenneth a servant—a being of a different sphere—not to be overworked, certainly, to be well fed and sheltered . . . but beyond this she never went. . . . Janet belonged to an inferior order. There was no common ground of womanhood or human needs on which these two could meet in this woman's thought." Janet is chagrined by Mrs. Kenneth's aloof treatment, which she had never encountered in "the sleepy old factory town." In the end Janet evades the seducer's grasp despite his blandishments, and the narrator intervenes to cement the moral of the story. "Has this 'story of Janet Strong' no significance for you my country women?" Townsend asks. "One common humanity holds you, oh mistress and maid, in its mighty grasp; the same great sorrows and joys—the same great hopes and fears prove you of one lineage and one race!"[72] That Townsend used the word "race" was significant in the context of late 1863: her intention was to call to the "white" race at a time when many were publicly debating the place that freedpeople would take. That "Janet Strong" was not Irish, as many domestics of the time were, compounded this message.

During the war, however, Townsend's most frank and unsentimental piece on women workers came when she learned of the disparity in wages paid to government workers of different sexes in Washington. She was appalled at the unchallenged assumptions of society that ranked the worth of a woman's work at less than half of men's. The assumption of women's dependence on men, and hence their supposed reduced economic need (an element of republicanism), made no sense in the material circumstances of the war. In "Women's Wages," she commented angrily, "There it is the world over, the strong taking advantage of the weak." This state of affairs, she claimed, undercut the vaunted nineteenth century's "new courtesy and deference" toward women. "Now we appeal to you, oh reader," she wrote, "is this just, or fair, or honorable?"

In taking up the issue of unfair wage scales, Townsend was also faced with the issue of the respectability, for women, of work outside the home. Here the assumption of male independence and female dependence, the central gender construct of republicanism, could not be sustained, and Townsend's arguments against it only suggest its continuing power. Not only did Townsend defend her working sisters, but she also reminded her readers of the many cases in which the woman was the primary breadwinner, unable to choose to stay in a comfortable home. Furthermore, she argued, there was only a limited field of competition between workingmen and -women, although "there are paths of good and faithful service where women can walk abreast with man without sacrificing in any degree her womanliness." She should not have to sacrifice her respectable class status either, Townsend stated. "I honor and pity the workers of my sex," she continued, "[d]elicate women and girls, with their frail health and strong hearts, going out in the world to do their labor there, and for that very reason losing often social caste where they should receive double honor, and doing their work so well that men are compelled to praise it, and then congratulate themselves on its being done—so cheap!"[73] Here Townsend deliberately mixed stereotypical images of workingwomen with those of middle-class women: those who work can be "delicate," too, rather than coarsened, with the "strong hearts" associated with the moral middle class. She created the "common ground of womanhood" she calls for in her story, but with "pity" as well as "honor" for the women who "go out in the world" to labor.

Both Fern and Townsend, in raising and analyzing issues of class and war, drew greater attention to the disparities of life between women with whom they assumed to share the same middle-class values. Neither writer described the workday of the industrial woman worker; they gave little sense that they were aware of the conditions that shaped the lives of workingwomen or even farm women outside of the city. What they were able to do was to identify another war going on between business owners and workers, a war that women were losing. And what they reveal is their own unease with an ideological system of meaning that, while useful in creating unity around a virtuous middle class, had little relevance to the material circumstances of midwar.

Rebecca Harding Davis's work went one step further than Fern's and Townsend's, taking her reader "right down with" her into the dirty, unsentimental lives of working people. Davis was impatient with the ideological truisms of the Northeastern elite, who had no idea of the suffering the war imposed on people whose lives in no sense matched their understanding. In August 1862, after returning home from a trip north, where she met the Concord intellectuals, Davis let her anguish about the war spill into a letter to Annie Fields. "These are sad lonesome days for us here," she admitted, "—the war is surging up close around us." She called to her friend to use her heart and see the pain and hurt—and right—on the other side. "O Annie if I could put into your and my true woman's hurt the ever present loathing and hate for it!" she wrote passionately. "If you could only see the other side enough to see the wrong, the tyranny in both!" Although she stressed that she could never have lived in a slave Confederacy, she granted the South the "right of revolution."[74]

Davis believed that there was more than one war being fought in America, and she drew her reader's attention away from the battlefield to the factory in her first full-length novel, stressing the importance of class injustice even in the midst of supposed unified national effort. "Your ears are openest to the war-trumpet now," the narrator of *Margret Howth* tells the reader. Set in the first years of the war and published in 1862, *Margret Howth* considered the evils of industrialization.[75] "I want you to go down into this common, every-day drudgery," she wrote, "and consider if there might not be in it also a great warfare. Not a serfish war; not altogether ignoble, though even its only end may appear to be your daily food."[76] As in *Life in the Iron Mills*, the narrator of *Margret Howth* assumes a readership from above, who will "go down" into a "nightmare." Part of that nightmare will be in readers realizing their complicity in it.

Davis's novel ultimately focused on this war of industrialization and consequent demoralization, but her opening made a profound statement about the meaning of both wars and their relative importance. The selfishness revealed by her portrait was not that of the workingman or -woman, she suggested, but of the capitalist; the blindness that made it possible was not that of the workingman or -woman, but of the middle-class reader who persisted in seeing only one civil war and ignoring the realities of capitalism. Pointing out the class inequities even in the present conflict, she continued: "You must fight in it [the class war]; money will buy you no discharge from that war."[77] Unlike Townsend or even Fern, Davis refused to flatter her readers by allowing them to place themselves comfortably on the "right" side.

Most significant in revealing her opinions on the war were Davis's short stories published in the *Atlantic Monthly* in 1862 and 1863. Her depictions of the struggles of farm women in the West Virginia hills in "Paul Blecker" and "David Gaunt" are carefully nuanced. Although the stories gently suggest that the Union is the appropriate choice, figures on both sides are compelling and sympathetic, and the real villain is the war itself. "There are no thoroughbred villains, out of novels," she wrote. "Even Judas had a redeeming trait (out of which he hanged himself)."[78]

Davis's stories, as *Life in the Iron Mills* and *Margret Howth*, bridge the gap between the domestic novel, with its careful rendering of emotion, and the emerging tradition of realism, with its careful attention to even ugly detail. Grey Gurney and Theodora (Dode) Scofield are not the classically beautiful and talented heroines of the domestic novel; they are gritty, uneducated workingwomen but with a warmth that causes all to draw nearer to them. These women are hardworking and dutiful, yet stymied by lives that offer them nothing. This despair hangs over both stories and to some extent explains the protagonists' response to the war. Dode erupts into "passion-fits" on occasion, though she controls them. They "were the only events in her life. . . . If her heart and brain needed more than this, she was cheerful in spite of their hunger." Though considered a "shy home-woman" and described as having "no public sperrit," she is clearly mystified by the war and, in the words of her father, "don't take sides sharp . . . 'n fact, she isn't keen till put her soul into anythin' but lovin'."[79] It is her moral vision that the reader is urged to adopt.

Ironically, the war is also an outlet for the hunger of women. The other women in Dode's town—and all over the country—are drawn to discussions of the war as a respite from their cramped lives. The women fill the village meeting to discuss the war, for "they had taken the war into their whole strength, like their sisters, North and South: as women greedily do anything that promises to be an outlet for what power of brain, heart, or animal fervor they may have, over what is needed for wifehood or maternity." This does not, however, imply a patriotic fervor. Dode and "these women had seen their door-post slopped with blood,—that made a difference." This makes Dode reject the vaunted patriotism of the Methodist preacher who loves her and the war itself: "[S]he talked plain Saxon of it [the war], and what it made of men; said no cause could sanctify a deed so vile,—nothing could be holy which turned honest men into thieves and assassins."[80] Grey Gurney of "Paul Blecker" is equally at a loss in choosing sides in the war. She leaves the decision up to God, "knowing how stupid she was, near-sighted, apt to be prejudiced—afraid to pray for one side or the other there was such bitter wrong on both."[81]

In both stories Davis pits men who know each other on opposing sides. War, she thus implies, is always personal. In "David Gaunt," the title character—a preacher—faces the only man who loves him—Dode's father—on the battlefield. He shoots and sees him fall. Thus Gaunt is faced with the "eternal truth, a humanity broader than patriotism" that Dode has held fast, that "no cause could sanctify." His choice devastates him, and he turns from fighting to nursing. In "Paul Blecker" the title character is confronted with the wounds of the estranged husband of the woman he loves and wishes to marry, a man he knows to be a cad. As a doctor, he could turn away, but he does not. In both cases Davis depicts a war with no easy targets, a war within communities and within families. There is no honor and glory here.

This grim realism of a war with no easy choices was both new and compelling in a context of perceived crisis. Davis was against slavery, as her stories demonstrate, but antislavery concerns did not play a central role in her public war work. Her war was a war of the ruling class against the oppressed, poor rural and urban working folk, white and black, connected by their common oppressor. The enemy, ironically, was both the audience for which she wrote and the reason she wrote. In this uneasy state she was almost alone.

Davis's work contrasted sharply with that of other antislavery writers who painted their subjects and concerns with more dramatic colors and in more dichotomized ways. That polemical vision, as Lydia Maria Child might have argued, suited the language to the political purpose: it created no confusion or sympathy for the oppressor or for the South. Davis also contrasted with other writers in her absolute rejection of accepted republican ideology and comforting truisms about the war's moral meaning. Her characters are not self-sufficient rural folk, or an urban upper class that needs to find common cause through self-generated virtue; these are people mired in capitalism or destroyed by the complexities of a war that has no clear logic.

THE MIDDLE YEARS of war were shaped by a profound sense of dislocation. Women writers looked to the ideological truisms of their world to see where the damage had occurred, and thereby to fix it. With few exceptions, they believed in the North's ability to rise to this challenge through soul-searching rather than structural change. For more conservative and classbound writers, like Gail Hamilton and Mrs. O. S. Baker, the "thrill of dread" meant a crisis of will and womanhood, and demanded a reassessment of its meaning and power. For others, like Fanny Fern and Rebecca Harding Davis, the inequity in economic conditions that resulted in disunity needed to be confronted in order for positive social change to occur.

Yet whether writers called for the nation to bind or to examine its wounds, the midwar years represented a profound wrench in focus, language, and message. Lydia Maria Child would never recapture her hope in a nation that took a moral step for practical reasons; Harriet Beecher Stowe would consider the slavery question largely solved and move on to new issues; Frances Ellen Watkins Harper would turn from antislavery to activism in support of freedpeople, for whom she devoted the rest of her life. Younger writers Louisa May Alcott and Rebecca Harding Davis explored issues of class, race, and womanhood with greater freedom after midwar, and recognized in the nation's divisions the concerns that would shape their later careers.

I have now been absent two years almost, and have just got letters from my friends in Auburn, urging me to come home. My father and mother are old and in feeble health, and need my care and attention. I hope the good people there will not allow them to suffer, and I do not believe they will. But I do not see how I am to leave at present the very important work to be done here. Among other duties which I have, is that of looking after the hospital here for contrabands. Most of those coming from the mainland are very destitute, almost naked. I am trying to find places for those able to work, and provide for them as best I can, so as to lighten the burden on the Government as much as possible, while at the same time they learn to respect themselves by earning their own living.—Harriet Tubman, Boston *Commonwealth* (July 1863)

{ CHAPTER FIVE }

Trying to Find Places

The Question of African American Freedom in the Late War

IN JULY 1863 the Boston *Commonwealth* published one of Harriet Tubman's only written legacies of the war years, an "as-told-to" letter to her New England friends, describing her work in the South. She was, at that time, working in several capacities at Hilton Head in the South Sea Islands: as a nurse for ill and wounded African American soldiers, as a volunteer worker with destitute freedpeople, and as a spy for the Union army. A remarkable facility for disguise, coupled with the dismissive ways in which older African American women were viewed in the North and South, made Tubman very valuable to the Union cause, just as she had been very valuable to the antislavery cause in the 1840s and 1850s in spiriting away hundreds of Maryland slaves to freedom.[1]

The letter was carefully crafted and seems sufficiently consistent in tone and style with Tubman's later "as-told-to" narrative as to make it likely that much of the shape, and clearly the content, were her own.[2] In it she asked for a bloomer dress, since she was short of clothes and had fallen on her skirt when she was running during one of her expeditions south. She also commented on the accounting of the Combahee River Expedition, a successful raiding mission she worked on with Colonel James Montgomery. "Don't you think we colored people are entitled to some credit for that exploit?" she asked. "We weakened the rebels somewhat on the Combahee river, by taking and bringing away *seven hundred and fifty-six* head of their most valuable live stock, known up in your region as 'contrabands,' and this, too, without the loss of a single life on our part, though we had good reason to believe that a number of the rebels bit the dust."[3] The critique as well as the humor and irony here would be evident to her readers: the Rebels were weakened more than "somewhat"; the "live stock" brought away were *people*; and the entire expedition would have been impossible without African American intervention, without which so many slaves would have never boarded an unknown ship for parts unknown.

Yet the reform message touched upon (the bloomers) and the critique leveled at the Northerners (their reporting and their use of the word "contraband") were not the only messages in Tubman's public letter to Boston. In her final paragraph she described the nature of her work in Hilton Head, explaining why she could not return to New York and take care of her elderly parents (whom she freed from Maryland a dozen years or so before). "I do not see how I am to leave at present the very important work to be done here," she told her amanuensis. She was looking after the ill among the freedpeople, as well as trying to get them clothing and food. In addition, she concluded, "I am trying to find places for those able to work, and provide for them as best I can, so as to lighten the burden on the Government as much as possible, while at the same time they learn to respect themselves by earning their own living."[4]

Tubman sounded the note that became increasingly insistent during the final two years of the war: "trying to find places" for African Americans not only in the liberated South, but in a Union that was largely hostile to them. Her appeal was again carefully couched: her work was meant to "lighten" the government's, undoubtedly out of her knowledge that the government, when pressed, would not supply the needs of the freedpeople, and because any effort to get such aid would anger the North. In a war that was fought for, among other things, a free labor ideology that was rapidly becoming less viable, Tubman may have felt compelled to present a picture of freedpeople able and eager to pull themselves up by their proverbial bootstraps, freedpeople who would only "learn to respect themselves" when doing just that.[5]

The Context

The work of "trying to find places," as Tubman put it (or "What Are We Going to Do with the Negro?" as paternalist whites put it), characterized the discussion of African Americans in the North during 1863–65. The New York draft riots were precisely about the place that freedpeople would inhabit: in a world in which wage labor had overtaken traditional master-apprentice relationships, white workingpeople foresaw that their interests would not be served by a war that would add to the numbers seeking paying work. Their attacks were not only on a government that did not recognize their dilemmas—soldiers' wages could not support large families, even when they were paid on time—but also on antislavery activists and African Americans themselves.[6]

The argument that slavery was wrong and should therefore end no longer took center stage (Fanny Kemble's *Journal*, discussed below, notwithstanding). Abraham Lincoln helped make that happen by declaring over three million slaves "forever free," even if they were still in Confederate hands, and by allowing blacks to enlist in the Union army and fight for their own freedom. When the war ended, slavery would, in fact, be dead.

Indeed, it was dying already. The Combahee River Expedition may have been unusual in the number of people liberated at one time, but the numbers of freedpeople within Union lines grew daily. Thousands flooded into Washington, many of whom moved into quickly established refugee camps, where Sojourner Truth, among others, worked. These refugee camps, like the one in Hilton Head, were filled with destitute, starving, and poorly clad people, few of whom had chances at jobs, even doing manual labor. That they were able to sustain themselves, by hiring themselves out as laborers, or by making food for soldiers and civilians, in no way detracts from the extremity of their situation.[7]

Newly freed and refugee blacks were viewed with suspicion and anger by many whites. The midterm elections in November of 1862 had returned more Democrats than Republicans to office, though Republicans were still in the majority. Jim Crow laws in the North, although slowly dismantled during the war, persisted in reminding African Americans of pervasive racial prejudice. That prejudice meant that some soldiers refused to reenlist in a war purportedly now to end slavery. And the enlistment of blacks into the Union army in late 1862 and early 1863—numbering, by the end of the war, over 180,000—angered some whites even more, excluding only those who thought it good that black soldiers die in lieu of white.[8] As one Cincinnati paper put it in 1865: "Slavery is dead, the negro is not, there is the misfortune."[9]

Emancipation Rhetoric and Fanny Kemble's Journal: The War Turns a Corner

How Sambo figures on the historical canvas, now! Nobody can overlook him, whether they wish it or not; he is *every* where. This is one of the principal advantages gained by this war; if not *the* principal; and it is a vantage ground which never can be lost.
—Lydia Maria Child to friend Mary Stearns (December 22, 1862)

A heightened sense of the significant transition under way in the war's meaning, brought about in part by the Emancipation Proclamation, was the context in which Frances Ann Kemble's *Journal of a Residence on a Georgian Plantation* was published in 1863. Like earlier narratives on fugitive slaves written by white women in form but completely unlike them in content, Kemble's *Journal*, published twenty-four years after it was written, drew a great deal of attention upon publication. Written by a British woman, its factual bite and the standing of its author in antislavery and upper-class circles gave the book credibility as well as notoriety. Fanny Kemble's *Journal* demonstrated how a nascent realist sensibility could be enlisted to promote fervor for war. Like Rebecca Harding Davis, Kemble drew her reader into the mud and reality of the thwarted lives of slaves and showed their right to a mighty anger.

Fanny Kemble was a well-known British Shakespearean actress whose divorce trial from the aristocratic Georgian Pierce Butler shocked the nation in 1849. The *Journal*, written while the married couple were visiting Butler's vast plantations, was thus of interest to its readers for more than just its depiction of slavery; some might have read it, one imagines, for its account of the Butler-Kemble marriage. They were not disappointed on either count. Passionate, angry, and anguished, Kemble's *Journal* reveals the war between her idealism and the last shreds of her loyalty and commitment to her husband. In some sense the personal conflict was the perfect metaphor in the eyes of many readers and writers for the nation itself undergoing a nasty "divorce," one whose nastiness was uppermost in 1863.

The antislavery community embraced Kemble's *Journal*. "Slavery never appeared so hateful, nor slaveholders so vulgar and brutal, as in these pages where a woman tells the world what the black women of the South have so long endured," editor Lydia Hasbrouck wrote in the *Sibyl*.[10] The Boston *Commonwealth*, representing a community that had supported Kemble through her divorce, ran three separate notices of the *Journal* in successive editions of the paper. "There is no excuse," the editor wrote in the first mention of Kemble's then forthcoming book, "no palliation of facts, but the whole system is laid bare and quivering before the eye." This is directly related to the war, the editor implied, for this diary "day by day" tells "the terrible truth . . . that this rebellion, to secure and perpetuate slavery, is an insurrection against human nature itself."[11]

In a letter to the London *Times* published in the *Commonwealth*, Kemble predicted another war unless slavery was ended in the United States. She also clearly depicted the slaves as intelligent and aggressive concerning their own freedom: "The liberty offered them [the slaves] is hitherto anomalous, and uncertain enough in its conditions; they probably trust it as little as they know it, but slavery they *do* know; and when once they find themselves again delivered over to *that* experience, there will not be ONE insurrection in the South—*there will be an insurrection in every State, in every country, on every plantation*."[12] Once skeptical of the antislavery community— Kemble argued in her book that emancipation should be undertaken only by slaveholders—she now joined the advance guard, stressing, far more than the women writers of the U.S. antislavery community, the possible consequences of denying emancipation.[13]

Antislavery activists recognized Kemble's work for its political potential. Lydia Maria Child, Kemble's friend of many years, had wished to publish the *Journal* years earlier when she was the editor of the *National Anti-Slavery Standard*. "I was disappointed at the time," she wrote to Oliver Johnson, the current editor of the *NASS*, "but I am very glad it did *not* appear then; for it would do a hundred-fold more good now. It came out in the nick of time. I think it will prove one of the most powerful of the agencies now at work for the overthrow of slavery."[14] Gail Hamilton agreed. In "Words for the Way," a wartime essay reprinted in her 1865 collection *Sketches and Skirmishes*, Hamilton recommended the *Journal* "as a specific for heart-sickness contracted by hope of victory long deferred." Kemble's book, she argued, will encourage people to remember what they are fighting against, and "thinking of this, we should reckon the sufferings of this present war not worthy to be compared with those under which the African race has so long groaned, being burdened."[15] Charlotte Forten was also impressed, in her journal calling Kemble a "noble woman" with "a keen sense of justice" and "true humanity." "Such a book," she prophesied, "such a thorough exposé of slavery must do good, in this land, and in England as well."[16]

It is not surprising that Kemble's passionate *Journal* was so well received. As Child noted, the Northern mood had shifted during the war, especially after the Emancipation Proclamation. What is surprising is the degree of passion that was now considered acceptable by editors (and, presumably, readers). This passion was focused on the plight of slave women in particular. In one of her last journal entries, Kemble summed up the situation she observed. "In considering the whole condition of the people on this plantation," she wrote, "it appears to me that the principal hardships fall to the lot of the women—that is, the principal physical hardships."[17]

Kemble's *Journal* was meant for women readers and assumed antislavery sentiments were natural to true womanhood. Written as a series of letters—thirty-one in all—to her good friend Elizabeth Dwight Sedgwick of Lenox, Massachusetts, the book seems to have been designed to appeal to an antislavery woman's greatest concerns. "Assuredly I *am* prejudiced against slavery," she wrote, before even leaving Philadelphia, "for I am an Englishwoman, in whom the absence of such a prejudice would be disgraceful." Nevertheless, she added, "I go prepared to find many mitigations in the practice to the general injustice and cruelty of the system—much kindness on the part of the masters, much content on that of the slaves."[18]

Yet Kemble recorded no mitigating factors and was frequently overwhelmed by horror and despair at the condition—physical, psychological, and moral—of the slaves. Her *Journal*, in fact, was a litany of indictments, the same ones the antislavery community had been broadcasting to the world for decades. By recognizing her complicity as the wife of a slaveholder and her powerlessness to improve their conditions (her husband refused to listen to her constant demands for their freedom or comfort), Kemble developed a critique of the slave system—and marriage—that resonated with Northerners in wartime. The *Journal* went into a second edition and was later reprinted in pamphlet form.[19]

Fanny Kemble's *Journal of a Residence on a Georgian Plantation* was crucial in questioning the assumed link between black and white women. Although Kemble herself identified with the slave women surrounding her, because of their shared experiences of childbearing and -rearing, she recognized painfully that they shared no other substantive experience, and that even her efforts to identify with them could and should be viewed with derision and contempt. How could she, after all, understand their pain? She was part of the problem, and they should and probably did feel only "murderous rage" for slaveholders—and their wives. This message challenged readers who assumed a facile ability to reach across the immense differences in privilege and experience to embrace a "common" womanhood in the name of unity.

He Is Every Where: Antislavery at Midwar

This was the world in which African American and white antislavery women writers worked, and they were well aware both of the promise of these years and its enduring evils. The sense that the North was becoming more receptive to antislavery literature—and accepting of Union general George McClellan's removal for his lack of vigor in promoting the war—was what convinced Lydia Maria Child that an important turning point had been passed. "How Sambo figures on the historical canvas, now!" she wrote a friend in December 1862.

> Nobody can overlook him, whether they wish it or not; he is *every* where. This is one of the principal advantages gained by this war; if not *the* principal; and it is a vantage ground which never can be lost. When I reflect how impossible it was, a few years ago, to get a word in Sambo's favor into any paper or periodical, except a few of the out-and-out abolition papers, from which nobody copied anything; and when I look round now, and see how the pro-slavery Harper pitches its tune; how new Magazines start with the best talent of the country singing in chorus for freedom; how pro-slavery Generals lecture in favor of arming the negroes; and when I write emancipation articles, and find them readily accepted by the Wheeling, Virginia, Intelligencer, and the St. Louis Democrat; when I take a view of all this, I cannot but thank God and take courage.[20]

To her nephew at the battlefront Child wrote that she tried not to be anxious, "because I have a prevailing belief that we are coming out right, *at last.*"[21]

While such euphoria did not last, the widespread discussion of "Sambo"—and Child's distorting lens of race prejudice was consciously and ironically used—did succeed in convincing the antislavery community that some progress toward universal emancipation was being made. To a great degree this belief changed the questions women abolitionists addressed in their public writings.[22] While they did not neglect to record the many injustices of slavery, and the worthiness of African Americans, they began to grapple more substantially with the question of what place freed slaves were going to fill after the war and emancipation.

Child was impatient with the emphasis this question was getting. "What can we do with the *slaves*? is a foolish question," she wrote to Senator Charles Sumner of Massachusetts. " 'Take them away from Mr. Lash and place them with Mr. Cash' settles that imaginary difficulty. But what we can do with their *masters* is a much more difficult problem to solve."[23] Not surprisingly, few held such a sanguine opinion of what emancipation would mean for African Americans or of the appropriate focus of postwar concern.

The question of what do with the slaves was complicated, even for people in the antislavery movement, by the issue of racial intermarriage and African American sexuality. During the later years of war women writers in general focused more attention on the manhood of freed slaves, describing them as eager for the chance to fight for their freedom. White women antislavery writers continued, to a lesser degree, to identify with women slaves, although they did not describe female slaves as becoming women in the same way they described male slaves becoming men.

After the Emancipation Proclamation, women writers more confidently depicted the war as a moral struggle to end slavery—and to prove the nation's manhood. In her essay "The Southern Hate of New England," Virginia Sherwood claimed that the war was not a war of sections but of ideas. "On one side," she suggested, there is "barbarism, slavery, injustice, ignorance, despotism, the woes and maledictions of the oppressed races, the carnival of fiends; on the other, civilization, freedom, justice, education, republicanism, the gladness and gratitude of redeemed humanity, the jubilee of joy among angels."[24] Slavery, "a dire wrong, a foul injustice, done to a whole race," imperiled the "virtue, the manliness, the moral vitality of the nation that allows it." But the end of slavery was required for more than justice alone: the United States needed to end slavery to win international status. "Ours is the moral lever that is to move the world, if we would have it so," she argued. "If we lose our moral prestige we are nothing." Her final call was to the men of the nation, a call she deferentially claimed did not ring "with the convincing tones of a prophet or an angel" but with the "weak voice of a woman." To men, however, she wrote: "Rise! quit you like men—be strong! Upon you the ends of the world have come. If you have manhood, assert it now!"[25] In this sense it was *white* manhood that would allow African Americans to be free; Sherwood did not imagine (or fear) that blacks would work to win their freedom, nor did she include them in her "men of the nation."

In a letter to the editor of the *Independent*, written in 1862, Harriet Beecher Stowe posed Child's question about the future status of the slaves.

In "What Is to Be Done with Them?" she laid down the central questions—with some answers—to the late war and postwar debate. "Many well-meaning people," she wrote, "can form no idea of immediate emancipation but one full of dangers and horrors." This is absurd, she argued, comparing the freed slaves to the untutored immigrants crowding American shores. Using the logic of proslavery advocates, Stowe argued that African Americans were "acclimated" to the hot sun so detrimental to the white man and that the production of cotton could not go on without them. In reply to the question posed by the letter, she answered: "What will you do *without* them? Do you want to stop raising cotton? And if you don't, do you want to send away the only class of men who know how to raise it?"[26] Stowe's response, easing fears of social equality and revealing her own lack of imagination and enduring racial prejudice, left freedpeople in much the same condition and station that they inhabited under slavery.

In the mid-1850s, Stowe had received a missive from England and Ireland supporting the antislavery movement, signed by over half a million women. Replying in the January 1863 *Atlantic Monthly*, she sought to encourage these same women to support the Union, engaged now in a "great moral conflict." Stowe marshaled all the evidence at her disposal to defend the war's purposes despite the government's reluctance to wholeheartedly support emancipation. She described relief efforts for freedpeople on the Sea Islands and the first examples of the bravery of African American men fighting for their freedom. She cited Confederate vice president Alexander Stephens's "cornerstone" speech, in which he made clear that the new government "is founded upon . . . the great truth that the negro is not equal to the white man; that slavery, subordination to the superior race, is his natural and moral condition." Stowe also wrote of the sacrifices American women were making in the struggle against slavery. Finally, she asked, "Sisters, what have *you* done, and what do you mean to do?"[27]

The response of the Englishwomen was also published in the *Atlantic* four months later. Like Stowe, they explained their antislavery activism through their womanhood, and thus their implied moral sensibility, and their response represented another public political act by women in wartime. They asserted that they could affirm the moral basis of society and not be distracted by political jealousies. In their "Rejoinder," they asserted their continued aversion to slavery. "We abhor it," they wrote, "judging especially as *women*, because of all the unspeakable wrongs, the hideous degradation, it has inflicted upon our sex" (thus implicitly disassociating themselves from African American men). They praised Stowe and the United States for their sacrifices, and claimed to be representing Englishmen and, "even more universally[,] the belief and hopes of the Women of England, whose hearts the complicated difficulties of politics and the miserable jealousies of national rivalry do not distract from the great principles underlying the contest."[28] In this way Englishwomen could speak publicly but *not* politically, remaining decorous while asserting their right to a (political) voice.

Martha Walker Cooke, an editor for the *Continental Monthly*, also addressed the future of emancipated slaves. In an editorial of September 1863, Cooke, like Stowe, adopted the stereotypes of slaves promulgated by slaveholders. But unlike Stowe, she outlined the persistent racial oppression the freedmen were forced to undergo, with the New York draft riots as her backdrop: "It has been said [that] the negro was lazy, and would not work without the lash; that he was incompetent, and could not work; that he was a coward, and would not fight: when it is found that he will work, he is to be deprived of labor; found that he can work, deprived of employment; that he is loyal, and will fight for his country, although she has often been but a stepmother to him; he is driven from his home; his goods plundered and fired; himself mutilated and hung."[29] The challenge facing the North, she argued, was putting down the rebellion North as well as South, and welcoming the freedmen as well as the Irish. Unlike other women writers, Cooke refused to elide the persistent prejudice of the North, even if it revealed the North's splintered unity.

Cooke argued that women's duty lay in taking care of the freedmen—who, though different from the Irish—were needy in a familiar childlike way. The freedmen had certain advantages over the Irish, she wrote, employing common racial stereotypes even as she imagined she was giving praise. Blacks, she wrote, were "irrepressible and joyous . . . full of comicality and drollery; of fun, jeers, jokes, yahyas, and merriment; and this element will be needed in our midst to temper our puritan and national seriousness." What may be more significant, however, is that in her view the freedmen were naturally self-segregating: "He is not ambitious, he likes to serve those who treat him kindly, and seeks no *social* equality, as do the Irish, whatever position they may hold."[30] The freedman was, she argued, ultimately like women in many ways, dependent, loving, and naive: "[I]n his wild but loving soul . . . the feminine element of passion generally predominates over sustained virile strength." Women, Cooke added, have thus a particularly significant role in opening the way for the freedmen. "Our women can do much," she wrote, "for men are widely severed in opinion; and the social element, women's true and noble sphere, must be made available to bring about a better feeling."[31]

Cooke ascribed the lack of unity in 1863 to men, giving women the moral high ground both in reasserting that unity and in overcoming the problems of racial prejudice in the North. Her solution, however, was much like Stowe's and eventually Child's (in her *Freedmen's Book*, to be discussed later): African Americans must learn middle-class values with a Protestant work ethic, and they must not aspire to social equality (or, by implication, to intermarriage). The tenor of the discussion revealed the tension evident in the antislavery community of women writers. Few had looked forward to the problems inherent in the end of slavery, and those problems led both to a further splintering and to a common unease.

A Shifting Subject: African American Men

During the 1850s and the early years of the war, antislavery writers most often focused on the evils confronting slave women rather than men. Uncle Tom, a notable exception, was drawn as feminine and passionless. More typically, Fanny Kemble's attention was most captured by the plight of childbearing women whose physical state was weakened by unremitting labor. By midwar, reflecting yet another shift in those years and a widening rift in the ways women wrote about women's work in wartime, many young writers took up the subject of African American men, trying to "make a place" for them but at the same time revealing their covert anxiety about sexual unions between white women and black men.[32]

This is not to say that writing about women across race lines disappeared. Two prose poems, both published in the *Continental Monthly* in 1863, demonstrate the continuing power of cross-racial gender bonding at least for white women at midwar. Yet the politics revealed in the poems are in some sense remarkably dissimilar despite their adherence to a common theme. The differences between them suggest the varying extent to which white women were willing to imagine social equality in a world after slavery.

Martha W. Cooke's "The Lady and Her Slave" implies in the title alone the class lines that will continue to separate two subjects already divided by race and experience. The poem is initially told from the perspective of the slave, who on her deathbed reveals to her mistress that they are sisters, and furthermore that the white woman's husband has raped her, and is the father of the girl child she has born.

The slave's account of the rape is tortured and remarkably angry and frank: "He came at midnight to my hut—abhorrent to my sense— / Force—threats of shame—foul violence—a slave has no defense!" Yet her description of her emotions is perhaps even more revealing: "Wronged—

soiled—and outraged—sick at heart—what right had I to feel? / He deemed his chattel honored,—God! how brain and senses reel!" Wronged by master and mistress (who had questioned her disapprovingly about the father of her then unborn child), the slave is given the space to express her anger but has still been delicate enough to wait to tell her mistress until her master is dead. If this woman is able to secure her child's freedom by telling her story, Cooke still draws the "lady" as the heroine of the piece when she recognizes her wrong and frees her slaves.

The second of the two poems demonstrates a different relationship between the two women, and gives a more equal status to the slave mother. In "The Two Southern Mothers," Isabella MacFarlane tells the story of the death of a Confederate soldier and the grief of his mother. "Woful mother!" she wrote, "who can borrow / Words to paint her frantic sorrow?" But MacFarlane then suggests that the reader's sympathy, if not entirely misplaced, should really be extended to the bereaved mother's slave. This other Southern mother is frank with her anger, if generous in forgiving her mistress. "As she mourned her slaughtered brave," MacFarlane wrote of the Confederate mother, "Came and spake her aged slave, / Came and spake with solemn brow: / Missis, we is even, now." The implicit irony lies in the "aged slave's" generosity in her accounting: the Confederate mother loses one child, while she has "lost" ten, all sold. The slave mother, now in the position of personal power, can express both her benevolence (in forgiving) and her righteous anger: "Thus she spoke, that sable mother; / Shuddering, quailed and crouched the other, / Yea! although it tarry long, / PAYMENT SHALL BE MADE FOR WRONG!" The poem reverses the image of the crouching slave and generous white lady in the antislavery emblem: here the white mother "quails" and "crouche[s]" at the feet of the African American mother. If this is a more just portrayal, there is also fear here: the readers will be among those who would "quail," unless they actively identify with the slave mother. To do so would require a leap of faith, out of the racial prejudice so pervasive in the North.[33]

The work of antislavery writers on African American men was equally splintered by the politics and fears of the writers. Two writers—Davis and Alcott—took up the question of interracial desire and sexuality during the war, going right to the center of much of white men's building anxiety. In her story "John Lamar," Rebecca Harding Davis describes the dawning of the male slave's manhood as an uncontrollable and understandable but dangerous moment, revealing her own buried worry that freedmen would think that they did not have to "choose a wife from [their] own color now." She was only one of a handful of white women expressing these anxieties publicly. Alcott, another of the few women to clearly address the issues of interracial sexuality and intermarriage during the war, described such possibilities in a more positive light in her stories. Keeping the course of the war pointed in a positive direction was the purpose of many women writers; they were likely responding to the racial fears of their communities (and themselves) by leaving the future's slippery questions aside.

Significantly, Davis and particularly Alcott also reflected another shift in the writing on antislavery. With the arming of African American men, and the emancipation of the slaves on the South Sea Islands at least, the questions facing the antislavery community changed significantly. As Stowe revealed in her letter to the editor noted above, "What Is to Be Done with Them?," whites became increasing concerned about African Americans' ability to support themselves in freedom. Given the conventions of gender in the mid-nineteenth century, this concern translated into questions about African American manhood. Many of the antislavery stories and narratives of the mid- to late war took up this question by focusing greater attention on African American men. The characters in these stories are most often—and not surprisingly, considering the political work they were meant to do—honest, hardworking, and self-segregating.

A few stories use the degradation of childlike or child slaves to argue that a war fought to improve their condition would be morally justified. Typically the objects of compassion are drawn as repugnant, perhaps to minimize their possible sexuality. Mattie Griffiths's "Ratie: The True Story of a Hunchback" and Rebecca Harding Davis's "Blind Tom," both published in November 1862, feature deformed African American children who have talents that lead Southern whites to exploit them. Griffiths and Davis employ the stereotyped language of antebellum fiction to describe their protagonists, whom they claim to be authentic. Ratie is "a hunchback and a dwarf, with an ugly black face"; Tom is "as repugnant an object as the lizards in the neighboring swamp," of "the lowest negro type."[34] The reader is to understand that even the lowest and most unattractive humans have something of God in them and are thus worthy of compassion. Yet the language reinscribes the concept of the racial other and maintains the position of author as benevolently responding to even this repulsive literary—or actual—object.

Griffiths and Davis emphasize the pain and sorrow that mark these lives. Both Ratie and Tom are oppressed by Southern whites, who, though fond of both children, use them as objects for their own purposes: Ratie "was much liked by all the family," and Tom "through his very helplessness, came to be a sort of pet in the family."[35] When Ratie's singing talent is discovered by a passerby who begs to buy her, the family sells her. With dignity but sadness, Ratie consoles her many friends (including whites) and goes off to New Orleans. There she dies of homesickness. Tom, by contrast, is not sold but displayed. His musical talent is the piano, which he plays by instinct. "I heard him sometime in 1860," Davis wrote, giving the story a ring of veracity. The narrator is struck by the sad little airs Tom played when no one was watching. "Some beautiful caged spirit," she wrote, "one could not but know, struggled for breath under that brutal form and idiotic brain. I wonder when it will be free. Not in this life: the bars are too heavy."[36]

These stories have clear didactic purposes. Blind Tom cannot be helped, Davis asserts; "all the war is between you." But that does not relieve the reader of the necessity for compassion, because "in your own kitchen, in your own back-alley, there are spirits as beautiful, caged in forms as bestial, that you *could* set free, if you pleased." "Don't call it bad taste in me to speak of them," she adds, "You know they are more to be pitied than Tom,—for they are dumb."[37] If positive in tone and message—if not in her use of demeaning stereotypes—Davis's work overlooks African Americans in the North who were *not* unable to speak publicly for themselves, among them Harriet Jacobs and Frances Harper, and she offers as white women's work a kind of paternalism: the setting free of Northern African Americans. She also, most clearly, describes African Americans as "caged" by their "bestial forms," reinscribing a racism that could see beauty only in whiteness.

Yet in both cases these stories ironically functioned as progressive politics in the antislavery community, reinforcing the work that white women could and should do to end racial prejudice and slavery. Lydia Maria Child cited Griffiths's purpose—of demonstrating the moral worth of even the most unlikely slave—in a letter she wrote to her friend praising the story. She knew its political potential and wanted more like it. "I wish you would illustrate in a story," she added, "the kindness, devotion and religious trust of some old slave you have known." For her the political thrust of Griffiths's writing was clear: "The great variety of new openings for pleading the cause of our poor oppressed slaves, and the many proofs that the people are really beginning to understand the subject at last, go far toward reconciling me to all the horrors of this war. It needed an earthquake to shake down the walls of prejudice and let in the light into dark places."[38] Griffiths was credited with shining some of the light, even as she denigrated her subject in order better to exalt it.

In all her writings, Davis meant to suggest the essential murkiness of the war, and she promulgated a complex understanding of the South and the costs of slavery. In so doing she generally went further than other writers in allowing for unease and anxiety to exist alongside direct forceful political messages. At the same time, however, she continued to use stock portraits of enslaved African Americans in degrading positions: if "white" was complicated, "black" was not. One month after "Blind Tom" was published in the *Atlantic Monthly*, she followed with "John Lamar," a story meant to suggest that the war was far from a simple struggle of good against evil. Lamar's slave Ben is worthy of justice, but he is not the kind, devoted, and religious character Child wants to see. An initially trustworthy slave who has been planning to aid his captured Rebel master to escape, Ben is persuaded by an abolitionist guard to take his freedom. Instead of aiding his master he kills him and flees north. Yet the culprit in the story is not Ben—whose brutal mind cannot ultimately comprehend the immorality of the act he commits—nor the master, who is paternal with Ben and forgives him even as he lies dying. Rather, the villain is the abolitionist, who has "enlisted to free the Uncle Tom's, and carry vengeance to the Legree" and who has projected these characters onto Ben and his master.

Here, as elsewhere in the story, Davis stops to remind her readers of the similarities between themselves and Ben, yet with the sense of difference always there at the same time. "There was a pain in [Ben's] head," she describes, as he looked north toward freedom. "[H]is nerves grew cold and rigid, as yours do when something wrings your heart sharply: for there are nerves in these black carcasses, thicker, more quickly stung to madness than yours."[39] "These black carcasses" are touched with humanity but are related to animals. The war will end slavery, but it will not end due to fanaticism, but rather to justice even to those of a lower order.

Ben's master dies with biblical phrases on his lips and reproach in his eyes. The ex-slave now has a new sense of manhood—and brutality. The story's moral is expressed by the abolitionist, who reconsiders his false dichotomy of good and evil. This act of reconsidering is what Davis wants of the reader. The desperate unfairness of both trampled lives—African American and white—strikes the repentant abolitionist, and "the war, which had become a daily business, stood suddenly before him in all its terrible meaning." Repeating Stowe's, Child's, and clearly Davis's belief, he mutters, "The day of the Lord is nigh, . . . and who can abide it?"[40]

In Alcott's stories of race and of war, there is less of this subtlety and interior conflict.[41] Significantly, Alcott's African American male characters are not repugnant but physically beautiful, suggesting a possibility for interracial sexual interest (rather than anxiety) that was foreign to most writings by women at midwar. More familiar metaphors of antebellum antislavery writing were suggested as well as challenged. In "M. L.," "An Hour," and most significantly "My Contraband" (later called "The Brothers"), heroic men and generous women draw closer because of their love, and thus in some way solve what Alcott sees as the central problem: racial prejudice. All three stories were published in the Boston *Commonwealth* along with Alcott's later famous set of sketches on her Washington nursing experience, "Hospital Sketches."

"M. L.," written before the war but never accepted for publication because of its antislavery (and radical) theme, fits the late war mood, if not the expectations of its readers. In depicting interracial romance and marriage Alcott went further than any other woman writer at that time, laying the groundwork for postwar explorations of the same theme. Yet she still hedged her bets. The energy in her African American characters comes from their white fathers, a familiar motif in antislavery literature. Paul Frere, the African American lover in "M. L.," "passes" for white and has established himself as a music teacher in, but not of, an aristocratic community. He is hardworking and proud but not grasping and never presuming; the first signs of love come from a young white woman, who has rejected many other suitors until she meets Paul Frere, the quintessential image of the self-made man.

Frere is thus the image of righteous manhood, and unlike many of his literary forebears, he is not first demeaned by a damaging physical description. His face is "pale bronze" with "black locks" that "streaked an ample forehead, black brows arched finely over southern eyes as full of softness as of fire." His pain and the history of his oppression "was the secret charm he owned, this giving him the simplicity that dignified his manner, the sincerity that won in his address; this proved the supremacy of character over culture, opulence and rank, and made him what he was—a man to command respect and confidence and love." In addition, he has a great love and respect for women; it is his white sister who has given him his freedom.[42] He is, literally, a "brother" (a *frère*) to white (abolitionist) women.[43]

He is also an ideal husband. This, then, is a new African American character, and the love between him and his white fiancée cannot be denied. Accepting the scorn of her community gracefully, she marries Paul Frere for the worthiness of his character and thereby wins Alcott's—and, Alcott hoped, the reader's—praise in following the dictates of her conscience and not her culture.

Paul Frere returns in the image of Robert Dane, or "Bob," the escaped slave in Alcott's "My Contraband," and it is here that the manhood of African American soldiers is celebrated in its most complete version. "Bob," like Paul, is saved by a beneficent white woman. He is literally given a new name—and a new manly identity—by nurse Dane, the narrator, who discourages him from killing his white Confederate brother for stealing and raping his wife. It is love for that wife that turns Robert from his murderous purpose, "for when all other means of salvation failed, a spark of this vital fire softened the man's iron will until a woman's hand could bend it."[44] Instead of killing his half-brother, he will go on to face him in combat at Fort Wagner. Here, where Colonel Robert Shaw was immortalized by the antislavery community as the white leader of a regiment of brave African American soldiers, Robert faces and is fatally wounded by his brother. His compatriot, a freedman from Boston, kills Robert's brother and risks his own life to carry Robert to safety, for, he tells the narrator, "we boys always stan' by one another."

By setting Robert within a context familiar to her readers—"Every one knows the story of the attack on Fort Wagner"—and mentioning Robert Shaw's often eulogized story in passing, Alcott legitimized Robert and his struggle while personalizing the incident itself. She sought to persuade the doubtful reader of the African American's essential worthiness by including him in her vision of the appropriate future when the "fight" is won: "The future must show how well that fight was fought; for though Fort Wagner still defies us, public prejudice is down; and through the cannonsmoke of that black night the manhood of the colored race shines before many eyes that would not see, rings in many ears that would not hear, wins many hearts that would not hitherto believe."[45] The reader, Alcott thus assumed, does believe—and the "fight" is against more than just the South; it is also against racial prejudice.

As with the other two stories, the sexual attraction between whites and African Americans is the central tension of "An Hour." Here is a story of an aborted slave insurrection—aborted because of the unexpressed love between a mulatto slave woman and the young master who refuses to own or exploit her. In this case, however, if the appropriately named master, "Gabriel," saves his white stepmother and half-sisters, he himself is saved by the beautiful slave Milly. In this story Alcott turned again to the power of love as a motivator, and of whites as the well-meaning saviors of African Americans. She thus attempted to soothe possibly frightened readers, allowing them to feel their own benevolent and continuing power even while she suggested a new kind of equality based on love.[46]

Younger writers like Davis and Alcott portrayed new dangers and pleasures in a society that freed its slaves. If at first authors tried to convince the reader of the moral necessity to call for an end to slavery, by the last two years of war women writers were suggesting the positive good that African Americans could offer to a postemancipation society. Although few blacks would go as far as Alcott implied in her stories, their message of benevolent whites connecting with moral blacks grew more appealing as her status in the literary community rose.

What Will We Do with the Negro? Wartime Strategies for Reconstruction

In the last years of war, abolitionist women writers offered visions of a reunited country reconstructed by love and goodwill—if the love did not, in general, result in marriage. Connection between the races would emerge naturally, out of common needs and white generosity. Largely, however, the races would live happily separate, content with sharing the opportunities of capitalism. This dramatizing of the future, complete with its racial fantasy of comfortable hierarchy and social segregation, seemed drawn specifically to ease the expressed fears of many white Northerners.

Most writers suggested that the distance between postemancipation blacks and whites would be based more on class and social status than geography. In Emily C. Pearson's 1864 novel *The Poor White; or, The Rebel Conscript*, the answer to the question of African American status is clear: the main African American character, Trolo, is a self-made man, like Alcott's Paul Frere, and will live on in his cabin in the Dismal Swamp far from whites. In other stories and novels with prominent African American characters, this premise is more explicit (and racist): they will work in some menial position, for which they are deemed particularly fitted. In Jane G. Austin's 1864 novel *Dora Darling*, for example, young Dora's faithful companion will live in a house provided for him, where he will garden happily for the white families nearby just as he did when he was a slave. Dora, even at twelve the epitome of the benevolent white woman of antislavery literature, emphasizes his childlike dependence: "But we shall always take care of him, of course," she writes to a friend.[47]

Some antislavery women asked the same questions about postwar life for freed slaves and answered them with action: they worked at home in freedmen's aid societies and they went to the South Sea Islands and began the experiment of Reconstruction. A few of these activists supplemented their work with moral suasion through writing about the experience. By persuading their home communities of the worthiness of their experiment and the freedpeople, they hoped to excite further support for, and ease fears of, total emancipation.

Some of the most significant activism involved teaching on the South Sea Islands, but many more women helped by providing food and clothing for freedmen's aid societies. Lydia Maria Child joined in this effort early, hearing with pleasure that hers was the *first* box of supplies to arrive at Fort Monroe for the use of fugitive slaves. Writing to Francis Shaw in January 1862, Child expressed her eagerness to be of help. "My interest in the 'contrabands,' everywhere, is exceedingly great," she wrote, "and at this crisis, I feel that every one ought to be willing to do their utmost."[48] This interest led to her concern over the exploitation of the contrabands. "The 'contrabands' ought to be employed," she told Shaw, "on such terms that the more they *do* the more *money* they get. I wish white people could get rid of the idea that they must manage *for* them."[49] Child called the Boston Educational Commission's work in sending teachers to Port Royal one of the "green spots in our blood-red landscape." "I shall do all I can for it," she wrote to Sarah Shaw, the mother of the soon-to-be martyred Robert.[50]

Other women writers joined in the chorus by lauding the efforts on behalf of contrabands and freedpeople. In 1864 Alcott reprinted in the Boston *Commonwealth* the grateful letters of African American soldiers to their teachers. "To any who find time heavy on their hands, who have a prejudice to conquer, or who long to help on the great transition, we would say become a teacher in the Readville barracks and earn a lasting satisfaction through the duties and pleasures of a just work generously performed," she wrote in conclusion.[51] These efforts had their detractors, however. The Democratic press hinted that women had gone to flirt with the officers in "a manner not consistent with morality," prompting the editor of the *Continental Monthly* to launch an angry defense of the women who went south to Port Royal. "Florence Nightingale," the editor argued, "undertook nothing nobler."[52]

Two major accounts of the Port Royal experiment written by women who had gone there to observe or to teach appeared during the war. The first, Austa French's *Slavery in South Carolina and the Ex-Slaves; or, The Port Royal Mission*, appeared in 1862. French went with her husband, the Reverend Mansfield French, to aid him in his efforts on behalf of the American Missionary Association. Though one of her colleagues called her "cracked," and her African American driver was known to have a chuckle at her expense, French maintained her evangelistic zeal in the experiment.[53] Her book, written in the style of a rousing sermon, focuses on the oppressions that the Sea Island slaves had undergone and functions as a call for emancipation. The other major work, "Life in the Sea Islands," a series of articles written by Charlotte Forten in 1864, was published first in the

Liberator and later that year in the *Atlantic*. Forten's pieces gracefully emphasize the dignity and ability of the slaves, whom she compares favorably to New Englanders. Her articles clearly demonstrate her belief both in the justice of their liberation and their positive contributions to national life.

The accounts reveal two entirely different perspectives on antislavery literature and politics. Like Kemble, French pays a great deal of attention to the plight of the slave women, although the question of manhood also looms large. Forten, on the other hand, seems more concerned with describing the bravery and competence of African American men, now donning the blue uniforms of Union soldiers in large numbers. French more clearly reflects the concerns of the early war years, Forten those of the later.

French explained that *Slavery in South Carolina* was written quickly to inspire others to equally great efforts. "Well intentioned, but faultering [*sic*] measures will not answer, now; none but the strongest, sternest, unselfishest."[54] Her work was specifically meant for women. "Something must arouse the ladies of the North," she explained, "for if we can get the strong influence at the fireside right, all will soon be done." The sweeping, evangelical quality of her prose was designed for this purpose: "The object in this writing, and in the cuts, is to make deep, vivid impressions."[55]

French's primary interest seems to be the loss of manhood, both white and African American. By manhood she means self-respect, self-control, and self-realization. "The direst evil slavery has brought upon the North is not the thousands of millions it has, and will cost, not the suffering, not even the glorious deaths of the noblest, bravest, dearest, officers and men," she claims. "No. It is IN THE LOSS OF MANHOOD—of free, noble, honest outspeaking. This is the dire, dire loss."[56]

Yet French lingers longer on the trials borne by slave women. Here she describes some of the most despicable crimes—like pregnant women beaten, buried up to their necks, and left for hours—of which the book is full. "Slavery, has been dignified as an awful sin long enough. It ought to be treated as it is, as the most despicable, of all meannesses," she writes.[57] It was field work, however, that destroyed the quality of life for slave families. "There is not a spot of the globe," French claims, "where woman toils equally with man in the field, and they live in a civilized manner. It is impossible, utterly so."[58] Although field work left slave women unable to clean their cabins or clothes, or to adequately prepare the food for their families, it did not leave them unwomanly: "Here, you will see woman uncultivated in some respects, it is true, but, she is woman." Furthermore, French argues elsewhere, slave women maintained a "heart chastity" despite their sexual victimization. "The fact is, these women have not parted with true delicacy, true virtue. That is evident, whatever they have suf-fered."[59] Her emphasis on women and field work, read in the context of the times, chastises the government for forcing women to persist in this work despite their newly achieved freedom. Their new lives should include, she believes, some of white women's privileges.[60]

French implies that unlike African American or white women, neither of whom have lost their womanhood, white men, the perpetrators of slav-ery, have suffered the loss of their manhood, and African American men have been robbed of theirs. Yet if slave women are womanly, they still need direction, especially where cleanliness is concerned. At one point, French describes how she ordered a slave woman worried about getting rations and tending her child to wash her dying nephew. Here French's "benev-olence" crosses the line into imperious condescension. "We said to the poor woman, 'We pity you more than we blame you. We keep our sick little ones as clean as this dear little one is now; but we do not have to work in the field as you do. Still, you want to learn to do things right, don't .you?'"[61] White women, she suggests, know how to do things right, and not only because of their improved circumstances.

In her position as observer, and with her expressed purpose as inspira-tion, French uses the Sea Island slaves as evidence to assign characteristics to the African race writ large. In so doing she reinforces stereotypes. In advancing moral arguments for the end of slavery, she describes slaves as victims dependent on whites to aid them. While advancing economic arguments for the end of slavery she depicts freedpeople as spendthrifts: "The Colored, in freedom, will not hoard but spend money. They will dress, and ride, in good style. . . . Imagine the trade set in motion the moment they get wages. What brisk market for everything conceivable."[62]

Charlotte Forten, by contrast, describes Sea Island slaves as hardy agents in their own destiny, even as she explicitly records the oppression they had to endure. The child of a long tradition of free Philadelphia African Americans, Forten came to the islands for a different purpose than French; her articles are more of a travel diary than an impassioned sermon. She is far more respectful toward her subjects. They are men, women, and chil-dren, not "the Colored." Even as she shies away from some of their more unfamiliar cultural practices like the "shout," a spiritual dance of the Sea Island slaves, she claims these people for her own, even going so far as to adopt their expressive ways of speaking. In describing her joy at meeting an old friend on the islands, Forten writes, it was " 'too much, too much,' as the people here say, when they are very much in earnest."[63]

Forten's relationship with the subjects of her narrative are interactive.

She comes to teach the slaves how to read; they offer her something equally valuable in return: a sense of purpose. "My heart sings a song of thanksgiving," she exclaims at the end of her second essay, "at the thought that even I am permitted to do something for a long-abused race, and aid in promoting a higher, holier, and happier life on the Sea Islands."[64] Her journal, written at the same time but published after her death, echoes this sense of accomplishment and mission.[65]

"Life in the Sea Islands" also challenges the stereotypes that French employed in *Slavery in South Carolina*. In describing Cupid, who acts as Forten and her companion's "right-hand man," Forten tempers a negative description with a respectful and almost tender approval: "The face nearly black, very ugly, but with the shrewdest expression I ever saw, and the brightest, most humourous twinkle in the eyes. . . . One glance at Cupid's face, showed that he was not a person to be imposed upon, and that he was abundantly able to take care of himself, as well as of us."[66] Forten praises the music, manners, and style of the Sea Island residents, and marvels at the excitement shown by old and young about learning. "I never before saw children so eager to learn," she exclaims, "although I had had several years' experience in New England schools."[67] Forten also directly challenges the notion that African Americans are "inferior" in any way: "One cannot believe that the haughty Anglo-Saxon race, after centuries of such an experience as these people have had, would be very much superior to them. And one's indignation increases against those who, North as well as South, taunt the colored race with inferiority while they themselves use every means in their power to crush and degrade them, denying them every right and privilege, closing against them every avenue of elevation and improvement." It is racism and degradation, not lack of talent, that impedes "the colored race," Forten argues.[68]

In describing the ability, competence, and bravery of the African American men setting off to fight for their newly adopted country, Forten gives dignity to their position and draws attention to their sacrifice. Like others in her community, she was taken with Colonel Robert Shaw and Colonel Thomas Higginson, both of whom commanded African American forces. Forten and her companions watched Shaw's regiment march on dress parade shortly before the attack on Fort Wagner, and she remarked on its "remarkably fine and manly appearance." Nursing the wounded soldiers of the Massachusetts Fifty-fourth after the battle, she sewed up the holes in their uniforms, some of which had been torn to pieces. Despite their losses, they still maintained a "brave, cheerful spirit." "Already, they, and the regiments here, as well, have shown that true manhood has no limitations of color."[69]

A comparison of the politics of Austa French and Charlotte Forten reveals the divergent sensibilities within the antislavery community generally. While both clearly were well meaning and active in their desire to aid the freedpeople, French was paternalistic and managerial, while Forten was eager to learn from as well as to teach the contraband. French's work, like that of the narratives written by white women in the early part of the war, perpetuated stereotypes that Charlotte Forten challenged. Above all, French's involvement seemed to confirm her sense of racial order, while Forten's moved her to a new understanding.

"WITH MALICE TOWARD NONE; with charity for all, with firmness in the right, as God gives us to see the right, let us strive on to finish the work we are in," said Abraham Lincoln in his famous second inaugural on March 4, 1864. Many observers in the century and a half since have noted the deeply religious sensibility that pervades this speech; fewer have noted the extent to which Lincoln's words represent a vindication of the views of women antislavery writers, who framed the war in the moral terms the president had initially resisted. "Fondly we do hope—fervently we do pray—that this mighty scourge of war may speedily pass away," Lincoln said. "Yet if God wills that it continue, until all the wealth piled by the bond-man's two hundred and fifty years of unrequited toil shall be sunk, and until every drop of blood drawn with the lash, shall be paid by another drawn with the sword, as was said three thousand years ago, so still it must be said 'the judgments of the Lord, are true and righteous altogether.'" In the end, the vagaries of electoral politics did not prevent Lincoln from seeing the same "hand of God in the tempest" that Lydia Maria Child did.

The last years of war were difficult for Lydia Maria Child. Although she was enthusiastic about the work being done on the Sea Islands, and elated at full emancipation in Maryland, the treatment of the contrabands still filled her with bitterness. "The state of the country has never weighed so heavily upon *me*, as it does this Spring," she wrote another antislavery advocate in 1864. "I get more and more sensitive about the cruelties and the sufferings; and the mean conduct of the government toward the negroes fills me with shame. I think we shall ultimately be saved as a nation; but I have painful doubts whether we are *worth* saving."[70] As she was throughout the war, Child remained an excellent litmus test for the antislavery women writers as it ended. Ahead of her generation in terms of racial prejudice (although certainly not free from it) and critical of Union self-congratulation, she was reflective about her community in equally significant ways.[71]

One of Child's last literary projects on behalf of African Americans, *The Freedmen's Book*, written near the end of the war and published shortly thereafter, demonstrates and sums up some of the most salient themes of women's writing on slavery during the war years. As usual, Child was clear about the book's political purposes from the beginning. Unlike any of her earlier writing, it was assembled specifically for the freedpeople, not for whites. Noting the absence of *"suitable"* reading, Child wished to provide a compilation of short stories, essays, hymns, poems, and biographies for the freedpeople, to give them a sense of pride in their own history as well as some pointers for their future. She wanted it "to have a *good moral* effect, and an *encouraging* effect." All profits from the book—which was meant to be sold at a low price—would go to buy books for the freedpeople's schools.[72]

The book included excerpts from Harriet Jacob's *Incidents in the Life of a Slave Girl*, Harriet Beecher Stowe's *Uncle Tom's Cabin*, Charlotte Forten's "Life on the Sea Islands," all of Mattie Griffiths's short story "Ratie," and Frances E. Watkins's poems "Ethiopia," "Bury Me in a Free Land," and "The President's Proclamation" and her prose piece "The Air of Freedom." It claimed a large space for the contributions of women antislavery writers, implying their significant influence on the war's outcome. At the same time, a note of patronizing benevolence crept in, as Child's simplistic essays condescended to their subjects. In essays on animals (equating slaves to badly treated oxen!), health, the training of children, and freedom, Child sounded an all too familiar note of the most negative kind of maternalism, which assumed a childlike audience, even as it urged freedmen not to "rebel, but stand up for your rights 'in a manly way.'"[73]

Child also included a poem, "John Brown and the Colored Child," about the man who had refired her own enthusiasm. Brown was a common subject, especially in the war's waning years. Charlotte Forten taught the popular song "John Brown's Body" to her young charges at her school on the Sea Islands, and her companion, Laura Towne, "told them the story of the brave old man who had died for them."[74] Gail Hamilton, in her book of essays published in 1865, *Sketches and Skirmishes*, also recalled the raid on Harpers Ferry. Now, she wrote, "a hundred thousand men, imbued with John Brown's spirit, and armed by the law which he broke, march past his gallows-tree, and Freedom is avenged. He wrought ill for a noble cause....

But the good that he did lives after him, and the evil is interred with his bones."[75]

Despite this sense of the good that John Brown did, Lydia Maria Child shared with others a feeling that the war, for all its desperate suffering, had not accomplished the end of racism. Even the Emancipation Proclamation was not carried out in the proper spirit. Child never felt any sustained confidence in the government, and thus could never truly celebrate the end of slavery. She wrote sadly in August 1865 to Colonel Shaw's grieving mother:

> If I had been told, thirty years ago, that Slavery would be abolished in my day, I should have anticipated such enthusiastic joy as would have set me half crazy. But in reality I have felt no enthusiasm, no exhilaration. I have been thankful to God for the wondrous change; but, what with the frightful expenditure of blood; and emancipation's having been forced upon us by *necessity*, instead of proceeding from the repentance of the nation; and the shameful want of protection to the freedmen since they have been emancipated; there has been no opportunity for any out-gushing of joy and exultation.[76]

Many of Child's colleagues, and Child herself, with the novel *The Romance of the Republic* in 1867, went on to attack the racism of the North and the South during Reconstruction. Others in the postwar period recounted their experiences during the war or wrote about other heroic women, African American and white, who had contributed to ending slavery, if not racism.

Yet during the war years, women writers, largely entirely separate from the antislavery activists, described the war more as an opportunity and even an adventure than as moral struggle. For these women, the war opened up new space for *them*, space where they could imagine a new kind of woman and a new kind of work. These women offered Florence Nightingale as their model, trying to create unity behind an English, and thus perhaps more conventionally acceptable, figure. Yet their work, while engaged in a kind of effort toward unity, revealed further the schisms of the mid- and late war: here were women who explicitly rejected the limits of separate sphere ideology altogether, either by imagining it gone or by entering directly into male spaces of hospital, camp, and occasionally even battlefield.

'Tis woman's part of glory

To shroud the pulseless clay.

From which the soul of bravery

Has proudly soared away.

That lofty life, perchance, hath won

A plaudit from the years;

But dimmed existence mourns its sun,

And woman's part are tears.

—Sarah E. Carnnshall,

Peterson's Magazine (March 1864)

{ CHAPTER SIX }

Woman's Part of Glory
Love, Death, and Work in Women's Writing, 1863–1865

IN HER 1896 autobiography, *Chapters from a Life*, Elizabeth Stuart Phelps recalls the moment when she first heard the nation was at war. It was a gray day in April, and in the midst of a frightening lesson, she heard the tinkle of laughter. A young and pretty girl whirled a newspaper above her head and, dancing around the room, cried happily, "War's begun! *War's begun!*" With horror an older girl remonstrated, "Oh, how *can* you?" putting her hand over the younger girl's lips and saying, "Hush, hush, *hush!*"[1]

Phelps's recollection illuminates the schism in Northern white women's writing that, while it widened throughout the war, became significant after 1863. On the one hand was excitement at the war's opportunities and romance, embodied in the young and pretty girl; on the other was a sense of the war's great and lasting tragedy, which an older girl immediately recognized. Even in Phelps's own work, which began in earnest with a war story in January 1864, there is some sense of this ambivalence, although she was generally far more apt to express the pain of war than to celebrate its opportunities.[2]

Phelps is also emblematic of a younger generation whose literary and intellectual life was shaped by the crucial issues that the war uncovered. "At this time," Phelps said later of the war's beginning, "I had no interest at all in any especial movement for the peculiar needs of woman as a class." It took the war's killing scythe to cut away her "old ideas of womanhood," which she "had not to any important extent begun to resent."[3] One result was that Phelps took up the concerns of workingwomen after the war's end, an interest that derived from a confluence of the war's effect on women, the writing of contemporaries like Davis, and her own investigation into the collapse of the Pemberton mill in Lawrence, Massachusetts, which buried dozens of working girls alive.[4]

What Phelps did not recognize, and could not have represented, however, were the barriers to active participation that many women discovered in the course of their war work. These issues were also explored in the late war years by a group of women who continued to ask and answer the pressing early war question of "What Can Woman Do?" The narratives of nurses and United States Sanitary Commission (USSC) workers on the field suggest the contributions that women were making and the ways in which those contributions were diminished and their efforts thwarted by both men and institutional bureaucracy.

These three responses to the war—a sense of challenge, excitement, and opportunity; grief and pain over rising numbers of war dead; and pride in accomplishments made and resistance overcome in work for the wounded—overlapped and coincided late in the war. Writing by white women increased significantly in these years, as more participated in a struggle to define the meaning of the war and women's place within it. In some sense this outpouring was understandable, given the needs of a publishing industry short on male writers. Yet it might also be explained as an effort to take the war's meaning and direction away from the freed slave in the wake of the Emancipation Proclamation. It may have been a way, perhaps, to assert the war as a white woman's war, much in the way Northern men had claimed it as a white man's war in the first years of the conflict.[5]

Elizabeth Stuart Phelps (Ward) (1844–1911). Phelps began her career by writing Civil War fiction and became famous with *The Gates Ajar* (1868), a novel that offered solace to the many who lost kin, but especially to women. Her reinterpretation of heaven angered ministers but appealed to readers, making her novel a major best-seller. (Photo used by permission of the Schlesinger Library, Radcliffe College.)

Woman's Place in War: Women-Nurses

By 1863 women had established their right to work for the war effort. USSC workers had gained more positive press coverage as the effects of this organization became clear. Although in most cases Sanitary Commission leaders were men, it was mainly women who carried out its objectives. Writing pamphlets describing the goals and intentions and chronicling the work of the commission was one of their tasks, and nurses and organizers used their pens in the later years of war to remind the people of their continuing needs.

The writing of nurses and sanitary workers was significant for several reasons. First, like the work of Louisa May Alcott praised by Rebecca Harding Davis ("she knows hospitals"), its ring of authenticity gave such writing credibility and interest. Second, it documented popular resistance to women's intervention directly into public life. Women could do only what it was deemed appropriate that they should do, unless they fought for the privilege in struggles that figured prominently in these writings. Third, issues of class that were already moving to the fore in the minds of social critics became clear in the narratives of women-nurses[6] and sanitary workers as they assessed the implications of women being paid for work that was defended as an extension of home. And finally, this midwar writing of women's experiences was the first wave of the many postwar narratives that constituted an effort toward a women's history of the war.

Although women "enlisted" as nurses from the opening weeks of the war in various capacities, it was not until the later years that their contributions to the war effort became both well known and culturally accepted. On the Union side alone, approximately 8,000 women worked as nurses during the Civil War. Of that number, some 3,200 were officially appointed by Dorothea Dix, who was named the Superintendent of United States Army Nurses on June 10, 1861.[7] Other women working in hospitals volunteered independently, were recruited specifically by doctors, were sent by local aid committees, came to nurse relatives, or were formerly enslaved and had fled to military camps and stayed to nurse.[8]

Nurses also came from disparate class backgrounds. Historian Susan Reverby notes that "many were working-class women—domestics, laundresses, or nurses—for whom hard physical work and even some nursing were not new experiences. Others were middle-class women who had nursed family members or neighbors, but who never had worked for wages, seen the inside of a hospital, or been responsible for the physical care of strangers."[9] Jane Woolsey, a nurse in various hospitals throughout the war, commented afterward that women-nurses "were of all sorts and came from various sources of supply," many remaining "without any clear commission or duties," all "set adrift in a hospital, eight to twenty of them, for the most part slightly educated, without training or discipline."[10] Her comments were disparaging: she exalted the well-trained elite women that she represented and indicated her disassociation with other women-nurses not of her class and status.

The duties undertaken by these nurses varied. As Elvira Powers explains in her 1866 narrative, *Hospital Pencillings*, she had "charge of the diet," covered crutches and procured pads for amputated limbs, filled petitions for furloughs and back pay, wrote letters and read to patients, organized singalongs, baked an occasional cake, arranged prints for the walls, and "tried to have something on a little stand, which should represent or bring to mind a cabinet, to make them think of home. In short, have tried to make my ward look as Miss B. expressed it, 'as if there was a woman in it.'"[11] Other tasks typically taken on by nurses included washing patients, aiding the doctor in changing dressings, and, perhaps most often recorded, speaking to dying soldiers of biblical teachings of a world to come. A few took on tasks generally reserved for doctors, including assisting at amputations or changing dressings, depending on need and the dispositions of the doctors with whom they were working.

Other nurses established themselves on and near the battlefield. Clara Barton, working outside the jurisdiction of the government, brought food to the wounded, aided fallen soldiers, and spent hours both writing to the kin of the deceased and helping relatives find out what happened to their sons, husbands, or brothers.[12] Nurses like Annie Wittenmyer helped establish special diet kitchens for the wounded who could not stomach regular army fare. Her success was so widely acknowledged that she was appointed superintendent of all army diet kitchens.[13] Mary Ann (or "Mother") Bickerdyke was renowned for her work in Cairo, Illinois; she insisted on more thorough and consistent habits of cleanliness and ordered incompetent assistants dismissed or reprimanded. It was said in jest that General Ulysses S. Grant, when approached by a disgruntled officer who complained about Bickerdyke, exclaimed: "My God, man, Mother Bickerdyke outranks everybody, even Lincoln. If you have run amuck of her I advise you to get out quickly before she has you under arrest."[14] While Grant's jest purportedly demonstrated how men deferred to powerful women, it also sought to reassure by making clear that Bickerdyke was an exceptional—and exaggerated—case. Struggle over power between men and women in the hospital was common.

Northern efforts to open the field of nursing to women began just after Fort Sumter but were consistently hindered by public opposition. Dr. Elizabeth Blackwell established a training program for nurses in New York under the auspices of the Women's Central Relief Association. When the post of superintendent was created, however, Blackwell and her sister, also a doctor, were both bypassed because of the hostility of many men toward women doctors. The sisters withdrew from their initial leadership positions in order to minimize hostility toward women working in other capacities, such as nursing. As Dr. Emily Blackwell explained in a June 1861 letter, "The jealousy of the physicians of the City [New York], and the fear of many of our leading managers lest our name should make the work unpopular if we took any prominent part became so marked that we have to a great degree withdrawn as the affair went on."[15] The services of other women doctors throughout the war were consistently rebuffed, although Dr. Esther Hill Hawks and Dr. Mary Walker found work outside official channels that ultimately brought them some recognition.[16]

Dorothea Lynde Dix imposed her own restrictions on women-nurses to the extent that she could. Dix, whose age (fifty-nine) at the outbreak of the war both gave her authority and diffused sexual anxiety, had for years worked on behalf of the insane in asylums North and South, and offered her "gratuitous" services to the government on April 20, 1861. In her capacity as superintendent, Dix acted as a gatekeeper barring those she saw as romantic young women. Her nurses were required to be "plain-looking," over thirty, and devoid of hoops, jewelry, curls, and light dresses. They were also expected to be Protestant, although a considerable number of Catholic nuns evaded her control and spent many hours nursing during the war.[17]

Some of the most famous nurses of the Civil War period—Barton, Bickerdyke, Wittenmyer—were unsanctioned by any official authority. Narratives of war nursing include many by such "unofficial" nurses: Jane Swisshelm was an unpaid volunteer; Mrs. Edmund Souder was sent by her Relief Association; and even the famous Woolsey sisters, although they ultimately made their peace with Dorothea Dix, were never formally accepted as Union nurses until after they were established in formal positions by their well-connected male friends.

The conditions confronting the various nurses differed as well. Hospitals were originally established mainly in Washington. Later, field hospital stations were built at Point Lookout, Maryland, and City Point and Brandy Station, Virginia, among other locations, as well as along the western front.[18] Even in relatively well populated locations in Washington, given the rudimentary understanding of disease and poor facilities, hospital conditions varied widely. In *Hospital Sketches* Tribulation Periwinkle (Louisa May Alcott's protagonist in her fictionalized account of nursing) compared the Hurly-Burly (Union) Hotel and the Armory Hospital in Washington. At the latter, "order, method, common sense and liberality seemed to rule in a style that did one's heart good to see; at the former, disorder, discomfort, bad management, and no visible head, reduced things to a condition which I despair of describing."[19] Yet Periwinkle (and Alcott) landed at the Hurly-Burly, and her depiction of disorder only heightened the role for women that she sought to valorize.

Whatever the condition of the Hurly-Burly, field hospitals were considerably worse. In the accounts of the battlefields at Shiloh, Fredericksburg, and Gettysburg, nurses recall scenes of incredible carnage. In one autobiographical story, Belle Z. Spencer describes nursing in a Shiloh hospital while it was being shelled and after the battle searching for her husband on the bloody battlefield.[20] At Antietam, Clara Barton leaned over a wounded soldier, felt a bullet passing through her clothes, and found that the soldier had fallen back dead from the shot.[21] In a letter to her cousin written from the battlefield at Gettysburg three days after the shooting stopped, Cornelia Hancock said simply: "[T]here are no words in the English language to express the sufferings I witnessed today." When she and her friends arrived to nurse the wounded, no one remarked on their coming or told them what to do. Without utensils or a stove Hancock made a meal of broken bread and jelly, spread on with a stick, which she distributed to the wounded. The air, heavy with "putrefaction," was difficult to breathe. "To give you some idea of the extent and numbers of the wounds," Hancock wrote, "four surgeons, none of whom were idle fifteen minutes at a time, were busy all day amputating legs and arms."[22] In those spaces, women-nurses simply assisted in any way they could—and were generally accepted without comment as another pair of hands.

Nurses also had to fight off contagious disease. Hannah Ropes, who worked at the Union Hospital, died while she was collecting her own letters and journal for publication. In a sadly ironic letter to her son, penned eleven days before her death, Ropes wrote, "I am doing my last work now. The tax upon us women who work for the love of it is tremendous when we have a new arrival of wounded. . . . [A fellow nurse] has had to go to bed, one knee refusing to walk or bend."[23] Alcott, who worked under Ropes's supervision, came close to dying of typhoid fever at the same time. Of the six nurses that made up Eudora Clark's "happy sisterhood," she recounted in 1867, she was the only one left.[24]

While nurses at the front experienced the war firsthand, women writers were informing the public about their work. After two years in which few nurses appeared in the popular press, the public discussion of women's nursing on the battlefront increasingly began to infiltrate story lines. But that wasn't the only kind of working being discussed. Following a tradition of sensational literature on women acting in adventure stories as men, a number of writers introduced fictional women soldiers and spies to the reading public. These more daring stories contrasted with continuing images of self-sacrifice back home, as women writers tested and transgressed the limits of respectability.

Women on the Fictional Battlefront

"I have enlisted for the war, you know."
—Nora Perry, "Margaret Freyer's Heart," *Harper's New Monthly Magazine* (June 1863)

"You are my ideal of a *real woman*; you are one of the best soldiers in the army I hope you'll get promoted."

"Perhaps I shall, Katie, but not in his army. Woman's promotion is not in this world. It is in a higher army that we must look for honor, because, no lesser glory can ever content us."—*Kate Morgan and Her Soldiers* (1862)

The fictional heroines of the midwar illustrate a widening gap in the understanding of the ideal response of Union women to war. If culture is, in a sense, a rehearsal for politics, distinctly different versions of political authority were enacted in these dramas. Traditional understandings of women's role in society, around which there had been a greater consensus in 1861, now persisted side by side with newer versions. If the war seemed a battlefront for the acceptance of nursing as a role particularly suited to women, Louisa May Alcott's loving and humorous Nurse Periwinkle was the first clear victory. By the end of the war the role of woman as nurse was a familiar and acceptable choice for heroines searching for an object for their energies. At the same time, outside of mainstream magazine literature came narratives telling even more "thrilling" tales of women on the battlefield itself as vivandières, soldiers, and spies. Here were the most challenging renditions of the patriotic woman.

As in Katherine Williams's "Tableaux Vivants," where an "army" of women, young and old, works together for the soldiers, many wartime women authors stressed their own "enlistment" in the war effort. Each woman must do her part, Mary Eastman advises in her prose poem about the Gettysburg heroine, Jenny Wade. Busy making bread for the troops, Wade does not flee as the battle begins. This is her duty, she claims, "for all have work to do" under "war's dark shadow." She tells the Union officer who begs her to leave, "Farewell! I stay to do my part / In this dire struggle, though my hand / Hold not a sword; my loving heart / Throbs for an undivided land."[25] As she checks her bread later, a minié ball kills her.

For some writers, it was enough that men carried the memory of them to the battlefront: this was a way to demonstrate authority but no impropriety. Louisa May Alcott suggested this aspect of woman's role in her 1864 short story "On Picket Duty." The story revolves around four Union soldiers who think and talk about their wives during a quiet spell. One remarks their fortune for both the quiet spell and the influence of good women: "Fortunate for us that we do get [the quiet spell], and have such gentle bosom guests to keep us brave and honest through the trials and temptations of a life like ours."[26] One of the soldiers, who has been posing as a Virginian, reveals that he entered the war as a Confederate and is really from Alabama. He tells his comrades that when wounded earlier in the war he was brought to a Quaker's house in Pennsylvania, where a beautiful

Virginia girl was visiting. Although they fell in love, the girl said, "I will not love what I can't respect!" He rethinks his position, writes to his father, and enlists as a private in the Federal army. "There's no treason in the camp, for I'm as fierce a Federalist as any of you now, and you may thank a woman for it," he assures his mates.[27]

This vision of women's influence implied a power and role in society not widely accepted outside the pages of women's fiction, but it denied them (except in Wade's case, since her house *was* a battlefield) a physical space at the front. Yet during the war, especially after the publication of Louisa May Alcott's "Hospital Sketches" in the Boston *Commonwealth* in May of 1863, wartime authors allowed their heroines more scope in their search for something useful to do. Nursing, although described in some stories as a choice likely to be opposed by family, was ultimately justified as a task particularly suited to women, who would bring gentleness and emotion to the bedside of the wounded and make of the hospital a home.

In art, as in life, women went to the front as nurses for a variety of reasons. For some, it was a response to grief: many a heroine went to Washington hospitals after hearing of the death of their kin in order to assuage the pain of their loss through hard work. A few other characters enlisted out of boredom or restlessness. Finally, a few were described as choosing to work for the war in this fashion because, as Alcott put it in a letter to her grandmother: "I want to help if I can."[28] Duty to the war effort meant taking on a rewarding but difficult task. Both Alcott and Belle Z. Spencer, both of whom were writing their fictionalized accounts out of their own experience at battlefront hospitals, used this scenario to explain their choices.

"I want something to do," Tribulation Periwinkle says at the beginning of Louisa May Alcott's "Hospital Sketches," reflecting a widely held sentiment.[29] A neighborhood friend suggests nursing after family members run through a list of other possible choices: writing, teaching, acting, and marriage. For other literary heroines, the choice of nursing is even more reluctantly offered and in some cases resisted. In "A Daguerreotype in Battle," Ellen Rodman "quietly made her preparations in spite of all opposition." In Rodman's story "An Angel of Mercy," a doctor asks a family friend who has enlisted as a nurse, "Is this not an imprudent step? Are you not afraid of the consequences?"[30] Leslie Walker, in "Ray Amyott," is even more explicit when her senior surgeon warns Miss Heath of the consequences of becoming a hospital nurse: "[F]or your sake, let me remind you how unusual and strange is the step you are about to take. You are exposing yourself not only to the countless disagreeablenesses of this sorrowful place, but to the smallest misconstruction from those who see you here, and the gravest censure of your friends and acquaintances. Let me beseech you to think again before you take a final resolution."[31] The heroines in these stories, of course, accept the consequences and succeed at their new-found task while winning the approval and sometimes the love of men.

While women characters in these stories typically begin their nursing careers to aid relatives, the needs of other patients cause them to widen their vision, suggesting that, for women, national needs derive from domestic ones. This is clearly the implied message of Leslie Walker's story "Ray Amyott." Walker's heroine, Margaret Heath, goes to her fiancé, who has been hospitalized, and while she is nursing him, she also soothes and aids those around him. In Spencer's "One of the Noble," a friend of the narrator loses father and brother to the war and grieves for three days, after which she goes on with her work, saying: "Can I be idle when the work is yet unfinished they died trying to accomplish? No."[32] War work offered not only an opportunity but an imperative, pulling women into national consciousness. What is propriety, these writers implicitly ask, when "the work is yet unfinished"?

Yet women are also described as driven by their desire to leave home, as was Tribulation Periwinkle. In Miss Alice Gray's provocative story "A Part of the Mission of Harper's Ferry," a Northern girl who has lost her brother, a "young quadroon girl," and a wealthy Southern belle find themselves working in the same hospital. The Yankee is acting out of grief; the quadroon girl has escaped from slavery. But the Southern girl is "wearied of the round of society, without aim of object in life, discontented and morbid. She wanted occupation, an object. A mighty struggle was going on. Might not her heart and mind here find room to live?"[33] In this great conflict she could find occupation, and if insignificant, "it was, at least, a part in the vast whole, a post near the center of influence, impossible but that she must feel its throbs."[34] This story suggests not only the Northern perception of morbidity of an elite class of white women in the South but also the allure of being "a part in the vast whole." Here the North is truly democratic, a place where disparate women can find "room to live."

These women are described as finding a satisfaction in nursing that was missing in their earlier lives. In Rodman's "An Angel of Mercy," Helen Jimpson explains her response to her new life to the doctor questioning her choice: "When I think of the silly, useless life I led—without aim and without reward—and compare it with the honorable life of labor and usefulness before me, I feel I have passed from darkness into light."[35] Nora Perry's heroine in "Margaret Freyer's Heart" would agree. When a suitor suggests to her that there are enough nurses and she is not needed, she responds, "I should be sorry to think I was not specially needed by some natural fitness for this work. I have been glad to believe that it was so. Do not, I beseech you, by a single word, try to shake this belief; for I have found in it a contentment, a relief."[36] There is a weariness with war here as well as a need for an "aim" in life, a tussle between a meaningful life centered around a perhaps too wasteful enterprise. Action to assuage the wounded is offered as a relief from passivity. Waiting has lost any appeal it might have had.

For Belle Spencer, the wife of a Union officer, nursing was a way to assuage her feelings of uselessness and anxiety while waiting for her husband during the battles of the Army of the Southwest. Her stories are mostly based on her experiences before and during the battles of Shiloh and Corinth. "A Soldier's Wife" begins when the main character's husband leaves for the battle of Shiloh, and she is left to wait in Paducah, Kentucky. Feeling strong when he leaves, she weeps afterward and then asks herself, "What shall I do?": "And the answer came so quickly that my cheek was dyed with shame," the heroine says. "What should I do, with three hospitals within sight of my window? No need to ponder long. The call of duty was loud and strong, and I obeyed it without delay."[37] Nursing in a hospital away from home and bathing the bodies of men ranging from a gruff Irishman to a young white drummer-boy was constructed by Spencer as *duty*, making the unfamiliar role not merely acceptable but virtually an obligation.

In these stories the care that women give to the wounded is portrayed as particularly significant and successful, coming as it does from the gentle hands of delicate ladies. Their gender ensures their success because of woman's essential qualities of warmth and emotion. In "A Soldier's Wife," the narrator recalls a surgeon telling her she will assuredly be helpful: "Your voice is soft, your hand light and skillful—all women's are—and I have no doubt but your eyes will be quick to see what should be done."[38] Tribulation Periwinkle asserts that wounded men particularly need the affection of a woman's nature, even strong manly souls like her favorite Virginia blacksmith, "John." At first she is shy of him because he seems so self-contained, but she sees him crying silently when his wound is being dressed and ultimately realizes his need. "I had forgotten," she says, "that the strong man might long for the gentle tendance of a woman's hands, the sympathetic magnetism of a woman's presence, as well as the feebler souls around him."[39]

Alcott's and Spencer's stories brought a kind of authority to the wartime discussion of nursing, for in their hospital renderings they legitimized both their message (that middle-class women can "enlist" as nurses without losing caste or femininity) and their medium (which can safely harbor truths for women in an imagined form). The moral of their fictional and fictionalized accounts of nursing for the reader is clear: despite possible opposition, here is something women can do well for the nation.

While nursing won gradual, if grudging, acceptance from men, other experiences of battle remained beyond the pale, giving them their "thrilling" or titillating character. Venturing onto the battlefield to look for kin or help bury the dead, for instance, was explicitly denied as an acceptable role.[40] It could, however, inspire characters to develop a maturity they had earlier lacked. The Southern character in Miss Alice Gray's "A Part of the Mission of Harper's Ferry" goes looking for the son of a friend, and the gore shocks her. The experience, she explains later, changes her: "Well, from that place of horrors I came back a woman—the morbid, discontented girl was laid to rest that night."[41] Writers like Gray seemed to argue that realism, in the form of a battlefield, cut through sentimentality (even as they used a sentimental form to do so).

More obviously, "thrilling" narratives of adventuresome women had both a prewar history and an emphatic class character.[42] Sensationalism was already a well-established fictional genre by 1861, but its new subject gave it new drama: war was the most sensational setting of all. This writing belongs to a different literary community than Phelps's, but it clearly influenced middle-class writers, like Alcott and Davis, who often wrote for disparate audiences. (Alcott herself wrote a series of thrillers under a pseudonym.)

Sensational stories of women on the battlefield appeared in greater numbers by the war's last years. The first, the anonymously published "Lady Lieutenant," concerned a woman who, through her love for her sweetheart, cross-dresses and fights by his side, becoming a "lady lieutenant" because of her battlefield valor and ability. Published in 1862, it echoes an earlier narrative written about the Mexican War in 1851, *The Female Volunteer*.[43]

Women as spies seemed to particularly capture the reader's fancy, as the numbers of spy stories written during the Civil War suggest. The idea of women, considered to be innocent, moral, and truth-telling, becoming duplicitous implied a world gone deliciously mad. Charles Wesley Alexander's 1863 "narrative" *Pauline of the Potomac* tells the "true" story of a woman who became a Federal spy. He followed this with two more short novels in pamphlet form: *Maud of the Mississippi* and *Wenona, Gen'l Sherman's Indian Spy*. A year later the anonymous *The Thrilling Adventures of Pauline Cushman*, about "Major" Pauline Cushman, an actress who played the role of a Southern sympathizer in New Orleans while collecting information for the Federal Army, was published in two parts.

Cross-dressers and other women who fought on the battlefield were more common subjects in the late years of the war. These women challenged the social order in a direct way: they and their example suggested that gender was more a matter of appearance than of existential difference. Sara Emma Edmonds's 1864 fictionalized narrative of her experiences on the battlefield dressed as a man, *Nurse and Spy* (one edition was titled *The Unsexed*), sold an impressive 175,000 copies.[44] Jane G. Austin's *Dora Darling*, about a young girl who becomes a vivandière, and Abby Longstreet's *Remy St. Remy; or, The Boy in Blue*, about a woman who cross-dresses and fights to protect her family, were published in 1864 and 1865, respectively.

All these titles are redolent of the space that the war opened up for both men and women to reimagine gender. Within these stories gender is both fluid and fixed; the characters often move from one gender to the other in a single text, from the tender, emotional, fragile woman to the stern, stalwart, unflappable man. This is no neutral androgynous character, but a hybrid, which has the best traits of both genders. While on the battlefield this woman/man gently tends to the wounded even as bullets fly around her, and yet when faced with an enemy—particularly when defending a friend—she/he is courageous, competent, and inspiring to other men.

This gender dualism is perhaps most compellingly portrayed in Elizabeth Stuart Phelps's 1865 story titled "Margaret Bronson." Most likely written as the war ended, Phelps's story uses the war to challenge and play with women's traditional roles. Here she is less concerned with the war's tragedy, which plays such a crucial part in most of her writing on the conflict. The narrator begins by reminding the reader of the nation's "bloody baptism" and apologizes for this "fresh reminder." But, she continues, "my story does not concern a battle, but a woman; and how can I help it if she lived down there on the border, so surrounded and hemmed in by conflict and combatants, by scenes of peril and blood and death, that they must necessarily interweave themselves with the controlling events of her life?"[45] Margaret Bronson is "strong-minded," the community decides, and not without reason: "People were rather dubious on the subject of a young woman who carried pistols, had no desire to marry, and was not afraid of guerrillas. It was outré, it evinced discontent with her sphere."[46] Yet Bronson cares little for their assessment, and although bequeathed slaves by her father, she frees them all after his death and works the plantation alone, with only those freedpeople who choose to stay and whom she can afford to pay. Even though she clearly loves a Union private named McGinley, she spurns his advances, determined to battle on alone.

But Margaret Bronson breaks more rules than these. When a loyal servant—once a slave, now freed—tells her that her lover's camp is to be attacked by Confederate guerrillas, she acts. "Divest[ing] her dress of some of its feminine encumbrances," she takes a pistol and leaves for the camp. Once there she refuses to stay meekly in the bushes and await the outcome of the skirmish. "I will not hide here in the bushes and die like a coward," she tells her suitor, "no, not even for a look like that, Mr. McGinley." When the sergeant orders her out of the ranks she answers him indignantly: "If you can tell me any reason, Sir, why I should *not* fight, I should like to know it."[47] When his back is turned she returns to her lover's side with her pistol ready.

The woman who emerges is the best of man in womanly form, fearless and tender: "The picture, bright in the fitful glare, was one long to be remembered—the woman with her colorless, calm face and eyes on fire, the shadow of a smile still lingering on her lips, her black hair fallen low on her shoulders, and the fearless aim of the hand so womanly, so dazzling, so foreign to its deadly work. She fought like a veteran."[48] Margaret asks McGinley to teach her how to fight, and he does as they move forward together. He is not dismayed but inspired: "[I]n that hour when she seemed to have thrown off her womanhood, he knew that she was nearer to him than ever in all her life before."[49] When he falls she helps him to her house and nurses him back to health. (And, pointedly, it is he who falls.) Afterward she washes her hands convulsively and trembles before him, a contrast to "this woman who had gone into battle with a smile."[50] Love and fear of his conventionalism, not danger, make her weak. Her lover, of course, does not reject her as she thinks he will.

Phelps's implicit suggestion is clear: here is a woman who can be all that a man can be and still retain the virtues of womanhood. In the middle of the story Phelps promises her audience that her subject is authentic: "You think I am telling you of a woman who belongs only in poetry and romance. I assure you I am not." Margaret Bronson is principled about slavery, even if trained not to be by her father; she is courageous in battle, even when warned off by an officious officer; and yet she is tender and loving as a nurse to her sweetheart. Unlike the heroines in other "thrilling" narratives of women soldiers, Phelps's employs no disguise; she is woman even as she is soldier. In the end, despite her strong-mindedness, she is also more than acceptable to her lover.

Most of the women writers who used the later war years to extend the limits of the separate spheres did so in imagination only. These writers did not suggest equality with men but a certain kind of transcendence: women could be gentle, compassionate, competent, *and* soldiers, if need be. These authors both gave power to their characters' assumed natural attributes as women and suggested that these very attributes should cause that sphere to be extended into public life.

A Place for a Woman: Nurses Make Their Way

I found it *was* a place for woman. All of men's boasted ingenuity had been expended to devise terrible engines with which to kill and maim God's own image; and if war was right, it was right for woman to go with brothers, and husbands, and sons, that in the time of peril the heart might not faint with the thought of an untended death-bed in the crowded hospitals, where no hand but the rough soldier's should close the dead staring eyes.—Sarah Palmer, *The Story of Aunt Becky's Army-Life* (1867)

Over two dozen narratives of women's nursing experiences appeared early in the war in newspapers and magazines and toward the end of the war and thereafter in book form. These narratives reveal a persistent struggle for authority between female nurses and a variety of men in positions of authority.[51] On the one hand, nurses described resistance to their leaving home, recalcitrance from doctors when they arrived at hospitals, and at times peremptory dismissals by government officials once they had been established. On the other hand, they emphasized both their right to be in the hospital and the good work they provided while there, work that derived from the natural attributes of their womanhood.

Perhaps the most frank and revealing early essay regarding the strains of authority between doctors and nurses was written by Georgeanna Woolsey. In her 1864 essay "How I Came to Be a Nurse," Woolsey recounted her hospital training and the series of confrontations she endured with what she came to call the "evil Regular Army Bogie," or the government's official red tape, wielded by a succession of officials, including doctors and even other women, like Dorothea Lynd Dix. Woolsey used humor and irony to defend the value of the woman-nurse, but her main point was clear: women are right for the hospital and should be treated with respect, *especially* those nurses who have the natural intelligence of the elite.

"How I Came to Be a Nurse" was printed in *The Spirit of the Fair*, a USSC newspaper published for the Metropolitan Fair, a fund-raising event held in 1864. Woolsey was a natural person to ask for contributions after the success of an earlier essay, "Three Weeks in Gettysburg," in garnering support for the USSC. Her description of her struggles to find a central place in the war experience was written against the backdrop of three years' service in many different locales. In a few instances her services were specifically requested by certain surgeons, and most involved battlefront or near-battlefront conditions. Woolsey's background was likely to be known by many New York readers—she was from a prominent and wealthy New York family—and while her essay was written anonymously, given her prominence it probably did not remain that way for long. Her collected letters, published in 1899, contained excerpts of the essay. Some of the playful elements were cut; Dorothea Dix's name, tactfully omitted in the 1864 version because of the criticisms leveled at her then, was added in 1899. Remaking the story, it seems, meant both making it more serious and more precise in its details.

Initially Woolsey met resistance to her choice of nursing, although she played down her family's opposition in her published work. From the first, she claimed, she was a born doctor. (The disparity between the position of nurse and surgeon was never taken up, only suggested.) Woolsey humorously explained that as a child she was the one to whom the family members turned when their dolls were out of sorts: "I was selected by the other children as the family physician to the whole row of pink-cheeked rag babies." When she wanted to be a nurse at the beginning of the war, however, her family was not quite as supportive. "It was hard work getting myself acceptable and accepted, what with people at home, saying 'Goodness me! a nurse!' "[52]

Her published letters suggest that the opposition was rather more significant. To her sister Eliza she wrote, "So, my dear, be keeping the little plan [of going south to nurse] in view in making your arrangements, and don't say a word to anybody about our being at the Hospital; I don't want to have to fight my way through the course, and be badgered by the connection generally, besides giving a strict account of myself at home."[53] In calling it "a little plan," Woolsey minimizes the significance of her war work even to herself. She was clear that to be a nurse meant to "fight her way" into the public life she desired.

But family objections were trivial compared to the resistance of the medical community. In her essay on Gettysburg, Woolsey described her training in New York, given by physicians who always came late and left early. Again, although she was playful—"It was necessary that we should understand the mysteries of the saucepan"—her lighthearted banter still carried a sting. Why were the trainees treated with such disdain? "No one knows," she wrote frankly, "who did not watch the thing from the beginning, how much opposition, how much ill-will, how much unfeeling want of thought, these woman-nurses endured. Hardly a surgeon whom I can think of, received them with even common courtesy."[54]

Woolsey's pride and respect is reserved for the women who persevered amid such adversity. The hospital was marked by self-described lines of battle between the sexes. She saw the resistance of the surgeons as a "cool calculation" "to break up the system." The "Government had decided that women should be employed" so the army surgeons, "unable, therefore, to shut the hospitals against them, determined to make their lives so unbearable that they should be forced in self-defense to leave." The woman-nurses refused. "Some of the bravest women I have ever known were among this first company of army nurses," she wrote proudly, noting that they were "pioneers" paving the way for women in the future. In the end, Woolsey concluded, the women prevailed. The surgeons, seeing the results of their work, knew that "they could not do without the women-nurses." Moreover, the women knew that they knew it, and so there came to be a tacit understanding about their indispensability. Still, this victory had been costly; it came only after "great indignities," and although the nurses were "happy and assured at last . . . the fight for it was hard, and gray hairs are their lines of battle."[55]

Woolsey's own personal turning point in this larger battle occurred early in her nursing career, when she faced off with the "evil Regular Army Bogie," at this point describing Dorothea Dix as the army's gatekeeper. Dix, in Woolsey's eyes, took on many of the negative qualities Woolsey attributed to the doctors. She had been sitting by the side of a dying soldier, fanning him, when she was faced with her first "small Bogie," who fixed her with an icy stare. The "Bogie" then got "another one to help him" (in the letters, "Miss Dix" is substituted here) and the two "Bogies" told her to leave and "*never return.*" For Woolsey, however, "the moment of action had arrived." She was not to be forced out: "I rapidly reviewed my position, notified myself that I was the Benevolent Public, and decided that the sick soldiers were, in some sort, the property of the B.P." She then informed the "Bogies" that her carriage was coming at an appointed hour and that she would not leave until then. This caused them to retreat— perhaps it was her owning a carriage?—and a half an hour later, "Profession Etiquette made a most salutary repast off its own remarks."

Later in the war Woolsey would again break the rules by establishing, without orders, a small hospital camp. There she "utterly ignored the existence of the evil spirit, and did as I pleased." In the last analysis, however, Woolsey suggested that deference and charm would work the best. "Bogie is a fixed fact," she lamented, "and on the whole, more good may be accomplished by mildly stroking him the right way, than by punching his head, much as I should frequently prefer the latter proceeding."[56] "He" in this case could also be "she" when Woolsey referred to Dix.

In defending women's right to work in a hospital, Woolsey derived her authority from hard experience. For a "sensible" woman, "[h]ospitals *are* the right places," she wrote, despite the "great deal of nonsense" talked, the "grave disapprobation" of men, and the "romantic patriotism" of women.[57] Women, or, she was quick to add, "persons possessing the common sense, the native tact, the goodness of feeling, the facility of movement which are indispensable alike in parlors and kitchens," had a feeling for the work that rough men in most cases do not, and should not be barred from doing what their ability equips them for.

However, by 1863, even as Woolsey was writing, stories and poetry on the war topic began to sound a new note of disenchantment. The bitter edge to the early stories of waiting grew alongside the numbers of war dead, and women writers reflected the mood of the North at large as they began to retreat from the patriotic and sentimental phrases of the early war. "In contrapuntal fashion," historian James McPherson argues about another moment during the war, "developments on the homefront responded to the rhythm of events on the battlefield."[58] If this was true throughout the war, it may never have been more true than in 1863 and afterward. The patriotic woman now, increasingly, had to face the death of kin, and writers depicted this crisis as the most crucial of the war. In their stories some allowed for a sense of closure with a suggestion of a heavenly reunion, but in their poetry many echoed the nation's pain with little reference to the honor that seemed to sustain them in the early war.

A Crisis of Faith: An Internal Critique

A song these weary times? My restless pen
Seems dipped in human blood . . .
—L[ottie] L[inwood], "Verses," *Peterson's Magazine* (May 1863)

Patriotism, adventure, or public identity aside, hundreds of thousands of Northern (and Southern) women were forced to take stock of lives that were devastated emotionally and economically by the loss or crippling of relatives. For some households, gender roles changed dramatically as a result. Under these conditions, the last years of war were dominated by the image of the sorrowing woman who cared little for national glory and much for an individual man. Stories, and especially poetry, told grim tales unrelieved by celebrations of sacrifice for the national good. For white women unwilling or unable to directly critique the changing war aims—embodied in the Emancipation Proclamation and then in the Thirteenth Amendment—poetry clothed in the indirection of sentimentality offered a way to question the meaning (or even value) of the struggle. Here was an internal critique—perhaps as severe as would be published—suggesting that the war might be won at too great a cost.

By late 1863 women characters in stories were still waiting, but their anticipation had taken on a frenzied quality, since many expected the worst. Their poetry and stories emphasized their impotence to act as integral to their pain and anxiety. In "No Letter Yet," Helen Augusta Browne laments: "Oh days drag on their weary lengths / And weeks together knit, / Still, still I watch, and hope, and wait, / And still in doubt I sit."[59] In "Waiting," Emma Garrison Jones sounds a similar theme: "I sit alone, in the twilight gloom, / Waiting, watching, alas! in vain; / Down the winding path, through the clover bloom, / Willie will never come back again."[60] Months after the war's end, some families still had no word from their kin. " 'Living or Dead?' there was not a line / To tell us to which our thoughts might turn," Clara B. Heath wrote in her 1865 poem. " 'Wounded or Missing,' the record said— / And that was all we could ever learn."[61]

Some stories were grimmer. In January of 1863 Mary Denison wrote "The Dead Soldier's Ring," a vignette of unrelenting pain. A fiancée learns her lover's leg will be amputated; subsequently she learns of his death. She then goes to his mother to break the news and promises to live with her and support her as he would have done. Rather than claiming her son's glorious part in the war, the angry mother says, "Why did he ever go to this dreadful war? It has broken my heart."[62] The fiancée puts the dead soldier's ring on her finger and vows never to marry while his mother still lives. In "Send Them Home to His Mother"—said to be factual—the plot is simply that a young and vibrant nineteen-year-old dies in the hospital and sends his valise and sword home to his mother. The only consolation afforded the mother by the author is the thought that they will be separated "only a short while," as the gates to Heaven are "left ajar."[63]

Wartime authors were particularly interested in the altered behavior now required of women who had to adapt to crippled husbands, sons, and sweethearts. In Clara Augusta's "A Game of Fortune," a soldier returns from war without an arm and feels that he cannot win the love of the beautiful Miss Wellington because he is "deformed." If the arm was lost for the sake of his country, the author reminds us, "it is still a very hard thing for a strong man to lose anything from the perfect strength of his manhood."[64] Yet Miss Wellington, adapting to the situation, is quite forward in expressing her interest in the soldier. In L. J. Dunlop's "Halt," a woman insists that her fiancé marry her despite the loss of his leg. As his wife, she addresses her audience at the end of the story with what she considers the appropriate response to his injury: "My husband wears a cork-leg, and I am proud of it. It is his badge of honor. Had he lost an arm too, in the service of his country, for my *own* sake, I should not have cared."[65] In her story "Captain Charley," Louise Chandler Moulton similarly stresses men's need to know they are still wanted despite their condition. A mother's weeping by her son's bedside causes the son to ask her whether she loves him still, despite his having lost all his youthful symmetry with his arm. "God is good," she answers, and puts aside her maternal grief at his loss.[66]

Even more painful were lost kin, and dirges to the dead filled the pages of literary magazines with an increasing sense of despair. If the earliest poems mention the glory of war, and the worthiness of sacrifice, the later poems mention only the loss. From a political tragedy came an even more overwhelming domestic tragedy. Lottie Linwood's "Dead" stresses the latter. "Our house is dark," she writes, "no light is there; / Softly we gaze on the vacant chair."[67] In "Dirge," Ella Ellwood rejects the consolation of patriotism: "What care I for the dear-bought name / of hero?"[68] Laura C. Redden's "After Vicksburg" also questions why such sacrifice was demanded: "Ah God! Shall tears, poured out like rain, / And deathly pangs, and praying breath, / And faith as deep and strong as death, / Be given—and all in vain?"[69] This note of anger—"and all in vain?"—was new.

These writers emphasized that mothers suffered the most from wartime losses. Sister and betrothed mourn their fallen, Mrs. F. A. Moore writes in "Killed Instantly," but the mother will never stop: "Ay, peace for these young, grieving hearts / Till time shall bring them gentle glee: / The wounds on young flesh quickly heal. / But mother, who shall comfort thee?"[70] "There's comfort yet" in tears, Sylvie A. Speery writes in "Mother, Weep!": "Mother, Weep! thy boy is sleeping; / Ne'er shall battle-thunders wake. / Winds a funeral dirge are sweeping / O'er the mounds our soldiers make. / Weep! there's comfort yet in weeping. / Weep, mothers! weep!"[71] The implication here, however, is that while there is comfort left in weeping, there will come a time when even that comfort is not enough.

Many wartime poets argued that life was empty for women after tragedy struck. Phila Henrietta Case, in "Weary," stresses that for those left behind life is far harder than for those felled by death: "Oh! darling, the damp valley-clods, / Press not so heavy on thy head / As do the ills of life on mine. / And sweeter far thy lowly bed, / Than thus to live—and thus to bear / The cross, and know that thou art dead."[72] In her story "In War Time," Fannie B. Manson sounds a similar note. Her sweetheart, killed at the beginning of the war, has left her bereft: "[A]s the last sods fell upon the coffin, I felt that life held nothing more for me."[73] In Emilie Lester Leigh's "A Woman's Fame," a woman finds fame and fortune as a writer after her husband's death. But it is not enough: "What is fame to a woman who remembers a far-away grave that has widowed her life?"[74] The war, then, was "widowing" the lives of women, making the grief-filled but passive noun into an active verb.

A few of the poems and stories that chronicled the sorrow of losing family and friends sound a note of promise in their last stanzas or sentences, predicting a reunion in heaven. Martha Remick even suggests in "The Home in Heaven" that it will include Southerners as well: "On all sides broken households, / Sorrow and change go past! / But in the home of Heaven / We all shall meet at last."[75] In Mary A. Lee's poem "Missing," a young woman whose sweetheart is never found reflects, finally, "Oh Walter, / You will not be *missing* forever! For that I bless God and am glad."[76] Edith M. Clarke's "Will's Orange-Flowers" reflects on the common tragedy brought by the war and predicts a happy end after the grave: "Ah! there's many a Maggie among us; / Some waiting for Will to come; / And some—oh! the sorrow and darkness— / Mourn in a desolate home. / Some time, in God's beautiful justice, / With Heavenly love replete, / Somewhere, in bright sunshine and gladness, / These Wills and Maggies shall meet."[77] With earthly honor diminished as a reward, only heavenly reunions seem to validate these writers' loss.

For others this faith was not so easily won, requiring a period of unsettled questioning and of "heart-breaking agony." In these "crisis of faith" stories and poems, the protagonist, always a woman, goes through a period of almost angry rejection of peace and, through this time of longing and despair, comes to believe again that God understands and will aid her to live out her life in quiet acceptance. This trial, of course, echoes Christ's own struggle in the last moments of his death, when he questioned the God that gave him such pain and then accepts it with faith in the judgment and goodness of the Lord. What is notable in these evocations of an age-old story is that women unironically give themselves the role of Jesus.

Few doubted that the later years of the war were a significant time in testing the limits of woman's faith. Harriet Beecher Stowe addressed this crisis directly in the first of her "Chimney-Corner" series in the *Atlantic Monthly*: "What can we say to you in those many, many homes where the light has gone out forever?"[78] She seems to be answering Mary A. Lee's question in "Missing"—"Is heart-breaking agony wrong?"—when she says: "There is a certain amount of suffering which must follow the rending of the great chords of life, suffering which is natural and inevitable."[79] After this suffering and questioning, there will be peace, she promises.

This promise is echoed in the wartime stories, which move from cajoling women to action to soothing their overwhelming sorrow. "My Thanksgiving," written in 1863, articulates in one wife's reflections on hearing of her husband's death the pain and loss that many women felt: "I had not yet been long enough under its influence to have acquired the habit of faith and submission; and under this deadly blow I knew nothing, felt nothing Christian, or acquiescent, except the ever-present conviction that even in this whirling storm God was somewhere—not with me, or for me, but still living, and unchanged, and just, though all His world slipped away from under my feet like the sliding earth of a night mare dream."[80] Unlike most of the later war stories, the husband returns, but only after the wife has come to some sense of acceptance through a struggle with her faith.

In Elizabeth Stuart Phelps's "A Sacrifice Consumed," and to a lesser extent in her stories "My Refugees" and "The Bend," a similar but more wrenching spiritual crisis is faced by her heroines. Phelps's message about the redeeming power of faith centers around women, who are understood to be the primary caretakers of faith. As a result, when their resolution falters, the void is even deeper. All three of Phelps's stories revolve around working-class or lower-middle-class women impoverished by the war. In "A Sacrifice Consumed," an orphaned seamstress named Ruth, desperately working to support herself, gives in to a moment of overwhelming loneliness. The narrator, asserting the veracity of her story and comparing it to other forms of writing, tells the reader: "I am giving you no sickly sentimentalism when I let you into the secret of this moment of pain. The heart of every woman calls to God out of its own solicitude, in such a life as hers, with a bitterness only He can fathom."[81] Ruth, like "every woman," yearns for a family and is answered with the love of John Rogers. After their engagement, the war begins, but Phelps does not focus on the moment of parting like the authors of so many early wartime stories. "Why should I linger over the parting?" the narrator asks the reader. "Thousands of pale women know its sacredness, and need no picture of that which 'entereth within the vail.'"[82]

Instead, like other authors in the last years of war, Phelps focuses on the moment when Ruth learns of her *final* parting from John. She suggests that those who die are not the only heroes. Women who stay at home and continue on bravely, despite terrible loss, are also heroic.[83] Ruth struggles at first, for she is "no philosopher," and she grieves for her soldier; "she could not always see how it *could* be right—thinking, you know, that she had loved her soldier so." Met finally by one "who had himself wept and struggled alone on the hillsides of Judea for her," she finds peace, if no earthly companion.[84]

While some writers argued that the war provided a test of faith from God for women, others saw it as a national lesson from which the country would emerge renewed. Both Harriet Beecher Stowe, in "The Chimney-Corner," and Gail Hamilton, in her essay "Anno Domini," both in the same issue of the *Atlantic Monthly*, recognized this grief and pain as a necessary passage to the millennium. "The great affliction that has come upon our country," Stowe wrote, "is so evidently the purifying chastening of a Father, rather than the avenging anger of a Destroyer, that all hearts may submit themselves in a solemn and holy calm still to bear the burning that shall make us clean from dross and bring us forth to a higher national life."[85] Both suggested that the war was a great teacher, that it had brought out the best in the nation, and particularly in women. Gail Hamilton (typically) criticized and praised the nation before making further recommendations. Her praise, however, was mainly for women: "Out of the strong has come forth sweetness. From the helmeted brow of War has sprung one fairer than Minerva, panoplied not for battle, but for the tenderest ministrations of Peace. Wherever the red hand of War has been raised to strike, there the white hand of Pity has been stretched forth to solace."[86] This commendation, however, may have been intended more as self-fulfilling prophecy than realistic description, given the timing of its release. The Union still had the bloody Petersburg campaign to finish before Appomattox marked the official end of the war.

Other women writers used the historical moment to influence a change in men rather than women. In Helen Pierson's "Tom's Education," the narrator—a teacher who loses her position because of the war—returns home to find her charming but heedless brother there being thrown out of school following a night of fun. Although thinking him selfish, the narrator still gives him the diamond ring left her by their mother to pay his debts. He enlists instead, and thus gets the "education" that formal schooling and loving sisters have been unable to give him. Tom, the narrator observes, "learned to suffer and be strong; and it seemed to me that to some the war was a great educator, terrible in its lessons, but thereby enduring." Women and the country at large also felt these greater lessons; the war "lighted the fires of philanthropy and universal love to the suffering; it called out self-devoted women who had never found their true life-work till they stood with ministering hands by the sick and dying. Ah! I thought, there is good as well as evil in the war."[87] If women were also taught by the war, the war helped them find their "true life-work." Men like Tom, Pierson shows, undergo a necessary transformation when they begin to value that love and sympathy they took for granted before the war.[88]

A few late war writers focused on the work that war had made possible, suggesting the ways in which it had been successful. Instead of images of death, these authors created images of life beginning. Such strategies were typical of antislavery activists, who with the Emancipation Proclamation and the early work at Reconstruction on the South Sea Islands, celebrated freedom for African Americans. The direction of the politics in antislavery literature of the late war period reflects this shift in focus as women worked to ready the public for emancipation.

MORE CLEARLY THAN most, antislavery women understood the war as a political event. They shaped their message for certain effects: to praise or criticize a congressman; to encourage British support; to further illuminate the ills of slavery; to reassure the fearful of African American self-reliance and self-segregation; to suggest efforts at assisting freedpeople to adopt middle-class values of frugality, modesty, and hard work. In the process they revealed their deepest assumptions about the difference between the races and similarity between the genders. While African American women were seen as inhabiting a distinctly subordinate place in society, there was nonetheless a persistent belief in a shared inherent morality that ran through the writings of many white antislavery women. That belief was tied to an understanding and embrace of separate sphere ideology and represented the way in which this limiting ideology could become a powerful political tool.

Yet women writers throughout the war struggled with and against the dichotomies of social life in three ways. Most fundamentally they argued that public and private lives were not separate. Those at home were not, and could not be, protected from the war's deadly and public hand, nor could they affect public change without resistance and remonstrance.

Clearly, the Civil War was a time when the diverging expectations of men and women in society were most starkly etched. Traditional expectations placed women in passive roles—as spectator, refugee, victim—that women writers continually referred to and analyzed. In response, women writers rejected their passive roles by creating heroines who waited actively, who worked for the war at home, who went to the front to nurse, who went south to teach, and who even fought. Yet they also clearly lamented their status as the war's victims: each bullet, they reminded their readers, wounded someone at home.

Finally, women infused meaning and power into their conventional roles, as well as challenging them. As moral guardians they ascribed to the war moral dimensions, a way to teach the country at large the lessons of Jesus, to suffer and yet accept suffering, to die for the sins of others, and, in dying, to save the country. The war, then, symbolized both pain and opportunity, both limitation and expansion, and it was claimed by women, as Delphine Baker terms in it her metaphorical novel of 1862, as a "domestic *and* political tragedy."[89]

As I passed through the first hospitals of wounded men I ever saw, there flashed the
thought—*this* is the work God has given *me* to do in this war. While in the midst of so
much excitement, in the times which form *history*, we were unconscious of it all: it was
our daily life. Now, in these peaceful days, we begin to realize where we have been, and
in *what* we have taken part.—Anna Holstein, *Three Years in the Field Hospitals* (1867)

{ CHAPTER SEVEN }

The Times Which Form History

Writing the War, 1865–1868

THE END OF THE WAR, beginning with the capture of Richmond, Virginia, on April 2 and the surrender of General Robert E. Lee to General
Ulysses S. Grant on April 9, was greeted with joy by women writers. "Hur-
rah!" Louisa May Alcott wrote in her journal, "Went to Boston & enjoyed
the grand jollification."[1] Eleven days later Lydia Maria Child sounded a
note of anxiety. "I am rejoicing over the good news, which promises cessa-
tion of slaughter," she wrote to her good friend Lucy Osgood, "but I
rejoice with trembling."[2] Will the nation reconstruct so as to protect the
freed people and poor whites from the white ruling class? she wondered.
Presciently, she added, "If they have any power left, they will certainly use
it to keep down the poor whites and emancipated blacks."[3]

When the news of President Abraham Lincoln's death spread north-ward, Child saw the hand of God in it. "The assassination of our good President, shocked and distressed me," she wrote to Sarah Shaw, another close friend, but she reported that five minutes later she had wondered if "the wonderful guidance of Providence" was not at work. "The kind-hearted Abraham, was certainly in danger of making too easy terms with the rebels."[4] Mary Abigail Dodge did not assess the political ramifications of Lincoln's death so swiftly (even if she had agreed with Child's hopes for Reconstruction). "There is doubtless good to come from this great calam-ity and wickedness," she wrote in a letter dated April 15, "but it as yet is impossible to see what the good is."[5] Alcott thought she saw that good on the streets of Boston. "Saw the great procession," she wrote in her journal, "& though colored men were in it one was walking arm in arm with a white gentleman & I exulted thereat."[6]

THE DISARRAY of the late war years, its complicated mix of hope, fear, and possibility, gave way to multiple agendas for postwar women writers. The crisis of faith that was sounded in late war poetry was abandoned with a renewal of writing celebrating glory and honor. Given the need for national celebration and the end of battlefield deaths, this perhaps made sense.

What also made sense was the degree to which the history of the war, particularly the role women played in it, was immediately contested. What these histories—largely if not exclusively written by men—emphasized, glossed over, wrangled about, and left out was the subject of public scru-tiny and anxiety. It is not surprising, then, that two years after the war, not one but two huge volumes on Union women's contributions to the war ef-fort were published (both by men)—or that fifteen years after that the au-thors of *The History of Woman Suffrage* would make their own interpretation.

In these and other accounts, the key issue was how women's contribu-tions to the war effort would be framed: As a springboard to greater free-doms and responsibilities? As aberrations that forced temporary changes on naturally domestic and private women? As a narrative of early senti-mental unity, followed by a crisis of confidence at midwar, and then a combination of late war anxiety and play?

Whatever the tenor of these accounts, they were written in a broader early postwar climate that was initially full of promise for women and African American men but also socially unstable, and, ultimately, repres-sive. The men who compiled the huge histories worked hard to recreate a universal woman whose experience of the war would not ruffle national

"Each ready to do her part to hasten the coming of the happy end."

This illustration, by Sol Eytinge, was included in Louisa May Alcott's 1873 novel *Work* and represents Alcott's greatest hopes for the future. That future, of social justice, would come about through the collective work of women—white, black, and Irish; working class, middle class and upper class; young and old—here drawn with hands clasped. Significantly, each woman in the novel speaks for herself and those she represents, even as Alcott speaks for them all; the rhetoric of unity here in the postwar period is more supple than earlier renditions, even though it is still shot through with ironies.

feathers and who represented the most respectable of middle- and upper-middle-class white women. The universal woman could, when stretched benevolently, include a poor, white seamstress, but these were exceptions. The larger intent was both to exclude and to smooth over difference, in a return to a rhetoric of unity that would emphasize the war's inevitable victory and the unshakable gender and racial conventions that (supposedly) sustained it. In writing the history of the war, by contrast, women looked to the past as a way of getting their due in the present. Their postwar histories were more contentious than they were earlier or came to be later— edgier, with a glimmer of anger breaking through the Victorian veneer.

Given that the novel was early on considered a women's genre, it is not surprising that novelists were the most numerous of the female historians of the war. Some claimed that their stories were based on fact; others simply used the war to lend legitimacy to their tales. Either way, they argued about the ideological meaning of the war with stories rather than by recounting factual information, and believed themselves to be relaying truths about their country, its recent tragedy, and its meaning for women in general. And despite the patent sentimentality and the muddled quality of the worst of these novels, all were clearly written with a goal of documenting the transformative effect of the war on women's lives.

However they narrated them, women-nurses heralded their experiences as a kind of truth and authority previously unknown in their lives. Rejecting the tone of official affirmation by the men who also wrote about nurses, the nursing memoirs focused considerable energy on the conflict between men and women, and between classes of women-nurses. Unlike Louisa May Alcott's *Hospital Sketches* and other wartime narratives, nurses' memoirs were serious, detailed, and even angry remembrances. Their message was directed at the history-writers and authority figures who had made their war work difficult; they were carrying on a struggle that continued after Appomattox.

Taken together, these novels and narratives seem at once suggestive and limited. Rather than looking forward to new challenges facing women in a new era, as novelists in the early 1870s used the war to do, most of these works look backward to chart where women had been. Nursing memoirs were framed with flowery statements of women's natural nurturing ability and emphasized self-sacrifice and pain rather than authority and strength. Even those novels that grappled with postwar fears (such as the fear of intermarriage between whites and blacks, the subject of which is taken up in Chapter 8) did so with a political understanding rooted in prewar assumptions. And all of them gave center stage to the middle-class white woman of the North, a hardworking, order-oriented, compassionate, and moral exemplar of the restored Union.

At the same time that these works harkened back to past ideals of harmony, they also anticipated coming changes, particularly in the ways in which they emphasized class distinctions. War novels included heroines of

"Peace" from *Harper's Weekly*, July 8, 1865. The end of the war is depicted through both traditional and nontraditional images of men and women here: On the one hand, there are joyous women kissing returning soldiers, in positions of supplication and deference and as purveyors of hope, prosperity, and peace, throwing garlands and offering wheat as a symbol of plenty. On the other hand, the main figure looms over the others and suggests the central role women will play in restoring the Union to fertility and reunion. (From the author's collection.)

more scope and public bravery than previously imagined, and they referred to women's rights with more sympathy, prefiguring the more independent new woman of the late nineteenth century. The directly political writing of the abolitionists suggested the style, if not the content, of later social protest novels. And though nursing narratives began and ended with flowery sentiment, they contained stories and statements of an angry realism. It is this persistent dualism between the politics of the past and the budding process of change for the politics of the future that is most compelling in works published during the early years of Reconstruction.

Writing Women and the War: Transitions

The years 1865 and 1868 provide useful boundaries for an analysis of women's writing on the Civil War. The sense of political possibility and promise in 1865 waned as the country lurched forward; by 1868, when the last Southern state was readmitted to the Union, disillusionment with the war and its outcome had set in. Still, in 1865, a series of significant events demonstrated how far the nation had come and how great its tragedy was. The Thirteenth Amendment, ending slavery, overcame Democratic resistance in December of 1864 but still involved a year of state-by-state decisions before becoming law. Less than a week after Lee's surrender at Appomattox Court House, President Lincoln, whom even many radical abolitionists had come to grudgingly respect, was assassinated.

Early Reconstruction was shaped by conflict between Lincoln's successor, Andrew Johnson of Tennessee, a former slave state, and an increasingly radicalized Congress. The meaning of the Civil War was at the heart of political debate in these three years as the president and Congress divided on the proper procedures for readmitting the seceded states to the Union. After what abolitionists saw as a good beginning, the former Democrat Johnson's lenient course toward the South became increasingly clear. Although he felt an obligation to reestablish the voting power of the states through presidential pardons, Johnson felt no comparable desire to grant new African American citizens their right to suffrage. It would take political crisis, attempted impeachment, and the election of a new president in 1868 before their civil and voting rights were at least minimally protected.[7]

The South itself was a dangerous place to be African American and a stultifying one for white women in the years after the war. As historian Susan Lebsock notes, "The central facts of southern life after the war were poverty and troubled, volatile relations between the races, and it is worth inquiring how much the status of women could have improved under these conditions." It was in these years that what Lebsock calls the "mythology of rape" emerged as a rationale for the debasement and murder of black men.[8] Such an ideology, and the fears it represented and stirred, made it difficult for women of the North to absolutely condemn Southern white relations with the freed slaves, even as the need for intervention and reform continued and even intensified.[9]

The two years between the end of the Civil War and the passage of the Fourteenth Amendment (granting citizenship to African Americans) were marked by significant changes in reform communities generally and in suffrage reform specifically. Women who had not previously supported women's rights now joined the struggle, and suffrage seemed like a real possibility. The experience of the war led women reformers to pin their hopes on the federal government rather than to focus political attention on state legislators. No longer a repository of suspicion for harboring slavery, and now deemed capable of enormous and (to their mind) laudable change, the national center was viewed (at least temporarily) with renewed hope.

Still, the rhetoric, strategies, and membership of these movements were largely those of the prewar North. Suffrage reformers marshaled arguments about universal rights in an effort to link women's and African American suffrage in the minds of legislators—to create unity by eliding difference, an early war tactic—but these were arguments that had been used successfully to extend suffrage in the days of Andrew Jackson. Men and women reformers who had first rubbed shoulders in antislavery days, and then worked side by side during the Civil War in freedmen's aid societies and other local and national efforts, now made one last push.[10]

It took the defeat of woman suffrage by Congress to finally splinter these old networks, a splintering with profoundly negative effects. With the addition of the word "male" in the Fifteenth Amendment, woman suffrage reformers' hopes were dashed, leaving the activists bitter and angry over the sacrifices they had made during the war to establish their right to national representation. Reformers like Lydia Maria Child sided with Lucretia Mott and Frederick Douglass in insisting that African Americans' voting rights should get political priority. Elizabeth Cady Stanton and Susan B. Anthony, among others, disagreed, and their subsequent reform efforts and racial statements took a new direction in 1869 with the establishment of their political magazine *The Revolution*. Though their determination to work collectively with only white women ultimately bore the fruits of a deeper feminist consciousness, their racist statements in lectures and print soured the movement from that moment forward, establishing the suffrage movement as a white women's organization and hampering cross-racial alliances for years to come.[11] Stanton and Anthony's politics in this period laid bare the internal divisions in a reform community that had long used the idea of unity in a facile way.

Reform communities were not alone in experiencing such fragmentation. Literary trends begun during the war intensified during the late 1860s and early 1870s. With the proliferation of dime novels during the 1860s and the emergence of the cheap "nickel libraries" of working-class sensational fiction in the 1870s, a time of widespread class cross-over in literary reading material had ended by 1868. Subsequent cultures of letters, as literary historian Richard Brodhead terms them, were now more loosely connected.[12]

The Civil War figured prominently in all forms of literary production from 1863 to 1869: stories and poems in literary magazines; sensational, sentimental, and realistic novels; and narratives of soldiers and nurses, as well as general histories. Writers scrambled to record and assess what would be the monumental national event of their lives. If the writing in these novels showed no decisive shift to new literary forms, nor presented entirely new ideas, it nevertheless represented, in the words of one scholar, "the seedtime of a new period."[13]

The chaos of Reconstruction was reflected in the lives of many women writers as they struggled to make sense of this national tragedy. Generational position notwithstanding, the nine women considered in this study were all undergoing significant changes from 1865 to 1868, many of which were in direct response to the war. Writers from an older generation, including Lydia Maria Child and Frances Ellen Watkins Harper, were joined by Rebecca Harding Davis in a continuing effort to secure social justice for now freed African Americans. For these writers, the war was centrally about slavery and its demise, and their work served to reinforce this conviction, retaining many prewar arguments and prejudices. Harriet Beecher Stowe and Gail Hamilton, by contrast, turned away from direct political intervention to different social questions, although in neither case was this retreat complete. Both writers faced public and private crises in the late war and postwar years that absorbed their energies and re-focused their positions on the place of women in society. Mrs. E. D. E. N. Southworth, alone among these writers, used the postwar period to *begin* publicly exploring the issue of the Civil War in her fiction. Although Southworth nursed a few soldiers in her home on the Potomac during the war itself, she had not written about the conflict directly.[14]

Meanwhile, in a shift that would have profound consequences for the postwar period, other writers like Fanny Fern, Louisa May Alcott, and Elizabeth Stuart Phelps turned from the war toward an interclass exploration of the position of women in society. Fern analyzed the commonality as well as the inequities between women immediately after the war, followed in turn by Alcott and Phelps.[15] Harper, while retaining an image of the central middle-class woman figure in her stories, worked to make that figure more representative of African Americans and her stories more illustrative of their conditions and concerns. This movement represented an effort to look beyond the war to new efforts, strategies, and ideas.

In this chaotic period of early Reconstruction, however, most writers focused their attention on what had happened during the war years rather than on its implications for the future. Child, Davis, and Southworth joined many other women writers, particularly nurses, in assessing the meaning of the Civil War factually and imaginatively.

Women's Histories:
Reinscribing the "Universal" Woman for Posterity

Men's effort to contain the meaning of the war for women began almost immediately. Frank Moore (*Women of the War*) and Dr. L. P. Brockett and

Mrs. Mary C. Vaughan (*Woman's Work in the Civil War*) published the first collective histories of Union women in wartime in 1866 and 1867, respectively, mixing individual vignettes of notable women to create a collective sense of a universal, stalwart, and, above all, respectable white, middle-class woman.[16] Moore's volume, subtitled "Heroism and Self-Sacrifice," was echoed a year later by Brockett and Vaughan, who modified it to "Heroism, Patriotism and Patience." "Never," Brockett and Vaughan wrote in the first page of their preface, "had the gentle and patient ministrations of women been so needful as in the last year of war; and never had they been so abundantly bestowed, and with such zeal and self-forgetfulness."[17] In both cases, it is the "self-forgetfulness" that Moore and Brockett and Vaughan laud.

These books purported to represent all women of the war, yet class and racial biases are threaded throughout.[18] In listing the efforts of women on behalf of the war, Brockett and Vaughan note approvingly "the heroic souls who devoted themselves to the noble work of raising a nation of bondmen to intelligence and freedom" along with those who "attempted the still more hopeless task of rousing the blunted intellect and cultivating the moral nature of the degraded and abject poor whites."[19] The implications here, of course, are that interacting with the "bondmen" was a heroic act; that they were unintelligent; that poor whites were unpatriotic, ignorant, and immoral; and that the women working in these capacities were neither black nor poor.

Yet Brockett and Vaughan's text in particular is laced with ambivalence. Moving from a wartime crisis that sought to enlist all women collectively and minimize their differences, they had to negotiate between the rhetoric of unity that characterized their rendering of the war years and the more class-conscious postwar mood. So, for example, when introducing the work of Bridget Divers, who was called "Irish Biddy" by some, they described her as "another remarkable heroine who, *while from the lower walks of life, was yet* faithful and unwearied in her labors."[20] Others "of this class of heroines" were hard to find, they added later, particularly when "they failed to maintain that unsullied reputation without which courage and daring are of little worth."[21] Few working-class women, then, truly brought honor to the Union through war work: most were prostitutes.

Those women who worked for pay were less heroic: their participation in the marketplace took them outside true womanhood (although soldiers, despite their pay, would never be so designated). When Dorothea Dix had to reject elite or middle-class volunteers, on account of youth, beauty, or frivolity, Brockett and Vaughan wrote, this "necessitated the

The frontispiece from Linus P. Brockett and Mary C. Vaughan's *Woman's Work in the Civil War*. The image, a postwar celebration of Northern women's efforts during the Civil War, illustrates (ironically) their effort to limit the significance of women's work. Women, in this illustration, protect—but remain—at their homes, and call upon the traditional respect due to women. The Southern men look respectfully at the stalwart woman brandishing the flag; there's no threat of violence. This illustration also subtly emphasizes that Northern women had to defend property the way Southern women did; during the war the latter were portrayed as having more to lose. (Photo from Brockett and Vaughan, *Woman's Work in the Civil War*.)

appointment of many from another class" (who, one infers, would not have been otherwise considered). Because these young women were "generally from the humbler walks of life," they had to be paid. While it was clear that Brockett and Vaughan regarded this as unfortunate, it was also clear that they considered such women passably patriotic—unlike, perhaps, the striking seamstresses in New York.[22]

Overall, however, Brockett and Vaughan, along with Henry Bellows, who wrote a second introduction for *Women's Work in the Civil War*, sought to remember the conflict as one of uncontested unity, where the courage and loyalty of *Southern* women were maligned. "In the course of a year, the zeal of the Southern ladies cooled, and they contented themselves with waving their handkerchiefs to the soldiers, instead of providing for their wants," Bellows argued.[23] Northern women, Bellows wrote, "were nearer right and more thoroughly united [by their work for the war] . . . than the American men." Their work engendered a "homogeneousness of feeling between the soldiers and the citizens, which kept the men in the field, civilians, and made the people at home, of both sexes, half-soldiers."[24] The women simply never doubted their government or their purpose: "Amid discouragements and fearful delays they never flagged, but to the last increased in zeal and devotion."[25] The war thus became, Bellows suggested, four years of sustained purpose in the North, unbesmirched by doubt.

Bellows, who, given his post, undoubtedly knew very well of the conflict between nurses and doctors in the hospital, tried at once to acknowledge it and to minimize it, even as he worked to establish nursing as both natural and unnatural to women. Women-nurses, he admitted, had to be both good at nursing and at gentle deference. "The honest, natural jealousy felt by the surgeons in charge, and their ward masters, of all outside assistance," he wrote, "made it necessary for every woman, who was to succeed in her purpose of holding her place, and really serving the men, to study and practice an address, an adaptation and a patience, of which not one candidate in ten was capable."[26] Moreover, in order to be nurses, women had much to overcome: they "conquered their feminine sensibility at the sight of blood and wounds; their native antipathy to disorder, confusion and violence; subdued the rebellious delicacy of their more exquisite senses; lived coarsely, and dressed and slept rudely; they studied the caprices of men to whom their ties were simply human—men often ignorant, feeble-minded—out of their senses—raving with pain and fever." Furthermore, he asserted, they did so alongside arrogant and undertrained doctors (although Bellows softens this with a footnote commending many surgeons). In exalting women-nurses, Bellows exaggerates their transformation: delicate middle-class women were not *meant* to be wartime nurses; they had to overcome who they were to do it; this was not natural—and hence would not last.

This emphasis on the unnatural quality of women's war work was the primary distinction between the history Moore, Bellows, and Brockett and Vaughan wrote of the war and the one that Elizabeth Cady Stanton, Susan B. Anthony, and Joslyn Gage, editors of the *History of Woman Suffrage*, did a number of years later. Volume Two of the *History*, published in 1882, included plenty of exaltation and praise. But the men's emphasis on temporary disruption in otherwise conventional gender relations was replaced by the notion that women had somehow had to remake themselves. The revolution of women portrayed in *History of Woman Suffrage* was a learning process that did not efface the natural delicacy of women but enhanced it. "Through the withdrawal of so many men from their accustomed work," the editors wrote, "new channels of industry were opened to [women], the value and control of money learned, thought upon political questions compelled, and a desire for their own, personal liberty intensified."[27] The change, these authors argued, came from the circumstances—doors were *opened*. Bellows and Brockett make no such claims for opening doors, nor for resulting revolutions.

For Stanton, Anthony, and Gage these changed circumstances "created a revolution in woman herself, as important in its results as the changed condition of the former slaves, and this silent influence is still busy." Notably, the women changed are not *among* the former slaves; their revolution is separate and at least equal in impact. This insistence on white women's history standing alone, and not being implicated with that of freedpeople, is significant in a historical moment in which race relations were approaching their nadir and emphasized the similarity in this history to the earlier ones: universal woman meant white, middle-class woman. This is the "woman" in "a revolution of woman herself."

Nursing Histories: Women's Authority and Class Conflict

By the end of the war, nurses had established a place for themselves in the mythology of victory. Sentimental biographical compendia praised nurses one after another for their "womenly" attributes and abilities.[28] Yet many of the nurses' own writings, particularly those written between 1865 and 1868, belie that comfortable praise with sharp social commentary. Rather than simple tales of submissive and compassionate nurses happy to serve, such as those common to earlier work, these narratives describe clashes between doctors and nurses and between nurses of different social classes over issues of policy, respect, and authority. For these nurses, the war was a testing ground for the definition of a (often sorely contested) new career. At the same time, the narratives themselves swing between florid posturing and a more gritty realism, retaining much of the tenor of past romantic writing even while suggesting a style more suited to the secularized context of the postwar.

Far more than for writers like Brockett, Vaughan, and Moore, these narratives depicted an ongoing class struggle between women-nurses. A significant number of the Civil War nurses were from elite families and saw their efforts in the war as the beginnings of a professionalized and respectable career for women. As historian Susan Reverby puts it, "A small coterie of urban upper-class women, who either had nursed during the war or actively participated in the Sanitary Commission or other relief activities, returned from their war efforts eager and confident that feminine virtues and organizational skills had a larger role to play in society."[29] The values behind this professionalization were efficiency, cleanliness, order, and education, values that would come to dominate an unsettled middle class in the nineteenth century. What was lost or minimized in this transition were values of compassion over efficiency; individual need over orderly care; and natural empathy rather than education. The nurses in the narratives analyzed here reflected those older values, yet they still demanded new authority for women.

In many ways nurses also embodied accepted prewar conceptions of womanhood. Their complaints were rarely offered as evidence of a need for women's rights, and they based their right to be in the hospital not on some conception of personal freedom but on gender roles well established as the social norm. Men go out to die and women go out to save, one nurse pointedly wrote in a poem prefacing and closing her narrative.[30] The problem comes only when men try to keep women from performing their duty.

Postwar narratives were significantly more critical than most of those published during the war, barring only Georgeanna Woolsey's essay "How I Came to Be a Nurse," which shared many of their other attributes. Postwar narratives were not propaganda for the Sanitary Commission, as were many published during the war, and hence they may not have had the same editorial constraints. The conflict within the hospital between doctors and nurses, and among nurses themselves, was revealed in a more unadulterated fashion. Postwar writings are equally far removed from Louisa May Alcott's somewhat irreverent and humorous *Hospital Sketches*; they represent at once a more trenchant critique of hospital life and a less nuanced and careful writing style. These are angry and pointed narratives that on the one hand catalogue the sacrifices made for individual soldiers, and on the other bitterly recount the difficulties of moving into a public sphere controlled by men. If women's efforts during wartime were an attempt to bridge the distance between the public and private spheres, here were exposés of the authority figures patrolling those bridges.

Among the nursing narratives published after the war, there are three that remark directly and consistently on power relations between men and elite women and the nurses that worked with them. These narratives make clear the hierarchies within nursing itself that emerged during the war years and demonstrate the control that upper-class women sought to impose over lower-middle-class and working-class women. To establish nursing as a respectable career, it seems, elite women had to restrict it to those women who would act "appropriately" by respecting authority. Significantly, little is known about the three authors of these narratives—Elvira Powers,

Sophronia Bucklin, and Sarah Palmer—all of whom were older women who had been dismissed from their positions at least once, or were self-described as confrontational on behalf of the wounded soldiers. These were neither romantic young ladies, as Tribulation Periwinkle might be imagined to be, nor powerful elite women, like the Woolsey sisters of New York.

Perhaps the best illustration of the deference demanded by doctors came in Elvira Powers's *Hospital Pencillings*, published in 1866. Powers nursed in more than one locale, and after a few incidents with doctors and chaplains was assisted by Mary Livermore in finding a new post. The major interest of her narrative derives from the specificity with which she analyzed her confrontation with one doctor who dismissed her from service. Powers, it seems, transgressed in matters not of medicine but in issues of language and manner.

Powers's narrative illustrates the penalties for a woman taking too critical and authoritative a stance in the hospital; as a woman she should have simply been grateful for the opportunity to be there. From the first Powers was critical of the men with whom she dealt, beginning with the ministers, whom she felt did not do their job in visiting the many dying in the wards. Of one particular man, she reported, "I was indignant and determined to report him, but was given to understand by more than one Christian minister, that the expression of indignation was considered a bad omen for my future success in hospitals." Curbing her "expression," she wrote, would be hard for one by "nature and birth an outspoken New Englander."[31]

The focal point of Powers's narrative is her dismissal from the small pox hospital, and the manner in which it was executed. Here she reveals not only her struggle with authority figures but also the absolute method they adopted in dealing with her. Rather than being confronted with her "transgression," Powers was abruptly terminated, further underscoring the power arrangement between men and women. Doctors and administrators needed no excuse to dismiss a nurse. "I've done something but havn't [*sic*] the least idea what, to displease somebody and haven't the least idea who," Powers wrote after being told that her place was being filled by another woman. Rather than giving up, she remained nearby waiting for a pass, working as a volunteer nurse in the hospitals and a teacher at a school for freedpeople. After describing some of her experiences as both a volunteer and a teacher, she explains the emerging reasons for her previous dismissal. "I have been very cautiously, and little by little, and with many charges not to tell any body, informed of the terrible crime for which I was tried, convicted, sentenced and banished, while all the time in blissful ignorance of the crime itself," she wrote. "This is the way of managing affairs here, I am told, and it is called military style." "I like it," she continues, with irony; "it saves one all the trouble and worry of defending one's self. And that might make one nervous and excited. It also saves confusion in the mind of the adjudging party."[32]

The "grave charge" for which Powers was accused involved her assumption of authority over a patient's care. "[U]pon a certain occasion," she wrote, "I presented myself before the surgeon of the division and told him with an authoritative air, that I wished he 'would see that a certain patient had a mustard poultice on his chest, because he wanted it.'" This is not the way Powers remembers the incident. She was much more deferential, she explains, and brusque only because she

> recollected hearing that some physicians were offended by even a request, and hesitated. Then thinking of the moans and apparent danger of the sufferer, I proceeded. These contradictory emotions, I can now realize, gave an unusual brusqueness to my manner, as I said:—
>
> "Doctor there is a patient in the third tent below, on bed, No. 9, who is in great pain and wants a mustard poultice. Will you see if he needs it? If so, I can make it."
>
> There was a flash in his eyes, as he replied:—
>
> "*I* will attend to the man. As for the mustard poultices, it is not necessary that you should attend to them, as the men nurses do that."

The problem was not with her assumption of authority—she denied assuming any—but with his hasty and unfair interpretation of her words. "This trouble was caused simply by a misunderstanding," Powers asserted. "He used the word *want* for *need*, so that when I said the man 'wanted' it—meaning that he *asked* for it, he interpreted it so as to convey the idea of my assuming the responsibility of saying, 'he needed' it. He also understood me to order him to 'see' that the man had it, when I simply asked if he would 'see if he needed it.'"[33] The degree of conflict that could emerge over both word choice ("want" and "need") and inflection (her "brusqueness") suggests the tension simmering between surgeons and nurses.

Powers was more unabashedly assertive in a confrontation with a minister, for which she made no apologies. In some sense this was more her moral duty, and thus more acceptable coming from a woman. The chaplain neglected to visit several dying patients, despite being asked to by Powers on successive occasions. One day she saw him "pitching quoits," and other ladies told her that he was acting as clerk for the surgeon in charge. "So here was a chaplain neglecting the sacred duties of his own profession," Powers exclaimed to the reader, "although amply paid for the same and earning more of the filthy lucre, to the neglect of dying men!"[34] "Thus endeth the defence," Powers wrote frankly. "Mrs. Gala Days [Gail Hamilton], you were entirely correct in your assertion that one must go abroad and see the world, to have 'personal experiences,'" she added. Those personal experiences could be revealing, as in this case of male insecurity and wrongdoing.

Powers's defense was woman's natural right to be in the hospital, a right based on her essential quality of compassion. "Notwithstanding that there is much feeling upon the subject [of women's influence in the hospital] of her real or imagined interference with professional duties," Powers wrote, "yet there are very many wise and noble surgeons in the service who rightly appreciate woman's influence in a hospital, and have assisted her in every noble word and work." And, she added, "a pure, true woman is amply repaid for working her way quietly and kindly against opposite influences, as she may feel assured that her efforts are blessed to the sick boys in her care." It is enough, Powers asserted, when a nurse "may so overcome the prejudices of a physician" that he will say: "You have been a blessing to the patients and a help to me—have attended to your own duties as nurse without interfering with those of mine as physician. And there are those whose lives are due to your care." These assurances, together with those of a patient redeemed from an irreligious life, can "amply repa[y]" a nurse for her struggles against "opposite influences."[35]

Sophronia Bucklin, a nurse three times dismissed by "opposite influences," challenged the "manliness" of anyone who blocked women from entering the hospitals.[36] Perhaps as a result of those dismissals she was never memorialized in any of the biographical compendiums (nor was Powers). Significantly, Bucklin used the conventions of manhood against the obstructionist doctors. If women, acting in traditional and compassionate ways, wished to fulfill their duty as nurses, how could any right-thinking man stop them? "No man of generous heart," Bucklin wrote, "wished women shut out from the doors of field or city hospitals.... It was only the ruffians who feared the just censure of compassionate women, who wished to exclude these from performing the labors, which kept our feet on the ground from early morn to the setting of the sun."[37] To challenge Bucklin's words would earn the critical reader a label of unfeeling selfishness, thereby making him unmanly.

Bucklin was explicitly critical of those with whom she dealt on a daily basis. Her tone was frank, eschewing the overflow of flowery sentiments that opened her narrative. Surgeons, she complained, could make the lives of nurses miserable. "It was in [the ward surgeon's] power to make our paths smooth, or to throw disagreeable things in the way which would make our positions extremely unpleasant, and subject us to not ordinary annoyance," she recalled, "[y]et no murmur or complaint dared pass the lips of a hospital nurse, for disgrace and dismissal only awaited the beck of his authoritative hand." Bucklin considered herself a victim of the oppression of unfeeling men, and her record of dismissals, then, becomes more of an indictment of them than of herself. Her criticism got even more pointed when she discussed the habits of some of the surgeons who were routinely drunk and examined patients in that condition. "Often we felt it was an insult to our womanhood to be constrained to give an outward show of respect when within there was nothing but loathing and detestation," she said of them.[38]

The confidence that women-nurses had in the good work they could and did do was often implicit in contrast to their more explicit descriptions of confrontations. Most narratives focused a good deal of attention on the stories of individual soldiers, significantly on their struggles with death. Rather than adopting a professional model of hospital decorum and treating wounded and sick soldiers as nameless patients, nurses sought to retain some sense of the soldier's individual pain. At the same time they used their own ability to soothe and comfort the wounded in their last minutes of life, an ability they assumed their reader would hold in high regard.

Ultimately, it seemed that many nurses felt as Elvira Powers did: that women were a crucial boon to soldiers suffering from the emotional wounds of homesickness, wounds only women could tend. At some points, these emotions were described as being the "only reasons" a certain patient was not recovering. Powers recalled one instance in which a head nurse (a man training to be a surgeon) told her of two patients on whom he had given up. They were given into her care, and survived.[39]

In a similar incident, nurse Sarah Palmer described being accosted by a doctor when she was trying to revive what he called a "dead man." Despite his "rude sneers," Palmer aided the soldier, taking up "the tangled thread of work which [the doctors] had promised to do." The patient recovered. In many cases in other narratives, as in this one, women claimed they drew on their essential compassion and empathy to effect a cure that men could not.

Many nursing narratives also revealed the degree to which the practice of nursing was a contested terrain *between* women. At issue was the degree to which middle- to upper-class women would control the terms under which nursing was practiced. Wealthy, well-known women, such as the Woolsey sisters and Katherine Wormeley, an elite young woman from Newport, Rhode Island, who wrote a history of the USSC, were invited by male relatives and friends to work as well as to supervise other nurses. Compared to the nurses hired by Dorothea Dix, who were earning forty cents a day, they had considerable power to define what kind of profession nursing would be. Their efforts to professionalize their endeavors undercut the efforts of less well educated women-nurses, who saw the task as emotional and nurturing rather than scientific. The best example of the elite perspective is Georgeanna Woolsey's "How I Came to Be a Nurse," an essay that subsequent narratives seemed to be working to refute. Sophronia Bucklin and Sarah Palmer expressed anger with the privileges and power that occasional lady nurses exhibited to their detriment and sought to establish their authentic relationship to war work despite their paychecks.

Despite Woolsey's uncompromising portrayal of the gender conflict in the hospitals, she was quick to deny that women-nurses were truly radical. These were aristocratic ladies, she reminded the reader. "None of [the early nurses] were 'strong-minded,' " she wrote; all were respectable, both politically and in terms of class status. "Some of them were women of the truest refinement and culture; and day after day they quietly and patiently worked, doing, by order of the surgeon, things which not one of those gentlemen would have dared to ask of a woman whose male relative stood able and ready to defend her and report him." "White hands," she recalled, scrubbed floors, washed windows, and performed other "menial offices." Women's resistance, then, took the form of patient, nonconfrontational persistence.

The exemplary nurse, Woolsey argued, was refined, moral, clean, and robust, but, above all, practical. "Put a sentimentalist, or a delicate creature whose head is full only of the romance of the work, in a ward," she prophesied, "and she will soon discover that she is in the wrong place." Yet "it is her head and her heart that we want, not her hands so much." Emotion, however, was not the problem, for the best nurse was the one to whom the rough soldiers confided, describing their pictures of home. The natural compassion of women, who remembered the small but significant comforts, Woolsey argued, also befitted the role of nurse. The "acceptable ministering angel" must not sympathize or expect romance but must use her "true kindness of heart and clearness of head" to "secure the greatest comfort and the speediest recovery for the sick, and for the well or convalescing, the best moral restraint."[40]

Working-class or less-educated women could not expect to offer "moral restraint," Woolsey argued. These were not the women that should be allowed authority in the public sphere. "When I say, 'women,' " she wrote explicitly, "I don't mean exclusively persons of forty-five, who prefer to pin their clothes on, rather than fasten them securely with buttons—persons who bend over a patient's bed, shedding inadvertent needles and scraps of thread into his gruel—persons who write 'To and Teast,' meaning tea and toast, etc., etc. These are not essentials calculated in themselves to fit a person for the position of army nurse, though from the specimens found in many hospitals, one would think total ignorance a qualification provided for in the army regulations." The appropriate nurse would be refined, for "the rougher the man, the more important is true refinement in his woman nurse." A rough soldier "recognizes and respects the *lady* in his nurse." Above all, Woolsey advised, no "great, rough scrub woman" would do for "ministering angel," for "put such a woman in a hospital, and her ignorance and coarseness tell at once on the moral tone of her ward."[41]

Although Sarah Palmer and Sophronia Bucklin were hardly "great, rough scrub women," they did represent the older, less-advantaged nurses of whom Woolsey spoke. Both clearly wrote out of a sense of their relative powerlessness, and they wrote believing that their hard and dirty work was more valuable than the delicate offerings of the ladies they encountered in the hospitals. Their appropriate nurse—although they never defined her explicitly—would be unafraid of blood and dirt, compassionate and motherly with the boys, and direct and forthright with the doctors.

Sarah Palmer's 1867 narrative, written by her niece, Sylvia Lawson Covey, and based on interviews with Palmer and her diary of three months, was unique in questioning the morality of war itself while considering the men who fought in it (at least the privates) as being heroic. Palmer mixed an acerbic realism with a mournful and religious sentimentalism; she talked frankly of lice and gently of the last moments of men. Unlike Woolsey, Palmer called herself a "common woman" rather than a lady, and was proud even of her utilitarian but highly unfashionable "bed-tick" dresses (held on with pins and not buttons). Her description of camp life revolved around the clashes between surgeons, chief cooks, ward masters, and her indomitable self. Palmer and Bucklin, who were equally revealing of internal conflicts, were less often the self-described victors. They did not see themselves as genteel "ministering angels" but "right-minded" workingwomen who described cleaning wounds far more often than deathbed conversions.[42] Yet they also drew on the traditional image of the nurse, grieving their regiments' losses as mothers even as they claimed their place in the war's larger story.

The persona of Sarah Palmer emerges from the text as a middle-aged, competent woman, impatient with the dainty affectations of upper- and middle-class women. She comes to do a job—a dirty one—and she will see that it is done. Palmer seems proud of her pay and describes to her niece her refusal to leave the paymaster's office until it is given to her. She relates with some pride that her garb is clean but crude, her straw hat only lasts until some soldier needs it, and her shoes are three sizes too big. "[A]s I had not matrimonial designs on that motley throng of men, it was all the same," she explains, "and they welcomed me with my hands full of rations as kindly as though clad like a queen."[43]

Although Palmer described the common soldiers as heroes, her position on the war was uncommonly negative for a published work. "[L]et noone [sic] say," she explains early in the narrative, "if war and its attendant sufferings be Christian, that where men are in the midst of this dreadful work, 'it is no place for women.' " Later, in the short diary included in the text, she makes her case even more forcefully. "Something is wrong somewhere," she writes after hundreds of dying men have been brought to the Ninth Corps Hospital at City Point. "God never made man in his image to be thus mutilated and murdered by the hand of his brothers. His mighty curse rests on the slayer's head, and shall those who wrought this killing go unscathed?" Even battlefield success holds no charms for her: "The poor wounded are now being brought in from the Fifth Corps—the loss is said to be heavy—and yet they call it 'victory.' "[44]

Palmer was under no illusions about the war: it devastated the lives of women as well as men, destroying all they held dear. Her narrative, in places, represents an entire rejection of sentimentalism. This is never more true than in the deathbed scenes she recalls. "War knows none of the comforts of peaceful death," she records. "No friends and family can watch with anxious eye the struggles of the soul to free itself from earth. War breaks down all the sweet charities which Peace nurtures into life, and dead men lie like dumb cattle in a slaughter-house, scarcely heeded, unless some tie of blood or spirit bound the living to the cold, inanimate corpse when life warmed it." As the "Harvester gathered them in," from Southern prisons and Northern hospital beds, Palmer remembers always that "some woman's heart cherished them."[45]

The catastrophic nature of war was precisely the reason that "it *was* a place for women," Palmer argued, refusing to challenge embedded conventions of womanhood. "All of men's boasted ingenuity had been expended to devise terrible engines with which to kill and maim God's own image," she added. "If war was right, it was right for women to go with brothers, and husbands, and sons, that in the time of peril the heart might not faint with the thought of an untended death-bed in the crowded hospitals, where no hand but the rough soldier's should close the dead staring eyes." Had more women been there to help, Palmer added, "many a brave man, whose bones moulder beneath the green turf of the South, would have returned to bless the loved ones left in the dear old home behind him." She agreed, however, that the soldiering could never be right for women: "[S]*he* could not give those dreadful wounds."[46]

Palmer not only clashed with surgeons; she also fought with ward masters and chief cooks (and nurses, whose food Palmer on occasion appropriated for the soldiers). Palmer gloried in her ability to thwart authority figures. One chief cook in particular was known for his stinginess, Palmer related, and she foiled him by sneaking out food when she went to eat. After a while she confessed to an "almost absolute hatred" for this man. "Thus men of low calibre," she recalled bitterly, "and full of wretched self, often get into places of trust, and caused us much annoyance in the exercise of their authority to withhold. . . . One right-minded woman . . . could have wrought far better work in their distribution than these great, unfeeling men, who get fat on the rich spoils," Palmer argued.[47] Women, she implied, were less likely to be selfish.

Despite her unabashed anger, Palmer describes herself as successful in resisting the authority of men. In fact, by her own account, she almost always won. When an officer blocked her way onto a transport ship going to Fredericksburg she boarded at another place, to his chagrin. Another surgeon refused to let a consumption patient be moved to Washington. Palmer ordered it, and the patient recovered and was discharged. Even in the case of the chief cook, Palmer was able to sneak out the delicacies (if not the brandy) she wanted for the soldiers. On one occasion, Palmer was given the money of a private for safekeeping. Hearing he was to be transferred, she rushed to the transport ship to give him back his money but was blocked from boarding by a recalcitrant surgeon. Enlisting the aid of a guard, she sneaked aboard and returned the money. Afterward, she could not resist "the inclination to let [the surgeon] know that a woman had set his authority at naught, and thanking him for his kindness, I added that the boys looked very comfortable." Palmer rejected that authority, claiming that the only "red-tape" she could endure "was sewn on the white ground-work with many stars, and floated in the free air of heaven."[48]

All women, however, were not kindred spirits, and Palmer recognized it when her efforts were checked or dismissed by upper-class women. At one point, exasperated at being the only woman in her hospital, she wrote: "I am so tired of seeing only men, that I could go to the other extreme and become a nun with good conscience." Yet when upper-class women accompanied Abraham Lincoln to visit her hospital (shortly before the president's death), Palmer became deeply conscious of the differences between them. "My bed-tick dress made a sorry contrast to [a volunteer's] costly-attired figure," she mused, "but I looked at my hands, which were not afraid to touch the dirty blouse of a wounded soldier, and wondered if her jeweled fingers would shrink at the contact." She concluded that she preferred her own situation. "I am not sure but wealth and position transform people into other beings," she wrote, "but if they would have rendered me insensible to the miseries of poor humanity, God be praised that he has withheld them from my hands."[49]

Even as she successfully negotiated with recalcitrant men, and claimed that her priorities were more morally sound, Palmer still felt and noted the restraint that accompanied her role as a woman. She blamed this sense of restraint, however, on biology. "I think my heart should have had a broader breast to beat in," she wrote in her diary, "because it feels cramped and confined as it is, and I am eager to do something which will tell amongst my fellow-creatures, and my slender woman's frame still holds me in check." Still, throughout the narrative, she claims for herself a position that "told" amongst her "fellow-creatures," and as she put it at the beginning, "It was something to brave popular opinion, something to bear the sneers of those who loved their ease better than their country's heroes . . . while a soldier's rations, and a soldier's tent made up the sum of our luxurious life."[50]

The introduction to Sophronia Bucklin's work echoed this anger at lady nurses who lived apart from the soldier's rude life. Written by "S. L. C.," the introduction is perhaps more caustic than the text itself. S. L. C. asserted that Bucklin "deserves a foremost place" in the history of the Civil War for leading "the life of an actual soldier," with its "rude fair," "unsubstantial tents," "weary marches," and "exposure to sun and dews." The writer argued that she was "in all things, save the wild, deadly charges of battle, A TRUE SOLDIER OF THE UNION."[51]

This writer also focused anger on upper-class women and "shoulder-strapped officers," much as Bucklin's narrative did. Bucklin did the real work while upper-class women got the praise. S. L. C. defended Bucklin for receiving pay for her work. Again, comparing her to privates, the author asked, "Who says, because they were *paid*, the sacrifice which they laid on their country's smoking altar was not a voluntary one?" Rather than "gratif[ying] a taste for romantic adventure," or seeing the Capitol, Bucklin went to work, S. L. C. argued, thus setting the image of her against that of the fictional image of the sentimental nurse. About this tension S. L. C.

was specific: "The well-ordered hospital, in which every sight which might shock a sensitive nature was carefully hidden—where lemonades, and jellies, and fruits, and flowers could, at fixed hours, be distributed by their fair hands—*was not* the field hospital, into which men were brought direct from the awful place of carnage, with the dirt of rifle pits mingling with their own gore, unable to meet nature's demands, with worms rioting over the putrifying flesh. Yet, it was in the field hospitals that Miss Bucklin did her greatest work."[52] The realism of Bucklin's work was given authenticity alongside the limited and conventional image of the refined heroine; in juxtaposing the two S. L. C. tapped into the prejudices of readers who might have discounted the importance of the sentimental vision.

Bucklin was equally critical of upper-class women who seemed to accrue all the glory of the ministering angel role, with none of the drudgery of the common nurse. This was particularly true of Wolf-Street Hospital in Alexandria, where the surgeons tried "to drive them from the service . . . by a systematic course of ill-treatment toward women-nurses." There were, however, ten women-nurses, herself among them, who "were here relieved within a year, many of them recognized and efficient helpers of the Government, which provided that one-third of its hospital nurses should be women. To the class of *occasional* nurses, who, with teaspoon and tumbler of jelly, passed through the war giving a taste indiscriminately to every patient—the class who wrote long glowing letters of hospital life, and who never did a thing for the soldiers only what could be performed with gloves on jeweled hands—Wolf-Street Hospital seemed an abode of plenty and comfort for all under its roof." Bucklin disassociated herself from "that class" of nurse who wore gloves and jewels at the same time that she disassociated herself from the "long glowing letters of hospital life."[53]

In the postwar years, nursing narratives became alternative histories. Replete with conflict and reflecting the shift in language from a mainstream antebellum romantic style toward a more accepted postbellum realism, these narratives mark a transitional moment.[54] The war heightened these women's awareness of the limits that society imposed on their work and their authority. Their resentment was funneled into a form of political work.

Yet these nursing narratives, for all their gritty realism and empowering sentimentalism, and despite their illuminating views on class conflict, were histories of the past. Nurses did not use their experience in the war to argue for the establishment of nursing schools that celebrated their particular values of compassion, nor for added authority in the hospitals as doctors or administrators. Their efforts were focused on the past, not the future. A few went on to establish themselves in the profession—Clara Barton and her founding of the Red Cross is the best example—but their narratives, which were far more typical, did not suggest this direction.

A Woman's War: Postwar Novels and
Mrs. E. D. E. N. Southworth's How He Won Her

Once for all the demon of self was dethroned, not to be enshrined again during the few remaining years of her life; and the war, which searched and tried so many characters, proved that Mrs. Alston's was not the weak despicable thing it had seemed.
—[Isabella McLeod], *Westfield* (1866)

The Northern women's war novels that appeared between 1865 and 1868 helped to introduce the myth of transformation so established in the minds of the authors of *The History of Woman Suffrage* a decade later. These novels, meant for audiences that included the middle-class elite, the reform community, and the working-class reader, shared several assumptions and intentions. First, they took women as their central figures; it was *their* war they meant to describe. Second, women's novels uniformly challenged the dichotomies of society. Here, they said, was public life invading private, and here were private women making an impact on the course of public events. Third, many novels offered both traditional and nontraditional heroines, suggesting both the continuity with past domestic heroines and the beginnings of newer conceptions of womanhood. Finally and most significantly, the war was described as a transformative event for middle-class white women, who were characterized as the primary moral figures. Traditional heroines waited at home, but they waited with strength and patience; their fragility, their fear, and their arrogance slipped away, leaving them more generous and compassionate. Nontraditional heroines were placed in positions of danger, and they responded to them with courage, demonstrating in the process the wide range of woman's ability.

Each of these common themes suggests more than one interpretation, some quite conventional, others more daring. The unity that characterized the rhetorical work of the early years fell away, as distinctions between women, even when commonalities were patronizingly offered, became the rule. This is clear in Isabella McLeod's 1866 novel *Westfield*, for example, which claimed in a subtitle to be "A View of Home Life in the American War." McLeod, whose background is unknown, provides a history of the impact of the war on one Northern community. Most of the men have gone to war, and in their absence the women demonstrate their own abilities and value. McLeod's women are politically minded, pious, cheerful, and strong, mixing convention with authority; the heroine, and community ideal, is a middle-class rural housewife, Aurora, who draws together disparate women.

The plot centers on Aurora's household. She is a new wife, recently having married a widower with two grown daughters. In her home the entire household participates in political discussions, thus McLeod's position on women and politics is established from the beginning. The women of the family, with "light fancy-work" in their busy hands, "in common with all intelligent American women . . . followed with deep and appreciative interest every movement in the political history of their country, forming their own opinions, and never hesitating to express them. Even quiet little May would contribute her share to such conversation between her father and his guests, never dreaming that in some parts of the civilized world she would have been looked at in silent amazement, or rebuked for a violation of feminine propriety."[55] The notion that there is a "common" view of the relationship between women and politics is tempered with the qualification "intelligent." Those too giddy with wealth, or too degraded by poverty, are not included.

When the men go off to war, the women take over their functions. Aurora, despite just having given birth to twins, manages her husband's farm with alacrity. She also helps one day a week at the Sanitary Commission in town. The head of this Sanitary Commission, the wife of the village doctor and herself a model housekeeper, is also more than competent. She is "quite in her element overseeing and directing a host of workers and finding a famous field for the display of her particular talents." The village's most independent and strong-minded female, who refuses to get married, finds her career in nursing. "I have found my mission," she tells Aurora. "[I]t lies most evidently in the sick-room. Nothing so subdues my impractical temper as having to do with people who are dependent on me, and too weak to oppose me. I shall offer myself for duty in the hospitals."[56] The town's prettiest and richest belle finds her way as the treasurer of the Sanitary Commission, and even after she loses her brother she still goes to meetings and contributes her share, much to the surprise and admiration of the community. Here is a community of women transformed by selfless and collective work, inspired by the example of the middle class. The conflict between women, which the novel hoped to resolve, transpires before the war and before the story begins, in a community once rent by pettiness.

This image of the now ideal community bowing, despite differences, to the model of the middle class was common to the early years of Reconstruction. Unlike Isabella McLeod, Mary Jane Holmes was one of the nineteenth century's most well known and popular novelists; *Rose Mather* was only one of forty novels she wrote from 1854 to the turn of the century. Holmes's books had a directly didactic purpose: "I mean always to write a good, pure, natural story, such as mothers are willing their daughters should read, and such as will do good instead of harm," Mather claimed.[57] The good they will do, it seems, is to reinforce a mainstream middle-class understanding of moral value.

In *Rose Mather*, doing good means teaching middle-class daughters to disregard class differences even as they are constantly remarked upon. The war in Holmes's novel of Rockland converts a divided women's community into a supportive sisterhood. "They were bound together now by a common bond of sympathy, those four women, each unlike to the other, and for a time they wept in silence, one for her wounded husband, one for a child deceased, one for a captured brother, the other for a son."[58] After the working-class Widow Simms loses her saintly son Isaac, the aristocratic Rose Mather strives to help ease her pain, leading the narrator to comment: "The war was a great leveler of rank, bringing together in one common cause the high and the low, the rich and the poor, and in no one was this more strikingly seen than in the case of Rose Mather, who, utterly forgetful of the days when, as Rose Carleton, of Beacon Street, Boston, she would scarcely have deigned to notice such as the Widow Simms, now sought in many ways to comfort the stricken woman, going every day to her humble home, and once coaxing her to spend a day at the Mather mansion."[59] Although there is a sense of a return to the rhetoric of unity here, the significance of this compromise of class dignity gets noted too often to do anything but heighten its perceived importance. The Mather mansion, and Rose herself plays too central a part for the war's leveling to be complete.

In the work of McLeod, Holmes, and many other women novelists the war is a dramatic watershed.[60] It taught communities the middle-class patience and virtue they needed. Without ultimately challenging the structures of womanhood and manhood it gave women a greater stake in public life and demonstrated their abilities when tested. Yet there were distinct limits to this transformation. In *Westfield*, for example, the new order did not mean that Aurora would continue to run the farm, or that the doctor's wife would start a business and continue to develop her managerial skills. Even that novel's most independent woman, who becomes a nurse, is able to do so only because of her "impractical temper," which renders her unfit for marriage. Nor does Holmes suggest that Rose understands the basis of class differences, or that the way the capitalism that has made her rich might contribute to making Widow Simms poor.

This would not be an insight of Mrs. E. D. E. N. Southworth's, either, despite her large working-class audience. Southworth offered her only directly political novels in the postwar period with *Fair Play* (1865) and its sequel, *How He Won Her* (1866). These novels were a two-volume exploration of the roles that women played in the North and the South from 1860 through the Civil War and appeared first in serial form in the *New York Ledger*. A shift was under way in Southworth's vision and style in these novels, and her subsequent novels grew more thrilling and mysterious in a movement away from the conventional domestic novel toward the sensationalistic dime novel. Whether this shift was a conscious choice or an unconscious preference, it illustrated a larger movement within fiction itself, as class differences gradually separated audiences in the postwar years.[61] As the distance between the style and politics of working-class and genteel literature widened, Southworth chose the former. (Harriet Beecher Stowe, by contrast, grew ever more genteel.)[62]

This shift began in Mrs. E. D. E. N. Southworth's sensationalist novel of the Civil War. In *How He Won Her*, Southworth's buoyant child heroine Capitola matures in the figure of Britomarte, who becomes a woman's rights woman. Her counterpart is a minister's daughter, Erminie, whose own quiet ministry comforts and supports those around her. Yet Southworth adds two additional women characters to provide even greater contrast. Britomarte and Erminie are Northerners, but the spunky Elfrida and the elite Alberta are Southern, and each woman is meant to illustrate a possible choice of occupation and political position within the war context.

Southworth's Civil War novel is in many ways a distillation of earlier work; in the dozens of her novels, themes and personalities often overlap. Erminie, often called "the Lutheran minister's orphan child," is a classic demure heroine for Southworth. She is self-sacrificing and childlike in her innocent trust, and her fiancé, Colonel Eastworth, is an older man. During wartime, Erminie renounces Eastworth when he chooses the Confederacy and she becomes a nurse in Washington, where she lives.

The more complicated characters are the Southerners. Elfrida ("Elfie") Fielding, a Virginian, is also a classic Southworth creation, much like Capitola in her antics. She and her father are Unionists and barely escape to Washington when their farm is burned by angry Rebel neighbors (they are saved by the classic loyal slave). Elfie enlists as a soldier and shows up for her summons in her skirts, becoming peeved when she is turned away.

Her former lover is also a Confederate, and when he kidnaps Elfie and whisks her off with other guerrillas, she defies him by refusing to marry him. Alberta Goldsborough, the least developed of Southworth's four main women characters, is an aristocratic Rebel lady who will risk all—including her honor—for her husband and the Cause. She dies tragically, throwing herself in front of a bullet meant for her husband.

It is Britomarte, or the "Man-Hater," who suggests some attributes new to mid-nineteenth-century heroines. The narrator clearly prefers Britomarte, although she acknowledges to her readers that they might identify more with the demure Erminie. Britomarte is silent and brooding, brilliant but poor. She will reveal few of her thoughts, take no handouts—she earns her own living—and refuses to marry her obviously worthy lover, Justin, because of the appalling situation of women in marriage. Although humorously drawn as the angry woman's rights woman, she is also beloved within the story and is the most interesting character in the novel.

Other novels and narratives of this period feature women-as-men on the battlefield, but Britomarte is one of the most financially successful characters.[63] Disguised as Wing, a silent but able soldier with a curiously downy cheek, Britomarte follows her lover to battle. Wing saves Justin's life through courage and agility, fearlessly leads men into battle, and is promoted for valor. If Britomarte's reason for going to war—her love of Justin—is conventional, based on woman's essential commitment to connectedness, this motive does not negate her performance on the battlefield, a performance that earns her the title of "Destroying Angel" rather than "angel of mercy." At the end of a fierce battle, Britomarte reveals her identity to Justin (who knew all along). As she explains: "Justin, my beloved, I abjured my womanhood, disguised myself and followed you to battle; I have been by your side on twenty well fought fields; I have dared what woman never dared before, that I might ever be with you!"[64] The daring of the "twenty well fought fields" here is cushioned by the "adjured my womanhood" as well as the "followed." One could not fight or lead men, it seems, without denying womanhood.

Southworth's hero is also the most enlightened male character in these wartime novels. From the first he recognizes that only equal treatment will win him the love of Britomarte. At first he shudders to see her in the ranks but "reflected that [he] had no right to betray [her] secret, or restrain [her] free agency."[65] While he tries to protect her by procuring her a private tent and separate duties, there are times when he cannot (she becomes a spy). Justin, in acknowledging his own struggle, demonstrates his worthiness to Britomarte, and ultimately wins her (and perhaps the reader's) admiration.

In the end Britomarte confesses the reason for her passionate hatred of men—the men in her family have all been evil—and she agrees to marry her lover. Southworth, however, does not insist that she renounce her women's-rights ideals. Justin, in response, counters that the women in her family may well have been too gentle, that "too deep a submission" will spoil men as surely as too great a resistance. And Britomarte adds that if she individually wants only to be loved, she will always "advocate the rights of women—in general."[66] Southworth in this way appeals to both sides of the issues of women's rights: Britomarte has been tamed, is no longer a man-hater, and wants no rights. But Southworth also maintains the importance of recognizing collective grievances and offers a dramatic heroine who, despite and because of her gender, becomes a leader of men, and courageous enough to impress her lover with the error of his ways. There was political work done there as well.

"WHEN THE HISTORY of this war shall be written, (and *that* cannot be *now*)," Fanny Fern wrote in an essay titled "Soldiers' Wives" in 1862, "let the historian, what else soever he may forget, forget not to chronicle [the] sublime valor of the hearthstone all over our struggling land."[67] Fern was not alone in recognizing the struggles that women at home were undergoing. Those struggles—emotional, religious, domestic, and financial—were the main concern of the women Civil War novelists. Yet like the work of women-nurses and antislavery activists, these novelists wrote of middle-class white women and their particular concerns, and they wrote their moral politics into the war record. Their rhetoric of unity from the early war years was frayed, however, by their evident concern over middle-class control of the war's meaning and the place of the conventional woman. That ambivalence, coupled with the anger over class conflict embedded in nursing narratives, illustrates the strain over the labor question and the woman question that characterized the early postwar.

I'm not ungrateful, God knows . . . Freedom and clo's, and a home of our own, is much. But it's not all. Forgive me. A mudder kerries her chile's life on her heart when he's a man, jes as before he was born; you know dat. I wondered what was my boy's birthright in dis country. . . . Dar's four millions of his people like him; waitin' for de whites to say which dey shall be—men or beasts. Waitin' for the verdict, madam.

—Rebecca Harding Davis, *Waiting for the Verdict* (1867)

Still Waiting

Race and the Politics of Reconstruction

THE END OF THE Civil War gave women writers an opportunity to rewrite the past, one that gave special moral authority to the middle-class women who believed that they helped achieve the victory. Yet in writing the history of the war, they also had to come to terms with a new social order that included altered relationships between whites and blacks. Postwar novels often focused on these new definitions of whiteness and blackness, especially for those who might be able to "pass" from one to the other.[1]

The emphasis on whiteness and blackness in the years just after the war reflected the intense anxiety both conservative and progressive Northern white women had about the consequences of the war. If most were willing to declare that the end of slavery was morally and politically necessary to the health of the republic, they were not willing to share the power of defining that nation's well-being. Black characters, now again more likely to be black women, were not drawn as independent, authoritative, or nationally useful; stereotypes once criticized as Southern propaganda flourished as slavery's legacy.

Women writers diverged, however, in their use of whiteness and blackness as political emblems of the postwar discussion of race, as much as they had during the later years of the war. Mainstream writers, largely liberal, made the distinction between black and white severe, dramatic, and morally decisive. Abolitionist writers promoted a more just reapportionment of political power, especially in the South, creating a sense of a "moral whiteness" in "black" characters, albeit one still fettered by a largely unconscious racism that could not abandon racial difference.

In *Playing in the Dark: Whiteness and the Literary Imagination*, literary critic and novelist Toni Morrison focuses on seemingly subsidiary black characters in the novels of whites to suggest both their necessity to the plot and their suggestiveness about the nature of white fear and desire. She makes her case by using the work of Herman Melville, Willa Cather, William Faulkner, Gertrude Stein, and other major canonical writers, but it is clear that her insights can also be used to explore novels in which black characters are central. And in one sense, applying her insights to novels with black protagonists is apt when it comes to the fiction of white women abolitionists in the early Reconstruction period.

This is true despite the differences between these novels and those that Morrison studies. First, as noted above, in a number of these novels, black characters are not simply subsidiary but primary protagonists. Second, love and intermarriage between white and black characters—latent, if ever conscious, themes of much earlier white fiction—are explicit. The intertwined lives of black and white people become political messages about the failures and possibilities of national reunion and repair. Largely overlooked by political historians, these texts provide a glimpse into the tangled and contradictory ways antislavery white women imagined themselves and others in a nation rebuilding itself.

In this sense Morrison's insights reveal the schism at the center of these political visions: the ostensible aim of the novel is to reveal African American character, yet the result is to reveal white values. "The fabrication of an Africanist persona is reflexive," she argues; "an extraordinary meditation on the self; a powerful exploration of the fears and desires that reside in the writerly conscious. It is an astonishing revelation of longing, of terror, of perplexity, of shame, of magnanimity."[2] In this case, the Africanist presence, or black characters, are reflexive of not only a meditation on the self but on a nation rebuilding, a nation filled with "fears and desires."

That nation, like Lydia Maria Child five minutes after hearing of Lincoln's death, was preoccupied in the early postwar years with the questions and problems of Reconstruction. In 1867 and 1868, some of the challenges Northern women novelists posed were already being met. President Andrew Johnson's Presidential Reconstruction, an abysmal failure in terms of justice to the freedmen, had ended. The program of the radical Republicans, which was strongest in these years, had begun with the Reconstruction Acts and the Fourteenth Amendment. Reconstruction promised more protection for freedpeople from the newly formed Ku Klux Klan, and dismantled Black Codes, which had curtailed the personal and legal freedom of Southern blacks. The Fifteenth Amendment, granting universal male suffrage (a measure Lydia Maria Child specifically endorsed), was a year away and would be ratified in 1870.

Despite such measures, there was still much skepticism, even fear, on the part of white abolitionists and African Americans in 1867 and 1868. Redistribution of land had proved an illusive dream for the freedpeople, and the system of sharecropping, which promised freedom from daily direction from whites, dragged many into a spiral of fraud and debt. The results of the 1868 elections were also dismaying to freedpeople and their supporters. General Ulysses S. Grant won the presidency, but with the support of moderate rather than radical Republicans. As historian Eric Foner has noted, "The Radical generation was passing, eclipsed by politicos who believed the 'struggle over the negro' must give way to economic concerns."[3]

That economic concerns trumped moral ones during Reconstruction made the arguments of women writers less persuasive. Caught between rising Southern resistance and ebbing Northern energy these novels paired the political means of the prewar period with the radical ends of the postwar period. But these ends were largely beyond even what the more progressive legislators were willing to accept, never mind the attitudes of mainstream white America.

The volatility of the issue of intermarriage at the time that these writers first conceptualized and then published their work erupted in the struggle over a pamphlet published in 1863. In an effort to scare voters away from President Lincoln, and in the wake of the Emancipation Proclamation, Democrats artfully constructed *Miscegenation: The Theory of the Blending of the Races, Applied to the American White Man and Negro*.[4] In *Miscegenation*, where the word was coined, the ostensibly abolitionist author argues that intermarriage will solve the nation's racial problems by producing a better breed of children.[5] He declares that "whereas, the result of the last Presidential election has given the colored race on this continent its freedom, the next Presidential election should secure to every black man and woman the rest of their social and political rights; that the progressive party must rise to the height of the great argument, and not flinch from the conclusions to which they are brought by their own principles."[6]

Significantly, the pamphlet included "testimonies" from prominent abolitionists in an appendix, gleaned from their work. Harriet Beecher Stowe's novel *Dred* was among these, including quoted descriptions of her mulatto characters. For these political writers, the choices made by even women novelists were telling. The abolitionist community largely *did* flinch at "the conclusions to which they are brought by their own principles," however, rejecting the pamphlet wholeheartedly in some cases, and partially in others.

The question of intermarriage between blacks and whites, which had emerged during the war as a political concern, was a central preoccupation of both the white North and the white South. During the war, the American Freedmen's Inquiry Board suppressed testimony about liaisons between white women and black men out of fear that such information would threaten the goal of emancipation.[7] Although sexual and marital unions between blacks and whites had been a public subject to varying degrees in the antebellum North, the issue had been framed within a critique of slavery and centered around black women's vulnerability and resistance to rape by whites. In the postwar period, however, blacks were depicted as legal and social equals.

The specter of consensual unions was especially frightening for white men because it potentially undercut control over the bodies of women, both black and white. As historian Deborah Gray White observes about an earlier period, "Women and blacks were the foundation on which Southern white males built their patriarchal regime. If, as seemed to be happening in the North during the 1830s, blacks and women conspired to be other than what white males wanted them to be, the regime would topple."[8] That regime threatened to topple in the postwar period, and a few women writers worked to give it a push in what they believed was the right direction. The irony was that their effort itself reinforced the hierarchy they challenged.

Emphasizing Difference: Racial Whiteness in Postwar Fiction

For the majority of the postwar novels on war written by women, the newly free condition of African Americans was a point of self-congratulation.

The moral North, in these stories, triumphed over the evil South, and now slaves could happily find their place at the bottom of a "free" labor system. Despite well-meaning efforts to write black characters into the story of national life, these writers' first impulses seemed to encourage a kind of sunny complaisance about the relationships between white and black, one jarring in the aftermath of a cruel war. Whiteness, in their lexicon, unproblematically meant superiority, and if blackness was not evil, it was forever naturally separate. Any rhetoric of unity across race was meager and fleeting: black and white, if grateful and generous in their spheres, were drawn as unalterably different.

In her 1867 novella, "The Brownings," Jane Gay Fuller introduces a history of the war to young readers via a series of juxtapositions: the cold Christmastime cheer of the North in 1861 and the sunny glee of the South; a white girl in Georgia dressed in black, and a black girl dressed in white. The story concerns a family whose Northern mother has died, leaving her Southern husband a legacy of her antislavery politics as the war begins. The central question is, of course, how he will respond to this legacy. And furthermore what, ultimately, will happen to these white and black girls (one, his daughter, the other, his slave) as a result of his response.

The novella began the work of white rapprochement that would characterize the later phase of Reconstruction while maintaining the spirit of earlier antislavery sentiment.[9] "There is much error in the common belief that *cruelty* is the law of the Southern plantation," the narrator interjects at one point. "It is only an exception to the more general rule of care and kindness. Wrong as such a system of servitude may be in itself, great as are its attendant evils, nowhere perhaps in the world are found more careless, happy laborers than in the Southern United States."[10] The phrasing here is significant: the system is one of "servitude," not the grimmer "slavery"; "laborers," not slaves, were never resistant or aggrieved but "careless" and "happy"; and the region is not the "South," but the "Southern United States." In the end the white girl, Lucy, and the black girl, Teenah, are taken North out of the maw of war, one to join society, the other to educate herself to serve her "emancipated race."[11] Order is reestablished at the end of the story, with the discordant colors of the clothing now more appropriately rendered in consistent communities: white with white, black with black.

Even far more sympathetic stories in the immediate postwar period, including Harriet E. Prescott's October 1865 *Atlantic Monthly* story, "Down the River," constantly used the colors of white and black to represent good and evil, or at least fundamental difference. "Down the River" depicts the ideological enlightenment of a naive and foolish girl, "Flor" (called various names, none of them complimentary). She "was of pure race, black as her first ancestor," the author begins the story, and "her countenance was as unlovely as it is possible for one to be that owns the cheeriest of smiles and the most dazzling of teeth."[12] Flor is a dancer. She wears scanty clothing, dances with wild abandon to meaningless songs, and has no touch of religion—except a love of the earth—to hamper her. She wants nothing to do with freedom and loves her mistress, Miss Emma, more than herself.

Flor's coworkers infect her with a truer sense of her condition, and when she and her mistress get lost in a swamp, she meets the family butler, now free and living there. Before helping her return home with her mistress, he almost talks Flor into fleeing slavery, and only her steadfast loyalty to Emma (who is sleeping) restrains her. Emma's comment about her fear of the dogs that will be sent out to find Flor is striking, as is Flor's rather-wiser-than-she's-supposed-to-be answer: "Dey knows de diff'unce 'tween de dark meat and de light."[13] Emma promises to protect Flor but fails to, and when the two return to the plantation they are separated and Flor is flogged.

In the discussion between Flor and the butler, Sarp, over the unconscious body of Emma in the Great Swamp, images of white and black are bandied about in sometimes confusing and ambiguous ways. Sarp tells Flor that she can choose "the chance to make [herself] white in the Lord's eyes. . . . Refuse, and you take sin and chains and darkness." Flor won't believe that she could be white in heaven—"likely story, little black nigger like dis yere am be put in the groun' an' come out all so great an' w'ite an' shinin'-like!"—and when Sarp tries to convince her with an analogy using the image of a hard black bean and a white flower, she contradicts him: beans make beans, she tells him. He ends the conversation nonplussed, but she becomes convinced of the appeal of freedom nonetheless.[14]

The story ends after Flor, hearing of a Union battleship in the mouth of the river, steals a leaky stow, and despite waterfalls, desperate thirst, and frightening tides, makes her way there. Her fear and courage are palpable and laudable placed alongside her early frivolousness, and when she is taken half-fainting off the plank she is left with, there are "white faces crowding around her" like "pallid blots," but one "dark face" smiles, a beacon, below the flag, "whose starry shadow nowhere shelters a slave."[15]

If the moral of the story—a congratulation to the North for winning the moral high ground—is clear by the end, the black / white dilemma of Sarp and Flor remains. Does a black bean make a white flower, the reader might plausibly ask? No, Flor answers, it makes a bean, and if she's surrounded by white in the end, it is the black face that is smiling: Flor won't want to identify with "pallid blots," and maybe not even a shiny white heaven. To begin with "a pure race" of black, to emphasize its natural ugliness and frivolity, and to end by paternalistically rescuing it is a constant inner narrative of many stories, even in the reformist liberal pages of the *Atlantic Monthly*.[16]

Even stories that are ostensibly about different issues concern themselves with race and heredity and their meanings to the North. In Mrs. Hopkinson's "Quicksands," published in June 1866, the central question of the story is why Percy, a beautiful white widow "with a face as destitute of color as if it had been carved out of marble," will not agree to marry an earnest young Unionist. The reader learns, however, that Percy is no widow after all but married to the cousin of an English earl. She is of unknown racial origin until it is revealed she is the child of a French governess and this same English earl. In other words, she is pure white. Percy's husband has gone on a trip and is never heard from again, although he is sighted at various times. All believe he has left Percy because of her murky origins, but in the end he returns, an exultant Union officer, the victim of Japanese pirates and Confederate impressment, now made new.

What's the message here? The whiteness that gives Percy and her suitor, whose face is often described as "pale and resolute," their identity is contrasted with the Japanese pirate and the Confederate, and will endow status on those who inherit it: the new nation deserves such citizenship and has lost such white heroes—"shining marks for death"—in its remaking. Identifying courage and bravery with whiteness claims the war for white men and the future for white women.

The glorification of the war, a theme so prevalent in the early war years and so strained in the later ones, reasserted itself when the battles ceased. Stories routinely emerged that described the conflict as heroic, well fought and well won, some writers stressing the contribution of African American soldiers, others beginning the work of deemphasizing it and presenting the war as a white man's war. This insistence on whiteness and the work of white men in women's writing emerged from the frequent use of words like "fair" to describe the protagonists of these narratives.[17] So in "My Little Boy," a sentimental tale about an honorable younger brother lost to an older-sister-cum-mother-substitute, the "incarnation of loveliness" has a predictably "fair face." The good times are marked by "white memories," and the person who comes bearing the tale of the boy's death at the end of the war offers an "outstretched hand turned white with pity."[18]

Even stories or memoirs of the war work undertaken on behalf of the freedmen suggest a pity that stresses difference while it acknowledges shared womanhood and a crushingly difficult context. W. H. Palmer's "A Woman" is narrated by a white woman of indeterminate age who works helping to distribute contributions from the North to the freedpeople in Virginia. (Significantly, an early war story titled "A Woman" concerns a white woman. Here the universal measure of womanhood has expanded— at least in the title.) The "woman" of the title is a "pretty quadroon" (to suggest her lightness and, hence, "beauty" to the audience) who, it is re-vealed during the course of the story, was married before the war and was apparently abandoned by the husband who fled slavery, and is being cou-rted by another man, whom she tries—and ultimately fails—to resist. The suitor offers her the material comfort she cannot achieve alone. Yet this woman has been given the name "Eve" and is drawn as a betrayer of trust.

The setting of the story—Virginia—is symbolic: here is the devastated South, hindered by a kind of moral decay. The narrator is struck with the air of corruption: "[T]here came into my mind a morbid notion, an idea of moral wrongs bred like maggots in the dissolution of an evil, of stinging swarms, like the bees of Samson's riddle, lodging in the carcass of a slain system." The swarms, of course, are freedpeople, and the carcass, the slav-ery of the South. Yet the narrator (and the writer) hold the freedpeople curiously to blame, even when ostensibly absolving them.

This story was published in the *Galaxy*, a new liberal magazine filled with common and negative stereotypes that sharper-edged wartime writ-ing had challenged but were by now widely embraced. The suitor, possess-ing only "a simple nature," "lacked the self-assertion which the quadroon often has, but the mulatto seldom." His energetic pursuit of Eve is charac-terized by "a craving enthusiasm, a timid abasing, engrossing passion." She, of course, has a "voluptuous grace" and "lissom arrogance," but the author is swift to tell us that she is clearly marked: "in the delusive light, like a dusk chiselling out of the shadows."[19]

The message of the story is that the African American woman, al-though stuck in a world in which she cannot support herself with the work she is best suited for—her suitor tells her, "You ain't fit to work. You'se jus' like white folks"—is not fit for the moral work of the white middle-class narrator, either. Faced with the dilemma of an ardent suitor and comfort-able marriage versus sacrifice, hard work, and moral rectitude, Eve *tries* to do the right thing but fails. She takes herself away from her suitor to work on a farm for poor and crude whites, but she comes back several months later, beaten down physically and morally, and marries him.

It is at this point that her prewar husband returns, gaunt with the work of finding her and the guiding work he has done for the Union. The narrator is introduced to him as another "article not invoiced," sent from the North; an "article" she can use if she "want[s] any help." True to this kind of story, the just-remarried wife and the now-returned first husband meet over the body of the new, now-dead-in-an-accident second husband, a convenient if implausible settlement of the problem.

What is significant to this story, and bears exploration, is the deliberate intervention of the narrator, who feels empowered to interrupt what is clearly a personal conflict. Eve, she decides, is so "easily tempted, cowardly, with small power for enduring or resisting, that I dreaded the test to which she was about to be put."[20] Indeed, she argues implicitly, it is this cowardice that causes Eve to fail her husband, not the work that admittedly made her "wretchedly changed." The only real credit Eve is given is for her choice of black for a wedding dress, for "she had the taste to perceive how much black relieved her tawny complexion."[21] The narrator, discovering that the "article" is Eve's former husband, goes to Eve and asks her if she has been married before; when she says yes and asks if the narrator has seen her husband, her joy at being newly wed and comfortable is swiftly quenched. The narrator pities her ignorance and is dismayed by her pain (surprised by it, too). "I had not counted on her suffering—her womanhood," she admits.[22] Although the narrator "do[es] not know if [Eve] was worthy of forgiveness," she ends the story believing Eve has been forgiven. The story, ultimately, is about moral failing, not desperate circumstance; about whiteness and moral certitude and blackness and "temptation, resistance, eventual defeat."[23]

The writer (and, one imagines, the reader) can congratulate herself. Using the war as a frame, minimizing black resistance to slavery or contribution to the Union effort, white women writers could place themselves on moral high ground, as benefactors of a slavish race that is to be deeply pitied but also judged wanting—and irredeemably different. Eve is no Eliza, leaping across floating ice and thus risking death for her child. The war thus *confirmed* the superiority of whiteness as well as the superiority of the Northern interpretation of the Constitution and Northern capitalism, Northern ideas of order and the work ethic.

An Africanist Presence

Distinct from the work of more mainstream liberals was that of previous abolitionists and activists who were more directly concerned with the policies of Reconstruction. These activists strove to create a moral whiteness through stories of black Americans struggling to be free in the aftermath of the Civil War, as a way of sanitizing their social and political presence. One strategy for depicting this moral whiteness came from creating literal "whiteness" in black characters. While "passing" characters already had a significant presence in the work of both black and white authors by the postwar period, their use here had multiple meanings, suggesting solutions to national rupture.

Three novelists in particular directly confronted the fears of the post-war period with novels about the war. Each had her own relationship to abolitionism and hence advocated a different approach toward Reconstruction. By 1865 Lydia Maria Child had struggled and sacrificed in the fight against slavery for over thirty years; her *Romance of the Republic* (1867) suggested that intermarriage and personal efforts at education would successfully integrate blacks into white society. Anna Dickinson, a virtual newcomer to antislavery work compared to Child, argued in *What Answer?* (1868) not so much for intermarriage—her lovers are literally killed by prejudice—as for black suffrage. And Rebecca Harding Davis, who struggled to illuminate the complexities of the Civil War to her readers, suggested, in *Waiting for the Verdict* (1868), the most idealistic solution of all: that right-thinking, white individuals and families adopt the fortunes of less fortunate black families and live side by side with them in communitarian relationships. Her depiction of love relationships between the races, however, was more realistic: they fail because of deeply embedded, and lasting, racial prejudice. The shared strategy in these divergent visions was to imagine postwar life through romantic love between blacks and whites. For all three writers, Reconstruction had metaphorical possibilities with pointed political implications.

These women used history and criticism more directly than the numerous other postwar white women novelists.[24] As historian Martha Hodes notes, they understood "how sex between white women and black men [and marriage between white men and black women] came to be a deeply political issue connected directly to the maintenance of racial hierarchy from emancipation forward."[25] They knew that the end of the war marked only the beginning of a social revolution still largely to be achieved in race relations, and the fight over civil rights and voting legislation formed the backdrop for their writings. In many ways this work was more honest, bracing, and effective than that of later writers, yet it also revealed the difficulty of translating abstract abolitionist pieties into a workable postwar program. Like Willa Cather, who made what Morrison calls a "dangerous journey" to view the "void of racism," they did not arrive safely.[26]

Yet Child, Dickinson, and Davis need to be seen as part of a larger effort, one inspired by similar motives. Most of the Northern women writing novels on the war in the postwar period condemned slavery and celebrated its demise. In many cases, such condemnations and celebrations were made by white characters in their fiction, suggesting that the hero or heroine saw God's will in the whirlwind before the nation did. The heroine in A. O. W's *Eyewitness*, a novel written to record the efforts of white Southerners loyal to the Union, says to her cousin, "O Harry, what greater evil could be visited upon man than slavery? . . . God grant, if this war must be, that it may ultimately and completely do away with slavery."[27] Another loyal Southern Unionist, from Bella Z. Spencer's *Tried and True*, is equally convinced of slavery's wrongs before the war but despairs of change: "It is like attempting to overturn the world, for one woman to put her small strength against so mighty an evil as this evil of slavery." During the war she is forced to abandon home and child because of these views and her aid to a fugitive slave; she then turns her efforts to nursing the wounded near southwestern battlefields.[28]

Other novelists used white male characters to express their antislavery views, thus perhaps making political statements more acceptable. Louisa May Alcott commented on the evil effects slavery had on whites through a fictional soldier impelled to heroism by his love for a moral and loving white woman. Once a Confederate, her hero is now a Unionist, and he tells his fellow soldiers on the picket line: "Have I not cause to dare much?—for in owning many slaves, I too became a slave; in helping to make many freemen, I liberate myself."[29] In Mary J. Holmes's novel *Rose Mather*, a white boy with Southern sympathies completes the author's condemnation of slavery. He has fled the South with his Unionist sister, is dying of disease, and is confused and upset at the outcome of the war. He tells his sister: "I get terribly perplexed thinking it all over, and how it has turned out. I think—yes, I know I am glad the negroes are free. We never abused them. Uncle Paul never abused them. But there were those who did; and if slavery is a Divine institution as we are taught to believe, it was a broken-down and badly-conducted institution, and not at all as He meant it to be managed."[30] By choosing a character with Southern loyalties to make this statement Holmes stresses that even slaveholders themselves could admit the wrong they perpetrated.

The position that many of these novels established allowed for an embrace of the lost white South. If the Confederacy was wrong, as they assumed it surely was, the South was inhabited by valiant and true Unionists—many of whom were white women—who through love and influence would change the rest. And, as in Holmes's novel, this position accepted the moderate Southern view of simply a "broken-down" institution, not "as He meant it to be managed." Here, then, was a redeemable white South, where black characters were generally left comfortably in the background, distanced by the perceived needs of Northern white writers to forgive and forget.

In this context, white women writers who had black characters express their own arguments were rather startling. Even more startling was the fact that many of these characters expressed themselves as part of interracial relationships. Child, Dickinson, and Davis went beyond what historian George Fredrickson considers a "viable abolitionist position" on miscegenation in the postwar period (i.e., looking the other way when blacks and whites fell in love and married) and crossed the line by having their characters consciously contemplate intermarriage.[31]

The Politics of Intermarriage

Of the three novels, the implications of Lydia Maria Child's *A Romance of the Republic* were the most conservative. The plot concerns two octoroons who, until they are orphaned, live in ignorance of their racial background. In the aftermath of these characters discovering their background, most of the novel concerns their growing awareness of the difficulties of maintaining sexual purity and respectability while they are slaves, even ostensibly protected ones. By the end of the novel they have both married white Northerners, and the problems of slavery are largely solved by the Civil War.

The complacency and underlying racial hierarchy that inform the novel seem unlike Child, whose letters sound a far more rigorously critical tone concerning racial prejudice. What emerges is the sense that Child, for all her thirty years of work, including a history of religious beliefs that refused to exalt Christianity at the expense of other faiths, retains the notion of New England white culture as preferable to all others: for blacks to enter white society as equals, they must become white.

The issue of intermarriage revealed both Child's hopes for an end to racial prejudice and her own unquestioned sense of cultural and racial hierarchy. Her two heroines are unintellectual, named for flowers and surrounded by them, and have to be saved by men. In the one case in which a secondary white character (who believes he is black) marries a clearly dark-skinned woman, she is quickly taught how to act white. Child's central characters, Rosa and Floracita, two (appropriately) cultured African

Lydia Maria Child (1802–80).
Following the 1833 publication
of an antislavery pamphlet
titled *An Appeal in Favor of that
Class of Americans Called Africans*,
Child thereafter used her
public writing to do political
work: to urge the end of slavery,
the decent treatment of fugitives and freedpeople, and
fairness for Native Americans.
(Reproduced courtesy of the
Schlesinger Library, Radcliffe
College.)

American sisters, draw this woman, Harriet, into their circle in order to
teach her to become a lady lest she hold her husband back. Harriet learns
how to sew and copy in an elegant hand, for "belonging to an imitative
race, she readily adopted the language and manners of those around her."
Falling in with yet another racial stereotype, Child describes her as failing
to be truly beautiful because of "too crisp" hair: "Her features were not
handsome, with the exception of her dark, liquid-looking eyes; and her
black hair was too crisp to make a soft shading for her brown forehead. But
there was a winning expression of gentleness in her countenance, and a
pleasing degree of modest ease in her demeanor."[32] One of the white male
characters, returning home from the war, asks to see the extent of the
women's influence in affecting Harriet's transformation. After she leaves
the room he says paternally, "Really, this is encouraging," adding, "If half a
century of just treatment and free schools can bring them all up to this
level, our battles will not be in vain, and we shall deserve to rank among the
best benefactors of the country; to say nothing of a corresponding improvement in the white population."[33] "They," it seems, need to have their
culture and their traditions trained out of "them." Since "they" are an

"imitative" race, "they" soon adopt the appropriate styles of middle-class whites and light-skinned blacks. The irony, of course, is clear: his fellow civilizers (Rosa and Floracita) are actually among "them."

Child used these fictional marriages to refute the argument that whites and blacks naturally repel each other as love objects. With them she directly challenged Northern white resistance to the effects of African American freedom on white society. And yet, Child—as did Dickinson and Davis—created her African American characters as special, odd, exceptional. Rosa and Floracita talk in light, flowery phrases interspersed with words in French and Spanish. They are adept at music and art but are unable to take up sterner courses of study. They are remarkably naive and have to be helped out of their difficulties by others (darker black servants, a white woman from the North, white men). Child's heroines lack the backbone of Dickinson's and Davis's; instead they are embodiments of dependent, submissive, pious, true women. They are clearly victims—and clearly exceptions. And yet their final marriages to white Northern men are seen as a positive good, rather than as the tragic mistakes these unions seem to be for Dickinson and Davis.

Anna Dickinson's 1868 novel *What Answer?* followed Harriet Beecher Stowe's tradition of providing evidence to support her story with the addition of a bibliographic note at the end of the text. However, Dickinson's tale of the tragic marriage of a wealthy white-skinned black Philadelphian and a Civil War officer ends in a significantly different way than most midcentury domestic novels: The lovers are brutally murdered in the New York City riot of 1863 by unrepentant Irish racists (the male character's British father is equally racist). They die holding each other, with his head "from which streamed golden hair, dabbled and blood-stained—upon her faithful heart."[34]

In *What Answer?* Dickinson focused on intermarriage as a way to make a larger point about both Northern racism and social justice. Yet if her Francesca Ercildoune has the backbone that Rosa and Floracita lack, she, too, is portrayed as an exception. She is so beautiful that when Anglo-Saxon William Surrey sees her out of his window he chases after her down the street to meet her. Her courageous brother Robert earns the praise of even previously racist white men as he carries the flag in battle while suffering two wounds. (A member of the Massachusetts Fifty-fourth, Robert is a product of the careful research that Dickinson gave to her plot.)

Their marriage, ironically, is most faithfully defended by Jim Given, a white working-class character who is employed in Surrey's factory and who serves under Surrey during the war. In her portrayal of this character

Anna Elizabeth Dickinson (1842–1932). Dickinson was an antislavery and women's rights activist who lectured widely in the North during the Civil War. Her postwar novel *What Answer?* used the New York City draft riots as the backdrop for a love story that urged her readers to give African Americans the vote. (Photo used by permission of the Library of Congress.)

(and Given's sweetheart, Sallie), Dickinson complicates stereotypical renderings of a racist urban working class. By depicting loyal working people, Dickinson suggests that racism is not confined to the members of the working classes, who are subject to reeducation through interaction with (good) black characters. Thus, Given strenuously argues with another soldier on the picket line when he hears of the marriage. Nature has placed a barrier between blacks and whites, the soldier says. Not true, Given counters, pointing to mulattos. " 'T wan't the abolitionists; 't was the slaveholders and their friends that made a race of half-breeds all over the country; but, slavery or no slavery, they showed nature hadn't put any barriers between them,—and it seems to me an enough sight decenter and more respectable plan to marry fair and square than to sell your own children and the mother that bore them. Come now, ain't it?"[35] In any case, he continues, Ercildoune isn't really African American, just as another friend isn't Indian, despite his Indian ancestry. If the Anglo-Saxon race is the master race, he suggests, isn't Francesca's seven-eighths of white blood master over her one-eighth negro blood? Slavery, then, continues, with one blood "master" over the other.

After the lovers die, the novel continues for three more chapters, suggesting that the real solution to racial prejudice is not so much intermarriage as it is politics. The darker brother of the near-white heroine is permanently maimed in the war, yet despite this mark of his patriotism he is still taunted by whites when he goes to the polls. Looking at his white companion and friend, he asks, "1860 or 1865?—is the war ended?" "No!" his friend tells him, taking his arm. How it will end, he says, "is for the loyal people of America to decide." The suggestion is clear: African American men deserve the vote, and this is the answer "loyal people" should give.[36] That the vote would not include women, black or white, and that it alone would not solve a racial prejudice so deep that it pulled apart families, is never addressed. Dickinson, who was a lecturer and not a novelist, wrote only to speak to one issue: the vote.

Rebecca Harding Davis's novel is far more complex than either Stowe's or Dickinson's and represents a real advance on her earlier work with black characters. Instead of brutish (because they have been damaged by slavery), these characters are varied and capable of growth. Like Stowe, Davis tended to give the finer intellect to the whiter characters and the immediately nobler impulses to darker ones, although the yearnings were the same across the spectrum of color. Davis's characters, especially her central African American woman, are also more frank in their expectations of social justice: these are not the hopes of Eliza, who is content with slavery until the sanctity of her family is threatened. They want and they deserve some sort of stability and opportunity on U.S. soil (although in Davis's rendering clearly not complete parity).

In *Waiting for the Verdict* Davis tells the story of two families, one white and one black, whose lives are entwined. In the white family, a Northern working-class woman named Rosslyn marries Garrick Randolph, a Southern aristocrat. Rosslyn, a virtuous and religious woman, has to remake Garrick, who in an act of selfishness and cruelty sells Hugh, a faithful slave and the head of the second family of the novel, in order to silence him about a family secret. In order for Garrick to retain Rosslyn's affections, however, he has to undo the evil he caused, and he makes a pilgrimage to the South both to reconnect the family he broke apart and to tell the secret. The relatives of Hugh, in a parallel story, struggle to reunite during the war despite terrible odds (like Eliza in *Uncle Tom's Cabin*, a young mother escapes slavery and walks for miles carrying her son). In the end Rosslyn offers a home and land for all three generations—Hugh, his son Nathan and wife, Anny, and his grandson, Tom—as a kind of retributive act of justice.

The friendship between Rosslyn and Anny suggests the way Davis imagined social revolution. It is the African American character who gives the novel its title as the two women together discuss the future of their children. Anny questions whether her son will get the birthright of freedom and opportunity he deserves: "I'm not ungrateful, God knows . . . Freedom and clo's, and a home of our own, is much. But it's not all. Forgive me. A mudder kerries her chile's life on her heart when he's a man, jes as before he was born; you know dat. I wondered what was my boy's birthright in dis country. . . . Dar's four millions of his people like him; waitin' for de whites to say which dey shall be—men or beasts. Waitin' for the verdict, madam.' "[37] Davis wondered whether the spiritual hunger of African Americans would be fulfilled with material comforts alone. Her political solution—that individuals provide a home for those in their backyard—was based on a prewar hope for individual perfectionism. Yet if the solution offered property and security, it still relied on black submission (being grateful) and white action ("waitin' for de whites") rather than African American independence—or recompense for years of unremunerated labor.

Davis plumbed questions of class together with those of race in *Waiting for the Verdict*, and she held out far more hope in the transformative power of the war on particular characters than on social structure. Her novel was meant to change the minds of her readers by soothing their fears. Rosslyn explains these racist fears to Anny:

> "I think," Ross hesitated, "one reason for the coolness with which the whites listen to your cry for help is, the dislike to the thoughts of intermarriage."
>
> "Dar's no danger of many marriages," said Anny, gravely and significantly; "an' as for mixin' de blood, it's been the fault ob de whites when dat eber was done. Dar'll be less of it when cullored women is larned to respect themselves. O, Missus! dat talk of marryin' is sech a fur-off shadder! But the ignorance an' disgrace ob my people is no shadder!"[38]

While Davis brought black characters forward in her text, and gave them dignity in a way many of her contemporaries did not, she still mixed her messages, either out of her own racial prejudice or out of some sense of what her audience would bear. If "it's been the fault ob de whites when dat eber was done," still, Anny adds, "[d]ar'll be less of it when cullored women is larned to respect themselves," which is a contradiction. And Anny still does not call her friend "Rosslyn," but "Missus"; if the women lived side by side, and the implication of this was a kind of social equality, this depiction contains another message.

Davis outlined her view in a subplot that unfolds earlier in the novel. The truth of intermarriage as a "fur-off shadder" comes up between John Broderip (Hugh's son "Sap," renamed in order to "pass") and the resolutely Anglo-Saxon Margaret Conrad, bringing Broderip to a crucial dilemma. Davis allows Broderip to "pass" not only in the novel's story but for the reader as well, until the climactic scene. Broderip, a surgeon of considerable skill, is drawn as an eccentric, moody, yet endearing man, one with whom the profound, critical, and highly intelligent Conrad falls in love.[39] When Broderip's darker brother Nathan escapes from slavery after risking his life to save Rosslyn's grandfather and comes to find his brother "Sap," the reader becomes privy to Broderip's deep ambivalence: should he continue to "pass" in order to win the love of Margaret and thus forsake both his family and his race?

Here Davis used the sympathy toward Broderip she created in her readers to stress the nature of his struggle with prejudice. If Broderip recognizes Nathan, he loses everything he owns, his social standing, his lover. If he does not, he rejects family, honesty, honor. He is not a pure hero; he struggles with this question. In attending to his brother's wounded arm, Broderip briefly ponders the possibility of letting his scalpel slip, and "accidentally" killing Nathan, thus avoiding having to admit his race to the world. Broderip had finally determined to ask Margaret to marry him before Nathan's arrival. Margaret's subsequent refusal to consider marriage with the man she loves because of his race is thus all the more disappointing. Significantly, her blind father is supportive of the match, even after Broderip reveals himself: here it is the white woman who sustains racial prejudice.

By the end of the novel, after Broderip's heroic death (also with the Massachusetts Fifty-fourth), Margaret conquers much of her destructive prejudice and, despite the love of an honorable white man, waits only to join Broderip in heaven. Through love between black and white, Davis suggests that Margaret's refusal to acknowledge her love was the "unnatural" act. By leading white readers to identify and feel affection for Broderip, she worked more subtly to force them to confront their preconceived prejudices.

Turning Points

Like the authors of antislavery stories of the late war, Child, Dickinson, and Davis depicted active and honorable black men in order to counter fears about the future of the freedpeople. These men earn their rights as citizens and thus justify the war's outcome. Rather than creating frightening portrayals of justified anger, these novelists created men who resist the forces that oppressed them in "honorable" ways—going to fight for the Union forces or aiding Union soldiers behind the lines. Their anger is channeled in socially acceptable ways. The writers stressed that these black men fought like white men, earned their freedom, and subscribed to familiar conventional values (men go off to battle and women, when they can, stay home). These men seemed to be conscious counterimages to the growing white Southern myth of the black rapist.

Yet it is significant that when all three novelists treat the theme of intermarriage, it is rarely black men who figure in that portrait; in most instances white men fall in love with black women. To return to Morrison, black characters were used as ways to express ideas about racial whiteness. In most interracial relationships white authors reinscribed a kind of social order: white men still had their choice of women, black and white, and black women were allowed to be "true women" by virtue of white desire to continue marking them as malleable, domestic, and passive. But if black men aspired to white women, these acceptable markers of social status shifted: black men were thus sexualized, active, and assumed to be able to protect white women. To soften such a dramatic shift, then, Davis made Broderip effeminate and Margaret masculine, and yet their final images reverse this: he becomes a brave soldier, she a chastened teacher and mother figure. Yet their union cannot be consummated anywhere short of heaven.

For these writers their novels were something of a turning point in their careers. Lydia Maria Child put a great deal of hope and energy into a postwar novel meant to address persistent racial prejudice, in the North and the South. The antislavery struggle had been her life's work, and although she sympathized with suffragists, Child felt she had "fought through a somewhat long campaign" against slavery and had "little energy for enlisting in a new war."[40] A Romance of the Republic was her last major effort for the freedpeople, even though she continued to write editorials for political newspapers on the issues of the day. Exceptional by any standard of persistence and passion for social justice and activism, Child was representative of a generation of antislavery reformers whose energies waned after the war's end, even as they continued to hope for and work for the millennium they increasingly felt would never quite come.[41]

Anna Dickinson, who was nineteen when the war began, became a lecturer with power and influence during the war years, considering both national issues and narrower partisan ones, peaking in a 1864 lecture to Congress. Her style was passionate and inspirational, and it drew huge crowds of both men and women. Throughout the war, newspapers debated the propriety of her place behind the lectern, even as they announced her next engagement. Journalist Fanny Fern celebrated Dickinson's work and its larger meaning for women in the *New York Ledger* on more than one occasion, suggesting at the same time that it had been bitterly criticized.[42] *What Answer?* was considerably less successful than Dickinson's lectures, as evidenced by its largely negative critical reception and the fact that it was published in only a single edition.

"Peace must have put a sudden barrier in the way of many women's new found careers," Rebecca Harding Davis wrote to Annie Fields in March 1866, musing that she had not seen any work from Louisa May Alcott recently.[43] Certainly her own career demonstrated a similar brief decline as she recovered from the birth of her second son and quarreled with James Fields of the *Atlantic* over what seemed a breach of contract.[44] In this period of personal turmoil, however, Davis wrote what was her most ambitious novel to date, one that questioned the progress of Reconstruction, touched upon the thorny issue of miscegenation, presented an unvarnished working-class heroine, eschewed the "painted" histories of the Civil War for one less sentimental and more complex, and, as noted earlier, offered a depiction of African Americans that while not without flaws, represented an advance on the more demeaning characterizations of her earlier writing.[45] "The subject [of Civil War and Reconstruction] is one which has interested me more than any other and I wish to put whatever strength I have into that book and make it, if possible, different from anything which I have yet been able to do," Davis wrote of *Verdict* to the editors of the new magazine the *Galaxy*.[46]

For each of these writers, fiction became a political vehicle through which to move the nation forward. Child hoped to put the form of novel-writing to as good use as her friend Stowe. In her typically astute fashion she summed up the political intent of her novel to an African American correspondent and antislavery compatriot, Philadelphian Robert Purvis, who had written to her to praise it. "In these days of novel-reading, I thought a Romance would take more hold of the public mind than the most elaborate arguments; and having fought against Slavery, till the monster is *legally* dead, I was desirous to do what I could to undermine Prejudice," she wrote.[47] Her letter to Purvis sounded an optimistic note, but it preceded and followed others with a far more cynical and despairing tone. The novel's unenthusiastic reception was daunting for Child, sapping her energy for writing another. "[T]he apathy of my friends [for her novel] took all the life out of me, and has made me feel as if I never wanted to put pen to paper again," she confessed. In all, the work brought "a great deal of disappointment and humiliation" and little income, mainly, her biographer surmises, because of the subject of intermarriage.[48]

Dickinson's novel was also largely rejected in the press. Harriet Beecher Stowe praised the work and wrote to Dickinson as a member of an older generation passing the torch of social reform to a new one. "I lay on my sofa all alone on Saturday night and read your book all through, and when I got through I rose up mentally and fell on your neck and said, Well done, good and faithful Anna—daughter of my soul," Stowe exclaimed. "Your poor old grandma in this work rejoices to find it in your brave young hands." Later she added, "Don't mind what anybody says about it as a work of art. Works of art be hanged! You had a braver thought than that." The response of the *Nation* was more typical. "Whatever a novel should have, it lacks," the reviewer asserted, "and whatever a novel should not be it is. A thoroughly bad novel."[49]

The response to Rebecca Harding Davis's novel was also mixed, although it was seemingly treated with a bit more respect by her reviewers if only in their giving space in their newspapers for their critiques. Her biographer argues that her labors were not wholly in vain, for "*Waiting for the Verdict* is one of her best novels and, as an epic of the Civil War and its aftermath, an important literary document of the period."[50] Contemporaries disagreed. Stowe praised it, while the *Nation* reviewer, in this case Henry James Jr. (who perhaps wrote the review of Dickinson's work), dismissed it with contempt. James found her use of working-class and black characters curious and her clear-eyed realism distasteful. Yet James's distaste gave Stowe the determination to write Davis, which began their acquaintance. "*The Nation* has no sympathy with any deep and high moral movement—no pity for human infirmity," she wrote. "It is a sneering respectable middle aged skeptic who says I take my two glasses and cigar daily." As with Dickinson, Stowe believed Davis shared her political viewpoint. Stowe rightly saw Davis as engaged in reform through her writing rather than in creating elite literature, and she told her frankly never to expect sympathy from the *Nation* for "any attempt to help the weak & sinning & suffering."[51]

In courageously attempting to work against the grain of popular opinion—opinion that would subsequently harden—Child, Dickinson, and Davis perhaps not surprisingly failed to see the contradictory stances embedded in their own work. Child's cultural elitism; Dickinson's unrealistic faith in partisan politics; Davis's paternalism: each represented a clinging to some sort of racial order, even while the authors asserted much more than their audience allowed. The use of characters who "passed" into white society heightened that contradictory quality. Meant to suggest the common humanity that bound the races together—the elusiveness of difference—the idea of "passing" also valorized white beauty at the expense of black. It suggested, ultimately, that intermarriage did not so much solve the racial problems of Reconstruction as erase them.

IN HER 1865 Civil War sketch "Margaret Bronson," Elizabeth Stuart Phelps apologized to the reader for reviving the war in yet another story. By 1868 the waning interest she had prematurely noted three years before was well under way. Interest in the Civil War surged again in the 1880s and again at the turn of the century; subsequent revivals (like that of the late 1920s and 1930s) were mainly led by the white South. Few of the novels or narratives of this early postwar period survived this loss of interest.

Yet in this three-year period both the lives of many women writers and the literary history of which they were a part contributed to an important shift in style and content. The sentimental voice of romantic novels was evident. Yet the angry and realistic voices of nurses, the political and reformist thrust of antiprejudice novels, and the strong and involved Civil War heroines of home and battlefield left their mark on subsequent writers and women's writing alike. And, as Harriet Beecher Stowe passed her torch to a younger generation of women interested in the "weak & sinning & suffering," they chose new objects for their energy and attention.

The outlines of this shift, beginning at midwar, became clearest with novels only peripherally about the Civil War. These novels used the war to talk about the future rather than assess the past; these novelists created moral women but gave them new power. Unlike the writing of the immediate postwar period, which did not last in the public imagination, these novels caught the national fancy in lasting ways. Louisa May Alcott's *Little Women* and, most centrally, *Work*; Elizabeth Stuart Phelps's best-selling *The Gates Ajar*; and Frances Ellen Watkins Harper's *Iola Leroy* suggested that the war had truly transformed women; they were finally realizing the project of bridging the past and future.

"Perhaps this [acting as an interpreter between the classes] is the task my life has been fitting me for," [Christie] said. "A great and noble one which I should be proud to accept and help accomplish if I can. Others have finished the emancipation work and done it splendidly, even at the cost of all this blood and sorrow. . . . This new task seems to offer me the chance of being among the pioneers, to do the hard work, share the persecution, and help lay the foundation of a new emancipation whose happy success I may never see."—Louisa May Alcott, *Work* (1873)

{ CHAPTER NINE }

A New Emancipation

Interpreting the War for Tomorrow

AT THE END OF Louisa May Alcott's *Work*, her protagonist, Christie, sits surrounded by the women friends she has made since she set out from her aunt and uncle's home to make her fortune. She impulsively stretches her hands to her friends about her, "and with one accord they laid their hands on hers, a loving league of sisters, old and young, black and white, rich and poor, each ready to do her part to hasten the coming of the happy end." In the final moment of the novel, Christie's young daughter adds her own chubby hand, symbolizing a "coming generation of women," who will not "only receive but deserve their liberty."[1]

This triumphant finish represents what seem to be Alcott's hopes for the future and her fears about the present. Like Harriet Beecher Stowe, she asserts that the moral agency of women could change society; like Frances Ellen Watkins Harper, she asserts that this "brighter coming day" is on the national horizon. But like her contemporaries Elizabeth Stuart Phelps and Rebecca Harding Davis, Alcott seems convinced that women need first to connect with each other to ensure their right to labor and to liberty, particularly now across class and racial lines. And in order to connect they need to see and understand the problems faced daily by poor women, rather than insisting, simply, that women are all alike.

These hopes derived from an understanding of society shaped by the experience of the Civil War. A belief in moral agency and women's authority prevalent in the 1850s, heightened by *Uncle Tom's Cabin*, was strengthened by the sacrifices women made and experiences the war brought to women in the North, even as new values of professionalism and efficiency gained ground culturally. In 1861 Louisa May Alcott was frustrated by the limitations society put upon her gender, but by 1868 she had stretched those limits with her stint in Washington hospitals and had found a voice and a place in the public eye. Even as Alcott's career illustrates many publishing trends at mid-nineteenth century, as she moved from working- to middle-class audiences, her work also illustrates both the continuities and the changes in the public and political efforts of women writers.

The Civil War did not end the sense of millennial possibility for Northern women writers of either generation discussed here, nor did it close their dialogue on the appropriate work of women in politics. Rather, by the late 1860s the assumptions behind those arguments had changed. Instead of arguing over any involvement by women in national affairs, the question became *how* women would be involved.[2] Would they "influence" men as members of political units called families? Or would they themselves vote, as individuals with their own moral and political views? Increasingly, Northern women writers publicly supported the suffrage cause, even if they did not formally join it. With the exceptions of Gail Hamilton (an ironic antisuffragist) and Mrs. E. D. E. N. Southworth (whose views on the subject are not definitively known), the remaining seven writers—Stowe, Fern, Harper, Child, Davis, Alcott, and Phelps—publicly acknowledged their support for voting rights for women, a position few mainstream writers before the war had taken.

Also indirectly traceable to the war was a growing sense of gender solidarity among these middle-class and largely white women writers. Significantly, reform organizations segregated by gender grew more prevalent after the war. Societal constrictions that caused only personal resentment in writers like Phelps during the war years now seemed like collective grievances as the difficulties faced by women of all classes and races became clear. Surrounded by women mourning for lost fathers, husbands, brothers, and sons, destitute and without opportunities for work, Phelps and others developed a sharper critique of the larger society, even as they worked to expand the power of the middle-class woman.

Rather than rejecting the optimism implicit in such works as *Uncle Tom's Cabin*, the older generation as well as a younger generation of writers continued to place their faith in the power of essays, poetry, and stories to spur social change. What shifted—and this was crucial—were the parameters allowed to the ideal woman at the center of their writing. This "coming woman," described by Alcott in her novel *An Old-Fashioned Girl*, was "strong-minded, strong-hearted, strong-souled, and strong-bodied." She lived with a "purpose" as the heroines in this novel did, "which seemed to ennoble her womanhood, to give her a certain power, a sustaining satisfaction."[3]

Part of what Alcott called the "religion" of this group of heroines was sisterly solidarity and understanding. In her classic story of the March family on the home front during the Civil War, *Little Women*, and her subsequent novels *An Old-Fashioned Girl* and especially *Work* (a novel also set partially in wartime), this sense of shared gender responsibilities, power, and moral authority is clear. Elizabeth Stuart Phelps also used the war as a springboard for discussing the shared concerns and needs of women in *The Gates Ajar*, one of the most popular Civil War novels in the nineteenth century. Her novels that followed, *Hedged In* and *The Silent Partner*, solidified this stance.

Frances E. W. Harper, whose career showed no signs of abating, also called for sisterly solidarity but called as well for a more complex understanding of the relations between women of different races and classes. She called on middle-class white women to stop valorizing their position at the expense of others. In her fictional sketch "The Mission of the Flowers," published with her 1869 poem *Moses: A Story of the Nile*, she argued that the greatest bar to sisterhood was arrogance. In the story the rose bush (that is, the white woman) is given the opportunity to change all the flowers to roses, and soon learns to her dismay that this diminishes the garden considerably, causing the visits to dwindle. The rosebush learns then that she must "respect the individuality of her sister flowers, . . . to see that they, as well as herself, had their own missions." Harper followed this publication with *Sketches of Southern Life*, a collection of narrative poems retelling the story of the Civil War and Reconstruction; *Iola Leroy*, her last novel, records a similar journey twenty years later.[4]

Alcott, Phelps, and Harper were particularly notable in illustrating the directions in which war work could lead women. Unlike the sentimental compilations published just after the war, which praised and exalted, these writers offered critiques as well as celebrations. Each used the Civil War as a backdrop to understand what followed and emphasized that the war had both positive and negative ramifications for women's lives and the subsequent focus of their reformist energy. In the tradition of moral action to redress political and social problems, these writers took up new struggles: Alcott to educate and define the "coming woman"; Phelps to enlighten women readers to their responsibilities to workingwomen; and Harper to strengthen and inspire the African American community in its continuing struggle for social justice. What they collectively suggest is an effort made by a few persistent reformers to use the war to make change rather than to validate the status quo.

A Call for Women

I had no ambition for public life. . . . But my acceptance of an active membership in the Sanitary Commission carried me inevitably into methods of work different from any that I had before known. . . . Everywhere there was a call for women to be up and doing, with voice and pen, with hand and head and heart.

—Mary Livermore, *The Story of My Life* (1898)

The call to arms that stirred women in the North to war work from April 1861 did not diminish as expected in the postwar years, Mary Livermore asserts in *The Story of My Life*. The peace she assumed would follow her tremendous effort never came. Instead, the war taught her to see American society in a new light, and helped her grow emotionally and politically. The rhetoric of unity, or simply the war's insistent realities, led her to change her political understanding. "If there had been a time in my life, when I regarded the lowest tier of human beings with indifference or aversion," she wrote, "I outgrew it during the war." The need for women's political work became clear to her with that changed understanding. She saw that "[a] large portion of the nation's work was badly done, or not done at all, because woman was not recognized as a factor in the political world."

Reversing her prewar stance against voting rights for women, Livermore became active in the woman suffrage movement, and carried her wartime skills into postwar life as a writer and a lecturer. She was not alone. Women began to gather together to work on social issues from the education of themselves in clubs to their daughters in colleges, and from temperance to suffrage. Echoing her description of her wish at the Civil War's beginning, to be "a hand, a foot, an eye, a voice, an influence, on the side of freedom and my country!" she described a postwar life in which "[e]very-where there was a call for women to be up and doing, with voice and pen, with hand and head and heart."[5]

In the late 1860s and early 1870s women's activism and cultural criticism coalesced into three main issues: what contemporaries labeled the "woman question," the "labor question," and the "Negro question." All three were intimately connected to the war's legacy. The conflict had drawn particular attention to both men's and women's appropriate behavior, causing a widening of societal limits forced by the exigencies associated with the conflict. What that legacy would mean and how it could be written into history was debated in the immediate postwar years and thereafter.

The "coming woman" explored in the late 1860s and early 1870s was both like and unlike the heroines of novels and stories preceding the war. Moral, domestic, and sincere, she was also considerably more strong-minded, self-reliant, and astute. The centrality of the labor question also intensified in the North: the war sped the quickening pace of capitalism, worsened difficult conditions for workers in general, and opened some doors of employment to women—but at unequal wages to men's. Greater contact between classes as a result of the war led to both the solidifying of class distinctions and a few notably sincere, if often misguided, attempts to overcome those divisions. Of continuing concern to many Northerners, though waning in the general public view, was the Negro question. In these years African Americans and some whites, North and South, struggled to cement the gains of the war and to make freedom meaningful through civil rights and voting rights, despite the unrepentant prejudice of white Northerners and the constant and deadly harassment of white Southerners.

Perhaps the most consistent position emerging after the Civil War from the Northern women writers studied here was an insistence on woman's right to a voice in politics. For most this meant suffrage, perhaps not a surprising development considering the attention drawn to the issue with the proposing and passing of the Fifteenth Amendment.[6] Harriet Beecher Stowe, in a letter written to Fanny Fern, her former student, wrote in July of 1868 an ostensible answer to a question, "Yes, I do believe in Female Suffrage—The more I think of it the more absurd this whole government of man over woman looks." Stowe followed this unequivocal statement the next year with a series of articles in *Hearth and Home* publicly supporting suffrage.

While Lydia Maria Child clearly did not believe that woman suffrage was as crucial an issue as justice to the freedpeople, she also lent her written support to the struggle in a letter to Elizabeth Cady Stanton, which was published in the New York *Independent* in the fall of 1866. "Since you care to know my opinion of the cause you are advocating so zealously and ably," she wrote, "I will tell you frankly that I sympathize entirely with your views concerning women's true position in society, and I cordially wish you God Speed." Yet Child would not fight in the suffrage trenches. "I am old," she confessed, "and, having fought through a somewhat long campaign of reform, I feel little energy for enlisting in a new war."[7]

Fern, for her part, made a discussion of women's rights and oppression a staple of her editorial sketches after the war.[8] For Fern, however, what she called the "woman-question" never solely referred to the vote but to the cramped, dependent, anguished lives of women generally. Others concurred with this emphasis. In an essay responding to one titled "The Woman Question," supporting suffrage, Davis wrote "Men's Rights" for *Putnam Magazine*. Although, as Davis's biographer Sharon M. Harris argues, the article reveals Davis's ambivalence toward the woman's rights movement, it demonstrates her bedrock assumptions about women's need for a political voice. "It is too late for argument about it," Davis stated flatly, citing the desperate conditions of many women. These conditions— of prostitution, poverty, and women's "sale" of themselves on the marriage market—are the real problem, "a tragedy more real to me than any other in life." It was in 1868 that Davis's focus shifted from industrial life and Civil War tragedy to the lives and concerns of women specifically.[9]

Harris claims Davis was reacting in part to *Women's Wrongs: A Counter-Irritant*, a book by Gail Hamilton published in 1868. Despite Hamilton's frank call for an expanded understanding of women's sphere, her acknowledgement of women's political knowledge and women's need and right to independent time for self-fulfillment, she did not believe in granting immediate suffrage to women, although she expected women would and should win it eventually. Rather than push for the vote, she recommended that women work in other ways to address their concerns, revealing her own core beliefs about the beneficent role of capitalism and economic opportunity, and her narrow interpretation of republicanism. Hamilton argued that although suffrage might have been a right that women deserved, it would not help them solve the nation's problems, and restricting suffrage would have a more beneficial effect on the nation than expanding it. Hamilton was a Federalist of the old school, and she believed that voters should only be men of education and property.[10]

In 1871 Hamilton and Phelps went head-to-head over the issue of women working outside the home in a series of articles in the New York *Independent*. These articles demonstrate the natural bridge between the woman question and the labor question, and the central place of these controversies during the early postwar years. While Phelps argued for women's right to labor, and for the power that economic independence conferred upon them, Hamilton stressed the difficulty of motherhood and women's need for protection and support by men.

Phelps's position was clearly consistent with both her writing and her life to that date, but Hamilton's was not. As Mary Abigail Dodge, she had begun to support herself at least partially as a young woman, first by teaching and later by writing. Her voice, as she told her mother frankly in a letter in the 1850s, was an independent one, and she meant to be limited by no one. Although her alter ego, Hamilton, was opposed to voting rights for women, Dodge was a political insider beginning in the late 1850s with a stay at the house of Gamaliel Bailey, the editor of the *National Era*, and continuing after the war when she returned to Washington to live with her cousin Harriet Stanwood Blaine and her husband, future Republican presidential candidate James G. Blaine. In such settings, a contemporary noted, she interacted with "senators, cabinet officers, diplomats, the titled Englishmen of the High Commission, [and] the President himself." Hamilton's conservative turn, made in about 1871 when she was trading opinions with Phelps, has been attributed to the influence of Blaine, and she in turn was thought to have written many of his speeches. In her 1896 obituary, the *Women's Journal* summed up her life, describing "her entire literary career" as "an object lesson in women's capacity as a political thinker and writer."[11] What the writer might have added was that her trajectory was consistent with that of other elite women, who turned away from liberal reform toward a free labor ideology that shored up the expanding fortunes of the few at the expense of the many.

Mary Livermore's understanding of the woman question from her experience in the Civil War, by contrast, led her to the political left. Her belief in an expanded destiny for women, whose potential had been tried by the national conflict, was shared by many, historian Mari Jo Buhle has noted. In Livermore's work, and that of many of the writers studied here, a strengthened belief in "sisterly solidarity" emerged, a solidarity that acknowledged class differences and encouraged women to work to ameliorate the conditions of workingwomen.[12] Consciously echoing antislavery reformist language, women reformers, such as Caroline Dall in her prewar polemic on the subject, *Woman's Right to Labor*, called for women to join "in bonds as bound" across class lines.[13]

Coexisting with these middle-class reformers was another group of women who used reform to solidify class lines and who rejected sisterly solidarity for professional status. These women, historian Lori Ginzberg argues, took from their Civil War experience a belief in bureaucracy and government efficiency. They founded new organizations and "severed their own benevolent work from its traditional moorings in the ideology of gender difference even as they eschewed suffragists' concern for undermining that ideology; indeed, they seemed to free themselves entirely from awareness of their sex, demonstrating instead a newly explicit loyalty to their class."[14] Mary Abigail Dodge, or Gail Hamilton, is emblematic of this large and vocal cohort.

That these two communities of white women, ruling and middle class, were aware of each other is clear from the writings of Louisa May Alcott and Elizabeth Stuart Phelps. Alcott and Phelps explicitly challenged organizational reformers who rarely met the objects of their work and who had no knowledge of the conditions of poor women's lives. Their continued commitment to prewar moral reform, which mixed new ways of understanding women's potential and women's purpose, seemingly had great resonance with the middle class. If Stowe dominated the literary landscape for white middle-class women writers and readers in the 1850s, Phelps and Alcott did so in the late 1860s and early 1870s.

It is also true, however, that in exploring the labor question through its effects on women, these writers and more like them held onto their middle-class values and aspirations rather than seeking to understand alternative value systems as equally worthy. As Richard Brodhead has argued, Alcott's work of the 1860s and 1870s embodied a "larger cultural drama" as the publication of fiction became more class stratified. During the war years Alcott wrote for what were becoming diverse audiences: the elite readers of the *Atlantic Monthly*, a mixed regional audience for the Boston *Commonwealth*, and a more clearly demarcated working-class audience for *Flag of Our Union* and *Peterson's*. By the late 1860s Alcott had chosen her milieu and her audience by casting her lot with an emerging "middlebrow" or implicitly middle-class culture. Her work for adolescents and children, shaped by a moral vision that had much of the past woven within it, became the frame of reference for subsequent generations of middle-class readers.[15]

Other readers from an earlier generation were in sympathy with Alcott's message and her choice of audience. "In my many fears for my country and in these days when so much seductive and dangerous literature is pushed forward, the success of your domestic works has been to me most comforting," Harriet Beecher Stowe wrote her younger colleague in 1872. "It shows that after all our people are all right and that they love the right kind of thing."[16] "*Our* people," however, was not *all* people for Stowe, who increasingly retreated from her universalizing vision in *Uncle Tom's Cabin*.

The legacy of these women writers on the labor question was mixed. Despite their hard look at the conditions of workingwomen, Fern, Alcott, Phelps, and Harper clung to received ideas about society attributable to their middle-class status and education. Those ideas in Fern included an insidious and unquestioned prejudice against the Irish; in Alcott, a failure to include factory work as an option for women workers; in Phelps, a failure to face the implications of her harsh critique of capitalism; and in Harper, an assimilationist ethic that was common among middle-class African Americans at the turn of the century.[17] Nevertheless, the middle-class audiences that Alcott, Harper, and writers like them wrote for in the postwar period cannot negate their very real concern for the workingwomen. Their middle-class ideas about womanhood—what historian Mari Jo Buhle calls a "woman's culture forced to a political maturity during the Gilded Age"—offered possibilities for useful cultural criticism even as it narrowed and limited cross-class understanding.[18]

In addition, the "new emancipation" for women workers pursued by Alcott's protagonist Christie assumed an "old" emancipation had been complete. This assumption, and the reviews of *Work* that criticized Alcott's inclusion of a slave woman's story, demonstrate the shift the Northern public was making away from concerns about African Americans.[19] As historian Lori Ginzburg notes, "[T]he decline in Northern interest in the former slaves followed astonishingly soon after the war ended."[20] Harriet Beecher Stowe, for example, looked for other objects for her social analysis, arguing at one point that drunkenness brought about "a misery—a desolation—an anguish deeper than that of the slave."[21] Lydia Maria Child turned her attention to the plight of Native Americans, in 1868 publishing a pamphlet on the subject of their rights. That she was not alone in turning to this reform was clear to Lucretia Mott, who when solicited for support for teachers of freedmen in the South, wrote, "The claims of the Indians—so long injured & cheated & wronged in so many ways seem now, with many of our Friends, to take the place of the Freedmen."[22] When the subject of freedpeople came up in reform circles in these later days of Reconstruction, it was most often in relationship to another oppressed people, often as a point of reference now surpassed.

Yet Child in particular did not ignore the tragedy occurring in the South in the late 1860s and early 1870s, even as she shared her energies with reform on Indian policy. As freedpeople were caught in an ever tighter web of economic slavery with the sharecropping system, and active and successful African Americans were beaten, raped, or murdered, fewer Northern reformers were looking south to redress their injustices, and the political system seemed to have failed them again.[23] In 1872 Child wrote to her old friend Sarah Shaw that with a possible return to "self-government for the States," she feared that the perpetrators of outrages on the freedpeople, the newly established Ku Klux Klan, would be tried by judges and jurors who were themselves members. "I verily believe this Republic is in more imminent peril now, than it was in 1861. Oh, *can* it be that all that blood and treasure was expended in vain?" she asked Shaw.[24]

Frances E. W. Harper addressed such questions in her postwar lectures and poems. Her "coming woman" reconstructed the conventional middle-class white ideal, even as she challenged and encouraged a sisterhood that recognized the particular boundaries that society had placed around African Americans.[25] Harper's target audience, like Alcott's, was the next generation, and she worked in an emerging middle-class culture within the larger African American community that mixed radical and conventional ideas. Like Phelps, Harper believed in the agency of the individual, an agency inspired and sustained by God. Yet this was no sentimental, unquestioned faith but one built upon a realistic sense of the respective conditions of life for African Americans in the South and factory women in the North.

Alcott, Phelps, and Harper reflected and shaped a dialogue on the future using the past—their wartime experience—as a guide and drawing from the evident material circumstances they saw, experienced, and read about. Yet the event that shaped their understanding of that future was the Civil War; for them as for many other Northern women writers it was a turning point in their political lives.

The "Coming Woman": Alcott and the Woman Question

Some time ago we got into a famous talk about what women should be, and Becky said she'd show us her idea of the coming woman. There she is [indicating a sculpture], as you say, bigger, lovelier, and more imposing than any we see nowadays; and at the same time, she is a true woman.—Louisa May Alcott, An Old-Fashioned Girl (1869)

Ostensibly, *Little Women* is another novel of the battlefront at home. Certainly it contains many of the necessary ingredients: the novel is a recounting of a battle between selfishness and self-sacrifice, passion and self-control, and the men are located offstage while women are the central figures. And *Little Women* could also be seen as a retelling of the classic story of growing up, much like Susan Warner's *Wide, Wide World*. Yet *Little Women* is more than just a conservative story, offering limited power through self-knowledge, and it is not just another home-front tale. Jo's vibrancy and aspiration persist in ways that Warner's Ellen's do not, and while Jo is not the "coming woman" of Alcott's later imagination, she rides on the cusp of a new world while retaining much of the old.

This creative tension between limits and possibility, which gives the novel its enduring appeal, derives much of its energy from its wartime context. As literary critic Judith Fetterley notes, "The Civil War is an obvious metaphor for internal conflict and its invocation as background to *Little Women* suggests the presence in the story of such conflict. There is tension in the book, attributable to the conflict between its overt messages and its covert messages."[26] In this autobiographical novel, Jo finds her "true style" at last when she eschews the sensationalistic renderings of writers such as Mrs. S. L. A. N. G. Northbury (an obvious reference to Mrs. E. D. E. N. Southworth) and adopts a simple narrative with a clear moral. In a note to herself in her diary, Alcott identified *Hospital Sketches* as her parallel moment. "The Sketches never made very much money," she remembered in 1879, scribbling by her diary entry for 1863, "but showed me 'my style,' & taking the hint I went where glory waited me."[27] Glory, it is clear, could only "wait" for her through nursing, and more significantly, writing about nursing.

This political and literary style, learned through Civil War experience, was designed for a specifically middle-class audience. More than simply an artistic choice, Richard Brodhead has suggested, Alcott's turn to the center was dictated both by the *Atlantic Monthly*'s rejection of her work and her need to support herself and a growing extended family. And if, as Fetterley has noted, Alcott's later work for "Young America" became less contested and less nuanced—and less memorable—there was a crucial interlude in her work between 1868 and 1873 in which she produced three novels that connected with the still vibrant traditions of moral suasion of the past but with an emerging image of a new woman. That they were middlebrow is indisputable; but they were also pointed works of political and cultural criticism.[28]

Alcott and her contemporaries saw the years in which they were living as pivotal ones for women. In "The Women of 1867," Fanny Fern urged *all* women, despite age, social position, or education, to write to express their pain and anguish. To anyone who believes that women have little to complain of, Fern wrote sternly, "You should have read the letters I have received; you should have talked with the women I have talked with; in short, you should have walked this earth with your eyes open, instead of shut, as far as its women are concerned, to endorse this advice."[29] Look around, Fern tells her audience, and read the political message there.

Even Gail Hamilton, who in certain ways seems to have "walked this earth with [her] eyes" shut, still acknowledged that women reformers had much to reform. In *Women's Wrongs*, she argued that the opponents of suffrage use heinous and absurd points to make their case and assume the privileges of God in deciding women's nature. Further, she asserted, men cannot be trusted with the interest of women, for "the minds of women are dwarfed, their health ruined, their fortunes squandered, their hearts broken, by men who stand to them in the nearest and dearest relations."[30] If she did not believe in the political expediency of giving woman the vote at that time, Hamilton did believe in three crucial points: that women's opinions could have political power whether expressed by voice or pen; that women could achieve political gains by joining together; and that women had, in many cases, grievances to redress.[31] She, too, defined a "coming woman," much as she had in 1863. This woman would be robust, well-educated, comfortably dressed(!), politically astute, and energetic. She would define her goals and meet them despite prejudice and roadblocks; she would accept no charity nor political favors (this from a woman who previously had gladly accepted both).

Hamilton's and Fern's hopes for the woman of mid-nineteenth century were shared by Harper and others. Harper's short sketches in the African Methodist Episcopal Church publication *Christian Recorder* in 1873 illustrate the values and aspirations she deemed necessary for a young woman. Her protagonist for these sketches, Jenny, has gone to college, and after returning sits and talks to her aunt about her hopes for her future. Her aunt has feared that college would unsuit Jenny for housework and make her reject the associations of her youth. But although changed, Jenny still believes in domestic duty, self-sacrifice, and familial love; she sees her future as building upon that. "I think, Aunty, the best way to serve humanity, is by looking within ourselves, and becoming acquainted with our powers and capacities," she says earnestly. "The fact is we should all go to work and make the most of ourselves, and we cannot do that without helping others." For Jenny, self-realization will lead to greater good, and for this reason she also believes in woman suffrage.[32]

Alcott's *Little Women*, *An Old-Fashioned Girl*, and *Work* examine many of the same issues, and build upon each other. *Little Women* is the best known and perhaps best written, though the politics and cultural criticism are more overt in the later novels. In all three novels, for example, the comfort and strength derived from sisterhood is posited. But in the first the sisters disperse through marriage, while in the second even marriage does not separate the "sisters," and in the third the sisters are widowed, single, and married and join together nonetheless. Each offers an evolving sense of the possibilities and responsibilities of womanhood. "Polly" is "not intended as a perfect model, but as a possible improvement upon the Girl of the Period," Alcott wrote to her readers in a preface to *An Old-Fashioned Girl*.[33]

Of the four girls that constitute the little women, it is Jo whom readers most often refer to, and it was Jo who was drawn to represent Alcott herself. Significantly, it is the Civil War that figures most crucially in the first volume of *Little Women* in teaching Jo the value of self-control. More than any of her sisters, it is she who wants to break the limiting boundaries of appropriate behavior for girls. "Don't I wish I could go as a drummer, a *vivan*—what's its name? or a nurse, so I could be near him and help [Father]," she exclaims. Jo lists her wishes in order of their danger and adventure—a drummer leads armies without weapons, the most courageous of all; a vivandière, or "daughter of the regiment," helps the wounded on the battlefield and soldiers on the march; and a nurse binds the wounds in hospitals nearby. Yet Jo, unlike Alcott, has to stay home instead and fight battles within herself. This inner civil war with her temper "was a much harder task than facing a rebel or two down South."[34] It is after these rebellious thoughts that "Marmee," Jo's mother and teacher, gives her girls *Pilgrim's Progress* as their game, hoping to channel their energies into identifying and overcoming their particular faults: Meg's vanity, Jo's temper, and Amy's selfishness (Beth has no faults). In the chapter "Burdens," in which the sisters each deal separately with the family's poverty and the grind of work, Marmee mitigates their discontent with a story of the father she meets while sewing at the soldier's aid society. He has given all four of his sons to the war, two of whom have died, another who has been imprisoned, and the fourth who is sick in a Washington hospital.

The sense of duty associated with the Civil War helps Jo become the little woman both Marmee and her chaplain father expect. When Jo meets her "Apollyon" and is enraged by Amy's stealing and burning of her manuscript, her mother tells Jo of her own struggle with anger and duty, referring to the difficulty of giving up her husband to the war. Her mother's pain convinces Jo to continue fighting her own battles. And when a telegram from the front arrives, with the news that Jo's father lies sick in Washington, Jo makes the greatest sacrifice of all by selling her long, thick hair—her only feminine asset—for money to send with her mother. (Alcott herself also lost her hair to the war; it fell out during her long illness.)

The little women who emerge in the second volume, after the Civil War is over and the oldest, Meg, has been married, are wiser in self-control and self-knowledge. Each is taught a signal lesson. Meg, who immerses herself too entirely in child care, learns that women's sphere should not be too confining. "Don't shut yourself in a bandbox because you are a woman, but understand what is going on, and educate yourself to take your part in the world's work, for it affects you and yours," Marmee chides her.[35] Jo learns self-sacrifice and the virtue of domestic tasks with the crushing loss of Beth, whom she nurses to the end. In writing of this painful passage Jo finds her voice, much in the same way Alcott found her own in writing about the death of soldiers. The appeal of that voice, her father tells Jo, is its honesty (as Davis said of Alcott, "She knows hospitals"). Amy, who seems to change the least and get the most of all the girls, learns not to marry for money (although she ends up with a wealthy husband anyway).

Literary scholars have long argued over the meaning of Little Women both for the culture and for the course of Alcott's life. Many have concluded that Little Women is a conservative compromise, particularly because all the little women, including the independent Jo, marry in the end. "Jo should have remained a literary spinster," Alcott wrote to her friend Alf Whitman, but she bowed to the pressure of her readers, Alcott explained, even while refusing to marry Jo to her childhood sweetheart, Laurie.[36] Yet even if Little Women has a "middle story"[37] more subversive and challenging than its ending, Jo's marriage to the fatherlike Bhaer is still not an entire compromise of her earlier attractive rebelliousness. Granted, Professor Bhaer, an older German father figure and sincere moralist, criticizes Jo's writing of sensationalistic stories and is far less charming than her young lover Laurie (who marries Amy). But Jo greets his proposal of marriage by admitting her own strong-mindedness, wiping away *his* tears, and telling him resolutely, "I'm to carry my share, Friedrich, and help to earn the home. Make up your mind to that, or I'll never go."[38] For a mid-nineteenth-century novel, written to instruct young America, this is a strong message indeed.

Alcott's message became more emphatic in her two later novels. *An Old-Fashioned Girl*, written in 1869–70, begins as an excessively moralistic tale of Polly, a poor rural girl who comes to the city to visit her wealthy friend Fanny. The "old-fashioned girl" finds that the family she visits is very unhappy and misled by riches and status-seeking, and her values of respect and service help ease their worldly woes. Initially *An Old-Fashioned Girl* seems a marked declension from the more nuanced *Little Women*; Polly is a hybrid of all four March girls—she is as pretty as Meg; gets angry on occasion like Jo; can be saintly like Beth; and is at times as selfish as Amy— but lacks their internal tensions. It is the second half of the novel, when a grown-up Polly returns to the city to work to support her brother's education, in which Alcott seems to reveal her hopes for adult womanhood.

Polly is no unblemished heroine as a young adult; indeed, she emerges with the shift in tone and politics of the second half of the novel as a far more interesting character. Rather than simply content with her work as a music teacher, Polly feels her sacrifice for her brother acutely. But the worst obstacle she faces is class prejudice. "Another thorn that wounded our Polly in her first attempt to make her way through the thicket that always bars a woman's progress, was the discovery that working for a living shuts a good many doors in one's face even in democratic America," Alcott explains, making "our" Polly and her problems belong to the readers. As the friend of a wealthy girl, Polly had been received everywhere as a young woman; as a music teacher, she is ignored or patronized. The second half of the novel largely explores her struggle to come to terms with her position in the social order, allied with virtuous working-class women and impoverished once-wealthy women in a middle class that embraces a diversity of women if not of values, a parable of Louisa May Alcott's own life and struggle.

In order for Polly to find her way she has to learn the virtues of her independence. The competent and dignified spinster (Miss Mills), who owns the boardinghouse where Polly lives, takes in a young girl who has attempted suicide as an alternative to dying of starvation or becoming a prostitute, seemingly the only options left to her. On meeting this girl, Polly becomes transformed, seeing the even thornier "thicket" that surrounds another woman. "She had heard of poverty and suffering, in the vague, far-off way, which is all that many girls, safe in happy homes, ever know of it; but now she had seen it, in a shape which she could feel and understand, and life grew more earnest to her from that minute." Polly takes as a "principle of [her] life, to help up [her] sex as far and as fast as [she] could." In so doing, Miss Mills tells her, she is practicing "Christian charity," an old-fashioned virtue that cannot be impugned by calling it "rampant women's rights." Women, Polly's mentor says, must put aside the names that they get called for working for "whatever is going to fit their sisters and themselves to deserve and enjoy the rights God gave them."[39]

Later in the novel Polly meets and joins a group of women who more completely represent her politics and aspirations than Fanny's wealthy friends. Rebecca Jeffrey is a sculptor, her roommate Lizzie Small is an engraver, and Kate King, most likely meant to represent Alcott herself, is an authoress. Polly takes Fanny to meet them, and they discuss womanhood at the feet of a sculpture of the "coming woman" that Rebecca is carving. The sculpture is a representation of the past and the future, mixing strength and beauty. The group cannot decide what object to put in her hand. A scepter, they agree, is a classic evasion—"the kingdom given [her] isn't worth ruling"; a man's hand isn't needed, for this new woman will "help herself"; and an infant isn't right, for she must be "something more than a nurse"; "a ballot-box," on the other hand could sit at her feet, not in her hand, along with a needle, pen, palette, and broom "to suggest the various talents she owns" and to "show that she has earned the right to use them."[40] In the end they do not decide, and they sit silently "looking up at the beautiful, strong figure before them, each longing to see it done, and each unconscious that she was helping, by her individual effort and experience, to bring the day when their noblest ideal of womanhood should be embodied in flesh and blood, not clay."[41] This sisterhood, it is clear, will help along the coming of a new woman, and later in the novel Fanny and Polly ratify their own "Loyal League," to "stand staunchly by one another" in a new war.[42]

The connection between the Civil War and postwar efforts to redefine womanhood are made most explicitly in Louisa May Alcott's novel *Work*. Like *An Old-Fashioned Girl*, *Work* has two parts, each of which represents a different political perspective and literary approach. In the first part of *Work* Christie Devon strikes out on her own and finds employment first as a servant, then as an actress, governess, and companion, and finally as a seamstress in a mantua-making establishment. The chapter titles reinforce the sense of episodic experiences rather than transformative ones, although at most stages in her transformation Christie meets and is aided by women. Only the mantua-making position remotely resembles factory work, and it represents an ideological weakness on Alcott's part not to include such labor as an option for Christie. By the 1870s, factory work was not considered a choice for a middle-class workingwoman, and though Alcott stretched the boundaries of acceptability for the middle class in arguing for women's right to labor, there were clear limits in how far she was willing to go. Even in her democratic vision of America, certain class lines were not crossed.

Nevertheless, a "fallen" woman and her working-class friend bring Christie back from the edge of despair, suggesting that aid between women of differing class backgrounds works in both directions. Christie's emotional breakdown and her new beginning with the help of friends is a pivotal moment in the novel and demonstrates Alcott's best hopes for women's connection to each other. In the beginning of the second part of the novel, Christie has essentially become the impoverished young girl in *An Old-Fashioned Girl* who attempts suicide when blocked by prejudice and social strictures from finding work. Christie's descent begins with her support for another woman. In the mantua-making establishment, Christie meets and befriends Rachel, a shy and obviously genteel young woman. When Rachel is fired due to a spiteful coworker's discovery that Rachel years before had run off with a lover, Christie leaves in protest and struggles to find sewing work. This struggle leaves her months later at the edge of a river, where a renewed and strengthened Rachel finds her. Rachel takes her to the house of Cynthie Wilkins, a laundress and clear-starcher, the mother of numerous children and the wife of a spineless former drunk. Mrs. Wilkins gives Christie the home she needs and introduces her to "Mr. Powers," a minister who gives her hope through a true religion.[43] After a brief respite with these healing influences, Christie goes to work in the house of a Quaker woman and her son, where she begins again to make an independent and stable life for herself, this time with the help of friends. In *Work*, then, the central character thus learns the value of womanly support through the experience of suffering, not just—as in *An Old-Fashioned Girl*—through meeting a poor girl who has suffered.

The Civil War is the proving ground of Christie's new life. Rachel has been found to be the long-lost daughter of the Quaker family, and Christie is engaged to the Quaker son. The war's larger story is not recounted, for "it has been so often told," the narrator interjects. Here it is "touched upon" as "one of the experiences of Christie's life, an experience which did for her what it did for all who took a share in it, and loyally acted their part." In the early days of the conflict the women of the family "waxed strong in the new atmosphere," finding new objects for their energies. And after the need for soldiers grows, Christie and her lover are married, and *both* enlist, he as a private and she as a nurse. They take on this national task as they did their marriage, "shoulder to shoulder."[44]

Christie contrasts her war work with her acting. On the stage she only acted the "Amazon," with martial thoughts of Joan of Arc or Britomarte; "now she had a braver part to play on a larger stage, with a nation for audience."[45] Still, Alcott hints at the limitations within which women worked, even in the expanded stage of the war; although Christie proves herself rapidly, she has "bestowed upon her the only honors left the women, hard work, responsibility, and the gratitude of many men." She is no benevolent-but-blind upper-class woman, wanting only to swab foreheads delicately, but rather a strong, cheerful, motherlike nurse, who is not afraid to do dirty work. Her husband is not afraid to do dirty work, either; in the last year of the war, he is killed as he helps fugitive slave women and a boy escape.[46]

By the end of the novel Christie has emerged a mature woman, saddened by her loss but accepting of it after her child is born. The conclusion emphasizes the difference in this novel from other romances of the nineteenth century. Love and marriage figure in *Work*, but they do not dominate it, and the novel ends with a woman, well into her forties, surrounded by other women of various ages, classes, and races—and no men. Christie has found her *work* rather than her husband in the end; and this will be the object of her life. In a great meeting of women she stands on impulse and speaks of the value of labor and struggle, and the power that a shared effort of women will make. After speaking, she is acknowledged as just the mediator that is needed "to bridge across the space that now divided [wealthy women] from those they wished to serve," and she is respected by working-women because she has been one of them for most of her life. This "new emancipation" of women is the task, then, that her "life [had] been fitting [her] for," she thinks, "a great and noble one which I should be proud to accept and help accomplish if I can." Unafraid of what other women will say, she calls herself " 'strong-minded,' a radical and a reformer," and she draws together a "loving league of sisters" to accomplish her ends.[47]

Alcott used the Civil War to suggest the power of women coming together and the realized potential of this great national effort. Yet the war represented not only what women could do but what they were often blocked from doing. Still, despite the "thicket" that women faced, they made the most of themselves through self-control and earnest effort. Jo cannot enlist so she stays at home and makes herself a new woman; Polly joins her own "Loyal League," pledging to help her "sister" through her trials; and Christie goes to the war, proves herself despite the lack of honors women can win, and returns to take on a new work derived from the experiences of her life, an example to other women. The "coming woman" was hastened by the Civil War, but she still had not arrived, and the memory of what the war had meant helped her become purposeful and active in national life.

Woman As a Class: Phelps and the Labor Question

At this time, be it said, I had no interest at all in any especial movement for the peculiar needs of women as a class. I was reared in circles which did not concern themselves with those whom we should probably have called agitators. I was taught the old ideas of womanhood, in the old way, and had not to any important extent begun to resent them.
—Elizabeth Stuart Phelps, *Chapters from a Life* (1897)

In her article "Men's Rights," written for *Putnam's Magazine* in 1869, Rebecca Harding Davis returned to a feeling she had repeatedly explored in her writing, one she called "hunger." Hunger is what the sculpture of the workingwoman expresses, revealed in the stark lines shaped by the equally hungry artist-cum-workingman in *Life in the Iron Mills*. The slave Ben in "John Lamar" feels hunger, too, after he kills his master and goes north. This creative and desperate craving for soul sustenance and freedom was felt by old and young women alike, Davis argued. "Suffrage, or work, any of the popular cries among us, are but so many expressions of this mental hunger or unused power."[48]

Fanny Fern tapped a similar feeling. Although the workingwoman lived a miserable life, Fern suggested that she was not alone, that she shared an "unused power" with the more financially fortunate woman jostling her in the crowds on the New York City street. The "dainty fashionist" was ignored by father and husband, left to fill her days with trivialities. Which "lives the more miserable life," Fern asked, "the wealthy woman—or she—this other woman—with a heart quite as hungry and unappeased, who also faces day by day the same appalling question: *Is this all life has for me?*" Fern was implying that attention on the "dainty fashionist" was legitimate but too narrow, that what bound women together was their shared hunger, a hunger no novelist had been able to describe or even grasp. "Meanwhile women's millennium is yet a great way off; and while it slowly progresses, conservatism and indifference gaze through their spectacles at the seething elements of to-day, and wonder, 'what ails our women?' "[49] Fern answers for workingwomen: they live in tight, unventilated rooms with many others, eat little and work too much, and they have no hope. The realistic depiction of their lives, taken from visits Fern made to their factories, was her effort at shaking the complacency of the conservative spectacles, and helping them to see the truth. In this way Fern stood "at her post, like a good soldier," by "groaning over the wretched women."[50]

In "At Bay," a story written in 1867 for *Harper's New Monthly Magazine*, Elizabeth Stuart Phelps paid tribute to Davis's and Fern's vision. The narrator, a rural woman, praises Davis's Civil War story "Paul Blecker," which she has read "a good while ago," for having something "*real* to say." Davis's work speaks to the narrator despite her class and condition. In her own writing, Phelps followed Davis's lead in describing women whom others considered "too poor, or too uneducated, or too worn-out with washing days."[51] And yet unlike Davis or Fern, Phelps sensed that she would never truly understand what the lives of workingwomen were like and that, despite the emptiness of wealthy women's lives, they could not feel the depth of "unused power" that workingwomen did. Perley, the heroine of Phelps's 1871 novel *The Silent Partner* says as much, using Davis's and Fern's phrase. "There are few things [working people] do not need," Perley tells Fly, her upper-class and bewildered friend. "We do not understand that, I think,—we who never need. It is a hungry world, Fly."[52]

Grief from her own loss helped pull Elizabeth Stuart Phelps into writing. She was twenty years old in 1864 when she began writing one of the nineteenth century's most popular novels, *The Gates Ajar*, published four years later. The book was written for the women who had lost kin and lovers in the war, as Phelps herself had lost a young man whom some thought she would marry. It offered a direct challenge to religious patriarchs by bypassing their inadequate forms of comfort, assuming that only women knew best how to speak to women. She later claimed in her autobiography that the war and the experience of writing the novel transformed her, leading her away from the "old ideas of womanhood" toward an understanding and sympathy for "the peculiar needs of women as a class."[53]

For Phelps, *The Gates Ajar* was a form of therapy, an offering to a country "dark with sorrowing women." She later realized her intended audience encompassed womanhood itself: "I do not think I thought so much about the suffering of men—the fathers, the brothers, the sons—bereft; but the women,—the helpless, outnumbering, unconsulted women; they whom the war trampled down, without a choice or protest; the patient, limited, domestic women, who thought little, but loved much, and, loving, had lost all,—to them I would have spoken."[54]

Ostensibly, *The Gates Ajar* is the journal of a young orphan, Mary Cabot, who turns to writing when her brother Royal is killed on the battlefield. Mary is unable to find any peace or resignation as the novel opens, and she is irritated by the empty condolences of the deacon and the town minister, the pointedly named Dr. Bland. The God they offer is a stern one, whose punishments are meant to invigorate Mary but only devastate her. The heaven they imagine—only for the elect, which they delicately suggest Roy may not be—is largely formless, filled with spirits dressed in white, playing harps and singing endless paeans to God.

Phelps offers another vision of heaven to her anguished readers, a heaven glimpsed through the friendship of women rather than the ministry of men. Into Mary's life comes her mother's sister, Winifred Forceythe, who acts as a lay minister and suggests to Mary a new way of imagining heaven and God. Rather than an unfamiliar place of spirits, Winifred describes a heaven just like home, filled with beloved people who retain their memory of the days passed on earth. There Mary will find Royal, and there she will find a loving and compassionate God, who has not so much taken Royal away as taken him out of sight.

Winifred displaces the minister, just as Phelps's novel seeks to displace other ministers. When Mary needs consoling, Winifred in her compassionate and womanly way strokes her hair and promises: "I am going to help you, and you must tell me all you can."[55] As the minister preaches of an unrecognizable heaven, Winifred subverts it with murmured asides to Mary and a hand slipped into hers under her cloak. "Ah, Dr. Bland," Mary writes in her journal, "if you had known how that little soft touch was preaching against you!"[56]

Unlike other Civil War novelists, Phelps was not patriotic and had little interest in defending the war. In *Gates* it takes Mary's family away, and she is desperate, unwelcome, misunderstood, and lonely. She makes no attempt, as other heroines do, to celebrate sacrifice. When the war ends it brings only "bitter Peace," not social transformation. Indirectly commenting on the war's purposes, Phelps makes Mary one of the "unconsulted" that the war has left and demonstrates her suffering to be of central importance. This legacy of grief, and not the need to defend or further the war's objectives, is the focus of the book.

The Gates Ajar was strikingly popular, catapulting Phelps onto the public stage. It sold not only 80,000 copies in America but also over 100,000 in England. Phelps recorded in *Chapters from a Life* that it was translated into French, German, Italian, and Dutch. There was a "Gates Ajar" patent medicine, a "Gates Ajar" tippet and collar, and even the rumor of a "Gates Ajar" cigar. For thirty years after the first publication of her novel Phelps received letters from grieving women, whose "misery seemed to cry in my arms like a child who must be comforted."[57] She sat down to answer those letters, feeling, after a long week of reading this "large and painful mail," as if "the world were one great outcry."[58]

She also received raging reviews from the press. "Religious papers," she remembered, "waged war across that girl's notions of the life to come, as if she had been an evil spirit let loose on accepted theology for the destruction of the world." Phelps was "put to the question," she recalled. "Heresy was her crime and atrocity her name."[59] Accepted theology, of course, was constructed and promulgated by men, and the unaccustomed vision of a young woman acting as a lay minister, and an extremely popular one, was clearly shocking and disturbing.

This popularity and outrage, mixed with Phelps's own loss of her lover and her postwar investigation and depiction of the burning and collapse of the Pemberton mills in nearby Lawrence, Massachusetts, moved her from the issues of the war to issues of womanhood and labor.[60] She brought to each issue her belief in living a Christian life, but this alone would not solve the nation's ills. Each woman needed to see the problems around her and solve what she could, to treat each other with love and courtesy, and to try to understand what could never truly be understood about each other's lives.

Phelps's subsequent novels, *Hedged In* and *The Silent Partner*, demonstrate this evolving interest. *Hedged In*, like *Gates Ajar*, involves the relationship between a younger woman and an older one, but here the connection becomes far more complicated. Nixy (or Eunice, as she comes to be called after she sheds her working-class persona), is a fifteen-year-old working girl who has just given birth to an illegitimate son as the novel opens. Desperately trying to avoid the asylum to which she knows her doctor will send her, she sets out on her own for the country, carrying her three-week-old child. She is an unusual heroine for a mid-nineteenth-century novel because she feels no compassion for her child, whom she rightly sees as a terrible burden and the obstacle to her finding work. Nixy wanders about the countryside, creating dilemmas for all who rationalize why they will not help her. After she leaves her baby on the doorstep of a wealthy family and it is taken to an orphanage, she is hired as a maid there, until the connection is discovered. Further wanderings lead her to the home of Margaret Purcell and her daughter Christina, who are "God's-folks" and take her in.

Hedged In is not a sentimental novel. Though Margaret Purcell is a Christian, she is not instinctively generous; her decisions to take Nixy in and then to essentially adopt her as her own daughter are difficult for her, and her prejudice leads her to act in ungenerous ways. In a reversal of what one might expect, the shamed and fallen girl teaches the older woman a hard lesson. Nixy is no saint, even after she retrieves her child four years later. She does not love him—will not love him until after he dies—and although she returns to the city briefly and helps an old enemy, she never becomes an affectionate or entirely likable character. Nor does Eunice ever marry, even though the perpetrator of her troubles comes to find her to apologize and offers his hand. Her death in the end sounds an odd note of expediency, but her story is still a far cry from romantic fiction.

Instead of marrying, Nixy becomes a teacher both in the story and for the reader. The reader learns of the degrading influences of "Thicket Street," where she grew up; learns of the fear and loathing that poor women feel for "organized avenues of charity"; learns that many purportedly Christian women find it far easier to preach reform to a young girl than to give her another chance at life or even shelter and food for a night.[61] Phelps, in sum, uses Nixy to argue against the gospel of efficiency preached by wealthy benevolent women. *Hedged In* reveals Phelps's distrust of professionalized charity, one she shared with Alcott, because of its lack of loving attention and courtesy. When the wealthy Mrs. Zerviah Myrtle officiously wants to help a dying woman from Thicket Street, she has no understanding of where the woman has come from or what might help. Mrs. Myrtle's dress rustles loudly, and her Bible rests heavily on the woman's feet. It takes the hand of Eunice Trent, who has walked through the rain to get to her, to soothe her and help her believe in heaven.

In *The Silent Partner*, a novel written in 1871, Phelps more clearly elaborates her vision of moral activism for both bourgeois and workingwomen. *The Silent Partner*, like *Gates Ajar* and *Hedged In*, features two women as its central characters. In the figure of Perley the novel seems as much an apologia for Phelps herself as it is an exploration of the evils of capitalist exploitation. As the novel opens Perley is "delicate" and her face exudes a "sweet dimness." She is the daughter of a mill owner and the fiancée of another, and she has no interest or knowledge in their work. She lives as she was born, "in a dream" of luxury, education, and music. A chance meeting with a workingwoman changes her life. When Perley patronizingly tells this woman, Sip, that she should not go to the theater—it "is no place for you, my poor girl"—Sip follows her to the opera and asks her frankly, "What place is this for you?" The theater for the workers is more honest and frank, Sip tells her, only "the plating over" is the difference.[62]

Perley and Sip have things in common, Phelps argues implicitly. They both feel the hunger of unused power; Perley wants some purpose to her life, and Sip wants some justice in hers, but they are separated by a "fixed gulf" of experience.[63] Moreover both have fathers that die at roughly the same time, caught in machinery (Sip's in the mill, Perley's at the railroad), and both feel little at the death of relatives who cared little for them. Both are women and can thus feel each other's pain; when Sip's sister is diagnosed as going blind from millwork, Sip turns to Perley, instinctively needing "some women folks to cry to."[64] Yet as close as the two women get, they do not forsake who they are. Sip cannot leave the mills, despite Perley's efforts to get her work elsewhere; she belongs in the mills, she discovers, among her coworkers as a speaker and lay minister. And Perley, although she averts a strike through her moral influence over both the mill's director and the workers, knows that she cannot do what Sip can. "I undertook to help her at the first," Perley tells her friend Fly, "but I was only *among* them at best; Sip is *of* them; she understands them and they understand her; so I left her to her own work, and I keep to my own."[65]

This sense of connection is what Perley and Sip strive for with each other, and what Phelps sought in her novel. In each of the early conversations between them, they talk at cross-purposes, neither entirely comprehending the other. When Perley advises Sip not to go to the theater, Sip tells her that the theater is what she waits all day for, what keeps her going. Perley does not understand and says as much; Sip asks her then, and later at the opera, if she *sees* the point, because "you'd ought to. You're old enough and wise enough."[66] In the next conversation they have, by the side of the falls in the mill town where Sip works, they still do not understand each other. Again, Sip's experience is between them. Perley tells Sip of the healthiness of her occupation, echoing the words she had heard from her father. Sip tells Perley of the injuries sustained by her family: her mother, who returned to the mills two days after giving birth to Catty, died two days later, and her father was crushed in a machine. It takes Perley's journey through the boardinghouses and the mills themselves, and her acquaintance with a young boy who is himself later crushed in the mills, to open her eyes and allow her to hear what Sip is telling her.

Men and women do not connect with each other in *Silent Partner*, and they never get as close as women do, even across the "gulf" of experience. Perley learns the limits of her life when she innocently suggests that she become a partner in the mill that she partially owns. Her fiancé and his father block her every move (the chapter is called "A Game of Chess"), allowing her only the power of "woman's influence," which she quickly discovers means no power at all. They call her concern for the millworkers "pretty and feminine" but out of line for a capitalist system. "For the first time in her life," Perley "was inclined to feel ashamed of being a woman." At the end of the conversation, her fiancé exclaims in exasperation, "What is the use of talking business to a woman?" suggesting that the profit motives of a businessman can never make sense to a woman concerned with the quality of workers' lives.[67]

The war and the antislavery struggle before it forms a shadowy back-drop for the novel. In the course of Perley's journey toward understanding both the capitalist world and her place in it, she meets an old radical, Bijou Mug, who has been blacklisted for striking for a living wage. Sitting beside him at the almshouse where she has gone to visit, Perley learns of his loss of his entire family to sickness and to war. The war took his two sons, he says, thus reinforcing Phelps's view of the sacrifices working people made to a nation that treated them so badly. Phelps also draws parallels with antislavery, in subtle and unsubtle ways. In an ironic reference to the Dred Scott case, where the Supreme Court decided that slaves had no rights society was bound to respect, a wealthy matron muses on Perley's time-consuming efforts for the millworkers. "But Society," sighed Mrs. Silver, "Society has rights which every lady is bound to respect; poor Perley forgets her duties to Society. Where we used to meet her in our circle three times, we meet her once now." Phelps's choice of name—Mrs. Silver—and language reinforce her critique of "Society"; Perley has not forgotten but redefined her duties. Later in the novel Phelps makes the connection she feels with the past even clearer through Sip's rejection of her lover's offer of marriage. "I'll never bring children into this world to be factory children," she tells him frankly, "and to be factory boys and girls, and to be factory men and women, and to see the sights I've seen, and to bear the things I've borne, and to run the risks I've run, and to grow up as I've grown up, and to stop where I've stopped,—never. I've heard tell of slaves before the war that wouldn't be fathers and mothers of children to be slaves like them. That's the way I feel, and that's the way I mean to feel."[68] Millwork is a form of slavery, Phelps implies, ironically echoing the critique of Northern society made before the war by slavery apologists. To bring a child into degrada-tion and despair from which they could never be freed was wrong; like Eliza in *Uncle Tom's Cabin*, Sip protects her offspring but does so by never bringing them into the world.

By the end of *The Silent Partner* both Perley and Sip have evolved into women capable of facing and helping to solve the problems of capitalism. They represent for Phelps the "coming woman" who will address the "labor question." From a sweetly dim young lady, Perley has become a "swift, strong helpful figure." And from someone "not used to feeling at all," she has become "a feeler," echoing Harriet Beecher Stowe's injunction to her readers at the end of *Uncle Tom's Cabin* that "*they feel right.*"[69] Sip has grown in knowledge of her powers as well, and she speaks to her coworkers of the salvation she sees open to them, and what unites rather than divides her and Perley. Sip does not discount or deny the wrongdoing of the mill owners; she seeks to soothe the pain of the millworkers, not to check their efforts to resist the bosses. She has become a "little preacher" like Winifred in *The Gates Ajar* and like Phelps herself, and both she and Perley have chosen happy, active, public, and single lives.

Elizabeth Stuart Phelps began a long and productive writing career with the subject of the Civil War. Like Alcott, she saw the torch of one generation being passed to another, and she took as the objects of her moral activism women's right to labor and women's right to define Christianity and heaven. While the war was not the only influence on her development, it was central to her thinking. The matriarchs of the earlier struggle against slavery, Harriet Beecher Stowe and Lydia Maria Child among them, inspired her with their example to take up the struggle for fair and human working conditions for women, a problem illustrated dramatically for her with the collapse of a nearby mill.[70] Her religious training and the grief of the many after the war whose pain did not get public play led her to reinterpret the Bible in her own way, an interpretation that appealed to thousands in the postwar years.

The Threshold of a New Era: Harper and the Negro Question

From threads of fact and fiction I have woven a story whose mission will not be in vain if it awaken in the hearts of our countrymen a stronger sense of justice and a more Christ-like humanity in behalf of those whom the fortunes of war threw, homeless, ignorant and poor, upon the threshold of a new era.
—final note in Frances E. W. Harper, *Iola Leroy* (1893)

In 1866 another writer spoke of the transformation the war had wrought and illustrated that transformation in her own life and work. "We are all bound up together in one great bundle of humanity," Frances Ellen Watkins Harper told the audience of the Eleventh Woman's Rights Conference, "and society cannot trample on the weakest and feeblest of its members without receiving the curse in its own soul."[71] If the "grand and glorious revolution" commenced by the war would come to fruition, there would be "no privileged class" but "one great privileged nation." Harper told her largely white suffragist audience that in this revolution the proper targets must be chosen, and suffrage for the white woman should not be first among them. "I do not believe that giving the woman the ballot is immediately going to cure all the ills of life," she said. "I do not believe that white women are dewdrops just exhaled from the skies." Like white men, she explained, they were good, bad, and indifferent, and rather than their

Frances Ellen Watkins Harper (1825–1911). One of the most well known African American poets in the nineteenth century, Harper used her work to condemn slavery, racism, and economic peonage before, during, and after the war. (Photo used by permission of the Library of Congress.)

rights, she would speak of wrongs done to her and other African American women who could not even ride the streetcars without discourtesy. "Are there not wrongs to be righted?" she asked.[72]

Frances Ellen Watkins Harper put whatever strength she had into commenting upon Reconstruction. She had lost her husband in 1864 and thereafter resumed public work full-time, spending the rest of her long writing career exploring the transition from slavery to freedom.[73] However, an important shift in her work after the war is discernible, as she moved from idealistic celebrations of freedom to a harder-edged but still hopeful realism about persistent racial prejudice. Unlike the other writers discussed here, Harper exercised more than one form of activism. Although she believed strongly in the power of the written word to inspire right action and right thinking, she also used the oral word, and traveled the South as a lecturer for many years after the war. *Moses: A Story of the Nile*, first published in 1868, was an original and creative prose poem rendition of the biblical tale with particular significance and relevance for African Americans in the postwar period.

The experience of Reconstruction was a painful one for many writers, as the idealistic hopes of freedom gave way to the daily terror of life in the postwar South. This sense of disenchantment was particularly acute in the work of Frances E. W. Harper, who directly experienced the chaos she described. In a letter from the South in 1867 she described her life as a lecturer. "I meet with a people eager to hear, ready to listen, as if they felt that the slumber of the ages had been broken, and that they were to sleep no more," she wrote. Things by then were "a little more hopeful," Harper reported prematurely, for freedpeople seemed to be receiving better labor contracts, and there was less violence. "If we have had no past, it is well for us to look hopefully to the future," she wrote in an 1867 letter to the *National Anti-Slavery Standard*, "for the shadows bear the promise of a brighter coming day; and in fact, so far as the colored man is concerned, I do not feel particularly uneasy about his future."[74]

But Harper's confidence about blacks did not extend to whites, North or South. From an initially celebratory and emotional state with the Emancipation Proclamation and the ending of the war, Harper moved to a sharper critique of Reconstruction that originated with a stinging indictment of a society that would need such a war to cure itself. In "Lines to Miles O'Reilly," published in 1867, Harper took on Charles Halpine, an Irish immigrant and Union officer who wrote songs under the pseudonym (Private) Miles O'Reilly. In "Sambo's Right to Be Kilt," O'Reilly celebrated African American enlistment because African Americans could act as cannon fodder for whites. In her poem Harper defended the war efforts of African Americans. They did not rise in armed insurrection against women and children, which would have only drawn the condemnation of the North, but fought honorably for their own freedom. "Words for the Hour" called on Northern men to realize the continuing dangers in the South and the war there still to be won. "O Northern men!" she called, "within your hands / Is held no common trust; / Secure the victories won by blood / When treason bit the dust." In another poem, aptly titled "Retribution," she defined her own position on the war. Like many religious interpreters of the conflict, she saw it as God's careful action. Yet she saw it as vengeance, a deserved punishment and a warning, rather than a cleansing fire sent to improve an erring nation.[75]

Yet perhaps Harper's most moving and creative work in the immediate postwar period was designed specifically for African Americans. *Moses: A Story of the Nile* is like many of Harper's poems in that it directly interprets the Bible for contemporary use. In most ways, however, it is entirely different: Harper employs no rhyme, and her poem is longer than any of her others. *Moses* uses the story of that biblical leader of the Jews as a parable for African Americans. The Civil War becomes the series of curses meted out to the Egyptians, and the freedpeople are now lost in the desert.

Harper's poem offered four distinct messages to her readers. First, she called on all African Americans to "join / The fortunes of [their] race," as Moses did, and "to put aside / All other bright advantages, save / The approval of my conscience and the meed / Of rightly doing." Second, in the figure of Moses's mother, she offered a vision of the power women could have in shaping the future. The memory of his mother's words and their inspiration gives the strength to Moses when he most needs it. Third, in God's message to Moses, Harper took a lesson about the rights of the freedpeople. "Let our haughty rulers learn that men / Of humblest birth and lowliest lot have / Rights as sacred and divine as theirs, and they / Who fence in leagues of earth by bonds and claims / And title deeds, forgetting land and water, / Air and light are God's own gifts and heritage[,]" Harper wrote in a relevant passage for those who sought at the least forty acres and a mule. Finally, Harper spoke of the children, who she now felt were the best hope for this "brighter coming day." If those Moses led from Egypt "slumbered in the wild," and forgot the teachings of the past, "they died / With broader freedom on their lips, and for their / Little ones did God reserve the heritage / So rudely thrust aside."[76]

In a speech of 1875 Harper called for "another battle" to be fought, one not "of flashing swords and clashing steel—but a moral warfare, a battle against ignorance, poverty, and low social condition." She called young men and women to this battle, telling women in particular to "give power and significance to your own life," for "in the great work of upbuilding there is room for woman's work and woman's heart."[77] This was the note that Harper sounded for the rest of her career. The Civil War was the turning point for her and her people, and she constantly reminded them of its meaning. It was a moment they fought for and won, a moment of justice in the midst of decades of oppression, and it became her guiding light. God's vengeance was revealed in the war, as it had been for the Egyptians enslaving the Jews, and the right to freedom for the slaves demonstrated the right to freedom and power for women as well. In a poem on suffrage, published thirty years after the war, Harper still used her words to convince men of their duty to women: "The masters thought before the war / That slavery was right: / But we who felt the heavy yoke / Didn't see it in that light . . . Now if you don't believe 'twas right / To crowd us from the track, / How can you push your wife aside / And try to hold her back?"[78]

In Harper's work can be seen many of the questions confronting the writers of the late nineteenth century. Like Alcott, Harper worked to define a "coming woman" of power and dignity. And like Phelps, Harper believed in women's right to fair and just labor and in her need to define Christianity for herself. Yet Harper believed that the problem of racial prejudice and racial injustice was paramount for the nation even after the war, and she believed that it was a problem only African Americans could truly understand and translate. In what seems an obvious reference to Harriet Beecher Stowe, given that Harper praised her work earlier, Dr. Latimer in *Iola Leroy* tells Iola to "write a good, strong book" for the race, for although "authors belonging to the white race have written good racial books, for which I am deeply grateful, . . . it seems to be almost impossible for a white man to put himself completely in our place."[79]

Harper was aware that her message to African Americans was ignored or dismissed by whites. Louisa May Alcott's *Work* was itself criticized for bringing up the question of slavery again with the introduction of a character named Hepsey and a call for contributions to the freedpeople after the war, even though this was a minor character in a minor section of the book. In her speech of 1875, Harper noted bitterly the lack of interest by whites in the condition of the freedpeople. Whites do not seem to care when African Americans are murdered in the South, she noted. Where was the public opinion so aroused by the wartime outrages in Vicksburg and Louisiana? Regardless of its victories over slavery, Harper argued, American civilization lacked a sense of justice, humanity, and the knowledge that, despite arguments over the origins of the species, "we all come from the living God and . . . He is the common Father."[80]

Two major works by Harper illustrate her understanding of the war's legacy: a long narrative poem, *Sketches of Southern Life*, and *Iola Leroy*, a novel she wrote for schoolchildren. Like Alcott's *Work* and Phelps's *The Gates Ajar*, both use the war as a touchstone to make sense of the moral mission of women in the late nineteenth century. *Sketches* marks Harper's return to her popular rhyming style, and moves beyond the explication of the war and the end of slavery to a call for renewed battle against oppression and social malaise. *Iola Leroy* is a frankly historical work, an effort to instruct the young about the work their forefathers and -mothers did to free themselves from bondage as well as lead them to choose moral and active lives. In the note following the text Harper makes clear that her object was to instill the justice and humanity she called for twenty years before *Iola* was written, suggesting the consistency of her vision and her struggle.

Sketches of Southern Life, published in 1872, represents an interpretation of the history of slavery, the war, and Reconstruction. The series of poems takes as its central character and narrator a woman named Chloe who belongs to the generation before the war and serves as an example to the "coming woman" of postwar America. Slavery, as Harper tells it, is both a story of loss and of community support. Aunt Chloe, in a poem of that name, tells of the anguish she feels when her sons are sold away from her. Her crisis of faith is averted only with the help of a slave preacher who leads her back to God and to hope for the future. In the poem that follows, "Deliverance," the story of the war is told through Chloe's eyes; she feels "somehow or other / We was mixed up in this fight." She speaks of the split within the Southern plantations between the parlor, where "Mistus" prayed, and the cabins, where the slaves prayed, each willing a different outcome. When freedom came, she admits frankly, it was a difficult adjustment, but "we weathered through the tempest, / For slavery made us tough." The end of the poem criticizes freedmen who had sold their vote for candy, sugar, meat, or flour. "Women radicals" managed to save the day, however, by following their husbands to make them do right. But if some were greedy, most men knew, Chloe adds, that "their freedom cost too much / Of blood and pain and treasure, / For them to fool away their votes / For profit or for pleasure."[81]

The last four poems of *Sketches* outline Chloe's postwar life and are an argument for an active and thoughtful political life for women. Like the freedmen who vote with the interests of *all* freedpeople in mind, she knows and feels the cost of freedom and is determined to get as much from it as she can. In "Aunt Chloe's Politics," she reiterates her message to her people, urging them to use the vote wisely. "And this buying up each other / Is something worse than mean," she cautions, "Though I thinks a heap of voting, / I go for voting clean." Chloe also means to learn to read, even though she is now "rising sixty." This is all the more reason, she thinks, for she has "no time to wait." Her work, and the work of the preacher who led her to God, finally pay off in the happy ending to *Sketches*. The preacher speaks for the first and last time in a church built for him, and Chloe is reunited with her sons. She is "richer now than Mistus," for her sons were saved for her.[82]

Iola Leroy echoes many of the messages of *Sketches* and explicitly uses some of its anecdotes. Like *Sketches*, the later novel suggests that despite some affection between mistress, master, and slaves, they worked at cross-purposes: slaves may have been loving, but they were not fools. The prayers of the mistress, it is implied, were not heard because they were not just. Like *Sketches*, *Iola Leroy* stresses not only the importance of leadership and self-help, but also the support that the African American community gave to itself through slavery, the war, and afterward. As one slave character tells another during the war, "Tom, if we ever get our freedom, we've got to learn to trust each other and stick together if we would be a people."[83] The two characters do just that as soldiers in the Union army.

Iola Leroy goes beyond *Sketches*, however, in illuminating the meaning and the effects of the Civil War. In writing a history of the war Harper was herself trying to do as her characters suggest would benefit the race: to write a "good, strong book," to faithfully chronicle "all the deeds of daring and service" that her people undertook for their freedom and the Union army. Rather than waiting on the plantation, the characters of *Iola Leroy*, both young men and women, enlist in the effort itself. Iola is the daughter of a plantation owner and his wife, unaware that her mother is a former slave and hence that she and her brother are African American. When the war begins Iola's father dies, and she and her family are remanded to slavery. With the help of an ex-slave, now a Union soldier, who reports her story to a Union commander, Iola is freed and becomes a nurse.

Harper uses Iola and her family to illustrate the barrier that race represented both during the war and afterward, a barrier higher and more impenetrable than class. Iola's brother Harry discovers he is a slave when he is in the North at a private school. When he decides to enlist in the Union army to search for his family in the South and fight for his freedom, he learns that he must irrevocably choose what race he will henceforth be. "It was as if two paths had suddenly opened before him, and he was forced to choose between them." On the one path was a chance for advancement, power, and achievement; on the other was "weakness, ignorance, poverty, and the proud world's social scorn."[84] Harry, like Iola later, chooses to fight both with and for African Americans, a choice that Harper celebrates both here and in earlier work.

Such acts are the mark of true leadership for both women and men, Harper argues, because race will determine social status in a way class will not. This point is reinforced through the words of the white character Camille Lecroix, a Southern plantation owner who feels some sympathy for Iola Leroy as she is kidnapped from her Northern school and taken south to slavery. He marvels at her beauty and elegance but tells his friend, the lawyer who has come to get Iola, that "it would be easier for me to go to the slums and take a young girl from there, and have her introduced as my wife, than to have society condone the offense if I married that lovely girl."[85] For Harper as well as Phelps, society is at fault for its severe boundaries, but Harper makes the additional point that these boundaries forever block African Americans, however white their skin.

Iola Leroy becomes for Harper the ideal American woman even as Harry becomes the ideal American man. Iola refuses to marry a white doctor who has fallen in love with her, despite her obvious attraction to him; she chooses instead her "life-work . . . among the colored people of the South." Her "fiery ordeal of suffering" during the war has taught her true values, and helps her identify with her people. Moreover, she believes that "every woman ought to know how to earn her own living" and ought to work against her own "weakness and inefficiency" with remunerative labor.[86]

Like Alcott's and Phelps's, Harper's work supported reform through what one of her characters calls "a union of women," who will "with the warmest hearts and clearest brains . . . help in the moral education of the race." These women will teach in the classrooms and by example, like the teacher and "grand woman" Miss Delany, who will become Harry's fiancée. In a conversation on their hopes for the race Miss Delany and Iola Leroy add their own voices self-confidently, calling for a political involvement of African Americans based on a knowledge and understanding of the past, most significantly and particularly an "everlasting remembrance [of] our great deliverance."[87]

At the same time, however, Harper joined Alcott and Phelps in criticizing organized charity for its blindness and lack of Christian humanity. At one point in the novel, Iola reports that her mother, while working as a missionary in Philadelphia, had once found an outcast girl. She filed an application for the girl at a local asylum, which was refused because of her race. But when she tried again with a white girl in the same condition, the doors swung open. "It was as if two women were sinking in the quicksands," Iola explains, "and on the solid land stood other women with lifelines in their hands, seeing the deadly sands slowly creeping up around the hapless victims. To one they readily threw the lines of deliverance, but for the other there was not one strand of salvation."[88] Race prejudice mars these charitable institutions and undercuts attempts at sisterly solidarity.

Iola Leroy argued that the nation was on the threshold of a new era, but that only justice and Christian humanity will disperse the shadows of oppression and bring the "brighter coming day" that the war and the end to slavery promised. Such justice and humanity will come through the agency of men and women through labor for their race, labor defined as everything from educating children as a mother or a teacher to working as a saleswoman or writing a book.[89] The war that brought tragedy, Harper stressed, also brought family reunions and an end to slavery, and its memory must be continually refreshed in order to give hope and impetus to the coming generations.

LOUISA MAY ALCOTT, Elizabeth Stuart Phelps, and Frances Ellen Watkins Harper used the war as a way of framing their moral message for the future. Earlier novelists and narrators used the memory of the war to place women in the national past, to make history a province of women as well as men. Alcott, Phelps, and Harper went beyond a static remembrance of the war toward an understanding of it that would inform and shape future generations of Americans. For each author the war suggested a wider arena of authority for women who proved their worth in the midst of its chaos and tragedy. And each author used the war to offer a political and cultural critique of postwar America in outlining the particular problems women faced: Alcott, in becoming a strong woman, Phelps, in opening avenues of moral and just labor for women, and Harper, in overcoming the prejudice and oppression of race.

And thou shalt take their part tonight—

Weep and write!

A curse from the depths of womanhood,

Is very salt, and bitter, and good.

—Elizabeth Barrett Browning,

The Liberty Bell (1855)

{ CONCLUSION }

IN *Chapters from a Life*, Elizabeth Stuart Phelps confessed her inability to act publicly on the moral reforms she espoused in her writings. Her beliefs had brought her censure and pain, but she felt she had not truly thrown herself into the solving of the problems she saw because of her inclination to study and write and her abject fear of public speaking. Mary Livermore soothed her when she was so attacked by a woman activist, responding that "she works in another way from ours," a defense Phelps remembered gratefully.

Yet if Phelps had not worked in the trenches, her literary work was "fed, not famished" by the "moral agitations" of her day. And while she believed strongly that realism was important to the writer, she knew that without a moral compass fiction would lead nowhere. "In a word," she wrote, "the province of the artist is to portray life as it is; and life *is* moral responsibility. . . . Life is moral struggle. Portray the struggle, and you need write no tract." This was the political work of fiction.

Many mid-nineteenth-century women writers shared these assumptions. Writing about war and slavery, women's rights and responsibilities, working conditions and the postwar social order, Northern women articulated hopes and fears for themselves and their many readers. They employed a rhetoric that could serve to bring them all together—as women—and to distinguish them by class and race while working toward similar goals. The slipperiness of this rhetoric, and its power during a time of conflict and war, made it enormously useful. Their writings represent an important chapter in American reform; their characters and narratives created a base of images and ideas that later generations of women would build upon.

Their didacticism, their moralism, their sentimentality, and their insistence on gender difference can be grating to the modern ear. And yet if the tone of their work offends us, their efforts to participate in public life, to express ideas that might make positive change, are worthy of our notice. Political involvement for a woman at midcentury was not easy for a number of reasons, for, as Harriet Beecher Stowe remarked in 1850, "[n]othing but deadly determination enables me ever to write; it is rowing against wind and tide."[1]

Those, like Stowe, who "put their oars in the water" left traces behind. By claiming writing as a means for expressing "moral struggle" and imagining means for resolving such struggles, these women offered a unique vantage point on the country's most pressing social and political concerns at a pivotal moment in its history. At the center of those concerns was a question about the structure of society: What can and should women do? Their writings at midcentury represented a pitched battle over the answer.

Women writers were quick to claim that the Civil War represented a victory in this battle. As a result of the war, they claimed, women had demonstrated their abilities in a public sphere in a variety of ways, and henceforth they should be offered the freedoms and the rights in that sphere that they had previously been denied. As even antisuffragist Gail Hamilton put it in her 1868 essay *Women's Wrongs*: "We cannot always have a war in which to fuse out prejudices and puerilities, but we might learn from our experience during this one war that wifehood and motherhood are set within no narrow bounds, depend upon no external conditions, but spring from the heart, inhere in the nature. With all this glowing past just behind us, how can men stand up and preach their trivialities?"[2]

Women writers, then, claimed "a glowing past" and went forward to address new moral struggles, and to continue the old ones with new vigor and hope. From the 1850s, when women entered public and political dialogue in record numbers, to the 1870s, when the direction of women's work had changed, an important shift was under way in the interpretation of social structures like class and race and in the form of social and political expression. In the course of their political work, women writers did effect "a revolution in woman herself" in establishing a middle-class middle ground. Their work, impressive and flawed as it was, demonstrated the power of words and stories in creating opportunity through imagination. These writers made "the revolution in woman herself" as the war did. As Elizabeth Barrett Browning put it in 1855, in a missive to her American friends: "Weep and write! / A curse from the depths of womanhood, / Is very salt, and bitter, and good."

The urge to do collective work, to bring together women across lines of race and class, made sense in a nation rent by Civil War. But it also makes sense during peacetime. That these women were unable to see beyond their class or race does not deny the significance of what they were trying to do. That the rhetoric of unity was just rhetoric does not undercut that to try to create a kind of unity around a common goal may make good political sense. And that the fissures, arrogance, and racism that undercut this political project grew in the Civil War era should come as no surprise: those fissures are with us still.

Notes

Introduction

1. Livermore, *My Story*, 85, 92.
2. The U.S. Sanitary Commission (USSC) was organized early in the war as a voluntary association designed to help the Army Medical Bureau. Given official sanction in June 1861, it was staffed almost entirely by women, although led largely by men. Among other related tasks, the commission gathered money, food, and supplies of all kinds and distributed them to the soldiers.
3. Stanton, Anthony, and Gage, eds., *History of Woman Suffrage*, 23.
4. The experience of white and black Southern women during and just after the war is the subject of numerous and useful twentieth-century books and articles; see, among others, Bynum, *Unruly Women*; Clinton, *Tara Revisited*; Clinton and Silber, eds., *Divided Houses*; Forbes, *African American Women*; Hodes, *White Women, Black Men*; Hunter, *To 'Joy My Freedom*; Jones, *Labor of Love*; Rable, *Civil Wars*; and Whites, *Civil War*.
5. Phelps, *Chapters from a Life*, 97.
6. Gallman, *North Fights*, 107, 105.
7. See, especially, Forbes, *African American Women*; Jones, *Labor of Love*; and Lebsock, *Free Women*.
8. See Stanton, Anthony, and Gage, eds., *History of Woman Suffrage*; DuBois, *Woman Suffrage* and *Feminism and Suffrage*; Flexner, *Century of Struggle*; and Newman, *White Women's Rights*.
9. See Dublin, *Women at Work*, ch. 9, and Kessler-Harris, *Out to Work*, ch. 4.
10. For the notion of "cultural work" undertaken through literature, I am indebted to Tompkins, *Sensational Designs*; a similar understanding of "ideological work," also tremendously useful, is from Poovey's *Uneven Developments*.
11. My understanding of the parameters of the word "political" has been deeply shaped by Joan Scott. See Scott, *Gender and the Politics*. Rebecca Edwards argues that this expanded understanding of politics does not represent how nineteenth-century Americans thought. During the Civil War and in the decades before and after it, however, middle-class women who were writing for a public audience at times explicitly claimed their work to be political; at others they coyly claimed it not to be while it made demands about the direction of national politics (see, for example, Mrs. Bird in *Uncle Tom's Cabin*, one of the most political of novels). See Edwards, *Angels*, 9. In any case, if the women writers studied here did not consistently claim politics as their domain, they nonetheless participated in political discussions, writing for a public audience about issues of national concern in order to make change.
12. My understanding of rhetoric and its power has come to me through Plato's *Gorgias* and its explication by my colleague in the Philosophy Department at Sarah Lawrence College, Michael Davis.
13. See Elshtain, *Women and War*, and Joan Scott, "Rewriting History," in Higonnet

et al., eds., *Behind the Lines*, 26. See also Faust, "Altars of Sacrifice," 1200, as well as Faust, *Mothers of Invention*.

14. Elshtain, *Women and War*, 165.

15. This theme of locating the central story with women rather than men is common to much women's fiction in the mid-nineteenth century. See Baym, *Women's Fiction*.

16. Elshtain, *Women and War*, 22, 166.

17. Hall, "Notes," 76. See also Jameson, "Reification and Utopia."

18. On this point see Baym, *Novels*, 27.

19. Denning, *Mechanic Accents*, 3.

20. Lipsitz, *Time Passages*, 13.

21. As Elshtain says, "Politics is the work of citizens, human beings in their civic capacities" (*Women and War*, 227).

22. Lipsitz, *Time Passages*, 16.

23. Lydia Maria Child's and Harriet Beecher Stowe's "letters to the editor" of the *National Anti-Slavery Standard* and the *Independent*, respectively, are frank expressions of politics; didactic stories funded by religious societies and the earlier mentioned death poetry tended to be more covert.

24. Significantly it was during the Civil War that the first woman *did* speak in the congressional halls. Anna Dickinson, a young and popular political lecturer, spoke to assembled legislators in the House of Representatives in 1864, spontaneously recommending President Abraham Lincoln for reelection during the course of her talk.

25. See Harris, *Nineteenth-Century American Women's Novels*.

26. The literature on this ideology and its relevance to daily social life in the nineteenth century is vast. Of particular note are the following in order of appearance in the historical dialogue: Barbara Welter, "The Cult of True Womanhood: 1800–1860," *American Quarterly* 18 (1966): 151–74; Sklar, *Catharine Beecher*; Cott, *Bonds of Womanhood*; Douglas, *Feminization of American Culture*; Epstein, *Politics of Domesticity*; Smith-Rosenberg, *Disorderly Conduct*; Kerber, "Separate Spheres"; Cogan, *All-American Girl*; and Harris, *Nineteenth-Century American Women's Novels*.

27. The degree to which this ideology applied to lived experience has been challenged by historians. Mary Ryan, for example, in *Women in Public*, makes the argument that women led public lives despite conventional dicta.

28. Dodge, ed., *Gail Hamilton's Life*, 1:280.

29. "Meredith," "Woman's True Position," *New York Ledger* 16, no. 37 (Nov. 17, 1860): 4.

30. Gail Hamilton, "A Spasm of Sense," in Hamilton, *Gala-Days*, 271; the essay was first published in the *Atlantic Monthly*.

31. See Blumin, *Emergence of the Middle Class*, ch. 5. My understanding of class formation has also been informed by Stansell, *City of Women*, and Wilenz, *Chants Democratic*. For the impact of domestic ideology on ideas about women and work, see Kessler-Harris, *Out to Work*, 53.

32. See Sklar, *Catharine Beecher*, 165.

33. Stansell, *City of Women*, ix. For the relationship of workingwomen to the ideology of separate spheres, see also Alexander, "We Are Engaged," and Ginzberg, *Women and the Work of Benevolence*.

34. See Newman, *White Women's Rights*.

35. Horton, "Freedom's Yoke." See also Forbes, *African American Women*.

36. See Carby, *Reconstructing Womanhood*.

37. See Leonard, *All the Daring of a Soldier*.

38. McPherson, *For Cause and Comrades*, 12.

39. Ibid., 77.

40. Hess, *Liberty, Virtue and Progress*, 17, 50.

41. Ibid., 107.

42. Hamilton, *Skirmishes and Sketches*, 432.

43. Quoted in McPherson, *Ordeal by Fire*, 487.

Chapter One

1. Happily for the Fales family, Edmund Fales did return home. He and his father died within less than a month of each other in the spring of 1879, leaving Sarah, her daughter-in-law, and her grandchild to fare for themselves on the Middletown farm (Sarah E. Fales, Fales Letters, R.I. Historical Society, Providence, R.I). Family information from a personal letter from Nancy Pierce Lantz to the author, January 11, 1991. See also Lyde Sizer, "Civil War: Her Story," *Providence Journal-Bulletin*, D1, D8.

2. More broadly educated women did express republican sentiments shared by the men, but perhaps Sarah Fales is more representative of not only rural women but even many of the writers who did not receive such a traditionally male education. See Hess, *Liberty, Virtue and Progress*.

3. Stowe, *Life of Harriet*, 128. For an excellent biography of Stowe, see Hedrick, *Harriet Beecher Stowe*.

4. Quoted in Wilson, *Crusader in Crinoline*, 252. While that proviso—providing she lived—rings as self-pity to a twentieth-century ear, it was true enough. Well before and after the Civil War, death was a regular visitor to nineteenth-century homes.

5. Phelps, *Chapters from a Life*, 14–15.

6. See Strasser, *Never Done*, and Matthews, *"Just a Housewife."*

7. Child, *Selected Letters*, 258–59, 253–54. Biographical work on Child has been aided considerably by two biographies: Clifford's *Crusader for Freedom* and Karcher's magisterial *First Woman in the Republic*.

8. This section is informed by the work of Strasser, *Never Done*; Boydston, *Home and Work*; and Sutherland, *Expansion of Everyday Life*, among other texts.

9. Sutherland, *Expansion of Everyday Life*, 68.

10. Quoted in Strasser, *Never Done*, 57.

11. Ibid.

12. Boydston, *Home and Work*, 81.

13. Quoted in Boyle, "Mrs. E. D. E. N. Southworth, Novelist," 9.

14. Boydston, *Home and Work*, 134.

15. Ibid.

16. Strasser, *Never Done*; see in particular chapter titled "Boarding Out"; Warren, *Fanny Fern*.

17. James, ed., *Notable American Women*, 2:137–39; see also Boyd, *Discarded Legacy*.

18. James, ed., *Notable American Women*, 1:493–95; see also Coultrap-McGuin, introduction to *Gail Hamilton*.

19. This is still true today. With special thanks to my entire women's community. They know who they are.

20. Child, *Selected Letters*, 254.

21. Quoted in Brown, *Knowledge Is Power*, 176.

22. Ibid., 173.

23. Ibid., 285.

24. The following section on the history of publishing, etc., and its effect on the literary domestic I owe to Kelley, *Private Woman*, ch. 1, and Mott, *History of American Magazines*, vol. 1, ch. 1.

25. Kelley, *Private Woman*, 8, 19.

26. Ibid., 10.

27. Geary, "Scribbling Women," 4.

28. Kelley, *Private Woman*, 11.

29. See Kelley for specifics about each of these novels and authors. See also Brown, *Sentimental Novel*; Hart, *Popular Book*; Mott, *Golden Multitudes*; and Pattee, *Feminine Fifties*.

30. Swisshelm, *Half a Century*, 113; also quoted in Mott, *History of American Magazines*, 2:50.

31. Quotes in Geary, "Scribbling Women," 133, 121.

32. Child, *Selected Letters*, 253.

33. This is a reference to Roediger, *Wages of Whiteness*. See also Saxton, *Rise and Fall*.

34. Clifford, *Crusader for Freedom*, chs. 1 and 2; James, ed., *Notable American Women*, 1:330; Karcher, *First Woman in the Republic*. See also the older biographies of Child: Baer, *Heart is Like Heaven* (1964), and Meltzer, *Tongue of Flame* (1965).

35. Quoted in James, ed., *Notable American Women*, 1:331.

36. Child, *Selected Letters*, 193.

37. Quoted in Clifford, *Crusader for Freedom*, 225.

38. Child's argumentative style, in much of her political work, was much more influenced by male political rhetoric than female fiction. Her sentimental fiction, by contrast, was considerably less effective.

39. Fields, ed., *Life and Letters*, 131.

40. Wilson, *Crusader in Crinoline*, 259–60.

41. Fields, ed., *Life and Letters*, 136.

42. Henceforth I will refer to Parton as Fern, her preferred name by the end of her life.

43. In the North, Wilson's *Our Nig* (1859), arguably also a kind of slave narrative, predates Jacobs.

44. Warren, *Fanny Fern*, 222–24.

45. Ibid., 43, 44, 54, 70–73.

46. Ibid., 92.

47. Ibid.

48. Ibid., 100.

49. Quoted in Boyle, "Mrs. E. D. E. N. Southworth, Novelist," 9.

50. Harper, *Brighter Coming Day*, 6–8; see also Boyd, *Discarded Legacy*. No copies of *Forest Leaves* are known to exist.

51. See Yee, *Black Women Abolitionists*, for the context of Harper's activism and early life.

52. Harper, *Brighter Coming Day*, 8–10.

53. Ibid., 95.

54. Quoted in Still, *Underground Rail Road*, 786, and in Harper, *Brighter Coming Day*, 10.

55. Harper, *Brighter Coming Day*, 57; "Eliza Harris," 61. Watkins also wrote "Eva's Farewell" in response to *Uncle Tom's Cabin*. Reprinted in *Brighter Coming Day*, 75–76.

56. Harper, *Brighter Coming Day*, 58–59.

57. Ibid., 12, 11.

58. This notion of Transcendentalist's rebuked is Sharon Harris's. For the quote, see Davis, *Life in the Iron Mills*, 11, 14–15.

59. Quoted in Harris, *Rebecca Harding Davis*, 26.

60. Davis, *Bits of Gossip*, 33–34, quoted in Harris, *Rebecca Harding Davis*, 84.

61. Rebecca Harding Davis, *Bits of Gossip*, 36, quoted in Harris, *Rebecca Harding Davis*, 85–86.

62. Quoted in Harris, *Rebecca Harding Davis*, 119; Alcott references from Rebecca Harding Davis, *Bits of Gossip*, 38, quoted in ibid., 87; letter quoted in ibid., 117.

63. Dodge, ed., *Gail Hamilton's Life*, 1:280.

64. Ibid., 194.

65. Biographical information has been gleaned from James, ed., *Notable American Women*, 1:493–95, and Coultrap-McQuin, *Doing Literary Business*, and with help from Louise Newman, with whom I shared resources and information on Mary Abigail Dodge.

66. Dodge, ed., *Gail Hamilton's Life*, 2:64.

67. Ibid., 41, 66.

68. Alcott, *Journals*, 124 n. 27.

69. Ibid., 119.

70. Alcott, *Selected Letters*, 77, 78.

71. "Metarealist" is Harris's term for Rebecca Harding Davis. See Harris, *Rebecca Harding Davis*, 19.

72. Quoted in Coultrap-McQuin, *Doing Literary Business*, 106.

73. See, for example, Stern, *Double Life*.

74. Alcott, "With a Rose." As with Lydia Maria Child, there are many astute scholars of Alcott. For an elegant reading of Alcott's "double life," see Elbert, *Hunger for Home*, and the older but still useful biography by Martha Saxton, *Louisa May*. For a collection of some of Alcott's "blood-and-thunder" tales, see Stern, ed., *Behind a Mask*, and Showalter, ed., *Alternative Alcott*.

75. Alcott, *Journals*, 110.

76. Phelps, *Chapters from a Life*, 76, 75.

77. For biographical information, see James, ed., *Notable American Women*, 3:538–40; Buhle and Howe, afterword to *Silent Partner*, 353–86; Bennett, *Elizabeth Stuart Phelps*; Kelly, *Life and Works*; Coultrap-McQuin, *Doing Literary Business*.

78. Phelps, *Chapters from a Life*, 47, 50, 48, 131–40. See also Harris, *Rebecca Harding Davis*.

Chapter Two

1. Donald, *Lincoln*, 542.

2. Joan D. Hedrick dates the meeting and describes all that is known from contemporary accounts. See her excellent biography, *Harriet Beecher Stowe*, 306.

3. In making this argument I am in a sense challenging historian Lori Ginzberg's point that the 1850s saw the waning of "moral suasion" as political act. That this is

largely true for activist women is clear, but for women writers (who wrote as a kind of activism) moral suasion remained (and remains) a primary political tool. See Ginzberg, *Women and the Work*.

4. Southworth, *Retribution*, 62.

5. Ibid., 108.

6. Southworth's novel *Ishmael*, her personal favorite, is the best example.

7. This insight derives from a reading of Morrison's *Playing in the Dark*, which suggests that black characters in white novels are often used to illuminate aspects of racial whiteness.

8. Mott, *History of American Magazines*, 1:46–47.

9. For biographical information on Elizabeth Oakes Smith, see James, ed., *Notable American Women*; see also Conrad, *Perish the Thought*.

10. Smith, *Bertha and Lily*, 55, 56.

11. Russo and Kramarae, eds., *Radical Women's Press*, 63, 64, 65, from the *Una*, February 1855. See Warren, *Fanny Fern*, 120–42.

12. Conrad, *Perish the Thought*, 175.

13. McPherson, *Battle Cry*, 119–20.

14. S[towe], "Appeal," *Independent* 6, no. 273 (Feb. 23, 1854): 1. Reprinted in the *Liberator* on March 3, 1854.

15. S[towe], "Appeal," 1.

16. S[towe], "Mothers of the Men," *Independent* 8, no. 191 (June 19, 1856): 1.

17. Letter dated August 3, 1856, in Child, *Selected Letters*, 291.

18. Campaign songs quoted in Pattee, *Feminine Fifties*, 108–9.

19. For this shift in Northern sentiment, see McPherson, *Battle Cry*, 202–13.

20. Child, *Correspondence*, 3. Yellin makes similar arguments with regard to Child's reaction to the raid at Harpers Ferry in *Women and Sisters*. See ch. 3, esp. 62–64.

21. Child, *Correspondence*, 5.

22. Ibid., 6.

23. Ibid., 7.

24. Ibid., 12.

25. Factual information on the *Correspondence* was taken from the editorial note in Child, *Selected Letters*, 333.

26. Child, *Correspondence*, 16.

27. Ibid., 17–18.

28. Ibid., 26.

29. Ibid., 26.

30. Child, *Selected Letters*, 342.

31. Swisshelm, *Crusader and Feminist*, 34 n. 3. Quotes are from a lecture, the text of which was reprinted in the *Minnesota Republican* on November 19, 1858.

32. Child, *Selected Letters*, 336, 337.

33. My understanding of Jacobs's work has been very much informed by Carby's *Reconstructing Womanhood*.

34. Child, *Selected Letters*, 357.

35. Ibid., 357.

36. Ibid., 378.

37. See Child, *Selected Letters*, 375 n. 3.

38. Reprinted in Jacobs, *Incidents*, 247 (letter dated Oct. 8, 1860).

39. Jacobs, *Incidents*, 235, 236 (letters to Amy Post dated Apr. 4 and Oct. 9, 1853).

40. See Carby, *Reconstructing Womanhood*.

41. Jacobs, *Classic Slave Narratives*, 393.

42. Davis, *Life in the Iron Mills*, 40.

43. Ibid.

44. Ibid., 46.

45. Ibid., 34.

46. Ibid., 39.

47. Davis, *Life in the Iron Mills and Other Stories*, 55.

48. Ibid., 69–70.

49. Information on the *Independent* from Child, *Selected Letters*, 409 n. 1.

50. Stowe, "What God Hath Wrought," 1.

51. Ibid. Child also believed that this was a crucial time for public opinion and thus important for the production of antislavery literature, mentioning as much in many of her letters around this time. See her *Selected Letters*, ch. 7.

52. Child, *Selected Letters*, 312.

53. Langdon, *Ida May*, 453.

54. Child, *Selected Letters*, 388–89 n. 1.

55. "Miss Watkins and the Constitution," *National Anti-Slavery Standard* 19, no. 47 (Apr. 9, 1859): 3.

Chapter Three

1. Alcott, *Selected Letters*, 64, and *Journals*, 105.

2. The practice of packing lint into the bandages of wounds caused widespread infections and gangrene until it was stopped early in the war.

3. For an analysis of the meanings of the war for the soldiers, see McPherson, *What They Fought For*.

4. See Faust's excellent book on the subject, *Mothers of Invention*.

5. Massey, *Bonnet Brigades*, 30; see also Culpepper, *Trials and Triumphs*, 245.

6. For an analysis of the experience of these women, see Leonard, *All the Daring of a Soldier*.

7. For a short history of women's efforts in Rhode Island, see Sizer, "Civil War: Her Story," *Providence Journal-Bulletin*.

8. Ginzberg, *Women and the Work*, 140–41; Massey, *Bonnet Brigades*, 32, 33; Culpepper, *Trials and Triumphs*, 248–49.

9. Quoted in Culpepper, *Trials and Triumphs*, 246.

10. Ibid., 248.

11. Child, *Selected Letters*, 411. See 411 n. 1 for information on the freedmen's movement.

12. Clifford, *Crusader for Freedom*, 258–63.

13. Livermore, *My Story*, 148–49.

14. Quoted in Culpepper, *Trials and Triumphs*, 316.

15. Massey, *Bonnet Brigades*, 330–33.

16. Quoted in ibid., 48–49.

17. For a brief description of Spencer's efforts, see the introduction to her postwar novel, *Tried and True*.

18. See Massey's chapter on women soldiers, "Risked Everything." See also Lyde Sizer, "Acting Her Part: Narratives of Union Women Spies," in Clinton and Silber, eds., *Divided Houses*.

19. Massey, *Bonnet Brigades*, 89.

20. "The Lady Major," *New York Ledger* 18, no. 14 (June 7, 1862): 4. Reynolds, the wife of an army officer, went on to become a physician and worked for the Red Cross after the war; see Massey, *Bonnet Brigades*, 69, 353.

21. Quoted in Jones, *Labor of Love*, 47. It is Jones's argument that slave women worked with the best interest of their families foremost.

22. Quoted in Sterling, ed., *We Are Your Sisters*, 243.

23. See Taylor, *Black Women's Civil War*.

24. See Conrad, *Harriet Tubman*.

25. Clifford, *Crusader for Freedom*, 248.

26. Child, *Selected Letters*, 393, 394. For a further examination of the politics of the Emancipation League, see Sterling, *Ahead of Her Time*, 333–34.

27. I am indebted to Wendy Hamand not only for this quote but for the information in this section on the Women's National Loyal League. See Hamand, "Women's National Loyal League," 41.

28. Ibid., 48.

29. For a further analysis of the editorial policies of these publications, see Endres, "Women's Press," 31–53.

30. Dodge, ed., *Gail Hamilton's Life*, 1:398.

31. S. J. F., "The War—Our 'Retreat,' " *Sibyl* 5, no. 23 (June 1, 1861): 951.

32. Fanny Fern, "Election Day," *New York Ledger* 17, no. 43: 4. Reprinted in *Sibyl* 7, no. 7 (Jan. 1862): 1010, as "Fanny Fern on Election-Day."

33. [Lydia Sayer Hasbrouck], "Women and the Crisis," *Sibyl* 7, no. 3 (Sept. 1862): 1077. Men also proclaimed women's role in war and its significance, although rarely did they assign a transformative effect to it. In the humor magazine *Vanity Fair*, all comedy was put aside as the editor praised women for their part. "In this stupendous drama the Women of the Union will play no ignoble part," the editor predicted in May 1861. The part envisioned, however, was to "pack the knapsack, tie on the scarf, . . . give the parting kiss and whisper the parting blessing" as well as inspiring "many a heroic action." See "The Women of Our Union," *Vanity Fair* 3, no. 71 (May 4, 1861): 207.

34. Gertrude Karl, "Who Are the Brave?" *Sibyl* 6, no. 4 (Oct. 1861): 987.

35. "Our Brave Times," *Continental Monthly* 2, no. 1 (July 1862): 64.

36. Other historians of women and war have also noted a shift in sentiment in women's writing during the war years. Drew Gilpin Faust argues that Southern women had "deserted" the war ranks by the later years of war; Alice Fahs argues that the connections between home and nation made in the early years of war had begun to unravel by 1863; Kathleen Diffley also argues that the connections between home and state began to break down by 1863 as the home was "invaded" by war. See Faust, "Altars of Sacrifice," 1200–1228; Fahs, "At Home with the Flag"; and Diffley, "Where My Heart is Turning Ever," 627–58.

37. Cheseboro', "Ambassadors in Bonds," 299.

38. For a few examples of Southern Unionist homes devastated by war, see Victor, *Unionist's Daughter*; W[heeler], *Eyewitness*, and virtually all of the stories written by Davis in the *Atlantic Monthly*.

39. Mary Eastman, *Jenny Wade*, 23.

40. Victor, *Unionist's Daughter*, 186.

41. Stowe, "Getting Ready for a Gale," 1.

42. Mary C. Vaughan, "Wounded at Donelson," *New York Ledger* 18, no. 39 (Nov. 29, 1862): 2.

43. Diffley, "Where My Heart is Turning Ever," 630. See also Diffley, *Where My Heart Is Turning Ever*.

44. "The Army of Knitters," in the "Editor's Department," *Arthur's* 19 (Jan. 1862): 61.

45. Virginia F. Townsend, "Somewhat of the Story," *Arthur's* 21 (Apr. 1863): 229–30.

46. See, for example, Mary C. Vaughan, "Lu Dayton's Captain," *New York Ledger* 18, no. 27 (Sept. 6, 1862): 2; Mary C. Vaughan, "A Patriot Girl," *New York Ledger* 19, no. 24 (Aug. 15, 1863): 3; and Amy Randolph, "The Ordeal of Battle," *New York Ledger* 19, no. 27 (Sept. 5, 1863): 3. See also Kate Sutherland, "The Laggard Recruit," *Arthur's* 19 (Jan. 1862): 9–12.

47. Fanny Fern, "Soldiers' Wives," *New York Ledger* 18, no. 36 (Nov. 8, 1862): 4.

48. Rodman, "Daguerreotype in Battle," 188.

49. "A Loyal Woman's No," 727.

50. C. A. C. H., "A Reminiscence of '61," *Arthur's* 24 (Oct. 1864): 166.

51. See Massey, *Bonnet Brigades*, esp. ch. 2, and Culpepper, *Trials and Triumphs*, esp. chs. 1 and 3.

52. Rose Terry Cooke, "A Woman," *Atlantic Monthly* (Dec. 1862): 707.

53. Moulton, "Buying Winter Things," 803.

54. Moulton, "Captain Charley," 407, 408.

55. "My Thanksgiving," *Harper's* 26, no. 155 (Apr. 1863): 636, 637.

56. Moulton, "Buying Winter Things," 804.

57. Moulton, "Kitten," 696–99. This was a commonly expressed desire—to be a man, or to have the freedom to act like one—both in the literature and in diaries of women at the time. See Alcott, *Journals*, 107. For Confederate women, see Faust, "Altars of Sacrifice," 1207.

58. "My Thanksgiving," 642.

59. Harriet Prescott, "Ray," *Atlantic Monthly* (Jan. 1864): 27–28.

60. A feeling of "uselessness" and a desire to contribute to the effort also was sounded in the South at roughly the same time. See Faust, "Altars of Sacrifice," 1206.

61. Central heroines become nurses in "Kitten" and "One of Many." Quote is from "Captain Charley," 408.

62. Williams, "Tableaux Vivants," 699.

63. Spencer, "One of the Noble," 206.

64. Haven, "One Day," 669. Emphasis mine.

65. The eulogy given Haven after her death suggests she practiced what she preached. See Richards, "In Memoriam."

66. This is a point made well by Fahs, in "At Home with the Flag."

67. As far as I know, these are the earliest two novels published on the war by women, although Baker's is described in James Kelly, *American Catalogue of Books*, as a pamphlet.

68. The only biographical information I have been able to glean on Delphine Paris Baker is contained in Brockett and Vaughan's *Women's Work*, 754–59.

69. Ibid., 759.

70. James, ed., *Notable American Women*, 3:519–20.

71. For this point, see Harris, *Nineteenth-Century American Women's Novels*.

72. [Baker], *Solon*, 3.

73. Ibid., 9.

74. Ibid., 10, 11, 13.

75. Ibid., 15.

76. Ibid., 37, 38, 43, 44.

77. Ibid., 69, 70, 74.

78. This is ironically very much like abolitionist literature such as *Uncle Tom's Cabin* and *The Key*; *Dred*, like *Unionist's Daughter*, has an appendix.

79. Victor, *Unionist's Daughter*, v, vi.

80. Ibid., 36.

81. Ibid., 12.

82. Ironically, Victor mixes this stereotyped vision of the loyal slave with a rather knowing understanding of the deference ritual. She describes how Pompey puts off a mob of men looking to steal cotton and how another young slave woman concedes that she has lied to her mistress to conceal her political views. See ibid., 12, 152.

83. Ibid., 10–11, 25.

84. Ibid., 60, 25.

85. Ibid., 33, 174.

86. Ibid., 171, 206.

87. Ibid., 211.

88. Alcott, *Journals*, 118. For a thoughtful portrayal of Alcott, with a disturbing twist at the end, see Fredrickson, *Inner Civil War*, 87–89. He suggests, with regard to Alcott's near-fatal bout with typhoid, that "perhaps her sensibilities as well as her health were not equal to the strain" (88–89), implying a less-than-respectful agreement with the other antisentimentalist writers he studies (at far greater length), namely John W. De Forest and Oliver Wendell Holmes. They display what he (more admiringly) describes as a "hard-bitten stoicism" (87).

89. Elbert, *Hunger for Home*, argues that Alcott has not found her voice at the beginning of *Hospital Sketches* and that it is not until she comes forward with her true identity—a "woman's rights woman"—that her voice steadies and remains consistent. This is a provocative argument and does not conflict with my assertion that this early style is consistent with other women's writing at the time. *Hospital Sketches*, in an important sense, demonstrates the shift in voice within women's war literature in general.

90. Alcott, *Hospital Sketches*, 24, 27.

91. Ibid., 27, 30.

92. Ibid., 3, 4, 6.

93. Ibid., 29.

94. Ibid., 93.

95. Saxton, *Louisa May*, 279.

96. Alcott, *Hospital Sketches*, 78.

97. Quoted in Saxton, *Louisa May*, 290, 291.

98. Alcott, *Hospital Sketches*, 95.

99. Quoted in Saxton, *Louisa May*, 290.

100. This observation—that abolitionist women used their "natural" moral authority to justify their antislavery work—has been oft-cited, but it is still relevant,

indeed, even *more* relevant to war literature. It is mentioned in this context also by Hamand, "Women's National Loyal League," 42.

101. Stowe, "Valley of Humiliation," 1.

102. Child, *Selected Letters*, 391.

103. "Speech of Miss Mary Grew," *National Anti-Slavery Standard* 22, no. 15 (Aug. 24, 1861): 1; reprinted from the *Liberator*.

104. Hamilton, *Country Living*, 424.

105. See Boyle, "Mrs. E. D. E. N. Southworth, Novelist."

106. Harper, *Brighter Coming Day*, 18.

107. See Wilson, *Crusader in Crinoline*, 262.

108. Child, *Selected Letters*, 382.

109. Child, *Selected Letters*, 388–89, 387. Both Child and Stowe wished to commend a soldier who reportedly refused to send fugitive slaves back to their owners, Child reported in another letter written to discover the soldier's name.

110. For Alcott, see "Colored Soldier's Letters," 1.

111. Child, *Selected Letters*, 374.

112. Ibid., 381.

113. Lydia Sayer Hasbrouck, "The Season and the War," *Sibyl* 5, no. 21 (May 1, 1861): 932.

114. Lydia Sayer Hasbrouck, "Remarks on 'Fanny Fern on Election Day,'" *Sibyl* 6, no. 7 (Jan. 1862): 1010. Louisa Cone, a regular letter-writer to the *Sibyl*, in March 1862 likened slavery to a fox that an accused boy claims not to have stolen but is under his jacket, eating him up. "And so this government," she writes, "now on trial for slavery. For while it declares it knows nothing about slavery, has it not got that very fox under its coat, gnawing out its vitals; and if it continues to hug the monster to its heart, would it be strange, if, while passing out of court, it should fall down dead?" ("What Can or Ought," *Sibyl* 6, no. 9 [Mar. 1862]: 1027).

115. Lydia Sayer Hasbrouck, "What Can Women Do?" *Sibyl*, 7, no. 2 (Aug. 1862): 1066.

116. Stowe, "Letter to Lord Shaftesbury," 1.

117. Child, *Selected Letters*, 391.

118. Stowe, "The Man and the Hour," 1. Lydia Maria Child also wrote praising the Fremonts, most particularly Jessie; see Child, "A Letter from Mrs. Child to 'Our Jessie,'" *National Anti-Slavery Standard* 22, no. 23 (Oct. 19, 1861): 4.

119. Stowe, "The Man and the Hour," 1.

120. Child, *Selected Letters*, 404.

121. Child, "Mrs. L. Maria Child to the President of the United States," *National Anti-Slavery Standard* 23, no. 17 (Sept. 6, 1862): 4.

122. Child, "Mrs. L. Maria Child," 4.

123. Child, "How a Kentucky Girl Emancipated Her Slaves," was published first in the New York *Tribune*; reprinted in *Independent* 14, no. 695 (Mar. 27, 1862): 6–7; and reprinted in a longer version in *National Anti-Slavery Standard* 22, no. 47 (Apr. 5, 1862): 4. Quote is from *Independent* version, page 6.

124. Child, "How a Kentucky Girl Emancipated Her Slaves.".

125. Ibid.

126. S. C. Blackwell, "Fugitives at the West," *Continental Monthly* 1, no. 5 (May 1862): 584.

127. This incident later became the basis for Toni Morrison's novel *Beloved* (1987).

128. Blackwell, "Fugitives at the West," 589.

129. Ibid., 591.

130. For an elegant overview of the writing and concern for class issues through the war period, see Buhle and Howe, afterword to *Silent Partner*, esp. 363–70.

Chapter Four

1. Hamilton, *Country Living*, 444–45.

2. Davis, "John Lamar," 417.

3. Quoted in McPherson, *For Cause and Comrades*, 13.

4. Ibid., 82.

5. For a swift overview of this movement, see McPherson, *Battle Cry*, 490–510, among other, more expansive narratives.

6. Grimké, *Journals*, 428. January 1, 1863, when the Emancipation Proclamation went into effect, was celebrated with a ceremony, singing, and speeches on the South Sea Islands. See Rose, *Rehearsal for Reconstruction*, 196.

7. Child, *Selected Letters*, 419.

8. My understanding of Rebecca Harding Davis has been directly informed by Sharon M. Harris's *Rebecca Harding Davis*. I regard Harris's work as a model for intellectual portraiture.

9. For an overview of this argument, see Buhle and Howe, afterword to *Silent Partner*, and Buhle, *Women and American Socialism*, esp. ch. 2. For prewar attention to class differences, see Stansell, *City of Women*.

10. Quoted in McPherson, *Ordeal by Fire*, 279.

11. McPherson calls it a "tactical draw" but a "strategic defeat" for Lee. For figures, see ibid., 286. For a gory but illustrative history of the battle, see Sears, *Landscape Turned Red*.

12. The review of this exhibit in the *New York Times* is telling. "[But] there is one side of the picture that the sun did not catch, one phase that has escaped photographic skill. It is the background of widows and orphans, torn from the bosom of their natural protectors by the red remorseless hand of Battle. . . . Homes have been made desolate, and the light of life in thousands of hearts has been quenched forever. All of this desolation imagination must paint—broken hearts cannot be photographed" (quoted in McPherson, *Ordeal by Fire*, 284).

13. McPherson, *Ordeal by Fire*, 292–97.

14. Quoted in ibid., 305.

15. Paludan, *People's Contest*, 180.

16. Ibid. The best treatment of the draft riot is Bernstein's *New York City Draft Riots*.

17. Fite, *Social and Industrial Conditions*, 187. See also Penny, *Employment of Women*.

18. For mention of this phenomenon, see Blake, *Strike in the American Novel*, 6–7. Blake remarks the accuracy of the sentimental descriptions of over work, death from tuberculosis, and necessity for occasional prostitution. For an illustration of the chicanery of subcontractors during the war, see Kessler-Harris, *Out to Work*, 79–80.

19. See Massey, *Bonnet Brigades*, esp. ch. 6.

20. Kessler-Harris, *Out to Work*, 76.

21. Ibid.

22. Massey, *Bonnet Brigades*, 142.

23. Ibid., 132.

24. Ibid., 133.

25. Ibid., 72; Paludan, *People's Contest*, 184–85.

26. Fite, *Social and Industrial Conditions*, 184, 186; Paludan, *People's Contest*, 182–83.

27. Quoted in Culpepper, *Trials and Triumphs*, 270.

28. Ibid., 271. Phillip Paludan argues that the war accelerated trends in agriculture that were ultimately beneficial to many farmers and their families. He notes also that men leaving home for the war enhanced a woman's culture, which is best represented in Alcott's *Little Women*. See *People's Contest*, ch. 7, esp. 158.

29. Quoted in Culpepper, *Trials and Triumphs*, 270.

30. "Soldiers' Wives—A Sad Story," *New York Ledger* 18, no. 49 (Feb. 7, 1863): 4.

31. See Bernstein, *New York City Draft Riots*.

32. Massey, *Bonnet Brigades*, 144–45; see also Fite, *Social and Industrial Conditions*, 186.

33. Paludan, *People's War*, 182–83. Sewing women from Philadelphia had also written in January 1865. See Massey, *Bonnet Brigades*, 146.

34. Child, *Selected Letters*, 544; Mary C. Vaughan, "The Soldier's Wife," *New York Ledger* 17, no. 17 (June 29, 1861): 6. This story is about an unnamed war with the Indians but is left unclear until midway through. Vaughan went on to write regularly about the Civil War.

35. "Realizing sense" is Rebecca Harding Davis's phrase.

36. From Stanton, Anthony, and Gage, eds., *History of Woman Suffrage*, quoted in Keetley and Pettegrew, eds., *Public Women*, 176, 177.

37. Keetley and Pettegrew, eds., *Public Women*, 177.

38. Whipple quoted in Coultrap-McQuin, *Doing Literary Business*, 113.

39. Hamilton, "Lights in the Shadows," in *Country Living*, 456.

40. This latter essay is dated January 1862 but must be from January 1863, since Fredericksburg and pontoon boats are mentioned. It is included in Freidel, ed., *Union Pamphlets*, 321–25. Originally published in the *Congregationalist*.

41. Hamilton, *Gala-Days*, 251; originally published in the *Atlantic Monthly* in March 1863.

42. Hamilton, *Gala-Days*, 252.

43. For a particularly interesting study of war and gender, see Higonnet, Jenson, Michel, Weitz, eds., *Behind the Lines*.

44. The Loyal Publication Society began publishing pamphlets to sway public opinion on the war in late 1862 or early 1863. Most were written by men. A selection of these have been collected in Freidel, ed., *Union Pamphlets*.

45. Historian Alice Fahs suggested to me that this might be Stowe's. I have been as yet unable to verify this through biographies and papers.

46. For the historiography of the "separate sphere," not just separate sphere ideology, see Kerber, "Separate Spheres."

47. Hamilton, "A Spasm of Sense," in *Gala-Days*, 271; and Hamilton, "My Book," in *Skirmishes and Sketches*, 432. Both were previously published in the *Atlantic Monthly*.

48. Hamilton, *Gala-Days*, 252.

49. Ibid., 253.

50. Ibid., 255–56.

51. Ibid., 257.

52. Ibid., 262.

53. Ibid., 261–62, 263, 264.

54. "Few Words in Behalf of the Loyal Women," 767.

55. More than the other two, this author draws on both the Old and New Testament for defense and argument. This was a trend in many war writings by women. Biblical narratives were their model for expression as well as the means by which they interpreted their world. Historian Ruth Feldstein, in particular, has helped me to identify this point.

56. Hamilton is decidedly antislavery, although, notably, not in "A Call to My Countrywomen."

57. "Few Words in Behalf of the Loyal Women," 768, 769.

58. Ibid., 770, 775.

59. Ibid., 784–85. This writer may not be as naive as this quote makes her sound. As Faust convincingly argues, the strength of the South was significantly impaired when women "deserted" in the later years of war. See Faust, "Altars of Sacrifice."

60. "Few Words in Behalf of the Loyal Women," 785, 786.

61. The Ladies Loyal League *seems* to be the same thing as the Women's National Loyal League established in mid-1863 by prominent women's suffragists and abolitionists. For further information regarding this effort, see Hamand, "Women's National Loyal League," 39–58.

62. O. S. Baker, "The Ladies Loyal League," *Continental Monthly* 4, no. 1 (July 1863): 51, 52.

63. Ibid., 52, 53.

64. Ibid., 53, 54.

65. Ibid., 55.

66. Ibid., 55–56.

67. Davis, "Paul Blecker," pt. 1, p. 593.

68. Fanny Fern, "Things I Like to See," *New York Ledger* 18, no. 36 (Nov. 8, 1862): 8.

69. Fanny Fern, "Reason Versus Feeling," *New York Ledger* 21, no. 4 (Mar. 25, 1865): 8. See also her defense of women lecturers—most likely Anna Dickinson—in two columns, "Women Lecturers," *New York Ledger* 19, no. 12 (May 23, 1863): 8, and "Woman on the Platform," *New York Ledger* 20, no. 2 (Mar. 12, 1864): 8. In the first she is more moderate, observing, "For one, I am rejoiced when any new and honest avenue of interest or employment is pointed out for women." By the later date she was more impatient: "The great bugbear cry of 'unsex-ing' is getting to be monotonous. Custom sanctions every day a thousand things much more amenable than female lecturing to this objection, about which no such hue or cry is raised."

70. Fanny Fern, "Whose Fault Is It?" *New York Ledger* (June 25, 1864), from Fern, *Ruth Hall*, 327–28.

71. See, for example, Virginia Townsend, "Home Pictures of the Times" and "The Mothers of Today," *Arthur's* 18 (Nov. 1861): 233–38, and 263, respectively.

72. Virginia Townsend, "The Story of Janet Strong," *Arthur's* 22 (Oct.–Dec. 1863): 164, 277.

73. Virginia T[ownsend], "Women's Wages," *Arthur's* 23 (Apr. 1864): 214.

74. Quoted in Harris, *Rebecca Harding Davis*, 95. Harris argues persuasively that the Civil War marks a crucial turning point for Davis's literary theory.

75. Davis, *Margret Howth*, 271.

76. Ibid., 6.

77. Ibid., 7.

78. Davis, "Paul Blecker," pt. 2, p. 690.

79. Davis, "David Gaunt," pt. 1, *Atlantic Monthly* (Sept. 1862): 260.

80. Ibid., pt. 2 (Oct. 1862), 404.

81. Davis, "Paul Blecker," pt. 2, p. 678.

Chapter Five

1. Conrad, *Harriet Tubman.*

2. Although this is all speculation, I feel that it's justified by a close reading of works by and on Tubman.

3. Quoted in Keetley and Pettegrew, eds., *Public Women*, 176.

4. Ibid.

5. Sojourner Truth, in her work with the freedpeople of Washington, also worried that they were living "off the government" and told them so, earning their ire. Yet if Truth was telling this to freedpeople, Tubman was doing so to whites, perhaps as a way of deflecting their criticism of the freedpeople. See Painter, *Sojourner Truth*, 215.

6. See Bernstein, *New York City Draft Riots.*

7. See Forbes, *African American Women*, and Painter, *Sojourner Truth*, ch. 22.

8. Cullen, "I's a Man Now," 75–90.

9. Quoted in Foner, *Short History*, 14.

10. Lydia Sayer Hasbrouck, "Life of Slave Women," *Sibyl* 8, no. 3 (Sept. 1863): 1175.

11. *Commonwealth* 1, no. 42 (June 19, 1863): 4. *Journal of a Residence* is also mentioned with excerpts in *Commonwealth* 1, no. 43 (June 26, 1863): 2.

12. Review of Kemble's *Journal of a Residence*, *Commonwealth*, 1, no. 46 (July 17, 1863): 1–2.

13. Kemble, *Journal of a Residence.*

14. Child, *Selected Letters*, 435.

15. Hamilton, *Skirmishes and Sketches*, 233.

16. Grimké, *Journals*, 505.

17. Kemble, *Journal of a Residence*, 305.

18. Ibid., 11.

19. See editor's introduction, ibid., liii. See also Bell, *Major Butler's Legacy*, esp. chs. 15–21.

20. Child, *Selected Letters*, 422. Hasbrouck also makes this point—that the mood of the North had shifted in favor of antislavery—much earlier. See Lydia Sayer Hasbrouck, "The Question of the Hour," *Sibyl* 6, no. 1 (July 1861): 964.

21. Child, *Selected Letters*, 427.

22. This general shift in antislavery literature is suggested but not outlined specifically in Turner's still useful book, *Anti-Slavery Sentiment*, ch. 5.

23. Child, *Selected Letters*, 413.

24. Virginia Sherwood, "The Southern Hate," *Continental Monthly* 4, no. 3 (Sept. 1863): 244.

25. Sherwood, "Southern Hate," 250, 254.

26. Harriet Beecher Stowe, "What Is to Be Done with Them?" *Independent* 14, no. 716 (Aug. 21, 1862): 1.

27. Stowe, "To 'the Affectionate.'"

28. "Rejoinder," 526, 527.

29. C[ooke], "Editor's Table," *Continental Monthly* 4, no. 3 (Sept. 1863): 357.

30. Ibid., 358.

31. Ibid. This is very like the later one on women's sphere during the war generally, mentioned above, and thus leads me to suspect that Cooke also wrote that one.

32. See Hodes, *White Women, Black Men*.

33. See Cooke, "Lady and Her Slave," 330–33; MacFarlane, "Two Southern Mothers," 490–91. For an elegant analysis of the antislavery emblem see Yellin, *Women and Sisters*.

34. Mattie Griffiths, "Ratie," *Independent* 14, no. 730 (Nov. 27, 1862): 6; Davis, "Blind Tom," 581. Griffiths's "Ratie" was reprinted in *National Anti-Slavery Standard* 23, no. 33 (Dec. 20, 1862): 4, and in Child's *Freedmen's Book*.

35. See previous note.

36. Davis, "Blind Tom," 584, 585.

37. Ibid., 585.

38. Child, *Selected Letters*, 421.

39. Davis, "John Lamar," 411, 416.

40. Ibid., 423. In this story the abolitionist is the trigger for the action of the slave, and his unwitting oversimplification leads to what the reader is to see as tragic justice. That the abolitionist goes on to realize afterward the powder keg that is the racial dynamic of the South, and that the error lies in both the North and the South, separates Davis's vision from postwar vilifications of abolitionists.

41. Very few women writers discussed the theme of intermarriage at this time, and none so frankly as Alcott. Lydia Maria Child wrote an interesting letter on the topic (unpublished), in which she argues that there is no lack of "natural" affinity (see Child, *Selected Letters*, 414); Mrs. Austa French, on the other hand, devotes a chapter to it in *Slavery in South Carolina* and argues just the reverse—that there will be no intermarriage after emancipation. Ironically, French weakens her argument by following it immediately with stories of the sexual victimization of African American women and their resulting mulatto and near-white children.

42. Alcott, "M. L."; reprinted in Turner, *Anti-Slavery Sentiment*, app. A; citations are from pages 128, 130, 143.

43. With thanks to Emily Park for this point.

44. Alcott, "My Contraband," *Hospital Sketches*, first published in *Commonwealth* in 1863; also reprinted in McSherry, Waugh, and Greenberg, eds., *Civil War Women*. All citations are from there, page 25. See also Cohn, "Negro Character"; Stern, ed., *Critical Essays*; and Showalter, ed., *Alternative Alcott*, esp. intro.

45. McSherry, Waugh, and Greenberg, eds., *Civil War Women*, 27.

46. The relationship between Milly and Gabriel, however, is perhaps the least "equal" of the three—perhaps because in this case the woman is African American; in the three others, the woman is white. See also Cohn, "Negro Character," for an analysis of this story.

47. [Austin], *Dora Darling*, 369. For other stories on this theme see Dodge, "Our Contraband," 401; Helen Pierson, "In Bonds," *Harper's Monthly* 29, no. 172 (Sept. 1864): 488–97; and Cheseboro', "Ambassadors in Bonds."

48. Child, *Selected Letters*, 396, 401.

49. Ibid., 402.

50. Ibid., 411.

51. Alcott, "Colored Soldier's Letters."

52. "Editor's Table," *Continental Monthly* 1, no. 6 (June 1862): 728.

53. Willie Lee Rose, *Rehearsal for Reconstruction*, 54, 167.
54. French, *Slavery in South Carolina*, x.
55. Ibid., ix.
56. Ibid., 286.
57. Ibid., 99–104, 96.
58. Ibid., 105.
59. Ibid., 184, 185.
60. For this insight I'd like to thank my anonymous reader.
61. French, *Slavery in South Carolina*, 48.
62. Ibid., 308. See also Willie Lee Rose, *Rehearsal for Reconstruction*, 164–65.
63. Forten, "Life on the Sea Islands," 587–96; 666–76. See also Grimké, *Journals*. The articles are quite similar in tone and content to Forten's (later Grimké's) journal entries for the same time period.
64. Forten, "Life in the Sea Islands," 676.
65. Grimké, *Journals*. See Journals 3 and 4.
66. Forten, "Life in the Sea Islands," 590–91.
67. Ibid., 591.
68. Ibid.
69. Ibid., 675, 676.
70. Child, *Selected Letters*, 443.
71. See Child's letter on the damaging nature of racial stereotypes and of racial prejudice generally, in ibid., 408, 414.
72. Child, *Selected Letters*, 441.
73. Child, *Freedmen's Book*, 274.
74. Forten, "Life in the Sea Islands," 591.
75. Hamilton, *Skirmishes and Sketches*, 14.
76. Child, *Selected Letters*, 457–58.

Chapter Six

1. Phelps, *Chapters from a Life*, 66.
2. The best example of this ambivalence is Phelps's "Margaret Bronson," written just after the war ended, about a woman who took up arms when the war came to her doorstep.
3. Phelps, *Chapters from a Life*, 99.
4. See Phelps, "The Tenth of January," collected with *The Silent Partner*.
5. See Linderman, *Embattled Courage*; McPherson disagrees; see his *What They Fought For*.
6. Both Georgeanna Woolsey and Jane Woolsey referred to women who were nurses this way. See [Woolsey], *Three Weeks*, and Woolsey, *Hospital Days*.
7. Marshall, *Dorothea Dix*, 202–3; James, ed., *Notable American Women*, 1:488.
8. Schultz, "Women at the Front," 69, 70. See also Forbes, *African American Women*.
9. Reverby, *Ordered to Care*, 44. For class issues between nurses and the hampering effect that this has on feminist organization, see Melosh, *Physician's Hand*.
10. Woolsey, *Hospital Days*, 41. Also quoted by Schultz, "Women at the Front," 108.
11. Powers, *Hospital Pencillings*, 128, 129.
12. See Oates, *Woman of Valor*.

13. Massey, *Bonnet Brigades*, 50; Schultz, "Women at the Front," 95.

14. Quoted from Massey, *Bonnet Brigades*, 49. See also Nina Brown Baker, *Cyclone in Calico*, and Margaret Davis, *Mother Bickerdyke*.

15. Quoted in Culpepper, *Trials and Triumphs*, 322–23.

16. See Schwartz, ed., *Woman Doctor's Civil War*, and Snyder, *Mary Walker*; see also Schultz, "Women at the Front," 78, and Leonard, *Yankee Women*.

17. See Culpepper, *Trials and Triumphs*, 323; Massey, *Bonnet Brigades*, 47; and Schultz, "Women at the Front," 78.

18. Schultz, "Women at the Front," 77.

19. Alcott, *Hospital Sketches*, 65–66; Elbert, *Hunger for Home*, 153.

20. Spencer, "Soldier's Wife," 624.

21. Williams, *Clara Barton*, 79.

22. Jaquette, ed., *South after Gettysburg*, 10–11.

23. Brumgardt, ed., *Civil War Nurse*, 121.

24. Eudora Clark, "Hospital Memories," *Atlantic Monthly* 20 (Aug., Sept. 1867): 336.

25. Eastman, *Jenny Wade*, 19, 24.

26. Alcott, *On Picket Duty*, 3.

27. Ibid., 26.

28. Alcott, *Selected Letters*, 80. For another example of this, see Townsend, "Hospital Nurse," *Arthur's* 20 (Aug. 1862): 121–22.

29. Alcott, *Hospital Sketches*, 3.

30. Rodman, "Daguerreotype," 190, and "Angel of Mercy," 418. Another work that suggests opposition to nursing in more conventional terms is Howe's *Black Plume Rifles*.

31. Walker, "Ray Amyott," 346.

32. Spencer, "One of the Noble," 202.

33. Gray, "Part of the Mission," 102.

34. Ibid.

35. Rodman, "Angel of Mercy," 418.

36. Perry, "Margaret Freyer's Heart," 188.

37. Information on her war background is in the preface to her postwar novel *Tried and True*, v.

38. Spencer, "Soldier's Wife," 622.

39. Alcott, *Hospital Sketches*, 51.

40. Other such battlefield experiences for women are included in the following: Spencer, "Soldier's Wife"; Dorr, "Drummer Boy's Burial"; Longstreet, *Remy St. Remy*; and Howe, *Rival Volunteers*.

41. Gray, "Part of the Mission," 106.

42. For examples of women's autobiographical narratives that include those in what Jelinek calls the "sensational/exotic" style, see her *Tradition of Women's Autobiography*. For the context of midcentury sensationalist writing and its effect on the writers of the American Renaissance, see Reynolds, *Beneath the American Renaissance*.

43. Moore, *Lady Lieutenant*; Billings, *Female Volunteer*.

44. Lammers and Boyce, "Female in the Ranks," 30.

45. Phelps, "Margaret Bronson," 498.

46. Ibid.

47. Ibid., 500, 501, 502.

48. Ibid., 502.

49. Ibid.

50. Ibid., 504.

51. See Leonard, *Yankee Women*, which makes this point well with the story of Sophronia Bucklin.

52. "How I Came to Be a Nurse," pt. 1, *The Spirit of the Fair*, no. 1, Apr. 6, 1864, 29.

53. [Bacon and Howland, eds.], *Letters of a Family*, 2:79–80; quote from Georgeanna to Eliza, May 15, 1861, 86.

54. *The Spirit of the Fair*, no. 3, Apr. 11, 1864, 77; excerpts in [Bacon and Howland, eds.], *Letters of a Family*, 2:142–46.

55. *The Spirit of the Fair*, no. 3, Apr. 11, 1864, 77; excerpts in [Bacon and Howland, eds.], *Letters of a Family*, 2:142, 143, 144. The last quote was not included in the *Letters*.

56. *The Spirit of the Fair*, no. 4, Apr. 15, 1864, 125; excerpts in [Bacon and Howland, eds.], *Letters of a Family*, 2:144–46. The conflict described here is not only between the male medical authority and the women-nurses but also between the army in general and the philanthropic efforts of the public.

57. *The Spirit of the Fair*, no. 5, Apr. [?], 1864, 137.

58. McPherson, *Battle Cry*, 427.

59. Browne, "No Letter Yet." See also Kendall, "Fallen."

60. Jones, "Waiting," 336.

61. Heath, "Living or Dead?"

62. Denison, "Dead Soldier's Ring," *Arthur's* 21 (Jan. 1863): 14.

63. Minnie W. May, "Send Them Home," *Arthur's* 22 (Sept. 1863): 116–17.

64. Augusta, "Game of Fortune," 431.

65. Dunlap, "Halt," 433.

66. Moulton, "Captain Charley," 409. This theme is also addressed in Harriet Prescott, "Ray," *Atlantic Monthly* (Jan. 1864): 19–39; Walker's "Ray Amyott"; and Moulton's "Kitten."

67. Linwood, "Dead."

68. Ellwood, "Dirge."

69. Redden, "After Vicksburg."

70. Moore, "Killed Instantly," 366.

71. Sperry, "Mother, Weep!"

72. Case, "Weary."

73. Manson, "In War Time."

74. Leigh, "Woman's Fame," 235. Another poem on the subject is Pidsley's "Soldier's Widow," which ends: "She only knows that he has been / the sunlight of her home; / She only feels that she is left / To walk the world alone."

75. Remick, *Miscellaneous Poems*, 133.

76. Lee, "Missing."

77. Edith Clarke, "Will's Orange-Flowers."

78. Stowe, "Chimney-Corner," 109.

79. Ibid., 111.

80. "My Thanksgiving," *Harper's* 26, no. 155 (Apr. 1863), 643.

81. Phelps, "Sacrifice Consumed," 236.

82. Ibid., 238.

83. Ibid., 240.

84. Ibid. In Phelps, "Bend" and "My Refugees," women pass through moments of great spiritual struggle as a result of the war but do not, ultimately, lose their husbands or sweethearts.

85. Stowe, "Chimney-Corner," 114. This idea has a greater audience than just women, although I argue that women have a significantly distinct perspective on it. See Fredrickson, *Inner Civil War*, particularly ch. 5.

86. Hamilton, *Skirmishes and Sketches*, 263.

87. Pierson, "Tom's Education," 192.

88. These stern, almost angry voices on the (male) national sin, although dominating the January issue of *Harper's* were less common than the voices of sorrow. By the war's end many writers expressed the sorrow of Harriet Prescott. In "Peace," published in February 1865, she despairs that the earth's spring and renewal is not echoed in the war's progress toward peace: "On last year's blossoming graves, with summer's calm, / Loud in his happy tangle hums the bee; / Nature forgets her hurt, and finds her balm— / alas! And why not we?"

89. My emphasis.

Chapter Seven

1. Alcott, *Journals*, 140.

2. Child, *Selected Letters*, 451.

3. Ibid., 452.

4. Ibid., 453. Rebecca Harding Davis also saw the hand of God, but it seemed a grimmer one. See Harris, *Rebecca Harding Davis*, 123.

5. Dodge, ed., *Gail Hamilton's Life*, 1:494.

6. Alcott, *Journals*, 140.

7. For information on the Reconstruction period, see Foner, *Reconstruction*, and Montgomery, *Beyond Equality*.

8. Martha Hodes, in a more recent history of the sexual relations between white women and black men, concurs. See *White Women, Black Men*.

9. Lebsock, *Free Women*, 246, 248; on the coining of the phrase "miscegenation," see McPherson, *Ordeal by Fire*, 449.

10. Lydia Maria Child describes this ongoing work during the war. See Clifford, *Crusader for Freedom*, ch. 19. See also Karcher, *First Woman in the Republic*.

11. For an overview of the woman suffrage movement, see DuBois, ed., *Elizabeth Cady Stanton*, esp. 88–112. For a more positive earlier reading of the Reconstruction era, see DuBois, *Feminism and Suffrage*.

12. For these shifts, see Denning, *Mechanic Accents*, and Brodhead, *Cultures of Letters*.

13. For an analysis of the "waves" of interest in the Civil War, see Smith, *Civil War*. For a thematic study of many Civil War novels, curiously excluding many I have found, see Lively, *Fiction Fights the Civil War*; and for a very useful study of early Civil War novels and their authors, see Schuster, "American Civil War Novels."

14. This was likely to have been to some extent *New York Ledger* policy; before the war Robert Bonner had banned the use of the word "abolitionist" from his pages. Fanny Fern, however, rarely seemed hampered by Bonner's editorial stance. See Warren, *Fanny Fern*.

15. McPherson, in *Ordeal by Fire*, 376, argues that "the Civil War was both a climactic triumph of the free-labor ideology and the catalyst of a more class-conscious labor movement that eventually rejected this ideology as serving the interests of conservative capitalism." See also Montgomery, *Beyond Equality*.

16. Moore, *Women of the War*, iii, vi.

17. Brockett and Vaughan, *Women's Work*, 5.

18. Moore's book, seemingly more hastily assembled, has less scaffolding and explanation of its purposes and reports incidents without the political flourish and justification of the later book. It is for this reason that I focus more on Brockett and Vaughan, although the tenor of the two books is remarkably similar.

19. Brockett and Vaughan, *Women's Work*, 6.

20. My emphasis. Ibid., 771.

21. Ibid., 774.

22. Poor seamstresses appeared here, too, but not as strikers. One sewing girl—unnamed—was remembered as having given up the wages of two weeks work to the war effort, a paltry sum, but heartfelt. Her significance as a sewing girl is remarked, both to refer to the image of the beaten down, modest young girl of 1850s fiction, and to avoid the less "humble" rendering of the striker.

23. Brockett and Vaughan, *Women's Work*, 91.

24. Ibid., 64.

25. Ibid., 62, 63, 57.

26. Ibid., 61.

27. Stanton, Anthony, and Gage, eds., *History of Woman Suffrage*, 23.

28. See, for example, Moore, *Women of the War*, and Brockett and Vaughan, *Women's Work*.

29. Reverby, *Ordered to Care*, 47. Lori Ginzberg implies that this coterie was, in fact, larger and more significant in the postwar than I have found to be true. See Ginzberg, *Women and the Work*, chs. 5 and 6. George Fredrickson makes a similar argument about the bureaucratization that occurred as a result of the massive organization that the Civil War required. The women-nurses studied in this section, I argue, resisted that change in part because it would have disempowered them even further. See Fredrickson, *Inner Civil War*.

30. Powers, *Hospital Pencillings*, 1, 211.

31. Ibid., 19–20.

32. Ibid., 54, 63.

33. Ibid., 64, 65.

34. Ibid., 66.

35. Ibid., 209–10.

36. See Leonard, *Yankee Women*, for a fuller exposition on Bucklin.

37. Bucklin, *In Hospital and Camp*, 70–71.

38. Ibid., 91, 175.

39. Powers, *Hospital Pencillings*; vignettes are on 21–26.

40. *Spirit of the Fair*, no. 5, Apr. 1864, 137.

41. Ibid.

42. Palmer, *Story of Aunt Becky*, 147, 113. Palmer's depiction of herself as a "common woman," as well as Bucklin's similar implication, challenges Nina Bennett Smith's assertion that army nurses were primarily self-described "ladies." See Smith, "Women Who Went to War," intro.

43. Palmer, *Story of Aunt Becky*, 116.

44. Ibid., 98, 3, 148, 144.

45. Ibid., 90, 77, 80.

46. Ibid., 2, 44.

47. Ibid., 111, 112, 113, 114.

48. Ibid., 104, 105.

49. Ibid., 167, 186, 187.

50. Ibid., 154, 2.

51. Bucklin, *In Hospital and Camp*, 22. S. L. C. may be Sylvia Lawson Covey.

52. Ibid., 23–24.

53. Ibid., 124–25. She could be referring here to Mrs. Anna Holstein, who she mentioned in her narrative as one of the women she had to deal with. Holstein, whose (yes, "glowing") narrative I class with those on the more conventionally sentimental side of the nursing reminiscence, was published two years before Bucklin's.

54. Although this moment can be fixed, historically, at an earlier point (given Stowe's and Davis's writing, among others), I am talking about mainstream acceptance, an echo of a transition already under way.

55. McLeod, *Westfield*, 45.

56. Ibid., 120–21, 127.

57. James, ed., *Notable American Women*, 2:208–9; quote on 208.

58. Holmes, *Rose Mather*, 101–2.

59. Ibid.

60. For other examples, see [Warner], *Daisy*, and Townsend, *Darryl Gap*.

61. See Denning, *Mechanic Accents*, for an analysis of this shift.

62. For this change in Harriet Beecher Stowe, see Patricia Hill, "Harriet Beecher Stowe's Averted Gaze," in Clinton and Silber, eds., *Divided Houses*.

63. For an analysis of Northern narratives of women soldiers and spies, see Lyde Sizer, "Acting Her Part," in Clinton and Silber, eds., *Divided Houses*.

64. Southworth, *How He Won Her*, 440.

65. Ibid., 443.

66. Ibid., 308, 312.

67. Fern, "Soldiers' Wives," *New York Ledger* 18, no. 36 (Nov. 8, 1862): 4.

Chapter Eight

1. During this period, of course, race was a multivalent rather than a polarized concept: each ethnic identity was designated as a "race." See Jacobson, *Whiteness of a Different Color*.

2. Morrison, *Playing in the Dark*, 17.

3. Foner, *Short History*, 147.

4. Fredrickson, *Black Image*, 171–74; McPherson, *Ordeal by Fire*, 449.

5. Martha Hodes, "Wartime Dialogues," Clinton and Silber, eds., *Divided Houses*, 230.

6. [Croly], *Miscegenation*, 65.

7. Hodes, "Wartime Dialogues," 240.

8. White, *Ar'n't I a Woman?* 58.

9. For postwar sentiment in the North, see Silber, *Romance of Reunion*.

10. Fuller, *Brownings*, 35–36.

11. Ibid., 121.

12. Prescott, "Down the River," 468.

13. Ibid., 475.

14. Ibid., 478–79.

15. Ibid., 490.

16. For a similar message, see also "Poor Chloe" (*Atlantic Monthly*, March 1866), a story set in the North "in the olden time."

17. My argument is not that this word or its use was new, but rather that it would be understood in a pointed way given this context.

18. Moody, "My Little Boy," 361, 363, 364.

19. W. H. Palmer, "A Woman," *Galaxy* 2 (Nov. 1866), 413, 414.

20. Ibid., 416.

21. Ibid., 420.

22. Ibid., 422.

23. Ibid., 420.

24. Frances Ellen Watkins Harper's *Iola Leroy*, which was produced in and reacts to an entirely different—and even grimmer—political and social context, was at that time the only nineteenth-century Civil War novel published by an African American woman. See Chapter 9.

25. Hodes, "Wartime Dialogues," 242.

26. Morrison, *Playing in the Dark*, 28.

27. W[heeler], *Eyewitness*, 104.

28. Spencer, *Tried and True*, 282–83.

29. Alcott, *On Picket Duty*, 30.

30. Holmes, *Rose Mather*, 302–3.

31. Fredrickson, *Black Image*, 171.

32. Child, *Romance of the Republic*, 433.

33. Ibid., 434.

34. Dickinson, *What Answer?* 267.

35. Ibid., 195.

36. Ibid., 297.

37. Davis, *Waiting*, 354–55.

38. Ibid., 354.

39. Here, as elsewhere, I refer to the character the way the author does. Davis, particularly, always refers to her women characters by their first names, and her men characters by their last. Black characters, additionally, are always referred to by their first names in Davis's book unless they "passed," like Broderip. Nathan, for example, was always just Nathan.

40. Child, *Selected Letters*, 467.

41. Some antislavery reformers, like William Lloyd Garrison, felt that emancipation marked the end of the struggle. Others argued that Reconstruction was crucial in securing the war's promise and continued their work. In any case there was a palpable sense of an era's end, and many writers in the antislavery community celebrated this with memoirs and collective biographies of the war's greatest soldiers.

42. Fanny Fern wrote two columns on women lecturers in the *New York Ledger*, most likely in response to the fervor Dickinson was causing. See Fern, "Women Lecturers," *New York Ledger* 19, no. 12 (May 23, 1863): 8, and "Woman on the Platform," *New York Ledger* 20, no. 2 (Mar. 12, 1864): 8.

43. Quoted in Harris, *Rebecca Harding Davis*, 128.

44. For an analysis of their dispute, see ibid., 126–27.

45. In her autobiography, *Bits of Gossip*, 138, Davis calls many of the post Civil War histories of the conflict "painted."

46. In the end, however, Davis was not able to write the exact book she desired to, as the editors of the new magazine *Galaxy* became impatient with the length of *Waiting for the Verdict*. See Jan Atteridge Rose, *Rebecca Harding Davis*.

47. Child, *Selected Letters*, 482–83.

48. Quoted in Clifford, *Crusader for Freedom*, 281.

49. Quoted in Chester, *Embattled Maiden*, 106.

50. Harris, *Rebecca Harding Davis*, 132.

51. Quoted in ibid., 137. On this same page Harris refers to Henry James Jr. as the correspondent of Gail Hamilton; actually it was his father, Henry James Sr. Her point about James Sr.'s gender politics, however, seems equally applicable to his son.

Chapter Nine

1. Alcott, *Work*, 442, 443.

2. For a further exploration of politics in women's literature and reference to this point, see Bardes and Gossett, *Declarations of Independence*, esp. 155.

3. Alcott, *Old-Fashioned Girl*, 257, 258, 261, 264.

4. Harper, *Brighter Coming Day*, 230. On Harper, see also Boyd, *Discarded Legacy*.

5. Livermore, *My Story*, 85, 92; Livermore, *Story of My Life*, 485. The basis of my understanding of this period comes from Buhle, *Women and American Socialism*.

6. See DuBois, *Feminism and Suffrage*, for the changing strategies of women suffragists. After the war and the failure to include women in the Fourteenth Amendment—indeed their explicit exclusion—suffrage reformers turned away from the millennialist reform strategy of the Garrisonians to a more pragmatic and racist political realism, which included briefly joining the Democrats. When mainstream political alliances failed, suffrage leaders returned to their egalitarian roots in searching for a constituency among working people. See also DuBois's newer interpretation of this transition in *Elizabeth Cady Stanton—Susan B. Anthony Reader*. For an analysis of suffrage in postwar novels, see Bardes and Gossett, *Declarations of Independence*, ch. 6.

7. Child, *Selected Letters*, 467. In another letter to Theodore Tilton, however, Child makes it clear that she thinks political rights should go to black men *first*, it being for them "a present and very imperious necessity" (468).

8. Lydia Sayer Hasbrouck suggests that Fern might have lapsed somewhat in her public support for voting rights in the preface to a sketch reprinted in the *Sibyl*.

9. Quotes in Harris, *Rebecca Harding Davis*, 148. Her point about Davis's shift is made first on 143, in an analysis of Davis's gripping short story "In the Market," *Peterson's* 53 (Jan. 1868): 48–57. See also Harris, "Redefining the Feminine," *Legacy* 8, no. 2 (Fall 1991): 118–21.

10. See Hamilton, *Women's Wrongs*.

11. Quotes and interpretation of Hamilton's shift are in Coultrap-McQuin, *Doing Literary Business*, 112. See also "Gail Hamilton," *Women's Journal* (August 22, 1896).

12. For the most comprehensive overview of the woman question and the labor question in the postwar period to date, see Buhle, *Women and American Socialism*, ch. 2, esp. pp. 51 and 55.

13. Quoted in ibid., 55.

14. Ginzberg, *Women and the Work*, 190.

15. Lawrence Levine sees a similar gap emerging in popular culture as a whole in this period. See Levine, *Highbrow/Lowbrow*. Joan Shelley Rubin dates the emergence of middlebrow culture to the twentieth century between the world wars, although, as I am suggesting in this study, many of its elements were apparent earlier. See Rubin, *Making of Middlebrow Culture*. My assessment echoes Brodhead's in *Cultures of Letters*.

16. Quoted in Brodhead, *Cultures of Letters*, 104.

17. Jean Fagan Yellin takes Alcott to task for that omission, dismissing her novel *Work* as a failure as a result. While her point about the limits of Alcott's radicalism are certainly true, Alcott can be seen here as extending the boundaries of the possible for middle-class women at a time of flux, as well as limiting the definitions of acceptability. This is no apologia for Alcott, merely an approach to her position from a different angle of reference. What Alcott proposed for her audience was an innovation and a quite radical one given her context. See Yellin, "From *Success* to *Experience*." See the work of Kevin Gaines on this assimilationist ethic; he and his work have helped me see this position clearly.

18. Quote is from Buhle, *Women and American Socialism*, 93.

19. For a mention of the review condemning Alcott's inclusion of Hepsey's story, see Sarah Elbert's introduction to Louisa May Alcott's *Work*, xxxix, and Stern, *Louisa May Alcott*, 232.

20. Ginzberg, *Women and the Work*, 179.

21. Fields, ed., *Life and Letters*, 327.

22. Quoted in Ginzberg, *Women and the Work*, 179.

23. There is an enormous literature on this period in the South. For the single best overview, see Foner, *Reconstruction*. See also Painter, *Exodusters*, pt. 1.

24. Child, *Selected Letters*, 508.

25. See Carby, *Reconstructing Womanhood*.

26. Judith Fetterley, "*Little Women*," *Feminist Studies* 5, no. 2 (Summer 1979).

27. Alcott, *Journals*, 124n.

28. Alcott also continued to write for working-class and sensationalist presses and magazines, as Alcott sleuths are continually uncovering. Those works, however, were published under other names; Alcott's mainstream political work of this period, meant to reflect her public persona, was for middlebrow audiences.

29. Fern, *Ruth Hall*, 343, 344.

30. Hamilton, *Women's Wrongs*, 91–92.

31. Ibid., 93, 95, 103.

32. Harper, *Brighter Coming Day*, 227, 229.

33. Alcott, *Old-Fashioned Girl*, v–vi.

34. Alcott, *Little Women*, 9.

35. Ibid., 392.

36. For example, see Halttunen, "Domestic Drama." My interpretation has been deeply influenced by Elaine Showalter's excellent introduction to the 1989 reprint of *Little Women*. Quote is from Alcott, *Little Women*, xix.

37. The notion of a "middle story" is from Harris's, *Nineteenth-Century American Women's Novels*.

38. Alcott, *Little Women*, 480.

39. Alcott, *Old-Fashioned Girl*, 180, 207, 208.

40. Ibid., 257–58.

41. Ibid., 263.

42. Ibid., 354.

43. Elbert, *Hunger for Home*, 243.

44. Alcott, *Work*, 358, 360, 364.

45. *Work*, 384. Alcott may or may not have been aware of Southworth's novel titled *Britomarte; the Man-Hater*. Britomarte was not, however, a culturally current reference; this is the only other reference I have found to it within women's mid-nineteenth-century published writing.

46. Alcott weaves in several well-known stories of the war, including one about a slave mother who brings her dead infant with her into a Union camp, so that it might me buried in a free land. This story is likely to have inspired Frances Ellen Watkins Harper's well-known poem "Bury Me in a Free Land."

47. Alcott, *Work*, 430, 431, 430, 437, 442.

48. Quoted in Harris, *Rebecca Harding Davis*, 149.

49. Fern, *Ruth Hall*, 347.

50. Ibid., 337, 336.

51. Quoted in Harris, *Rebecca Harding Davis*, 105–6.

52. Phelps, *Silent Partner*, 301.

53. Phelps, *Chapters from a Life*, 99.

54. Ibid., 96, 97–98.

55. Phelps, *Gates Ajar*, 36.

56. Ibid., 49.

57. Phelps, *Chapters from a Life*, 127.

58. Ibid., 122.

59. Phelps, *Gates Ajar*, vi; Phelps, *Chapters from a Life*, 118, 119.

60. In 1860 a supporting beam of a large mill in the industrial city of Lawrence gave way, trapping dozens of workingwomen. A fire began and killed many of these women, who sang hymns as they awaited their deaths, inspiring many of the onlookers. Phelps had not been allowed to visit the scene when it happened, although her brothers were; after the war she investigated the collapse and fire, and wrote a story of a painful love triangle set within the history of the event. See a reprint of that story and analysis of its meaning and its effect on Phelps's life in Buhle and Howe, afterword to *Silent Parter*.

61. Phelps, *Hedged In*, 114.

62. Phelps, *Silent Partner*, 38, 25, 24, 29.

63. Ibid., 30, 21.

64. Ibid., 190.

65. Ibid., 293. This is a distinction that Alcott also makes. Because Christie has worked, she can speak for workers in a way other middle-class or genteel women cannot and should not. Experience gives her authority.

66. Phelps, *Silent Partner*, 24, 30.

67. Ibid., 59, 61, 64, 68.

68. Ibid., 287–88.

69. Ibid., 25, 217, 39, 241; Stowe, *Uncle Tom's Cabin*, 442.

70. Elizabeth Stuart Phelps wrote biographical vignettes of both Stowe and Child in her autobiography, *Chapters from a Life*.

71. Harper, *Brighter Coming Day*, 217. See also Boyd, *Discarded Legacy*.

72. Harper, *Brighter Coming Day*, 217–19.

73. Harper had a great deal of range in the topics she explored, but she continually returned and reexplored this crucial turning point for the nation.

74. Letters are excerpted in Harper, *Brighter Coming Day*, 122–25.

75. Ibid., 192–93, 185–86, 190.

76. Ibid., 139, 148, 162, 163.

77. Ibid., 221.

78. Ibid., 241.

79. Harper, *Iola Leroy*, 262, 263.

80. Harper, *Brighter Coming Day*, 220.

81. Ibid., 199, 200, 203, 204.

82. Ibid., 206–7, 208.

83. Harper, *Iola Leroy*, 34.

84. Ibid., 125, 126.

85. Ibid., 100–101.

86. Ibid., 234, 195, 205.

87. Ibid., 250–51.

88. Ibid., 231, 232.

89. Significantly, all middle-class tasks.

Conclusion

1. Fields, ed., *Life and Letters*, 128.

2. Hamilton, *Women's Wrongs*, 198–99, 200.

Bibliography

Primary Sources

Personal Narratives, Autobiographies, Letters, and Histories

Alcott, Louisa May. *The Journals of Louisa May Alcott*. Edited by Joel Myerson and Daniel Shealy. Boston: Little, Brown, 1989.

———. *The Selected Letters of Louisa May Alcott*. Edited by Joel Myerson and Daniel Shealy. Boston: Little, Brown, 1987.

[Bacon, Georgeanna Woolsey, and Eliza Woolsey Howland, eds.]. *Letters of a Family during the War for the Union, 1861–1865*. Vols. 1 and 2. Printed for private distribution, 1899.

Brockett, Linus Pierpont. *The Camp, the Battle Field, and the Hospital; or Lights and Shadows of the Great Rebellion*. Philadelphia: National Publishing Co., 1866.

———. *The Philanthropic Results of the War in America*. New York: Sheldon and Co., 1864.

———. *Woman, Her Rights and Wrongs*. Hartford, Conn.: L. Stebbins, 1869.

Brockett, Linus Pierpont, and Mary C. Vaughan. *Woman's Work in the Civil War: A Record of Heroism, Patriotism and Patience*. Philadelphia: Zeigler, McCurdy and Co., 1867.

Brumgardt, John R., ed. *Civil War Nurse: The Diary and Letters of Hannah Ropes*. Knoxville: University of Tennessee Press, 1980.

Child, Lydia Maria. *Correspondence between Lydia Maria Child, and Gov. Wise and Mrs. Mason, of Virginia*. New York: Anti-Slavery Society, 1860.

———. *Lydia Maria Child, Selected Letters, 1817–1880*. Edited by Milton Meltzer and Patricia Holland. Amherst: University of Massachusetts Press, 1982.

Coatsworth, Stella S. *The Loyal People of the North-West*. Chicago: Church, Goodman and Donnelley, Printers, 1869.

Davis, Margaret B. *Mother Bickerdyke and the Soldiers*. San Francisco: n.p., 1886.

Dodge, H. Augusta, ed. *Gail Hamilton's Life in Letters*. 2 vols. Boston: Lee and Shepard, 1901.

DuBois, Ellen Carol, ed. *The Elizabeth Cady Stanton–Susan B. Anthony Reader: Correspondence, Writings, Speeches*. Boston: Northeastern University Press, 1992.

Fern, Fanny. *Ruth Hall and Other Writings*. Edited by Joyce W. Warren. New Brunswick, N.J.: Rutgers University Press, 1986.

Fields, Annie, ed. *Life and Letters of Harriet Beecher Stowe*. New York: Houghton Mifflin, 1898.

Freidel, Frank, ed. *Union Pamphlets of the Civil War, 1861–1865*. Cambridge, Mass.: The Belknap Press of Harvard University Press, 1967.

Grimké, Charlotte Forten, *The Journals of Charlotte Forten Grimké*. Edited by Brenda Stevenson. New York and London: Oxford University Press, 1988.

Harper, Frances Ellen Watkins, *A Brighter Coming Day: A Frances Ellen Watkins Reader*. Edited by Frances Smith Foster. New York: The Feminist Press, 1990.

Holstein, Mrs. Anna Morris Ellis. *Three Years in the Field Hospitals of the Army of the Potomac*. Philadelphia: J. B. Lippincott, 1867.

Jaquette, Henrietta Stratton, ed. *South after Gettysburg: Letters of Cornelia Hancock, 1863–1868*. New York: Thomas Y. Crowell Company, 1956.

Kemble, Frances Anne. *Journal of a Residence on a Georgian Plantation in 1838–1839*. 1863. Athens: University of Georgia Press, 1984.

Livermore, Mary. *My Story of the War*. Hartford, Conn.: A. D. Worthington and Company, 1888.

———. *The Story of My Life*. Hartford, Conn.: A. D. Worthington and Co., Publishers, 1898.

McSherry, Frank, Charles G. Waugh, and Martin Greenberg, eds. *Civil War Women*. Little Rock, Ark.: August House, 1988.

Marshall, Helen E. *Dorothea Dix, Forgotten Samaritan*. 1937. New York: Russell and Russell, 1967.

Moore, Frank. *Women of the War*. Hartford, Conn.: S. S. Scranton and Co., 1866.

Palmer, Sarah A. *The Story of Aunt Becky's Army-Life*. New York: John F. Trow and Co., 1867.

Penny, Virginia. *The Employments of Women, A Cyclopedia of Women's Work*. Boston: Walker, Wise and Co., 1863.

Phelps [Ward], Elizabeth Stuart. *Chapters from a Life*. Boston: Houghton Mifflin, 1897.

Russo, Ann, and Cheris Kramarae, eds. *The Radical Women's Press of the 1850s*. New York and London: Routledge, 1991.

Schwartz, Gerald, ed. *A Woman Doctor's Civil War: Esther Hill Hawks Diary*. Columbia: University of South Carolina Press, 1984.

Stanton, Elizabeth Cady, Susan B. Anthony, and Matilda Joslyn Gage, eds. *History of Woman Suffrage*. Vol. 2. New York: Fowler and Wells, Publishers, 1882.

Stowe, Charles Edward, ed. *Life of Harriet Beecher Stowe, Compiled from Her Letters and Journals*. Boston: Houghton Mifflin, 1889.

Swisshelm, Jane Grey. *Crusader and Feminist: Letters of Jane Grey Swisshelm, 1858–1865*. Saint Paul: Minnesota Historical Society, 1934.

———. *Half a Century*. Chicago: Jansen, McClurg and Company, 1880.

Taylor, Susie King. *A Black Women's Civil War Memoirs*. 1902. New York: Marcus Wiener Publishing, 1988.

[Woolsey, Georgeanna]. *Three Weeks at Gettysburg*. New York: Anson D. F. Randolph, 1863.

Woolsey, Jane Stuart. *Hospital Days*. New York: D. Van Nostrand, 1868.

Slave Narratives

[Gilbert, Olive, and Frances Titus]. *Narrative of Sojourner Truth; A Bondswoman of Olden Time, Emancipated by the New York Legislature in the Early Part of the Present Century; With a History of Her Labors and Correspondence Drawn from Her "Book of Life."* 1878. Salem, N.H.: Ayer Company, 1990.

Jacobs, Harriet. *Classic Slave Narratives*. New York: New American Library, 1987.

———. *Incidents in the Life of a Slave Girl*. Edited by Jean Fagan Yellin. 1861. Cambridge, Mass.: Harvard University Press, 1987.

Picquet, Louisa. *Louisa Picquet, the Octoroon; or, Inside Views of Southern Domestic Life*. New York: By the author, 1861.

Pierson, Emily Catharine. *Jamie Parker, the Fugitive. Related to Mrs. Emily Pierson*. Hartford, Conn.: Brockett, Fuller and Company, 1851.

Antislavery Poems, Tracts, Stories, Essays, and Collections

Alcott, Louisa May. "With a Rose, That Bloomed on the Day of John Brown's Martrydom." *Liberator*, Jan. 20, 1860.

Cabot, Susan C. *What Have We, as Individuals, to Do with Slavery?* New York: American Anti-Slavery Society, 1855.

Chapman, Maria. *The Duty of Disobedience to the Fugitive Slave Act: An Appeal to the Legislators of Massachusetts*. Anti-Slavery Tracts, No. 9. Boston: Published by the American Anti-Slavery Society, 1860.

——. *How Can I Help to Abolish Slavery? or, Counsels to the Newly Converted*. New York: American Anti-Slavery Society, 1855.

Child, Lydia Maria. "The Kansas Emigrants." In *Autumnal Leaves: Tales and Sketches in Prose and Rhyme*. New York: C. S. Francis & Co., 1857.

—— *The Patriarchal Institution, Described by Members of its Own Family*. New York: American Anti-Slavery Society, 1860.

——. "The Quadroons." In *Fact and Fiction: A Collection of Stories*. Boston: J. H. Francis, 1846.

——. *The Right Way, the Safe Way: Proved by Emancipation in the British West Indies, and Elsewhere*. New York: Published and for Sale at 5 Beekman Street, 1862.

The Female Skeptic; or, Faith Triumphant. New York: Robert M. De Witt, publisher, 1859.

[Flanders, Mrs. G. M.]. *The Ebony Idol*. New York: D. Appleton and Co., 1860.

The Fugitive Slave Law and its Victims. Anti-Slavery Tract No. 15, New Series. New York: American Anti-Slavery Society, 1861.

Greenwood, Grace [Sarah Jones Lippincott]. "The Leap from the Long Bridge." In *Poems*. Boston: Ticknor, Reed, and Fields, 1851.

Griffith, Mattie. "Madge Vertner." *National Anti-Slavery Standard* 20 (1859–60).

Harper, Frances Ellen Watkins. *Poems on Miscellaneous Subjects*. Philadelphia: Merrihew and Thompson, 1857.

The Liberty Bell (1839–58).

McKeehan, Hattia. *Liberty or Death; or Heaven's Infraction of the Fugitive Slave Law*. Cincinnati: n.p., 1859.

Martin, J. Selba. "The Sentinel of Freedom." *The Anglo-African Magazine* 1 (1859).

Proctor, Edna Dean. "Harvest and Liberty." *Independent* 12, no. 616 (Sept. 20, 1860): 1.

——. "White Slaves." *Independent* 12, no. 587 (Mar. 1, 1860): 1.

[Putnam, Mary Lowell]. *Record of an Obscure Man*. Boston: Ticknor and Fields, 1861.

Stowe, Harriet Beecher. "The Church and the Slave Trade." *Independent* 12, no. 622 (Nov. 1, 1860): 1.

——. "Getting Ready for a Gale." *Independent* 13, no. 647 (Apr. 25, 1861): 1.

——. "Getting Used to It." *Independent* 12, no. 628 (Dec. 13, 1860): 1.

——. "The President's Message." *Independent* 12, no. 629 (Dec. 20, 1860): 1.

——. "What God Hath Wrought." *Independent* 12, no. 624 (Nov. 15, 1860): 1.

Victor, Metta Victoria. *Maum Guinea and Her Plantation Children; or, Holiday-Week on a Louisiana Estate, A Slave Romance*. New York: Beadle and Company, 1861; New York: Books for Libraries Press, 1972.

Watkins, Frances Ellen. "Bury Me in a Free Land," *National Anti-Slavery Standard* 19 (Dec. 1858).

Willard, Emma. *Via Media: A Peaceful and Permanent Settlement to the Slavery Question*. Washington, D.C.: C. H. Anderson, 1862.

Antebellum Anti- and Proslavery Novels

NORTH

[Brown, Mattie Griffiths]. *Autobiography of a Female Slave*. New York: Redfield, 1857.

Hale, Mrs. Sarah Josepha. *Northwood; or, Life North and South*. 1827. New York: H. Long and Brother, 1852.

Langdon, Mary [Mary (Green) Pike]. *Ida May: A Story of Things Actual and Possible*. Boston: Phillips, Sampson and Company, 1854.

Little, Sophia L. *Thrice through the Furnace; A Tale of the Times of the Iron Hoof*. Pawtucket, R.I.: A. W. Pearce, 1852.

Pearson, Mrs. Emily. *Cousin Franck's Household*. Boston: Upham, Ford and Olmstead, 1853.

Ropes, Hannah H. *Six Months in Kansas: By a Lady*. Boston: John P. Jewett, 1856.

Stowe, Harriet Beecher. *Dred: A Tale of the Great Dismal Swamp*. Boston: Phillips, Sampson, 1856.

———. *A Key to Uncle Tom's Cabin*. London: Sampson, Low, Son, 1853.

———. "Uncle Tom's Cabin." *The National Era*, 1851.

———. *Uncle Tom's Cabin*. 1852. New York: Bantam Books, 1981.

Wilson, Harriet. *Our Nig*. 1853. New York: Vintage Books, 1983.

ANTI-TOM NOVELS, NORTH AND SOUTH

Butt, Martha Haines. *Antifanaticism: A Tale of the South*. Philadelphia: Lippincott, Grambo and Co., 1853. *Southern*

Cowdin, Mrs. V. G. *Ellen; or, The Fanatic's Daughter*. Mobile, Ala.: S. H. Goetzel and Co., 1860. *Southern*

Eastman, Mrs. Mary. *Aunt Phillis's Cabin; or, Southern Life as It Is*. Philadelphia: Lippincott, Grambo and Co., 1852. *Southern*

[Flanders, Mrs. G. M.]. *The Ebony Idol, by a Lady of New England*. New York: D. Appleton and Company, 1860. *Northern*

Hale, Sarah Josepha. *Liberia; or, Mr. Peyton's Experiments*. New York: Harper and Bros., 1853. *Northern*

Hentz, Caroline Lee. *The Planter's Northern Bride*. Philadelphia: T. B. Peterson, 1854. *Transplanted Northerner*

———. *Ugly Effie and Other Tales*. Philadelphia: T. B. Peterson, 1853.

Herndon, Mary E. *Louise Elton; or, Things Seen and Heard*. Philadelphia: Lippincott, Grambo and Co., 1853. *Southern*

McIntosh, Maria J. *The Lofty and the Lowly; or, Good in All and None All-Good*. 2 vols. New York: D. Appleton and Co., 1853. *Southern*

[Rush, Caroline E.]. *North and South, Or Slavery and Its Contrasts*. Philadelphia: Crissy and Markley, 1852. *Northern*

Schoolcraft, Mrs. Mary Howard. *The Black Gauntlet: A Tale of Plantation Life in South Carolina*. Philadelphia: J. B. Lippincott, 1860. *Southern*

Antislavery Writing in Wartime

Alcott, Louisa May. "Colored Soldier's Letters." *Commonwealth* 2, no. 44 (July 1, 1864): 1.

———. *Hospital Sketches and Camp and Fireside Stories*. Boston: Roberts Brothers, 1869.

———. "An Hour." *Commonwealth* 3, no. 13 (Nov. 26, 1864), no. 14 (Dec. 3, 1864).

———. "M. L." *Commonwealth* 1, no. 21 (Jan. 24, 1863); no. 22 (Jan 31, 1863); no. 23 (Feb. 7, 1863); no. 24 (Feb. 14, 1863); no. 25 (Feb. 22, 1863). Reprinted in *Journal of Negro History* 14, no. 14 (Oct. 1929).

Cheseboro', Caroline. "Ambassadors in Bonds." *Atlantic Monthly* 13 (Mar. 1864): 281–303.

Child, Lydia Maria. *The Freedmen's Book*. Boston: Ticknor and Fields, 1865.

Clark, Luella. "À La Guerre." *Independent* 13, no. 648 (May 2, 1861): 2.

Cooke, Martha W. "The Lady and Her Slave." *Continental Monthly* 3, no. 3 (Mar. 1863).

———. "War Song:—Earth's Last Battle." *Continental Monthly* 3 (May 1863).

Davis, Rebecca Harding. "Blind Tom." *Atlantic Monthly* 10 (Nov. 1862).

———. "John Lamar." *Atlantic Monthly* 10 (Dec. 1862).

Dodge, Mary E. "Our Contraband." *Harper's Monthly* 27, no. 159 (Aug. 1863): 395–403.

Ellis, Elsie. "Ennobled Bondmen." *Christian Recorder*, Aug. 19, 1865.

Forten, Charlotte, "Life on the Sea Islands." *Atlantic Monthly* 13 (May, June 1864).

French, Mrs. A[msta] M. *Slavery in South Carolina and the Ex-Slaves; or, The Port Royal Mission*. New York: Winchell M. French, 1862.

Harper, Frances Ellen Watkins. *Complete Poems of Frances E. W. Harper*. Edited by Maryemma Graham. New York: Oxford University Press, 1988.

"Irrepressible Conflict." *Continental Monthly* 1 (Apr. 1862).

Kemble, Frances Anne. *Journal of a Residence on a Georgia Plantation in 1838–1839*. New York: Harper, 1863. See reviews in the *Harper's Monthly* 27, no. 159 (Aug. 1863): 416–17, and *Commonwealth* 1, no. 42 (June 19, 1863): 4; no. 43 (June 26, 1863): 2; no. 44 (July 17, 1863): 1–2.

MacFarlane, Isabella. "The Two Southern Mothers." *Continental Monthly* 4, no. 4 (Oct. 1863).

Olmstead, Mrs. Elizabeth M. "The Clarion." *Independent* 13, no. 662 (Aug. 8, 1861): 1.

[Pearson, Emily Clemens]. *The Poor White, or the Rebel Conscript*. Boston: Graves and Young, 1864.

Perry, Nora. "Clotilde and the Contraband." *Harper's Monthly* 24, no. 144 (May 1862): 764–71.

"At Port Royal." *Atlantic Monthly* 9 (Feb. 1862): 244–46.

Prescott, Harriet E. "Down the River." *Atlantic Monthly* 16 (Oct. 1865): 468–90.

Proctor, Edna Dean. "The Stripes and the Stars." *Independent* 13, no. 647 (Apr. 25, 1861): 1.

"Rejoinder to Mrs. Stowe's Reply to the Address of the Women of England." *Atlantic Monthly* 11 (Apr. 1863): 525–28.

Shepard, N. G. "The Sisters." *Harper's New Monthly Magazine* 29, no. 171 (Aug. 1864): 335.

Stowe, Harriet Beecher. "Getting Ready for a Gale." *Independent* 13, no. 647 (Apr. 25, 1861): 1.

——. "The Holy War." *Independent* 13, no. 649 (May 9, 1861): 1.

——. "Letter from Andover." *Independent* 13, no. 655 (June 13, 20, 1861): 1.

——. "Letter to Lord Shaftesbury." *Independent* 13, no. 661 (Aug. 1, 1861): 1.

——. "The Man and the Hour." *Independent* 13, no. 667 (Sept. 12, 1861): 1.

——. "Sojourner Truth, the Libyan Sibyl." *Atlantic Monthly* 11 (Apr. 1863): 473–81. See also Mrs. Frances G. Gage, "Sojourner Truth." *Commonwealth* 1, no. 35 (May 1, 1863): 1, and Sojourner Truth's letter to James Redpath printed in *Commonwealth* 1, no. 44 (July 3, 1863): 1.

——. "To 'the Affectionate and Christian Address of Many Thousands of Women of Great Britain.'" *Atlantic Monthly* 11 (Jan. 1863): 122.

——. "Valley of Humiliation." *Independent* 13, no. 666 (Sept. 5, 1861): 1.

Terry, Rose. "The New Sangreal." *Atlantic Monthly* 12 (Sept. 1863): 343–44.

Walker, Katherine. "Three Trophies." *Harper's New Monthly Magazine* 29 (1864).

Women's Fiction on the War

Akers, Mrs. Paul. "Spring at the Capitol." *Atlantic Monthly* 11 (June 1863): 766–67.

Alcott, Louisa May. "The Blue and the Gray." *Putnam's*, June 1868.

——. "Hospital Sketches." *Commonwealth* 1, no. 38 (May 22, 1863); no. 39 (May 29, 1863); no. 41 (June 12, 1863); no. 43 (June 26, 1863). Reprinted as *Hospital Sketches*.

——. *Little Women*. 1868. With an introduction by Elaine Showalter. New York: Penguin, 1989.

——. *An Old-Fashioned Girl*. 1869. Boston: Little, Brown and Co., 1997.

——. *On Picket Duty*. Boston: James Redpath, 1864.

——. *Work: A Story of Experience*. 1873. New York: Penguin, 1994.

Arey, Mrs. H. E. G. "Whither Away Does Our Good Ship Drift?" *Independent* 13, no. 655 (June 20, 1861): 1.

Arthur, T[imothy] S[hay]. "More Precious Than Gold." *Peterson's Magazine* 43, no. 2 (Feb. 1863): 155–56.

——. "The Soldier's Letter." *Peterson's Magazine* 43, no. 3 (Mar. 1863): 189–91.

Augusta, Clara. "A Game of Fortune." *Peterson's Magazine* 46, no. 6 (Dec. 1864): 430–31.

[Austin, Jane Goodwin]. *Dora Darling: The Daughter of the Regiment*. Boston: J. E. Tilton and Co., 1865.

[Baker], Delphine [Paris]. *Solon, or the Rebellion of '61*. Chicago: S. P. Rounds, Book and Job Printer, 1862.

Barker, Louise W. "Why I Wrote It." *Harper's New Monthly Magazine* 29, no. 169 (June 1864): 94–104.

Bouton, Elizabeth. "At The South." *Peterson's Magazine* 48, no. 1 (July 1865): 50.

Brewster, Anne M. "Lucy's Letters." *Atlantic Monthly* 17 (Jan. 1866): 64–69.

Browne, Francis. ed. *Bugle-Echoes*. New York: Frederick A. Stokes Company Publishers, 1886.

Browne, Helen Augusta "No Letter Yet." *Peterson's Magazine* 46, no. 2 (Aug. 1864): 136.

Bucklin, Sophronia. *In Hospital and Camp: A Woman's Record of Thrilling Incidents Among the Wounded in the Late War*. Philadelphia: J. E. Potter and Company, 1869.

Carnnshall, Sarah E. "Woman's Part." *Peterson's Magazine* 45, no. 3 (Mar. 1864): 193.

Carroll, Anna Ella. "The Relation of the National Government to Revolted Citizens Defined." In *Union Pamphlets of the Civil War: 1861–1865*. Vol. 1, edited by

Frank Freidel. Cambridge, Mass.: The Belknap Press of Harvard University Press, 1967.

Case, Phila Henrietta. "Weary." *Peterson's Magazine* 46, no. 1 (July 1864): 44.

Cheseboro', Caroline. "The Traitor's Wife." *Independent* 13, no. 648 (May 2, 1861): 1.

Child, Lydia Maria. *A Romance of the Republic*. 1867. Miami: Mnemosyne, 1969.

Clarke, Edith M. "Will's Orange-Flowers." *Peterson's Magazine* 48, no. 2 (Aug. 1865): 118.

Clyde, Miriam. "Clara's Hero." *Peterson's Magazine* 47, no. 1 (Jan. 1865): 27–28.

Dana, James H. "The Legion of Honor." *Peterson's Magazine* 40, no. 3 (Sept. 1861): 175–76.

Davis, Rebecca Harding. *Bits of Gossip*. Boston and New York: Houghton Mifflin, 1904.

——. "Ellen." *Atlantic Monthly* 16 (July 1865): 22–34.

——. *Life in the Iron Mills*. 1861. Boston: Bedford Books, 1998.

——. *Margret Howth*. 1862. New York: The Feminist Press at the City University of New York, 1990.

——. "Paul Blecker." Parts 1–3. *Atlantic Monthly* 10 (May 1863): 580–98; 11 (June 1863): 677–91; 12 (July 1863): 22–69.

——. *Waiting for the Verdict*. New York: Sheldon and Company, 1868.

Denison, Mrs. M. A. "Off to the War." *Peterson's Magazine* 42, no. 2 (Aug. 1862): 143.

Dickinson, Anna E. *What Answer?* 1868. New York: Books for Libraries Press, 1972.

[Dodge, Mary Abigail]. "Tracts for the Times. Courage!" (New York, 1862). In *Union Pamphlets of the Civil War: 1861–1865*. Vol. 1, edited by Frank Freidel. Cambridge, Mass.: The Belknap Press of Harvard University Press, 1967.

Dodge, M[ary] E. *The Irvington Stories*. New York: James O'Kane, Publisher, 1864.

——. "My Mysterious Foe." *Harper's Monthly* 26, no. 155 (Apr. 1863): 659–64.

——. "Netty's Touch-Stone." *Harper's New Monthly Magazine* 28, no. 166 (Mar. 1864): 517–19.

Dorr, Julia R. "The Drummer Boy's Burial." *Harper's New Monthly Magazine* 29, no. 170 (July 1864): 145–46.

Drille, Hearton [Jeannie H. Grey]. *Tactics; or, Cupid in Shoulder-Straps*. New York: Carleton, Publisher, 413 Broadway, 1863.

Dunlap, L. J. "Halt." *Peterson's Magazine* 43, no. 5 (May [June?] 1863): 431–33.

Eastman, Mrs. Clara. "The Soldier's Request." *Peterson's Magazine* 44, no. 3 (Sept. 1863): 212.

Eastman, Mrs. Mary (Henderson). *Jenny Wade of Gettysburg*. Philadelphia: J. B. Lippincott, 1864.

"Editor's Table." *Peterson's Magazine* 40, no. 1 (July 1861): 76; 40, no. 2 (Aug. 1861): 155; 43, no. 5 (May 1863): 398; 44, no. 4 (Oct. 1863): 311.

Ellwood, Ella. "Dirge." *Peterson's Magazine* 43, no. 5 (May 1863): 353.

"A Few Words in Behalf of the Loyal Women of the United States." In *Union Pamphlets of the Civil War: 1861–1865*. Vol. 1, edited by Frank Freidel. Cambridge, Mass.: The Belknap Press of Harvard University Press, 1967.

Fuller, J[ane] G[ay]. *The Brownings: A Tale of the Great Rebellion*. New York: M. W. Dodd, 1867.

——. "Quam." *Harper's Monthly* 26, no. 154 (Mar. 1863): 532–37.

Furness, Louise E. "The Real Cost." *Harper's New Monthly Magazine* 29, no. 174 (Nov. 1864): 741–44.

Gray, Miss Alice. "A Part of the Mission of Harpers Ferry." *Peterson's Magazine* 48, no. 1 (July 1865): 100–105.

Hamilton, Gail [Mary Dodge]. "Anno Domini." *Atlantic Monthly* 15, no. 87 (Jan. 1865): 116–22.

——. "A Call to My Countrywomen." *Atlantic Monthly* 11, no. 65 (Mar. 1863): 345–49.

——. *Country Living and Country Thinking*. Boston: Ticknor and Fields, 1863.

——. *Gala-Days*. Boston: Ticknor and Fields, 1863.

——. "Lights among the Shadows of Our Civil War." In *Country Living and Country Thinking*. Boston: Ticknor and Fields, 1863.

——. *Skirmishes and Sketches*. Boston: Ticknor and Fields, 1865.

Harper, Frances E. W. *Iola Leroy*. Boston: Beacon Press, 1987.

Hastings, Ellen A. "Abide in Faith." *Harper's New Monthly Magazine* 27, no. 161 (Oct. 1863): 595.

——. "Alas!" *Harper's New Monthly Magazine* 28, no. 166 (Mar. 1864): 449.

Haven, Alice B. "One Day." *Harper's New Monthly Magazine* 25, no. 149 (Oct. 1862): 660–69.

Heath, Clara B. "Living or Dead?" *Peterson's Magazine* 48, no. 5 (Nov. 1865): 357.

Heath, Natalie. "What I Owe the War." *Peterson's Magazine* 40, no. 3 (Sept. 1861): 200–202.

Holmes, Mary Jane Hawes. *Rose Mather: A Tale of the War*. New York: G. W. Dillingham, 1896.

Hopkinson, Mrs. "Quicksands." *Atlantic Monthly* 17, no. 104 (June 1866): 657–72.

Howe, Mrs. Julia Ward. "Battle Hymn of the Republic." *Atlantic Monthly* 9, no. 52 (Feb. 1862): 1.

——. "The Flag." *Atlantic Monthly* (Apr. 1863).

Howe, Mary Anne. *The Rival Volunteers; or, The Black Plume Rifles*. New York: John Bradburn, 1864.

Janurin, Mary W. "The Red, White and Blue." *Peterson's Magazine* 41, no. 3 (Mar. 1862): 217–20.

Johnson, Mrs. W. T. "On Picket Duty." *Atlantic Monthly* 13 (Apr. 1864): 495–97.

Jones, Emma Garrison. "Alice's Rose-Tree." *Peterson's Magazine* 47, no. 4 (Apr. 1865): 265–67.

——. "Waiting." *Peterson's Magazine* 47, no. 5 (May 1865): 336.

Kate Morgan and Her Soldiers. Philadelphia: American Sunday-School Union, 1862.

Kendall, Kate. "Fallen." *Peterson's Magazine* 44, no. 2 (Aug. 1863): 146.

Larcom, Lucy. "Reenlisted." *Atlantic Monthly* 13 (May 1864): 629–30.

Lawson, Mary L. "The Young Volunteer." *Peterson's Magazine* 16, no. 6 (June 1862): 480.

Lee, Mary A. "In Memoriam:—F. B. C." *Harper's Monthly* 27, no. 160 (Sept. 1863): 541.

——. "Missing." *Harper's Monthly* 27, no. 157 (June 1863): 119.

Leigh, Emilie Lester. "A Woman's Fame." *Peterson's Magazine* 47, no. 3 (Mar. 1865): 234–35.

L. L. [Lottie Linwood?]. "Verses." *Peterson's Magazine* 43, no. 5 (May [June?] 1863): 440.

Linwood, Lottie. "Dead." *Peterson's Magazine* 43, no. 4 (Apr. 1863): 302.

Longstreet, Abby Buchanan. *Remy St. Remy; or, The Boy in Blue*. New York: James O'Kane, 1866.

"A Loyal Woman's No." *Atlantic Monthly* 12 (Dec. 1863).

McLeod, Isabella. *Westfield. A View of Home Life during the American War*. Edinburgh: Edmonston and Douglas, 1866.

Manson, Fannie B. "In War Time." *Peterson's Magazine* 46, no. 2 (Aug. 1864): 137.

[Martyn, Sarah Towne Smith]. *Our Village in War-Time*. New York: American Tract Society, 1864.

Moody, Mrs. M. L. "My Little Boy." *Atlantic Monthly* 18 (Sept. 1866): 361–64.

Moore, Mrs. F. A. "Killed Instantly." *Peterson's Magazine* 44, no. 5 (Nov. 1863): 366.

Moore, Madeline [pseud.]. *Lady Lieutenant*. Philadelphia: Barclay and Co., 1862.

Moreton, Clara. "Parting." *Peterson's Magazine* 47, no. 5 (May 1865): 347.

Mornington, Maud. "The Nation's Dead." *Peterson's Magazine* 45, no. 5 (May 1864): 361.

Mott, Julia Eugenia. "Within A Year." *Peterson's Magazine* 41, no. 4 (June 1862): 29.

Moulton, Louise Chandler. "Buying Winter Things." *Harper's New Monthly Magazine* 25, no. 150 (Nov. 1862): 802–4.

———. "Captain Charley." *Harper's New Monthly Magazine* 27, no. 159 (Aug. 1863): 407–9.

———. "On Furlough." *Peterson's Magazine* 45, no. 1 (Jan. 1864): 38–41.

———. "Kitten." *Harper's New Monthly Magazine* 26, no. 155 (Apr. 1863): 696–99.

———. "The Last of Seven." *Harper's New Monthly Magazine* 29, no. 172 (Sept. 1864): 470–75.

———. "One of Many." *Harper's New Monthly Magazine* 27, no. 157 (June 1863): 120–21.

———. "A Woman's Waiting." *Harper's New Monthly Magazine* 27, no. 162 (Nov. 1863): 815–16.

"My Soldier." *Harper's New Monthly Magazine* 29, no. 174 (Nov. 1864): 734.

Neely, Kate J. "Letty's Proposal." *Harper's New Monthly Magazine* 25, no. 149 (Oct. 1862): 607–16.

Osgood, Kate Putnam. "In the Meadow." *Harper's New Monthly Magazine* 30, no. 175 (Dec. 1864): 51–52.

"Parting Hymn." *Atlantic Monthly* 8 (Aug. 1861): 235.

Perry, Nora. "Margaret Freyer's Heart." *Harper's New Monthly Magazine* 27, no. 157 (June 1863): 179–89.

Phelps, Elizabeth Stuart. "The Bend." *Harper's New Monthly Magazine* 29, no. 171 (Aug. 1864): 323–35.

———. *Chapters from a Life*. Boston: Houghton Mifflin, 1897.

———. *The Gates Ajar*. Cambridge, Mass.: Belknap Press of Harvard University Press, 1964.

———. *Hedged In*. Boston: Fields, Osgood and Co., 1870.

———. "Margaret Bronson." *Harper's New Monthly Magazine* 31, no. 184 (Sept. 1865): 498–504.

———. *Men, Women and Ghosts*. Boston: Fields, Osgood and Co., 1864.

———. "My Refugees." *Harper's New Monthly Magazine* 29, no. 174 (Nov. 1864): 754–63.

———. "A Sacrifice Consumed." *Harper's New Monthly Magazine* 28, no. 164 (Jan. 1864): 235–40.

———. *Silent Partner*. Ridgewood, N.J.: Gregg Press, 1967.

———. "The Tenth of January," in *The Silent Partner*. New York: Feminist Press, 1983.

———. *Walled In*. New York: Harper and Brothers, 1907.

Pidsley, Mrs. "The Soldier's Widow." *Peterson's Magazine* 46, no. 5 (Nov. 1864): 348.

Pierson, Helen W. "My Heart and I." *Harper's New Monthly Magazine* 27, no. 159 (Aug. 1863): 351–60.

———. "Tom's Education." *Harper's New Monthly Magazine* 30, no. 176 (Jan. 1865): 188–93.

Pollard, Josephine. "The Uprising." *Peterson's Magazine* 41, no. 4 (Apr. 1862): 326.

Powers, Elvira J. *Hospital Pencillings: Being a Diary While in Jefferson General Hospital,*

Jeffersonville, Ind., and Others at Nashville, Tennessee, as Matron and Visitor. Boston: Edward L. Mitchell, 1866.

Prescott, Harriet E. "Down the River." *Atlantic Monthly* 16 (Oct. 1865): 468.

———. "Madeleine Schaeffer." *Harper's New Monthly Magazine* 25, no. 145 (June 1862): 37–52; no. 149 (Oct. 1862): 651–60; no. 150 (Nov. 1862): 753–64.

———. "Peace." *Harper's New Monthly Magazine* 30, no. 177 (Feb. 1865): 281.

———. "Ray." *Atlantic Monthly* 13 (Jan. 1864): 19–39.

Proctor, Edna Dean. "Compromise." *Independent* 13, no. 657 (July 4, 1861): 1.

Redden, Laura C. "After Vicksburg." *Harper's New Monthly Magazine* 26, no. 154 (Mar. 1863): 518.

Remick, Martha. *Miscellaneous Poems*. Malden, Mass.: A. G. Brown, Steam Book and Job Printer, n.d.

Review of *The Battle-Fields of Our Fathers*, by Virginia F. Townsend. *Peterson's Magazine* 46, no. 4 (Oct. 1864): 295.

Richards, Caroline H. B. "In Memoriam: Alice B. Haven." *Harper's New Monthly Magazine* 27, no. 161 (Oct. 1863): 404–5.

Rodman, Ella. "An Angel of Mercy." *Peterson's Magazine* 47, no. 6 (June 1865): 416–21.

———. "A Daguerreotype in Battle." *Peterson's Magazine* 44, no. 3 (Sept. 1863): 187–90.

———. "Fanny's Flirtation." *Peterson's Magazine* 46, no. 1 (July 1864): 33–44, 116–17, 184–91.

Sangster, Mrs. George. "Lute Prescott's Engagement." *Peterson's Magazine* 45, no. 3 (March 1864): 194–97.

Sheffield, Frances Henrietta. "Lines." *Peterson's Magazine* 46, no. 1 (July 1864): 68.

———. "The Patriot Dead." *Peterson's Magazine* 43, no. 3 (Mar. 1863): 203.

Shirley, Anna W. "Tried and True." *Harper's New Monthly Magazine* 27, no. 162 (Nov. 1863): 835–39.

Southworth, Emma D. E. N. *How He Won Her. A Sequel to "Fair Play."* Philadelphia: T. B. Peterson and Brothers, 1869.

Spencer, Belle Z. "One of the Noble." *Harper's New Monthly Magazine* 29, no. 170 (July 1864): 201–6.

———. "A Soldier's Wife." *Harper's New Monthly Magazine* 29, no. 173 (Oct. 1864): 622–28.

———. *Tried and True*. Springfield, Mass.: W. J. Holland, 1866.

Spencer, Mary V. "I Was A-Hungered." *Peterson's Magazine* 46, no. 5 (Nov. 1864): 323–24.

Sperry, Sylvie. "Mother, Weep!" *Peterson's Magazine* 45, no. 6 (June 1864): 440.

Stanley, Carry. "The Volunteer's Wife." *Peterson's Magazine* 40, no. 5 (Oct. 1863): 256–59.

Stowe, Harriet Beecher. "The Chimney-Corner." *Atlantic Monthly* 15, no. 87 (Jan. 1865): 109–15.

———. "The Noble Army of Martyrs." In "The Chimney-Corner." *Atlantic Monthly* (Aug. 1865): 232–37.

Townsend, Virginia F. *Darryl Gap; or, Whether It Paid*. Boston: Lee and Shepard, Publishers, 1866.

"The True Heroine." *Atlantic Monthly* 9 (Jan. 1862): 27–28.

Victor, M[etta] V[ictoria]. *The Unionist's Daughter: A Tale of the Rebellion in Tennessee*. New York: Beadle and Company, 1862.

Walker, Leslie. "Ray Amyott." *Peterson's Magazine* 46, no. 5 (Nov. 1864): 339–48.

[Warner, Susan]. *Daisy*. Philadelphia: J. B. Lippincott, 1868.

Watson, Mrs. Sarah A. "My Brother." *Peterson's Magazine* 46, no. 3 (Sept. 1864): 198.

W[heeler], A. O. ("A. O. W."). *Eyewitness; or, Life Scenes in the Old North State, Depicting the Trials and Sufferings of the Unionists during the Rebellion.* Boston: B. B. Russell and Co., 1865.

Whitney, Mrs. A. D. "Peace." *Atlantic Monthly* 16 (Aug. 1865): 237–38.

Williams, Katherine F. "Tableaux Vivants." *Harper's New Monthly Magazine* 27, no. 161 (Oct. 1863): 698–704.

Secondary Sources

Aaron, Daniel. *The Unwritten War: American Writers and the Civil War.* New York: Knopf, 1973.

Abram, Ruth J., ed. *"Send Us a Lady Physician": Women Doctors in America, 1835–1920.* New York and London: W. W. Norton and Co., 1985.

Alexander, Ruth M. "We Are Engaged as a Band of Sisters." *Journal of American History* 75 (Dec. 1988).

Ammons, Elizabeth. "Heroines in *Uncle Tom's Cabin.*" *American Literature* 46 (1977): 166–79.

Aptheker, Bettina. *Woman's Legacy: Essays on Race, Sex and Class in American History.* Amherst: The University of Massachusetts Press, 1982.

Austin, Anne L. *The Woolsey Sisters of New York: A Family's Involvement in the Civil War and a New Profession (1860–1900).* Philadelphia: American Philosophical Society, 1971.

Bacon, Margaret Hope. *I Speak for My Slave Sister: The Life of Abby Kelley Foster.* New York: Thomas Y. Crowell, 1975.

——. *Mothers of Feminism: The Story of Quaker Women in America.* San Francisco: Harper and Row, 1986.

Baer, Helene G. *The Heart is Like Heaven: The Life of Lydia Maria Child.* Philadelphia: University of Pennsylvania Press, 1964.

Baker, LaFayette. *The Secret Service in the Late War.* Philadelphia: John E. Potter and Company. 1874.

Baker, Nina Brown. *Cyclone in Calico: The Story of Mary Ann Bickerdyke.* Boston: Little, Brown, 1952.

Bardes, Barbara, and Suzanne Gossett. *Declarations of Independence: Women and Political Power in Nineteenth-Century American Fiction.* New Brunswick, N.J.: Rutgers University Press, 1990.

Barton, William E. *The Life of Clara Barton, Founder of the American Red Cross.* New York and Boston: Houghton Mifflin Co., 1922.

Baym, Nina. *Feminism and American Literary History.* New Brunswick, N.J.: Rutgers University Press, 1992.

——. *Novels, Readers, and Reviewers: Responses to Fiction in Antebellum America.* Ithaca, N.Y.: Cornell University Press, 1984.

——. *Women's Fiction: A Guide to Novels by and about Women in America, 1820–1870.* Ithaca, N.Y.: Cornell University Press, 1978.

Bell, Malcolm, Jr. *Major Butler's Legacy: Five Generations of a Slaveholding Family.* Athens and London: University of London Press, 1987.

Bennett, Mary Angela. *Elizabeth Stuart Phelps.* Philadelphia: University of Pennsylvania Press, 1939.

Bennett, Nina. "The Women Who Went to War: The Union Army Nurse in the Civil War." Ph.D. dissertation, Northwestern University, 1981.

Benton, Josiah Henry. *What Women Did for the War and What the War Did for Women: A Memorial Day Address*. Boston, 1894.

Berg, Barbara. *The Remembered Gate: Origins of American Feminism—The Woman and the City, 1800–1860*. New York: Oxford University Press, 1978.

Berlin, Ira, Joseph P. Reidy, and Leslie S. Rowland, eds. *Freedom: A Documentary History of Emancipation 1861–1867*. 2nd ser. The Black Military Experience. Cambridge: Cambridge University Press, 1982.

Bernard, Jacqueline. *Journey toward Freedom: The Story of Sojourner Truth*. 1967. New York: The Feminist Press at the City University of New York, 1990.

Bernstein, Iver. *The New York City Draft Riots: Their Significance for American Society in the Age of the Civil War*. New York: Oxford University Press, 1990.

Biddle, Gertrude, and Sarah Dickinson Lowrie, eds. *Notable Women of Pennsylvania*. Philadelphia: University of Pennsylvania Press, 1942.

Billings, Eliza. *The Female Volunteer*. N.p., 1951.

Blake, Fay M. *The Strike in the American Novel*. Metuchen, N.J.: The Scarecrow Press, Inc., 1972.

Blumin, Stuart. *The Emergence of the Middle Class: Social Experience in the American City, 1760–1900*. Cambridge: Cambridge University Press, 1989.

Boyd, Melba Joyce. *Discarded Legacy: Politics and Poetics in the Life of Frances E. W. Harper, 1825–1911*. Detroit: Wayne State University Press, 1994.

Boydston, Jeanne. *Home and Work: Housework, Wages, and the Ideology of Labor in the Early Republic*. New York: Oxford University Press, 1990.

Boydston, Jeanne, Mary Kelley, and Anne Margolis. *The Limits of Sisterhood: The Beecher Sisters on Women's Rights and Women's Sphere*. Chapel Hill: University of North Carolina Press, 1990.

Boyle, Regis Louise. "Mrs. E. D. E. N. Southworth, Novelist." Ph.D. dissertation, The Catholic University of America, Washington D.C., 1939.

Braxton, Jeanne. *Black Women Writing Autobiography: A Tradition within a Tradition*. Philadelphia: Temple University Press, 1989.

Brodhead, Richard H. *Cultures of Letters: Scenes of Reading and Writing in Nineteenth-Century America*. Chicago and London: The University of Chicago Press, 1993.

Brown, Gillian. *Domestic Individualism: Imagining Self in Nineteenth-Century America*. Berkeley: University of California Press, 1991.

Brown, Herbert Ross. *The Sentimental Novel in America, 1789–1860*. Durham: Duke University Press, 1940.

Brown, Richard D. *Knowledge is Power: The Diffusion of Information in Early America, 1700–1865*. New York: Oxford University Press, 1989.

Buhle, Mari Jo. *Women and American Socialism*. Illinois: University of Illinois Press, 1981.

Buhle, Mari Jo, and Florence Howe. Afterword to *The Silent Partner*, by Elizabeth Stuart Phelps. New York: The Feminist Press, 1983.

Bynum, Victoria. *Unruly Women: The Politics of Social and Sexual Control in the Old South*. Chapel Hill: University of North Carolina Press, 1992.

Carby, Hazel. *Reconstructing Womanhood: The Emergence of the Afro-American Woman Novelist*. New York and London: Oxford University Press, 1987.

Chasson, Michael. "Harlots or Heroines?" *Virginia Magazine of History and Biography* 92, no. 2 (1984): 131–75.

Cheney, Ednah, ed. *Louisa May Alcott: Life, Letters and Journals*. Boston: Little, Brown, 1928.

Chester, Giraud. *Embattled Maiden: The Life of Anna Dickinson*. New York: G. P. Putnam's Sons, 1951.

Clarke, James B. "An Hour with Harriet Tubman." *The African Times and Orient Review* (Sept. 1912): 87–89.

Clausius, Gerard P. "The Little Soldier of the 95th: Albert D. J. Cashier." *Journal of the Illinois State Historical Society* 51, no. 4 (Winter 1958): 380–87.

Clifford, Deborah Pickman. *Crusader for Freedom: A Life of Lydia Maria Child*. Boston: Beacon Press, 1992.

Clinton, Catherine. *The Other Civil War: American Women in the Nineteenth Century*. New York: Hill and Wang, 1984.

———. *Tara Revisited: Women, War, and the Plantation Legend*. New York: Abbeville Press, 1995.

Clinton, Catherine, and Nina Silber, eds. *Divided Houses: Gender and the Civil War*. New York and London: Oxford University Press, 1992.

Cogan, Frances B. *All-American Girl: The Ideal of Real Womanhood in Mid-Nineteenth-Century America*. Athens: University of Georgia Press, 1989.

Cohn, Jan. "The Negro Character in Northern Magazine Fiction of the 1860s." *New England Quarterly* 43, no. 4 (Dec. 1970): 572–92.

Conrad, Earl. *Harriet Tubman*. New York: Paul S. Eriksson, Inc., 1943.

Conrad, Susan P. *Perish the Thought: Intellectual Women in Romantic America, 1830–1860*. Secaucus, N.J.: The Citadel Press, 1976.

Cooper, Helen M., Adrienne Auslander Munich, and Susan Merrill Squier. *Arms and the Woman: War, Gender, and Literary Representation*. Chapel Hill: University of North Carolina Press, 1989.

Coryell, Janet L. "Anna Ella Carroll and the Historians." *Civil War History* 35, no. 2 (June 1989): 120–37.

———. *Neither Heroine nor Fool: Anna Ella Carroll of Maryland*. Kent, Ohio: Kent State University Press, 1990.

Cott, Nancy. *The Bonds of Womanhood: "Woman's Sphere" in New England, 1780–1835*. New Haven: Yale University Press, 1977.

———. "What's in a Name? The Limits of 'Social Feminism'; or, Expanding the Vocabulary of Women's History." *Journal of American History* 76 (1989): 802–29.

Coultrap-McQuin, Susan. *Doing Literary Business*. Chapel Hill: University of North Carolina Press, 1990.

———. Introduction to *Gail Hamilton: Selected Writings*. New Brunswick, N.J.: Rutgers University Press, 1992.

[Croly, David G.]. *Miscegenation; The Theory of the Blending of the Races, Applied to the American White Man and Negro*. New York: H. Dexter, Hamilton and Co., 1864.

Cullen, Jim. "'I's a Man Now': Gender and African American Men." In *Divided Houses: Gender and the Civil War*, edited by Catherine Clinton and Nina Silber, 76–91. New York: Oxford University Press, 1992.

Culpepper, Marilyn Mayer. *Trials and Triumphs: The Women of the American Civil War*. East Lansing: Michigan State University Press, 1991.

Dannett, Sylvia, ed. *Noble Women of the North*. New York and London: T. Yoseloff, 1959.

Dannett, Sylvia G. L., and Katherine Jones. *Our Women of the Sixties*. Washington, D.C.: U.S. Civil War Centennial Commission, 1963.

Davis, Curtis Carroll. "Companions of Crisis: The Spy Memoir as a Social Document." *Civil War History* 10, no. 4 (Dec. 1964): 385–400.

Davis, Rebecca Harding. *Life in the Iron Mills and Other Stories*. Edited by Tillie Olsen. New York: The Feminist Press, 1972.

Denning, Michael. *Mechanic Accents: Dime Novels and Working-Class Culture in America*. New York and London: Verso, 1987.

DeVoto, Bernard. "Fiction Fights the Civil War." *Saturday Review of Literature*, Dec. 18, 1937, 3–4, 15–16.

Dickinson, Leon T. "Civil War Humor: Its Role in Novels on Slavery." *Civil War History* 2, no. 3 (Sept 1956): 49–65.

Diffley, Kathleen. *Where My Heart Is Turning Ever: Civil War Stories and Constitutional Reform, 1861–1876*. Athens, University of Georgia Press, 1992.

———. "Where My Heart is Turning Ever: Civil War Stories and National Stability from Fort Sumter to the Centennial." *American Literary History* 2, no. 4 (Winter 1990): 627–58.

Donald, David Herbert. *Lincoln*. New York: Simon and Schuster, 1995.

Douglas, Ann. *The Feminization of American Culture*. New York: Knopf, 1977.

Dublin, Thomas. *Women at Work*. New York: Columbia University Press, 1979.

DuBois, Ellen Carol. *The Elizabeth Cady Stanton–Susan B. Anthony Reader: Correspondence, Writings, Speeches*. Boston: Northeastern University Press, 1992.

———. *Feminism and Suffrage*. Ithaca, N.Y.: Cornell University Press, 1978.

———. *Woman Suffrage and Women's Rights*. New York: New York University Press, 1958.

Edwards, Rebecca. *Angels in the Machinery: Gender in American Party Politics from the Civil War to the Progressive Era*. New York: Oxford University Press, 1997.

Elbert, Sarah. *A Hunger for Home: Louisa May Alcott's Place in American Culture*. New Brunswick, N.J.: Rutgers University Press, 1987.

Elshtain, Jean Bethke. *Women and War*. New York: Basic Books, 1987.

Endres, Kathleen L. "The Women's Press in the Civil War." *Civil War History* 30, no. 1 (Mar. 1984): 31–53.

Enloe, Cynthia. *Does Khaki Become You? The Militarization of Women's Lives*. London: Pluto Press, 1983.

Epstein, Barbara Leslie. *The Politics of Domesticity: Women, Evangelism and Temperance in Nineteenth-Century America.* Middletown, Conn.: Wesleyan University Press, 1981.

Fahs, Alice. "The Civil War and the Construction of the Meaning of Work: Northern Civil War Nurses' Reminiscences." Paper presented at the Berkshire Conference of Women's Historians, June 1990.

———. " 'At Home with the Flag': Northern Sentimental Romances of War, 1861–1865." Unpublished essay, Aug. 1991.

Faust, Drew Gilpin. "Altars of Sacrifice: Confederate Women and the Narratives of War." *Journal of American History* (Spring 1990): 1200–1228.

———. *Mothers of Invention: Women of the Slaveholding South in the American Civil War*. Chapel Hill: University of North Carolina Press, 1996.

Fetterley, Judith, ed. *Provisions: A Reader from Nineteenth-Century American Women*. Bloomington: Indiana University Press, 1985.

Fite, Emerson. *Social and Industrial Conditions in the North during the Civil War*. New York: MacMillian Co., 1910.

Fladeland, Betty. *Abolitionists and Working-Class Problems in the Age of Industrialization*. Baton Rouge: Louisiana State University Press, 1984.

——. "Alias Franklin Thompson." *Michigan History* 42, no. 4 (Dec. 1958): 435–62.

——. "New Light on Sara Emma Edmonds." *Michigan History* 47, no. 4 (Dec. 1963): 357–62.

Flexner, Eleanor. *Century of Struggle.* 1957. Cambridge, Mass.: The Belknap Press of Harvard University Press, 1975.

Foner, Eric. *Politics and Ideology in the Era of the Civil War.* New York: Oxford University Press, 1980.

——. *Reconstruction: America's Unfinished Revolution, 1863–1877.* New York: Harper and Row, 1988.

——. *A Short History of Reconstruction.* New York: Harper and Row, 1990.

Forbes, Ella. *African American Women during the Civil War.* New York: Garland Publishing, 1998.

Fox-Genovese, Elizabeth. "Between Individualism and Fragmentation: American Culture and the New Literary Studies of Race and Gender." *American Quarterly* 41 (1990): 7–34.

Fredrickson, George M. *The Black Image in the White Mind: The Debate on Afro-American Character and Destiny.* New York: Harper Torchbooks, 1971.

——. *The Inner Civil War: Northern Intellectuals and the Crisis of the Union.* New York: Harper Torchbooks, 1965.

Freibert, Lucy, and Barbara A. White, ed. *Hidden Hands: An Anthology of American Women Writers, 1790–1870.* New Brunswick, N.J.: Rutgers University Press, 1985.

Friedman, Lawrence J. *Gregarious Saints: Self and Community in American Abolitionism, 1830–1870.* New York: Cambridge University Press, 1983.

Gallman, J. Matthew. *The North Fights the Civil War: The Home Front.* Chicago: Ivan R. Dee Press, 1994.

Gara, Larry. "The Fugitive Slave Law: A Double Paradox." *Civil War History* 10, no. 3 (Sept. 1964): 229–41.

Gardiner, Jane. "The Assault upon Uncle Tom: Attempts of Pro-Slavery Novelists to Answer *Uncle Tom's Cabin*, 1852–1860." *Southern Humanities Review* 12 (1978): 313–24.

Geary, Susan Elizabeth. "Scribbling Women: Essays on Literary History and Popular Literature in the 1850s." Ph.D. dissertation, Brown University, 1976.

Ginzberg, Lori. *Women and the Work of Benevolence.* New Haven: Yale University Press, 1990.

Gossett, Thomas F. *Uncle Tom's Cabin and American Culture.* Texas: Southern Methodist University Press, 1985.

Greenbie, Marjorie Barstow. *Lincoln's Daughters of Mercy.* New York: Putnam's Sons, 1944.

Hall, Stuart. "Notes on Deconstructing 'the Popular.'" In *People's History and Socialist Theory,* edited by Raphael Samuel, 227–40. London: Routledge and Kegan Paul, 1981.

Halttunen, Karen. *Confidence Men and Painted Women: A Study of Middle-Class Culture in America, 1830–1870.* New Haven and London: Yale University Press, 1982.

——. "The Domestic Drama of Louisa May Alcott." *Feminist Studies* 10 (Summer 1984): 233–54.

Hamand, Wendy F. "The Women's National Loyal League: Feminist Abolitionists and the Civil War." *Civil War History* 35, no. 1 (Mar. 1989): 39–58.

Hardesty, Nancy A. *Women Called to Witness: Evangelical Feminism in the Nineteenth Century.* Nashville: Abington Press, 1984.

Harris, Sharon M. *Rebecca Harding Davis and American Realism*. Philadelphia: University of Pennsylvania, 1991.

Harris, Susan K. *Nineteenth-Century American Women's Novels: Interpretive Strategies*. Cambridge: Cambridge University Press, 1990.

Hart, James D. *The Popular Book: A History of America's Literary Taste*. New York: Oxford University Press, 1950.

Hedrick, Joan D. *Harriet Beecher Stowe: A Life*. New York: Oxford University Press, 1994.

Henle, Ellen Langenheim. "Clara Barton, Soldier or Pacifist?" *Civil War History* 24 (June 1978): 152–60.

Herzog, Kristin. *Women, Ethnics, and Exotics: Images of Power in Mid-Nineteenth-Century American Fiction*. Knoxville: University of Tennessee Press, 1983.

Hess, Earl J. *Liberty, Virtue and Progress: Northerners and Their War for the Union*. New York: Fordham University Press, 1997.

Hewitt, Nancy A. *Women's Activism and Social Change: Rochester, New York 1822–1872*. Ithaca, N.Y.: Cornell University Press, 1984.

Higonnet, Margaret Randolph, Jane Jenson, Sonya Michel, and Margaret Collins Weitz, eds. *Behind the Lines: Gender and the Two World Wars*. New Haven: Yale University Press, 1987.

Hodes, Martha. *White Women, Black Men: Illicit Sex in the Nineteenth-Century South*. New Haven: Yale University Press, 1997.

Hogeland, Ronald W. " 'The Female Appendage': Feminine Life-Styles in America, 1820–1860." *Civil War History* 17, no. 2 (June 1971): 101–14.

Hollinger, David. *In the American Province: Studies in the History and Historiography of Ideas*. Bloomington: Indiana University Press, 1985.

Horton, James Oliver. "Freedom's Yoke: Gender Conventions among Antebellum Free Blacks." *Feminist Studies* 12, no. 1 (Spring 1986).

Hunter, Tera. *To 'Joy My Freedom: Southern Black Women's Lives and Labors after the Civil War*. Cambridge, Mass.: Harvard University Press, 1998.

Jacobson, Matt. *Whiteness of a Different Color: European Immigrants and the Alchemy of Race*. Cambridge, Mass.: Harvard University Press, 1998.

James, Edward T., ed. *Notable American Women*. 3 vols. Cambridge, Mass.: Harvard University Press, 1971.

James, Janet Wilson, ed. *Women in American Religion*. Philadelphia: University of Pennsylvania Press, 1980.

Jameson, Frederic. "Reification and Utopia in Mass Culture." *Social Text* (Winter 1979): 130–48.

Jeffrey, Kirk. "Reconstructing the Marital Experience of Lydia Maria Child." *Feminist Studies* 2 (1975): 113–30.

Jelinek, Estelle. *The Tradition of Women's Autobiography: From Antiquity to the Present*. Boston: Twayne Publishers, 1986.

———, ed. *Women's Autobiography: Essays in Criticism*. Bloomington: Indiana University Press, 1980.

Jolly, Mrs. Ellen Ryan. *Nuns of the Battlefield*. Providence, R.I.: Providence Visitor Press, 1927.

Jones, Anne S. *Tomorrow Is Another Day: The Woman Writer in the South, 1850–1936*. Baton Rouge: Louisiana State University Press, 1981.

Jones, Jacqueline. *Labor of Love, Labor of Sorrow*. New York: Vintage, 1985.

———. *Soldiers of Light and Love: Northern Teachers and Georgia Blacks, 1865–1873*. Chapel Hill: University of North Carolina, 1980.

Kane, Harnett T. *Spies for the Blue and Gray*. Garden City and New York: Hanover House, 1954.

Karcher, Carolyn L. *The First Woman in the Republic: A Cultural Biography of Lydia Maria Child*. Durham: Duke University Press, 1994.

———. *Shadow over the Promised Land: Slavery, Race and Violence in Melville's America*. Baton Rouge: Louisiana State University Press, 1977.

Kaufman, Janet E. " 'Under the Petticoat Flag': Women Soldiers in the Confederate Army." *Southern Studies* 23 (Winter 1984): 363–75.

Keetley, Dawn, and John Pettegrew, eds. *Public Women, Public Words: A Documentary History of American Feminism*. Madison, Wisc.: Madison House Publishers, 1997.

Kelley, Mary. *Private Woman, Public Stage: Literary Domesticity in Nineteenth-Century America*. New York: Oxford University Press, 1984.

———. "At War with Herself: Harriet Beecher Stowe as Woman in Conflict within the Home." *American Studies* 19, no. 2 (1978): 23–40.

Kelly, James. *The American Catalogue of Books (originals and reprints) Published in the U.S. from Jan. 1861 to Jan. 1871*. New York: P. Smith, 1938.

Kelly, Lori Duin. *The Life and Works of Elizabeth Stuart Phelps, Victorian Feminist Writer*. Troy, New York: The Whitston Publishing Company, 1983.

Kerber, Linda K. "Separate Spheres, Female Worlds, Women's Place: The Rhetoric of Women's History." *Journal of American History* 75 (June 1988): 9–39.

Kerber, Linda, et al. "Beyond Roles, Beyond Spheres: Thinking about Gender in the Early Republic." *William and Mary Quarterly*, 3d ser., 46 (July 1989): 565–85.

Kessler-Harris, Alice. *Out to Work: A History of Wage-Earning Women in the United States*. New York and London: Oxford University Press, 1982.

Kitchen, Oscar A. *Women Who Spied for the Blue and Gray*. Philadelphia: Dorrance and Company, 1972.

Lammers, Pat, and Amy Boyce. "A Female in the Ranks: Alias Franklin Thompson." *Civil War Times* (Jan. 1984): 24–30.

Leach, William. *True Love and Perfect Union: The Feminist Reform of Sex and Society*. New York: Basic Books, 1980.

Lebsock, Susan. *The Free Women of Petersburg: Status and Culture in a Southern Town, 1784–1860*. New York: W. W. Norton and Co., 1984.

Leonard, Elizabeth D. *All the Daring of the Soldier: Women of the Civil War Armies*. New York: W. W. Norton and Co., 1999.

———. *Yankee Women: Gender Battles in the Civil War*. New York: W. W. Norton and Co., 1994.

Lerner, Gerda. *Why History Matters: Life and Thought*. New York: Oxford University Press, 1997.

Levine, Lawrence W. *Highbrow/Lowbrow: The Emergence of Cultural Hierarchy in America*. Cambridge, Mass.: Harvard University Press, 1988.

Levy, Anita. *Other Women: The Writing of Race, Class and Gender, 1832–1898*. Princeton, N.J.: Princeton University Press, 1991.

Linderman, Gerald F. *Embattled Courage: The Experience of Combat in the American Civil War*. New York: The Free Press, 1987.

Lipsitz, George. *Time Passages: Collective Memory and American Popular Culture*. Minneapolis: University of Minnesota Press, 1990.

Lively, Richard A. *Fiction Fights the Civil War: An Unfinished Chapter in the Literary History of the American People*. Chapel Hill: University of North Carolina Press, 1957.

Loewenberg, Bert James, and Ruth Bogin, eds. *Black Women in Nineteenth-Century American Life: Their Words, Their Thoughts, Their Feelings*. University Park: The Pennsylvania State University Press, 1976.

Logan, Mrs. John A. *The Part Taken by Women in American History*. Wilmington, Del.: Perry-Nalle, 1912.

Lutz, Alma. *Crusade For Freedom: Women of the Anti-Slavery Movement*. Boston: Beacon Press, 1968.

Lystra, Karen. *Searching the Heart: Women, Men and Romantic Love in Nineteenth-Century America*. New York: Oxford University Press, 1989.

McDowell, Deborah, and Arnold Rampersand. *Slavery and the Literary Imagination*. Baltimore, Md.: Johns Hopkins University Press, 1984.

McGerr, Michael. "Political Style and Women's Power, 1830–1930." *Journal of American History* 77 (Dec. 1990): 865.

McLoughlin, William G. *The Meaning of Henry Ward Beecher: An Essay on the Shifting Values of Mid-Victorian America, 1840–1870*. New York: Knopf, 1970.

——. *Revivals, Awakenings and Reform: An Essay on Religion and Social Change in America, 1607–1977*. Chicago: The University of Chicago Press, 1978.

McPherson, James M. *Battle Cry of Freedom: The Civil War Era*. New York: Oxford University Press, 1988.

——. *For Cause and Comrades: Why Men Fought in the Civil War*. New York: Oxford University Press, 1997.

——. *The Negro's Civil War: How Americans Felt and Acted during the War for the Union*. Urbana: University of Illinois Press, 1965.

——. *Ordeal by Fire: The Civil War and Reconstruction*. 2nd ed. New York: McGraw-Hill Inc., 1992.

——. *Struggle for Equality: The Abolitionists and the Negro in the Civil War and Reconstruction*. Princeton, N.J.: Princeton University Press, 1964.

——. *What They Fought For, 1861–1865*. Baton Rouge: Louisiana State University Press, 1994.

McSherry, Frank, Charles G. Waugh, and Martin Greenbey. *Civil War Women*. Little Rock, Ark.: August House, 1988.

Massey, Elizabeth Mary. *Bonnet Brigades*. New York: Knopf, 1966.

Matthews, Glenna. *"Just A Housewife": The Rise and Fall of Domesticity in America*. New York: Oxford University Press, 1987.

Maxwell, William Quentin. *Lincoln's Fifth Wheel: The Political History of the United States Sanitary Commission*. New York: Longmans, Green, 1956.

Melosh, Barbara. *The Physician's Hand: Work, Culture and Conflict in American Nursing*. Philadelphia: Temple University Press, 1982.

Meltzer, Milton. *Tongue of Flame: The Life of Lydia Maria Child*. New York: Thomas Y. Crowell Co., 1965.

Montgomery, David. *Beyond Equality: Labor and the Radical Republicans*. New York: Vintage Books, 1967.

Moore, Frank. *Women of the War*. Hartford, Conn.: S. S. Scranton and Co., 1868.

Morrison, Toni. *Playing in the Dark: Whiteness and the Literary Imagination*. Cambridge, Mass.: Harvard University Press, 1992.

Mott, Frank Luther. *Golden Multitudes; The Story of Best Sellers in the United States*. New York: Macmillan Co., 1947.

——. *A History of American Magazines*. 5 vols. Cambridge, Mass.: The Belknap Press of Harvard University Press, 1957.

Newman, Louise. "Laying Claim to Difference: Ideologies of Race and Gender in the U.S. Women's Movement, 1870–1920." Ph.D. dissertation, Brown University, 1992.

——. *White Women's Rights: The Racial Origins of Feminism in the United States*. New York: Oxford University Press, 1999.

Norton, Ann. *Alternative Americas: A Reading of Antebellum Political Cultures*. Chicago: University of Chicago Press, 1986.

Oates, Stephen B. *A Woman of Valor: Clara Barton and the Civil War*. New York: The Free Press, 1994.

Osterud, Nancy Grey. *Bonds of Community: The Lives of Farm Women in Nineteenth-Century New York*. Ithaca, N.Y.: Cornell University Press, 1991.

——. "Rural Women during the Civil War: New York's Nanticoke Valley, 1861–1865." *New York History* (Oct. 1990): 357–86.

Painter, Nell Irvin. *Exodusters: Black Migration to Kansas after Reconstruction*. New York: Knopf, 1976.

——. Introduction to *The Secret Eye: The Journal of Ella Gertrude Clanton Thomas, 1848–1889*, edited by Virginia Ingraham Burr. Chapel Hill: University of North Carolina Press, 1990.

——. *Sojourner Truth: A Life, A Symbol*. New York: W. W. Norton and Co., 1996.

——. "Sojourner Truth in Life and Memory: Writing the Biography of an American Exotic." *Gender and History* 2 (1990): 3–16.

Paludan, Phillip. *A People's Contest: The Union and the Civil War, 1861–1865*. New York: Harper and Row, 1988.

Papashvily, Helen Waite. *All the Happy Endings: A Study of the Domestic Novel in America, the Women Who Wrote It, the Women Who Read It, in the Nineteenth Century*. New York: Harper and Brothers, 1956.

Parton, James, et al. *Eminent Women of the Age; Being Narratives of the Lives and Deeds of the Most Prominent Women of the Present Generation*. Hartford, Conn.: S. M. Betts, 1869.

Pattee, Fred Lewis. *The Feminine Fifties*. New York: D. Appleton-Century, 1940.

Pearson, Elizabeth Ware. *Letters from Port Royal*. New York: Arno Press and the New York Times, 1969.

Pease, Jane H., and William H. Pease. "Ends, Means and Attitudes: Black-White Conflict in the Anti-Slavery Movement." *Civil War History* 18, no. 2 (June 1972): 117–28.

Perry, Lewis, and Michael Fellman, eds. *Abolitionism Reconsidered: New Perspectives on the Abolitionists*. Baton Rouge: Louisiana State University Press, 1981.

Poovey, Mary. "A Housewifely Woman: The Social Construction of Florence Nightingale." *Uneven Developments: The Ideological Work of Gender in Mid-Victorian England*. Chicago: University of Chicago Press, 1988.

Rable, George. *Civil Wars: Women and the Crisis of Southern Nationalism*. Urbana: University of Illinois Press, 1989.

Reverby, Susan M. *Ordered to Care: The Dilemma of American Nursing, 1850–1945*. Cambridge: Cambridge University Press, 1987.

Reynolds, David S. *Beneath the American Renaissance: The Subversive Imagination in the Age of Emerson and Melville*. Cambridge, Mass.: Harvard University Press, 1988.

Reynolds, Moira Davison. *Uncle Tom's Cabin and Mid-Nineteenth-Century United States: Pen and Conscience*. Jefferson, N.C.: McFarland and Company, Inc. Publishers, 1985.

Riley, Glenda Gates. "The Subtle Subversion: Changes in the Traditionalist Image of the American Woman." *The Historian* 32 (Feb. 1970): 210–27.

Roediger, David. *Wages of Whiteness: Race and the Making of the White Working Class*. New York: Verso, 1991.

Rose, Ann C. *Transcendentalism as a Social Movement, 1830–1860*. New Haven: Yale University Press, 1981.

——. *Victorian America and the Civil War*. Cambridge: Cambridge University Press, 1992.

Rose, Jan Atteridge. *Rebecca Harding Davis*. New York: Twayne Publishers, 1993.

Rose, Willie Lee. *Rehearsal for Reconstruction*. New York: Oxford University Press, 1964.

Ross, Ishbel. *Angel of the Battlefield: The Life of Clara Barton*. New York: Harper, 1956.

Rubin, Joan Shelley. *The Making of Middlebrow Culture*. Chapel Hill: University of North Carolina Press, 1992.

Ruether, Rosemary Radford, and Rosemary Keller. *The Nineteenth Century: A Documentary History*. Vol. 1 of *Women and Religion in America*. San Francisco: Harper and Row, 1981.

Ryan, Mary P. *Cradle of the Middle Class: The Family in Oneida County, New York, 1790–1865*. Cambridge: Cambridge University Press, 1981.

——. *Women in Public: Between Banners and Ballots, 1825–1880*. Baltimore, Md.: Johns Hopkins University Press, 1989.

Sanchez-Eppler, Karen. "Bodily Bonds: The Intersecting Rhetorics of Feminism and Abolitionism." *Representations* 24 (Fall 1988): 28–59.

Saum, Lewis O. *The Popular Mood of Pre-Civil War America*. Westport, Conn.: Greenwood Press, 1980.

Saxton, Alexander. *The Rise and Fall of the White Republic*. New York: Verso, 1990.

Saxton, Martha. *Louisa May*. New York: Avon Books, 1977.

Schultz, Jane Ellen. "Women at the Front: Gender and Genre in Literature of the American Civil War." Ph.D. dissertation, University of Michigan, 1989.

Schuster, Richard. "American Civil War Novels to 1880." Ph.D. dissertation, Columbia University, 1961.

Scott, Joan W. "The Evidence of Experience." *Critical Inquiry* (Summer 1991): 773–97.

——. "Gender: A Useful Category of Historical Analysis." *American Historical Review* 91 (Dec. 1986): 1053–75.

——. *Gender and the Politics of History*. New York: Columbia University Press, 1988.

Sears, Stephen W. *Landscape Turned Red: The Battle of Antietam*. New Haven: Yale University Press, 1983.

Showalter, Elaine, ed. *Alternative Alcott*. New Brunswick, N.J.: Rutgers University Press, 1987.

Silber, Nina. *The Romance of Reunion*. Chapel Hill: University of North Carolina Press, 1994.

Sillen, Samuel. *Women against Slavery*. New York: Masses and Mainstream, 1955.

Simmons, Michael. " 'Maum Guinea'; or, A Dime Novelist Looks at Abolition." *Journal of Popular Culture* 10 (Summer 1976–77): 81–87.

Sklar, Kathryn Kish. *Catharine Beecher: A Study in American Domesticity*. New York: W. W. Norton and Co., 1973.

Smith, Elizabeth Oakes. *Bertha and Lily; or, the Parsonage of Beech Glenn*. New York: J. C. Derby, 1854.

Smith, George Winston, and Charles Judah. *Life in the North during the Civil War: A Source History*. Albuquerque: The University of New Mexico Press, 1966.

Smith, Nina Bennett. "The Women Who Went to War: The Union Nurse in the Civil War." Ph.D. dissertation, Northwestern University, 1981.

Smith, Rebecca Washington. *The Civil War and Its Aftermath in American Fiction, 1861– 1899*. Chicago: University of Chicago Libraries, 1937.

Smith-Rosenberg, Carroll. *Disorderly Conduct: Visions of Gender in Victorian America*. New York: Knopf, 1985.

Snyder, Charles McCool. *Mary Walker: The Little Lady in Pants*. New York: Washington and Hollywood, 1962.

Stampp, Kenneth. *And the War Came: The North and the Secession Crisis*. Baton Rouge: Louisiana State University Press, 1950.

Stansell, Christine. *City of Women: Sex and Class in New York, 1789–1860*. Urbana: University of Illinois Press, 1982.

Starling, Marion Wilson. *The Slave Narrative: Its Place in American History*. Washington, D.C.: Howard University Press, 1988.

Sterling, Dorothy. *Ahead of Her Time: Abby Kelley and the Politics of Antislavery*. New York: W. W. Norton and Co., 1991.

——, ed. *We Are Your Sisters: Black Women in the Nineteenth Century*. New York: W. W. Norton and Co., 1984.

Stern, Madeleine. *Behind a Mask: The Unknown Thrillers of Louisa May Alcott*. New York: Morrow, 1975.

——, ed. *Critical Essays on Louisa May Alcott*. Boston: G. K. Hall and Company, 1984.

——. *Double Life: Newly Discovered Thrillers of Louisa May Alcott*. Boston: Little, Brown, 1988.

——. *Louisa May Alcott*. Norman: University of Oklahoma Press, 1950.

Still, William. *The Underground Rail Road*. Philadelphia: Porters and Coates, 1872.

Strasser, Susan. *Never Done: A History of American Housework*. New York: Pantheon Books, 1982.

Sundquist, Eric J., ed. *New Essays on Uncle Tom's Cabin*. Cambridge: Cambridge University Press, 1986.

Sutherland, Daniel E. *The Expansion of Everyday Life, 1860–1876*. New York: Harper and Row, 1989.

Tallman, Robert. *Anna Ella Carroll, the Woman in Lincoln's Cabinet*. New York: Batter, Barton, Durstine and Osborn, 1941.

Taylor, William. *Cavalier and Yankee: The Old South and American National Character*. New York: G. Braziller, 1961.

Thomas, John L. *The Liberator*. Boston: Little, Brown, 1963.

Thompson, Lawrence S. "The Civil War in Fiction." *Civil War History* 2, no. 1 (1956): 83–95.

Tompkins, Jane. *Sensational Designs: The Cultural Work of American Fiction, 1790–1860*. New York and Oxford: Oxford University Press, 1985.

Trustram, Myna. *Women of the Regiment: Marriage and the Victorian Army*. Cambridge: Cambridge University Press, 1984.

Turner, Lorenzo Dow. *Anti-Slavery Sentiment in American Literature Prior to 1865.* Washington, D.C.: The Association for the Study of Negro Life and History, Inc., 1929.

Unger, Irwin, ed. *Essays on the Civil War and Reconstruction.* New York: Holt, Rinehart and Winston, Inc., 1970.

Venet, Wendy Hamand. *Neither Ballots Nor Bullets: Women Abolitionists and the Civil War.* Charlottesville: University Press of Virginia, 1991.

Walker, Peter F. *Moral Choices: Memory, Desire and Imagination in Nineteenth-Century American Abolition.* Baton Rouge: Louisiana State University Press, 1978.

Ward, William Hayes. "Fifty Years of *The Independent.*" *Independent* 8 (Dec. 1898): 1642.

Ware, Edith Ellen. *Political Opinion in Massachusetts during Civil War and Reconstruction.* 1916. New York: AMS Press, 1968.

Warren, Joyce W. *Fanny Fern: An Independent Woman.* New Brunswick, N.J.: Rutgers University Press, 1992.

Welter, Barbara. *Dimity Convictions: The American Woman in the Nineteenth Century.* Athens: Ohio University Press, 1976.

White, Deborah Gray. *Ar'n't I a Woman?* New York: W. W. Norton and Co., Inc., 1985.

White, Isabelle. "The Uses of Death in *Uncle Tom's Cabin.*" *American Studies* 26 (Spring 1985).

Whites, LeeAnn. *The Civil War as a Crisis in Gender: Augusta, Georgia, 1860–1890.* Athens: University of Georgia Press, 1995.

Wilenz, Sean. *Chants Democratic: New York City and the Rise of the American Working Class, 1788–1850.* New York: Oxford University Press, 1984.

Williams, Blanche Colton. *Clara Barton, Daughter of Destiny.* New York: J. B. Lippincott, 1941.

Wilson, Forrest. *Crusader in Crinoline: The Life of Harriet Beecher Stowe.* Philadelphia: J. B. Lippincott, 1941.

Wood, Ann Douglas. "Heaven Our Home: Consolation Literature in the Northern United States, 1830–1880." *American Quarterly* 26 (1974): 496–515.

———. "The Literature of Impoverishment: The Women Local Colorists in America, 1865–1914." *Women's Studies* 1 (1972): 3–45.

———. " 'The Scribbling Women' and Fanny Fern: Why Women Wrote." *American Quarterly* 23 (1971): 3–24.

———. "The War within a War: Women Nurses in the Union Army." *Civil War History* 18 (Sept. 1972): 191–212.

Yee, Shirley. *Black Women Abolitionists: A Study in Activism, 1828–1860.* Knoxville: University of Tennessee Press, 1992.

Yellin, Jean Fagan. "From *Success* to *Experience*: Louisa May Alcott's *Work.*" *Massachusetts Review* 21 (1980): 527–39.

———. *Women and Sisters: The Antislavery Feminists in American Culture.* New Haven: Yale University Press, 1989.

Young, Agatha. *The Women and the Crisis: Women of the North in the Civil War.* New York: McDowell, Bolensky, 1959.

Young, James Harvey. "Anna Elizabeth Dickinson and the Civil War: For and against Lincoln." *Mississippi Valley Historical Review* 31 (1944): 59–80.

———. "A Woman Abolitionist in the South in 1875." *Georgia Historical Quarterly* 32 (1948).

Index

stories of upward mobility, 39; relationship with slavery, 112; war's intensification of, 115, 132; separate spheres ideology as common ground, 124; as Davis (Rebecca Harding) literary emphasis, 139–40, 263; status of freed slaves and, 151; backgrounds of nurses, 170; reflected in male-authored histories of women's war activities, 201–2; reflected in nursing narratives, 204–6, 209–10, 213–14, 215; reflected in literature, 219; and women's professional status, 252; as Fern subject, 263. See also Middle-class white values; Upper-class women; Working class

Combahee River Expedition, 81, 142–43

"Coming woman" (Alcott term), 247, 254–62, 273, 274, 278

Compromise of 1850, 32, 35, 39–40, 54–55, 64

Concord literati, 42, 45–46, 137

Congregationalist (periodical), 43–44

Continental Monthly (magazine), 82–83, 105, 123, 130; Cooke editorship, 150–52; defense of Sea Island reconstructionists, 159

Cooke, Martha Walker, 150–52

Cooke, Rose Terry, 87

Corinth, battle of, 177

Correspondence (Child), 64–66

Cosmopolitan Art Journal, 91

Country Living and Country Thinking (Hamilton), 100

"Courage! A Tract for Our Times" (Hamilton), 83, 122

Covey, Sylvia Lawson, 211

"Daguerreotype in Battle, A" (Rodman), 86, 175

Dall, Caroline Healey, 57, 59–60, 251

"David Gaunt" (Davis), 138–39

Davis, Jefferson, 50

Davis, Lemuel Clarke, 42

Davis, Rebecca Harding, 14, 31, 50, 66, 144, 169; background and career, 37, 41–43; Life in the Iron Mills, 41–42, 66, 69–71, 138, 263; and Hamilton, 43, 45,

112; and Alcott, 43, 45, 169, 242, 258; and Phelps, 47, 168, 263–64; linkage of slavery and capitalism, 71; wartime writings, 110, 112–13; style and language, 112; midwar writings, 112–13, 133, 135, 137–40, 144, 152–55, 157; "Paul Blecker," 113, 138–39, 264; as most original voice among midcentury women writers, 133; on ruling-class oppression, 139–40; "John Lamar," 152, 155, 163; racial themes and characters, 152–55, 157–58, 232, 238–41, 242, 243; effect on Phelps's work, 168, 263–64; late war writings, 178; postwar writings, 200, 232, 233, 234, 236, 238–41, 242, 246, 263, 264; Waiting for the Verdict, 232, 238–40, 242–43; contradictory stances, 243–44; as woman suffrage supporter, 246, 250; "Men's Rights," 250, 263

Days, Gala (pseud. of Mary Abigail Dodge). See Hamilton, Gail

"Dead" (Linwood), 186

"Dead Soldier's Ring, The" (Denison), 185

"Deliverance" (Harper), 275

Delphine (pseud.). See Baker, Delphine Paris

Democratic Party, 143, 197–98, 225

Denison, Mary, 185

Denning, Michael, 6–7

Dickinson, Anna, 232, 233, 234, 236–38, 240, 241–42, 243–44

Diffley, Kathleen, 85

Dime novels, 6–7, 84, 199

"Dirge" (Ellwood), 186

Divers, Bridget ("Irish Biddy"), 201

Dix, Dorothea Lynd, 123, 170, 171–72, 181, 182, 183, 184, 201, 210

Doctors, women as, 171

Dodge, Mary Abigail. See Hamilton, Gail

Domestic work. See Housekeeping tasks

Dora Darling (Austin), 159, 179

Douglass, Frederick, 35, 59, 199

"Down the River" (Prescott), 225–27

Draft riots, 107, 115, 131, 134, 143, 150

Dred (Stowe), 60, 226

Dred Scott decision, 72, 269
Dunlop, L. J., 186

Eastman, Mary, 84, 174
Edmonds, Sara Emma, 179
Eldredge, Charles Harrington, 36, 45
Eldredge, Sara. *See* Fern, Fanny
Ellwood, Ella, 186
Elshtain, Jean Bethke, 5
Emancipation League, 81
Emancipation Proclamation, 81, 107,
  110–14, 122, 144, 185; Child's view of,
  110, 111, 165; shift in Northern mood
  after, 146, 148; shift in women's writ-
  ers aims after, 168; antislavery activ-
  ists strategies after, 190; intermar-
  riage issue following, 225; Harper's
  reactions to, 272
Emerson, Ralph Waldo, 42, 45–47
Eminent Women of the Age (Eldredge), 45
Employment. *See* Labor question; Nurs-
  ing; Teachers
Espionage. *See* Spies, women
Essays, 30 (*see also specific authors and titles*)
"Ethiopia" (Harper), 164
Eyewitness (A. O. W.), 233

Factory workers, women as, 22, 115, 116
Fair Play (Southworth), 219
Fales, Edmund, 17–19, 24
Fales, Sarah, 17–21, 24, 31, 47–48
Fanny Ford (Fern), 35
Farm families, 118, 138
Farrington, Samuel P., 36
Faulkner, William, 224
Female Volunteer, The (novel), 178
Femme, La (Michelot), 28
Fern, Fanny (pseud. of Sara Willis
  [later Parton]), 14, 29, 38, 50, 249;
  Ruth Hall, 24–25, 29, 32, 35, 57–59;
  consequences of widowhood for, 25,
  26–27; fictionalized autobiography,
  31–32; background and career, 35–37,
  43; meeting with Stowe, 36; as rebel,
  37; on Hamilton, 45; prewar work,
  57–60; war writings, 83, 86, 100–101,
  133–35, 137–38, 140; *New York Ledger*
  columns, 100–101; version of woman-

hood, 129; and workingwomen's
  issues, 133, 263, 264; on social inequities, 133–35, 263; postwar subjects, 200, 221, 246, 249–50, 253,
  263; on Dickinson's work, 242; as
  woman suffrage supporter, 246, 250;
  "Women of 1867," 255–6; and Phelps,
  263–64
Fetterley, Judith, 255
"Few Words in Behalf of the Loyal
  Women of the United States by One
  of Themselves, A" (anonymous),
  123–24, 127–30, 132
Fiction writing. *See* Novels; Short sto-
  ries; *specific authors and titles*
Fields, Annie, 43, 137, 242
Fields, James, 42, 43, 242
Fifteenth Amendment, 3, 199, 225, 249
Flag of Our Union (periodical), 252
Foner, Eric, 225
Foote, Shelby, 6
Forest Leaves (Harper), 39
Fort Donelson, battle of, 85
Forten, Charlotte, 8, 82, 111, 145–46,
  159–60, 162–63, 164
Fort Monroe, 159
Fort Sumter, attack on, 2, 55, 73, 78, 100,
  110, 128, 171
Fort Wagner, attack on, 157, 162
Fourteenth Amendment, 198, 225
Francis, Convers, 33
Francis, David, 32–33
Francis, Lydia Maria. *See* Child, Lydia
  Maria
Francis, Susannah, 33
Frederick Douglass' Paper (abolitionist
  newspaper), 41
Fredericksburg, battle of, 97, 98, 109,
  114–15, 172
Fredrickson, George, 234
Free blacks. *See* African Americans
Freedmen's aid societies, 158, 159
Freedmen's Book, The (Child, ed.), 151, 164
Freedmen's Bureau Offices, 118
Free labor ideology, 70. *See also* Slavery;
  Working class
Fremont, Jessie Benton, 62
Fremont, John C., 62, 103

Antislavery activism; Emancipation Proclamation; Race; Working class
Slavery in South Carolina and the Ex-Slaves; or, The Port Royal Mission, 159–63
S. L. C. (writer), 214–15
Smith, Elizabeth Oakes. *See* Oakes Smith, Elizabeth
Smith, Seba, 57
Social class. *See* Class divisions; Middle-class white values; Upper-class women; Working class
Social protest novel, 8
Soldier's aid societies, 78
Soldier's Orphans, The (Townsend), 135
"Soldier's Wife, A" (Spencer), 177
"Soldiers' Wives" (Fern column), 86, 134–35, 221
Solon, of the Rebellion of '61 (Baker), 90–93, 99
Souder, Mrs. Edmund, 172
South: border states writers' views of, 43; Northern divergences from, 50; Northern women writers' views of, 52–53, 55–56; women spies in, 80; Kemble's *Journal* on antebellum conditions in, 144–47; postwar climate, 198; basis of patriarchy, 226. *See also* Reconstruction; Slavery
"Southern Hate of New England, The" (Sherwood), 148
South Sea Islands. *See* Sea Islands
Southworth, Mrs. E. D. E. N. (Emma Dorothy Eliza Nevitte), 14, 29, 31, 41, 246; domestic concerns, 25–26; *Retribution*, 26, 38–39, 52–54; *The Hidden Hand*, 29, 100; background and career, 37, 38–39, 43, 52; Unionist spirit of novels, 38; literary themes, 39, 56–57; prewar opinions and work, 51, 52–54, 56; literary patterns and style, 52–53; war sentiments, 100; postwar subjects, 200, 219–21; *Little Women* reference to, 255
Southworth, Mrs., Frederick Hamilton, 39
Spartan mother image, 85, 87
"Spasm of Sense, A" (Hamilton), 10, 125
Speery, Sylvie A., 186

Spencer, Belle Z., 80, 89, 172, 175, 176, 177–78; *Tried and True*, 233
Spies, women, 80, 141; fictional accounts of, 178–79, 220
Spinner, Francis, 116–17
Spirit of the Fair, The (newspaper), 181
Stansell, Christine, 10
Stanton, Elizabeth Cady, 57, 59, 120, 203–4, 250; and "To the Women of the Republic," 81–82; woman suffrage and racial views, 199
Stein, Gertrude, 224
Stephens, Alexander, 149
Stephens, Ann S., 30, 82
Story of Janet Strong, The (Townsend), 135–36
Story of My Life, The (Livermore), 248
Stowe, Calvin, 101
Stowe, Fred, 101
Stowe, Harriet Beecher, 14, 31, 45, 65, 123, 238, 244; domestic concerns, 20, 21, 23, 25, 27; as schoolteacher, 25; and women's support network, 27–28; antislavery activism; *Key to Uncle Tom's Cabin*, 34, 68, 34–35, 40, 51, 54–56, 60–61, 72, 73, 99–100, 101–2, 149; career in 1850s, 34–35, 43, 54–55; Christian vision of, 35, 37, 38, 55, 103; and Fern, 36; Harper (Mary Ellen Watkins) poem to, 40; work compared to Phelps's, 47, 269–70; and Lincoln anecdote, 49–50, 71–72; and start of war, 50–52, 189; as prewar influence, 51–52, 252; and work of Southworth, 51–54; as political writer, 54, 60–61, 62, 70, 71–73; view of war, 60–61, 71–73; and Jacobs, 68; encouragement of women's war work, 84–87; Child and, 101–2, 242; early war activities, 101, 102; and Hamilton, 126; midwar work of, 140, 148–49, 151, 153, 155; on women's moral agency, 145–46; on future of freed slaves, 148–49, 153; late war work of, 164; on losses of later war years, 187–88; postwar social concerns, 200, 242–46, 249, 253; postwar literary style, 219; cited in *Miscegenation*, 226; as